T0211696

CISM COURSES AND LECTURES

The series presents lecture notes, monographs, edited works and proceedings in the field of Mechanics, Engineering, Computer Science and Applied Mathematics.
Purpose of the series in to make known in the international scientific and technical community results obtained in some of the activities organized by CISM, the International Centre for Mechanical Sciences.

INTERNATIONAL CENTRE FOR MECHANICAL SCIENCES

COURSES AND LECTURES - No. 347

ADVANCES IN DATABASE SYSTEMS
IMPLEMENTATIONS AND APPLICATIONS

EDITED BY

J. PAREDAENS
UNIVERSITY OF ANTWERP
AND
TECHNICAL UNIVERSITY OF EINDHOVEN

L. TENENBAUM †
RUSSIAN ACADEMY OF SCIENCES

SPRINGER-VERLAG WIEN GMBH

Le spese di stampa di questo volume sono in parte coperte da
contributi del Consiglio Nazionale delle Ricerche.

This volume contains 99 illustrations

In order to make this volume available as economically and as
rapidly as possible the authors' typescripts have been
reproduced in their original forms. This method unfortunately
has its typographical limitations but it is hoped that they in no
way distract the reader.

ISBN 978-3-211-82614-0   ISBN 978-3-7091-2704-9 (eBook)
DOI 10.1007/978-3-7091-2704-9

PREFACE

At the end of 1992 Prof. Lev Tenenbaum, from the Institute for Control Science in Moscow, took the initiative to organize a school of two weeks, "Advances in Database Systems, Implementations and Applications", in cooperation with CISM and Unesco.

CISM is the International Centre for Mechanical Sciences in Udine (Italy). For already more than twenty years it organizes schools and courses, with the purpose to favour the exchange of ideas and experiences among experienced and young scientists all over the world.

Lev asked me to coordinate the school together with him. From then on we had a fruitful cooperation, which resulted in the final program of the school which was held in Udine September 13-24, 1993.

Advanced information technology is pervasive in any kind of human activity - science, business, finance, management and others - and this is particularly true for database systems. Both database theory and database applications constitute a very important part of the state of the art of computer science. Meanwhile there is some discrepancy between different aspects of database activity. Theoreticians are sometimes not much aware of the real needs of business and industry; software specialists not always have the time or the opportunity to get acquainted with the most recent theoretical ideas and trends, as well as with advanced prototypes arising from these ideas; potential users often do not have the possibility of evaluating the theoretical foundations and the potential practical impact of different commercial products. So the main goal of the course was to put together people involved in different aspects of database activity and to promote active exchange of ideas among them.

Several specialists from all over Europe were invited to give one or more lectures: F. Arcieri (Rome), P. Atzeni (Rome), A. D' Atri (L'Aquila), H. Bruggemann (Hildesheim), R. Jungclaus (Braunschweig), B. Thalheim (Cottbus), P. Widmayer (Zurich), L. Tenenbaum

(Moscow) and J. Paredaens (Antwerp). The school was a success and was attended by about 30 people from Asia, Africa and Europe.

Less than three months after the school, in full preparation of the present proceedings, the Russian computer science community got a terrible shock: on December 6 1993, Lev Tenenbaum died in a fatal car accident in Moscow. In honour of my friend Lev, I finished the preparation of the proceedings with the help of many colleagues. Especially I thank Prof. Fuad Aleskerov from the same institute as Lev, who finished Levs paper that appears in this Volume. I also thank Paolo Serafini who was responsible for the administrative organization of the school and who did an excellent job.

I am sure that these proceedings can give an insight in some modern aspects of database systems to many readers and I hope they will always remember the Russian Computer Scientist, Prof. Lev Tenenbaum, who took the initiative and was the active motor of this work.

J. Paredaens

CONTENTS

Page

ACYCLIC HYPERGRAPHS AND RELATIONAL DATABASES
(A SURVEY)

L. Tenenbaum [†]

Academy Sciences of Russia, Moscow, Russia

ABSTRACT

Structural properties of hypergraphs and relevant features of relational databases having acyclic schemes were intensively investigated during 80s. The investigations resulted in impressive issues for hypergraphs and relational databases theory as well applications. Since interests of database community were switched over from relational to more complicated data models the interest to this topic has ceased. The survey summarizes results of acyclic hypergraphs and database investigations and gives short comparative analysis of different approaches.

1. INTRODUCTION

Hypergraphs formalism can be effectively used for describing structure of information being stored in relational databases (RDB). Such the description though being transparent and illustrative seems from the first glance to be superficial and little informative. But it proved that structural features of hypergraphs being used for such the description play important role in solving a raw of problems related to data manipulation in RDBs such as queries processing, testing some kinds of dependencies, maintaining universal relation interface, etc. [1,2,3,4]. A realizing this fact initiated during 80s a flow of investigations in the field of hypergraphs structural and its role in solving mentioned above problems. Unfortunately since switching the databases investigators attention over to more complicated data models like nested relations, complex objects and object oriented ones, the interest to hypergraphs structure investigations in connection with databases features has ceased; so all results which have been achieved in the field are connected with "classical" RDBs making use of flat relations (i.e. relations represented in the *first normal form*).

From the very beginning it became obvious that the most important (from the relevant databases properties viewpoint) feature of hypergraphs is their cyclicity/acyclicity. Even on intuitive level it was comprehensive that acyclicity (i.e. absence of cycles) of a hypergraph results in a raw of "desirable" properties of underlying RDB for example, related to query processing; that is why main efforts of researchers were concentrated first of all around investigation of structural features of *acyclic* hypergraphs. The interest just to acyclic hypergraphs was encouraged by a rather wide-spread point of view that cyclicity is generally unnatural for real world and cyclicity of a hypergraph being used for RDB description is consequence as a rule a results of failure RDB design and "semantically overloading" is of some attributes [5,6].

This paper summaries issues in the topic of acyclic hypergraphs and relevant RDBs properties.

Formalizing of hypergraph acyclicity notion proved to be not too trivial. Though hypergraph is nothing more than generalization of graph, a trial to identify hypergraph cyclicity with presence of closed paths in it (by analogy with graphs), and acyclicity - with absence of such paths proved to be little efficient. Class of cyclic hypergraphs under such approach unites both hypergraphs having complicated (from intuitive point of view) structure resulting in hard problems in solving the mentioned above databases tasks and hypergraphs with (intuitively) simple structure not leading to such problems; as for acyclic hypergraphs, their structure proved to be too trivial. In connection with this the following two approaches to the problem were outlined.

The first one is reduced in detailed classification of closed paths in hypergraphs based on their fine structural features as well as on the consideration each kind of such paths as the particular class of cycles. Each of the classes introduced in this way was denoted by a character according as a rule either to a name of the author who has introduced this class (for example B(Berge) - cycles) or to particular features of the class (for example T(tree) - cycles). Cycles which were introduced in this way may be generally called "θ-cycles" where "θ" has particular symbol value for particular class; hypergraphs having or not having θ-cycles are referred to as "θ-cyclic" or "θ-acyclic" correspondingly. Mentioned above approach further is referred to as θ - *approach (or θ - ideology)* and the classification - as θ - *classification*.

Alternative approach is based on the property of a hypergraph to remain connected (or to become disconnected) upon removing part of its nodes; this approach doesn't use explicitly closed path notion. In framework of this approach three classes of acyclic hypergraphs have been considered: α-, β- and γ- classes. Further this approach is referred to as *α-β-γ - approach (α-β-γ - ideology)* and corresponding classification - as *α-β-γ - classification*.

Taking into consideration restrictions on a size, the paper is not intended to give as complete as possible survey of all database aspects related to structural properties of underlying hypergraphs as well as the complete list of references; the main intention of the author was to supply a reader with main ideas and to provide orientation in the field. The paper is organized as follows.

In Chap.2 the hypergraphs formalism as the way of structure description of RDBs is shortly discussed as well as main notions of the hypergraphs theory and notations being used further are given. Chap. 3 is devoted to θ-approach: θ-cycles on hypergraphs and classification of θ-acyclic hypergraphs are considered. In Chap.4 the α- β-γ approach with corresponding classification of acyclic hypergraphs is discussed. In Chap.5 some RDBs problems which are influenced by structure of relevant hypergraphs are discussed. In Chap.5 short survey of algorithms for testing hypergraphs acyclicity is represented and conclusive Chap.6 summarizes the issues which have been considered in the paper.

Hereinafter familiarity of a reader with elementary foundations of RDB theory is supposed; we shall give below only minimum information directly connected with the main topic of the paper.

2. RELATIONAL DATABASES AND HYPERGRAPHS

2.1. Relational databases

Relational database (RDB) includes a set of (base) relations. Each relation is specified by its name, *scheme* (i.e. a set of relevant attributes) and in general by a set of *constraints* to which the information being contained in the relation must satisfy. Particular content of a base relation is represented by a set of tuples consisting of values of the attributes entering the scheme of the relation; each such a set is called *relation instance*. Different attributes may take values from different domains but in classic RDB, domains elements may be only atomic ones.

Database is specified by a set of base relations names, its *scheme* - i.e. a family of base relations schemes and by a set of constraints some of which may be interrelational[1]. *Database istance* consists of a set of base relations instances.

Supposing familiarity of a reader with foundations of RDB theory we don't give definitions of most relational notions e.g. relational operations, dependencies (e.g. *join* or *multivalued* dependencies), etc. All detailed information can be found in the paper of Paredaens Jan *Foundations of Database Systems* published in this book, as well in [7-9].

Schemes of different base relations may generally contain attributes with identical names. Hereinafter we shall assume implicitly that attribute names are *unique* which means that attributes with identical names belonging to different relations are defined on identical domains and have identical semantics. This assumption which is generally not mandatory in RDBs is known as *universal relation scheme assumption* (URSA, [10,11]).

2.2. RDB hypergraphs

Let $\chi = \{X_i | X_i$ is a base relation scheme} be RDB scheme. Union of all base relations schemes (*universum*) is denoted by U: $U = \bigcup_{\chi} X_i$.

Let W be a set. A *hypergraph* is a pair $\{W, \mathcal{Y}\}$ where $\mathcal{Y} \subseteq 2^W$; nodes of the hypergraph are elements of the set W, subsets $Y_i \in \mathcal{Y}$ of the set W which are elements of the family $\mathcal{Y}$ are referred to as *hyperedges* (or simply *edges*) of the hypergraph [12,13]. Hence any RDB can be described at the scheme level by the hypergraph $\{U, X\}$ which is further referred to as *hypergraph of the database*; its nodes are attributes of the database and edges are base relations schemes.

---

[1] Sometimes constraints are considered as part of database scheme

Hypergraph notion is generalization of graph notion: a graph is a particular kind of hypergraphs with $|X_i| = 2$ for any $X_i \in \mathcal{X}$. Like graphs, hypergraphs can be "visualized": in this, each edge is depicted as closed figure uniting all nodes belonging to the edge.

As an example let us consider a database "COMPANY" including three base relations: EMPLOYEES (Name, Position, Departement#, Salary); DEPARTMENTS (Department=, Department Name, Director, Number of employees); PERSON (Name, Sec.≠, Civil Status, Address). Attributes names constituting relations schemes are indicated in brackets after relations names. The following conditions could be constraints in the database: each department has the only director (DEPARTMENTS relation) and each employee is subordinated to a single director (DEPARTMENTS & EMPLOYEES relations). The hypergraph of this database is depicted on fig.1.

Further databases having cyclic or acyclic hypergraphs will be referred to as *cyclic* or correspondingly *acyclic databases*.

2.3. Denotations and main notions of hypergraph theory

The following denotations are used hereinafter.

Attributes' names (i.e. hypergraphs' nodes) are designated by small letters possibly indexed $(a, b, x_1, y_i \ldots)$. Attributes' sets (i.e. hypergraphs edges) are designated by capital last letters of the alphabet $(X_i, Y, Z, \ldots)$. Families of hypergraphs edges are designated by last handwritten capital letters of the alphabet $(\mathcal{X}, \mathcal{Y}, \ldots)$. Hypergraphs are designated by handwritten capital letter $\mathcal{H}$, possibly indexed $(\mathcal{H}_B, \mathcal{H}', \ldots)$.

Further we'll assume for each pair of hypergraph edges X_i, X_j that neither $X_i \subset X_j$ nor $X_j \subset X_i$ is valid, hypergraphs satisfying this condition are referred to as *reduced*. In databases having reduced hypergraphs each base relation is uniqly defined by its scheme; so we shall use as conventional relations names denotations r_{X_i}, $r_Y, \ldots$ using relation schemes X_i, $Y, \ldots$ as indexes; the letter "r" is used to distinguish between relations and their schemes.

Let $\mathcal{H} = \{U, \mathcal{X}\}$ be a hypergraph. We shall refer to the hypergraph $\mathcal{H}_U' = \{U', \mathcal{X}'\}$ where $U' \subseteq U$, $\mathcal{X}' = \{X_i \cap U'/X_i \in \mathcal{X}\} - \{\emptyset\}$ as *partial subhypergraph* of the $\mathcal{H}$, induced by the nodes' set U', edges $X_i' \in \mathcal{X}'$ as *partial edges* of the $\mathcal{H}$, induced by the set U'; the hypergraph $\mathcal{H}^* = \{U^*, \mathcal{X}^*\}$ where $\mathcal{X}^* \subseteq \mathcal{X}$, $U^* = \cup_{\mathcal{X}^*} X_i$ $(X_i \in \mathcal{X})$ as *complete subhypergraph* (or simply *subhypergraph*) of

$\mathcal{H}$. For example the hypergraph including 3 edges: {s#, n}, {n, d#} and {dn, d#} is the partial subhypergraph of the hypergraph depicted on fig.1 induced by the nodes set {s#, n, dn, d#}; hypergraph including two edges EMPLOYEES and DEPARTMENTS is a (complete) subhypergraph of the same hypergraph.

An edges' sequence $Y_{i_1}, Y_{i_2}, \ldots, Y_{i_m} = Y$ of the hypergraph $\mathcal{H}$ such that $\forall (1 \leq k < m): X_{i_k} \cap X_{i_{k+1}} \neq \emptyset$ is refered to as *path between* X_{i_1} and X_{i_m}, edges X_{i_k} and $X_{i_{k+1}}$ — as *neigbour* ones, "m" — as *lenght* of the path. Hypergraphs in which there is path between any two edges is referred to as *connected* (the example is the hypergraph on fig.1) hypergraph, and otherwise as *disconnected* one. Any maximal connected subhypergraph of $\mathcal{H}$ is referred to as its *connected component*.

A hypergraph $\mathcal{H}$ is *connected with respect to* (wrt) its nodes set $W \subset U$ iff the partial subhypergraph induced by the $U\backslash W$ is connected, and is *disconnected* wrt the same set otherwise (for example the hypergraph on fig.1 is connected wrt {dn,dir} but disconnected wrt {dn,d#}). Maximal subhypergraph of the $\mathcal{H}$ connected wrt set $W \subset U$ is referred to as *connected component of the* $\mathcal{H}$ *wrt the set* W.

Hypergraph $\tilde{\mathcal{H}}$ is the *reduction* of a hypergraph $\mathcal{H}$ iff $\tilde{\mathcal{H}}$ is obtained from $\mathcal{H}$ by deleting all its edges which are subsets of some other edges.

3. θ – CYCLES AND θ – ACYCLIC HYPERGRAPHS

3.1 Graphs cycles and hypergraphs edges cycles.

The hypergraph edge cycle notion [14,15,16,6] is a direct analogy with graph cycles; having been introduced later some other θ-cycles it was a trial to give something like "basic cycle" notion generalizing all kinds of θ-cycles. That is why we begin with this kind of cycles though this doesn't correspond to chronology of introducing θ-cycles in literature.

Let $\mathcal{H} = \{U, Y\}$ be a hypergraph. By analogy with graph cycles [17,18], any path of length $m \geq 3$ between edges X_{i_1} and X_{i_m} is referred to as *edge cycle* on a hypergraph iff it is "closed" that is $X_{i_1} \cap X_{i_m} \neq \emptyset$.

Examples of edge cycles are given on fig.2. As it is seen from the figure essentially different structures proved to be "cycles": beginning from hypergraph on fig.2a which is completely concording with intuitive idea on what does mean "cycle", to hypergraph on fig.2g which is not percepted as "cycle" at all and which can't cause some difficulties in solving database problems. As it was mentioned above this fact served a stimulus for introducting detailed classification of edge cycles basing on their fine structural features; this classification which was conventionally called "θ-classification" is discussed in the next section. We mention here only so called *pure cycles* which will be further frequently referred to. An edge cycle is *pure one* iff it satisfies the following conditions:

$$m=3: \quad X_{i_1} \cap X_{i_2} \cap X_{i_3} = \emptyset$$

$$m>3: \quad \forall j,k: (1 \le j, k < m, |j-k| > 1): X_{i_j} \cap X_{i_k} = \emptyset$$

The hypergraph on fig.2a is the pure cycle.

3.2. θ-cycles in hypergraph.

Let us pass to θ-cycles which have been introduced elsewhere. Note that though θ-classification, is pure "structural" one, in fact introducing any θ-class was always motivated by considerations on some "desirable" database properties induced by the absence of just this kind of cycles in database hypergraphs.

β-*cycles* [19; 20; 1; 15; 21; 2].
β-*cycle* is an edge cycle $C_\beta = \{X_{i_1}, \dots X_{i_m}\}$ such that the

sequence $C_\beta = \{X_{i_k} \setminus (\cap_{C_\beta} X_{i_j})\}$ is a pure cycle. Note that pure

cycles satisfy this condition and hence are β-cycles. Example of β-cycles are given on fig.2a,b.

Weak β-*cycles, G-cycles* [19,22;14,16].
Weak β-*cycle* is an edge cycle satisfying to the condition:
$$\forall(1 \le k \le m)\exists(a \in X_{i_k} \cap X_{i_{k+1}}):\forall(1 \le j \le m, j \ne k): a \notin X_{i_j} \cap X_{i_{j+1}}$$
G-*cycles* notion is equivalent to weak β-cycle one, it was introduced independently in [22]. By definition, G-cycle is an edge cycle satisfying the following condition:
$$\forall j, k \ (1 \le j, k \le m; j \ne k): X_{i_k} \cap X_{i_{k+1}} \equiv X_{i_j} \cap X_{i_{j+1}}$$
Hypergraphs on fig.2a-c are examples of weak β(G)-cycles[2].
Further we shall use termin "G-cycle" for short.

There is the following interrelationship between β – and G-cycles: any β-cycle is also G-cycle; any G-cycle contains subsequence which is β-cycle (see fig.2c); any not redundant G-cycle is β-cycle (see fig.2a,b).

γ.(γ. *aniolo*)-*cycles* [23;1,16].
γ-*cycle* is an edge cycle satisfying the condition:

---

[2] When k=m we shall mean hereinafter $X_{i_{k+1}} = X_{i_1}$.

$$\forall (1 \leq k \leq m) \exists (1 \leq j \leq m, \ j \neq k) : X_{i_k} \cap X_{i_{k+1}} \subseteq X_{i_j} \cap X_{i_{j+1}}$$

Hypergraphs on fig.2a-d are examples of Z-cycles.

T(*tree*) - *cycles* [16;14,15].
T-*cycle* is an edge cycle satisfying the condition:
$$\forall \ k,j : (1 \leq k, \ j \leq m, \ k \neq j) \ \exists \ (1 \leq l \leq m) : X_{i_l} \cap X_{i_{l+1}} \subseteq X_{i_k} \cap X_{i_j} .$$
Hypergraphs on fig.2a-e are examples of T-cycles.

γ-*cycles* [19; 20, 16].
γ-*cycle* is an edge cycle satisfying the following condition:
$$\forall \ (1 \leq k < m) \ \exists \ (a \in X_{i_k} \cap X_{i_{k+1}}) : \forall \ (1 \leq j \leq m, \ j \neq k): a \notin X_{i_j} \cap X_{i_{j+1}}$$
Formally γ-cycle is close to G-cycles, but unlike G-cycles, in γ-cycle one intersection of neighbour edges is allowed to be included in another one. Hypergraphs on fig.2a-e,f are γ-cycles; besides the subhypergraps consisting of the following edges sets are γ-cycles as well: $\{X_1, X_2, X_3\}$ and $\{X_1, X_3, X_4\}$ on fig.2d and $\{X_1, X_2, X_3\}$ on fig.2e.

Weak γ-*cycles* [19].
Weak γ-*cycle* is an edge cycle satisfying the condition:
$$(k=1 \ \& \ k=2): \exists \ (a \in X_{i_k} \cap X_{i_{k+1}}) \ \forall (1 \leq j \leq m, \ j \neq k): a \notin X_{i_j} \cap X_{i_{j+1}}$$
Hypergraphs on fig.2a-f are examples of weak γ-cycles.

There is relationship between γ - and weak γ-cycles similar to relationship between β- and G-cycles: any γ-cycle, is a weak γ-cycle; any weak γ-cycles contains a subsequence which is a γ-cycle (fig.2d,e); any not redundant weak γ-cycle is also γ-cycle (fig.2a,f).

S-*cycles* [24; 14,16].
A cycle which is either pure cycle or edge cycle (of length 3 satisfying the condition
$$(\exists a(a \in X_{i_1} \cap X_{i_3}):(a \notin X_{i_2}) \& (\exists b(b \in X_{i_2} \cap X_{i_3}):b \notin X_{i_1}) \& (\exists c:c \in X_{i_1} \cap X_{i_1} \cap X_{i_3})$$
is referred to as S-cycle; obviously class of S-cycles is a subclass of γ-cycles. Hypergraphs on fig 2a,f are examples of S-cycles.

B(*Berge*)*cycles* [12;14,15,21,2,16,25,1,19,20].
B-*cycle* notion being pure graph-theoretical by origin was introduced long before θ-classification; nevertheless it is fit well to θ-ideology. By definition B-cycle is closed sequence $\{X_{i_1}, x_{i_1}, X_{i_2}, x_{i_2}, \ldots, X_{i_m}, x_{i_m}\}$, $m \geq 2$ of different edges $X_{i_k} \neq Y$ and different nodes $x_k \neq U$ of a hypergraph $\mathscr{H} = \{U, Y\}$ satisfying the condition: $\forall (1 \leq k < m)$: $x_{i_k} \neq X_{i_k} \cap X_{i_{k+1}}$. Note that the main distinction of B-cycles from edge cycles is in the existence of *unique* nodes x_{i_k} in

sequence the mentioned above. Besides the length of B-cycle
may be equal to 2 : so any pair of edges having not less than
two common edges constitutes B-cycle for example, pair $\{X_1,$
$X_2\}$ on fig. 2b-d. From the other side it is not forbidden for
x_{i_k} to be common for more than one pair of neigbour cycle
edges. B-cycles of length 3 sometimes are referred to as
3B-cycles; hypergraphs on fig.2a-f are examples of 3B-cycles.
        B-cycles are obvious analogy of simple (e.g. not having
selfintersections) graph cycles: uniqueness of nodes
containingthe sequence in the B-cycle definition permits to
construct simple graph cycle on these nodes. Such cycles
constructed on nodes sets $\{a, b, c, d\}$ and $\{a, b, c\}$ are
depicted by dashed lines on fig.2a-f.
        The list of θ-cycles is exhausted on B-cycles. There is
partial order by inclusion on the set of θ-classes; but
because the main goal of this paper is a discussion of
acyclic hypergraphs as well as database problems connected
with such hypergraphs we leave to a reader an opportunity to
restore this order himself.

3.3. θ-acyclic hypergraphs.

        Acyclic graph (tree or forest) is a graph having no
cycles. By analogy it is natural to define *acyclic hypergraph*
as hypergraph having no cycles; but since in hypergraphs a
variety of cycles types may exist, speaking of *acyclic*
hypergraph it is necessary to indicate in respect to which
θ-cycle the hypergraph is acyclic. In this way the notion of
θ-acyclic hypergraph arises: a hypergraph is referred to as
θ-acyclic iff it doesn't contain just θ-cycles, where θ ∈ {B,
3B, "weak γ", γ, S, T, Z, G, β}.
        Note that would we try to introduce the "acyclic
hypergraph" notion on basis of "negating" edge cycles we
obtained too trivial hypergraphs structure: such the
hypergraphs could not contain nodes common to more than one
edges pair. Fig.3 depicts an example of such graph which is
really like a graph tree. Data bases having such hypergraphs
would have maximum of "desirable" properties but would hardly
be interesting in practice. Even hypergraphs of some
θ-acyclic classes have a rather simple structure. So
B-acyclic hypergraphs have no intersecting edges pairs with
more than two common nodes; γ-acyclic hypergraphs can't have
edges combination like depicted on fig.2f. In addition, B ,
3B - and γ-acyclic hypergraphs satisfy to some other though
not so strong restrictions.
        Besides θ-acyclic hypergraphs whose definition is based
only on "negating" corresponding θ-cycles other acyclic
hypergraphs whose definitions are connected withadditional
structural restrictions were considered in literature; they
may be included in θ-classification as well. Let us consider
two such examples introduced elsewhere.

H(*hierarhic*)-*acyclic hypergraphs* [16;14,15].
T-acyclic hypergraph is referred to as H-*acyclic* iff it is
hierarchical. Not giving here a strong definition of what
does mean *hierarhical* hypergraph we only notice that
structure of such hypergraph actually resembles the graph
tree structure. To clarify the idea we give an example of two
hypergraphs: hierarchical one on fig.4a and not hierarchical
– on fig.4b. Both hypergraphs are T-acyclic; hence the
hypergraph on fig. 4a is H-acyclic, on fig.4b – not.

S_k(*skeleton*) – *acyclic hypergraph* [16][3].

In the definition of these hypergraphs the following notion
is used: two edges are referred to as *equivalent by
intereseption* iff their intersections with other hypergraph
edges coincide; a subhypergraph of a hypergraph having only
one representative of each equivalency edges class, is
referred to as *skeleton* of the hypergraph. Hypergraphs having

T-acyclic skeletons are referred to as S_k-*acyclic*. Fig.5a

illustrates T-cyclic hypergraph with two pairs of equivalent
edges: $\{X_1, X_2\}$ and $\{X_3, X_4\}$, fig.5b – the skeleton of
mentioned above hypergraph which is T-acyclic. Hence the
original hypergraph on fig.5a is S_k-acyclic.

Obviously a hypergraph can be acyclic with respect to
one θ-class and cyclic – with respect to another one; this
essentially differs acyclic hypergraphs from acyclic graphs.
So hypergraphs on fig.2d-f are β-acyclic but T – and
γ-cyclic; hypergraph on fig.4b is β – and γ – acyclic but
B-cyclic; hypergraph on fig.5a is T-cyclic but S_k-acyclic;
etc.

There is partial order by inclusion on the set of
θ-acyclic hypergraphs classes; fig.6 with different acyclic
classes designated by corresponding letters illustrates this
order.

4. α-β-γ ACYCLIC HYPERGRAPHS

4.1. Preliminary remarks.

As it will be discussed further θ-approach based on
presence or absence closed paths (i.e. cycles) in hypergraphs
proved to be fruitful first of all in solving hypergraphs
covering problem related to query processing and creating
users views in databases. As for other problems related to
database features θ-approach proved to be not so effective:
as a rule θ-acyclicity could provide either sufficient or
necessary conditions for the features. It was obvious that
investigation of structural properties of hypergraphs
excluding wide complex of "cyclic" features is urgent which

---

[3] In [16] the "S-acyclic" termin is used.

---

[4] If a hypergraph is disconnected *wrt* some intersection set
of two, this set is referred to as *articulation set* and
corresponding edges pair – as *articulation pair*.

would hardly be done by enumerating all conceivable kinds of θ-cycles. In this way the α-cyclicity/acyclicity notion based on "strong connectivity" of a hypergraph emerged. This approach proved to be well compatible with other kinds of acyclicity equivalent to β- and γ-acyclicity which were considered in frameworks of θ-approach. In this way α-β-γ-classification of acyclic hypergraphs was introduced which is discussed below in this chapter.

4.2 α-β-γ acyclic hypergraphs.

α-acyclic hypergraphs.
α-acyclic hypergraphs notion is based on $block$ notion. $Block$ is a connected subhypergraph $H_B = \{U_B, X_B\}$ of a hypergraph H $= \{U, X\}$ satisfying to the following conditions:
— H_B is a reduction of partial subhypergraph of H induced by nodes set U_B;
— H_B is connected wrt intersection set $X_i \cap X_j$ for any X_i, $X_j \in X_B$.[4]

A block is trivial iff it consists of a single edge.[5]

A hypergraph containing only trivial blocks is referred to as α-acyclic and α-cyclic — otherwise [1,19,20].

For example hypergraphs on fig.2a-c are α-cyclic, hypergraphs on fig.2d-g are α-acyclic.

Alternative definition of α-cyclicity/acyclicity makes use of $closed$ $edges$ $subset$ notion. By definition, edges subset $X_B \subseteq X$ of a hypergraph $H = \{U, X\}$ is referred to as closed iff for each edge $X_i \in X$ there is an edge $X_{j_i} \in X_B$ such that $X_i \cap (\bigcup_{X_B} X_k) \subseteq X_{j_i}$; a hypergraph is α-acyclic iff any its closed edges set has no articulation pair. Both α-acyclicity definitions are equivalent [20].

Let us notice that a rather unnatural (from the first glance) ways of specifying edges set like "induced by nodes set" or "closed" in the definitions given above provide some "desirable" database properties which will be discussed in the next chapter.

The following definitions specify two additional hypergraphs classes which proved to be equivalent to α-acyclic ones [20,16,26,6,27]:

---

[5] In the paper "On analysis of arbitrary structure

— a hypergraph $\mathcal{H} = \{U, X\}$ is referred to as $J(joint)$-acyclic iff for any G-cycle in $\mathcal{H}$ there is an edge $X' \in X$ and triple of distinct integers $\{j, k, l\}$ such that

$$(X_{i_j} \cap X_{i_{j+1}}) \cup (X_{i_k} \cap X_{i_{k+1}}) \cup (X_{i_l} \cap X_{i_{l+1}}) \subseteq X'$$

where X_{i_s}, $s \in \{j, j+1, k+1, l, l+1\}$ are edges of the G-cycle;

— a hypergraph has a *running intersection property* - iff its edges set can be ordered as the sequence $\{X_1, X_2, \ldots, X_m\}$ such that for any i $(2 \le i \le m)$ there is an edge X_{j_i} $(j_i < i)$ such that

$$X_i \cap (\overset{i-1}{\underset{l=1}{\cup}} X_l) \subseteq X_{j_i} \; .$$ (In other words in such hypergraphs for each edge X_i there is "separating" edge such that the edge X_i and its "preceding" subsequence" $X_i, \ldots, X_{i-1}$ are in different connected components *wrt* the separating edge).

α-acyclicity of hypergraphs can be characterized as well by means of special graphs - *join trees* and hypergraphs *bisections*. Not being able to discuss this in details here we refer a reader to the original papers [20,28,29,30].

β-acyclic hypergraphs.

Not any edges subset in hypergraphs is closed or is induced by its nodes set. This fact can result phenomenon in hardly percepted intuitively and impossible for graphs: subhypergraph of α-acyclic hypergraph being considered as independent hypergraph proves to be α-cyclic. The hypergraph depicted on fig.7 illustrates this: the hypergraph is α-acyclic but its subhypergraph consisting of edges set $\{X_1,$ $X_2, X_3\}$ is α-cyclic (it is induced by its nodes set and has

hypergraphs and on some issues for relational databases" other notions of blocks introduced in literature will be discussed.

not articulation pair). This "Unnatural" situation motivated the introduction additional constraints being imposed on hypergraph structure in order to exclude such a phenomenon which resulted in the β-acyclicity notion [1,19,20]:a hypergraph is referred to as *β-acyclic* iff any its subhypergraph is α-acyclic, and *β-cyclic* otherwise.

So hypergraphs on figs.2d-g,3,4,5a are β-acyclic whereas ones on figs.2a-c, 7 - are β-cyclic.

Coincidence of just introduced notion with the "β-acyclicity" introduced in framework of θ-classification is not casual: both hypergraphs classes are equivalent.

Taking in the consideration the definition of α-acyclic hypergraphs the last definition can be reformulated in the following way: a hypergraph is β-acyclic iff any its (nontrivial) connected subhypergraph has articulation pair.

Remind that β-acyclic hypergraphs class is equivalent to "weak β" - and G-acyclic class (see Chap.3).

γ-acyclic hypergraphs.
A hypergraph is referred to as *γ-acyclic* iff any its intersecting edges X_i, X_j belong to distinct components connected *wrt* their intersection set $X_i \cap X_j$, and *γ-cyclic* otherwise. Like in β-acyclicity case just introduced hypergraphs class is equivalent to *γ-acyclic* one introduced in frameworks of θ-approach [19]. Examples of γ-cyclic/acyclic hypergraphs were considered in the previous chapter. One more γ-cyclic hypergraph is depicted on fig.7.

4.3 Degree of acyclicity and interrelation among α-β-γ-acyclic classes

There is a strong ordering on the set of α-, β-, γ-acyclic classes. Formally: $\gamma \subset \beta \subset \alpha$, where "α", "β" and "γ" are corresponding acyclic hypergraphs classes.

Informally, the weakest constraint being imposed on hypergraph structure is α-acyclicity: it "forbides" only "strong connected" hypergraph formations; that is why the α-acyclic class is the most wide. β-acyclicity imposes more strong restrictions forbiding "strong connectivity" for any subhypergraph of a hypergraph. The most strong restrictions are imposed by γ-acyclicity condition which forbides even such "harmless" edges combinations like depicted on fig.2f; this class is the most narrow. The formal relationship and informal considerations represented above explain the termin *degrees of acyclicity* introduced in [19]: γ-acyclic class has the highest degree of acyclicity whereas the α-acyclic one - the least.

Note in conclusion that sometimes B-acyclic hypergraphs (see Chap. 3) are included as well in the α-β-γ-classification: being strongly included in γ-acyclic class B-acyclic class has more degree of acyclicity than γ-class.

5. ACYCLIC HYPERGRAPHS AND DATABASE PROPERTIES

Being only a part of a database description the structure of data base scheme formalized by hypergraph nevertheless plays important role in solving a number of problems in databases. Seeking for so called context in query processing, creating user's view, testing constraints or universal relation hypothesis, some tasks of query processing optimization are examples of these problems. They are discussed below in this chapter.

5.1 Hypergraphs covering, query processing and users' views in acyclic RDBs

Hypergraph structure plays important role in seeking for coverings of a given nodes sets, i.e. connected subhypergraphs of the hypergraph containing a given nodes' set [14,15,31,32,28,29,33,34]; covering problem is in

turndirectly related to query processing and users views
creating in RDBs. Consider this in more details.

In formulation of a query to RDB, a query set attributes
set explicitly appearing in the query) and a subset of base
relations being used in query processing (which may be
specified by a subset of the database scheme) have to be
specified. For example let the case database "COMPANY" which
was described at the beginning of the paper is requested for
addresses of persons who are employees of some department,
say department "SUPPLY"; this query can be formalized as the
request for creating of single-attribute relation instance η_a

according the following formulae:

$$\eta_a = \pi_a \cdot \sigma_{dn="SUPPLY"} \left(\underset{\chi'}{*}, \eta_{x_i} \right)$$

where π, σ and "*" are correspondingly relational operations
of projection, select and (natural) join. Query set is
designated further "Q" (in this example Q={a,dn}) and a
database subscheme specifying the set of base relations
instances being involved in the query processing is $\chi' \subseteq \chi$ (χ
is the database scheme). In database literature the
subscheme χ' is referred to as context, or joinable set
[14,31,32]. Specification of a context is an important step
in queries formulation and evaluation. A context must
satisfy the following main conditions: query set must be
included in the context attributes set ($Q \subseteq \underset{\chi'}{\cup} X_i$): 2) it must
be connected.

In terms of hypergraphs the query set corresponds to
hypergraph nodes subset and the context corresponds to a
covering of the subset by a hypergraph.

Another important example of applying coverings in
databases is user's view creating problem i.e. specification
of a subdatabase to which the user addresses further his
queries. Attributes set of the view (which is an fact a union
of all potential queries sets of the user's queries) plays
similar role as query set for single query.

Trivial covering of any nodes subset which is
deliberately excessive is a whole hypergraph. But really a
covering should satisfy some additional demands; the most
important of them being its minimality (in respect to some
criterion) and acyclicity. Let us discuss this in more
details.

Minimal coverings. Covering *minimality* notion is
directly connected with *nonredundancy* one though these
notions are not equivalent. When dealing with cyclic
hypergraphs it may turn out there is a set of nonredundant
covering of specified nodes set and then it is natural to try
to find a covering minimal in some sense; so minimal covering
is always nonredundant but not vice versa. Three kinds of
minimal coverings were discussed in literature [14,15]:
- *edge-minimal* (e-minimal) covering with minimal edges
number: $|\chi'|$=min;

- *nodes-minimal* (n-minimal) covering with minimal nodes number $|\cup Y_i|=\min$;
γ'

- *size-minimal* (s-minimal) covering with minimal overall edges cardinality : $\Sigma|X_i|=\min$.
γ'

Each of mentioned above criteria has clear database orientation: e-minimal coverings provide minimal number of base relations being joined in query processing; n-minimal coverings provide minimal size of intermediate relations instances being created during query processing; s-minimal coverings provide minimal total size of relations instances being transmitted during query processing in distributed databases.

Generally each fixed nodes subset may have different minimal coverings (respectively to different criteria of minimality). For example consider the hypergraph on fig. 8 and nodes set $\{a,b,c\}$. This set has nonredundant coverings consisting of the following edges subsets of the hypergraph: $X_1=\{x_1,x_3,x_4\}$, $X_2=\{x_1,x_3,x_6\}$, $X_3=\{x_1,x_2,x_5,x_6\}$ and $X_4=\{x_1,x_2,x_4,x_5\}$. From these, X_1 and X_2 are e-minimal, X_1 n-minimal, X_1 and X_4 are s-minimal.

The task of finding minimal coverings of arbitrary nodes sets by a hypergraph of arbitrary structure is generally intractable. But the more strong constraints on hypergraph acyclicity are imposed the less complex this task is. So the complexity of finding e-minimal covers for α-acyclic hypergraphs is $o(|X|^2\cdot|U|)$ though finding n- and s-minimal covers for α-acyclic hypergraphs is yet intractable; a complexity of finding minimal covering for γ-acyclic hypergraph is polynomial of $(|X|+|U|)$ for any kind of minimality [4,14,15].

Unfortunately results on complexity estimations for minimal covering task are fragmentary and don't cover all the spectrum of acyclic hypergraphs classes (for example no results are published for minimal covering task by β-acyclic hypergraphs). Nevertheless taking into consideration inclusion relationships among different acyclic classes, an extrapolation on other classes can be done. (For example it may be surely stated that the complexity of finding e-minimal covering by Z-, H- and T-acyclic hypergraphs which are included in γ-acyclic class is not higher than polynomial of $(|U|+|X|)$).

Seeking for minimal coverings for hypergraphs in practice it is worth to keep in the mind the following structural features of acyclic hypergraphs [14,15]:- there is the unique e-minimal covering of arbitrary nodes set for B-acyclic hypergraph;- any nonredundant covering of arbitrary nodes set for a γ-acyclic hypergraph is e-minimal;- a number of different e-minimal covering of arbitrary nodes set for H-acyclic hypergraph $\mathcal{H}=\{U,\mathcal{X}\}$ doesn't exceed $|\mathcal{X}|$.

Acyclic coverings

In some practical applications it is desirable that a covering which is seeked for was acyclic. Such a problem arises for example in creating user's view to which the user will address further his queries; then it is natural to demand for structural simplicity of the user's view scheme which is in fact reduced to requirements of on a kind of acyclicity. Acyclic covering problem was extensively discussed in literature [35,4,25,36,37,38]. This problem is analogous to classic Steigner problem in graphs but for hypergraphs it is necessary to indicate in respect to which class the covering must be acyclic. So in the considered above example of covering the set $\{a,b,c\}$ for the hypergraph represented on fig. 8, the coverings X_1 and X_4 are α-acyclic, X_2 is α- and Θ-acyclic ($\Theta\neq B$), X_3 is B-acyclic.

It can happen that provided particular hypergraph and nodes set which is to be covered, acyclic covering from prescribed class doesn't exist at all; for example the node set $\{a,b,c,d\}$ has no α-acyclic covering by the hypergraph on fig.8. Hence the acyclic covering problem can be divided into two stages: 1) deciding whether acyclic cover exists and 2) finding minimal acyclic cover (if it exists). On both stages it is necessary to take in the consideration both acyclic class of the hypergraph and of the covering. We summarize estimations of complexity for both the stages which have been published in literature [4,25,36]. Unfortunately the results for minimal covering problem are also fragmentary but can be extrapolated for other acyclic classes.

As for the first stage, to decide whether there is Θ-acyclic covering ($\Theta=\gamma,B$) of a prescribed nodes set for an arbitrary hypergraph is NP-complete task. The problem whether there is B-acyclic covering given nodes set for a γ-acyclic hypergraph may be solved for the time $o(|\mathcal{X}|^2\cdot|U|)$; provided there is so called *Bachman diagram* for the hypergraph the answer can be obtained for the time $o(|\mathcal{X}|+|U|)$, [39].

As for the second stage the problem of finding acyclic covering of given nodes set for an arbitrary hypergraph is generally intractable. The problem of finding B – acyclic covering by B-acyclic hypergraph is solvable for the time $o(|\mathcal{X}|+|U|)$. The problem of finding covering for B- or γ-acyclic hypergraph is solvable for the time $o(|\mathcal{X}|^2\cdot|U|)$, though making use of Bachman diagram for the hypergraph reduces the estimation to $o(|\mathcal{X}|+|U|)$.

The following structural features of acyclic hypergraphs may be used in practicl to find acyclic coverings [29]:
- any subhypergraph of Θ-acyclic hypergraph with $\Theta\in\{B,Z,T,H,\gamma,\beta\}$ is Θ-acyclic;
- partial subhypergraph of B-acyclic hypergraph $\mathcal{H}=\{U,\mathcal{X}\}$ induced by any nodes set $U'\subset U$ is B-acyclic;

- maximal partial subhypergraph of Θ-acyclic hypergraph $\mathcal{H}=\{U,\mathcal{X}\}$ with $\Theta=\{B,H,T,Z,\gamma,\beta\}$ induced by any nodes set $U'\subset U$ is Θ-acyclic;
- any partial subhypergraph of Θ-acyclic hypergraph $\mathcal{H}=\{U,\mathcal{X}\}$ with $\Theta=\{T,\gamma,\beta\}\&\Theta\ne 3B$ is Θ-acyclic.

5.2 On equivalence of dependencies and some features in acyclic databases

Global and pairwise consistency

The *universal relation concept* which was popular in first half of 80s is one of the important concepts both from theoretical and practical points of view. The main idea of the concept is to create the interface giving to user an opportunity to consider the database not as collection of relations but as single relation containing overall information of the database such that each base relation is the universal relation projection on the corresponding attributes sets (actually this relation is virtual one). Such interface allows so "causal" users to formulate queries without being aware of database scheme and to address queries to the universal relation; then the database management software processes base relations to produce answer to the query.

For implementation of implementation ofuniversal relation interface a database must satisfy to *global consistencyy condition*. It means that for any admissible database instance there must exists some unique relation instance whose projections are the database base relations instances. Hence universal relation maintaining demands to test the database consistency for every database update; this task is generally untractable [42].

Close to global consistency is the *pairwise consistency* notion: a database is referred to as *pairwise consistent* iff for any its instance and for any its base relations instances pair η_{X_i} and η_{X_j} there exists a *relation instance* $\eta_{X_i \cup X_j}$ such that η_{X_i} and η_{X_j} are its projections on corresponding attributes sets X_i and X_j. This database feature is equivalent to the *"coincidence on intersections"* condition, which is formalized as follows:

$$\forall \eta_{X_i}, \eta_{X_j} (X_i \cap X_j \ne \emptyset): \eta_{X_i}[X_i \cap X_j] = \eta_{X_j}[X_i \cap X_j]$$

A complexity of testing pairwise consistency is obviously polynomial of database cardinality $|\mathcal{X}|$; that is why a possibility to reduce global consistency testing to testing of pairwise consistency is a very important practical problem [44-49]. Two kinds of consistency generally are not equivalent; but they are equivalent in α-acyclic databases [20]. Hence NP-complete testing of global consistency in α-acyclic databases may be reduced to testing of polynomial "coincidence on intersections".

Note that a hypergraph from any of class
acyclicity: is α-acyclic as well; hence last statement
concerns also with any kind of acyclicity.

6
Synonyms of the term in *global consistent (database)*:
joinable [40], *join compatible* [41], *join consistent* [42],
consistent [19] *decomposed* [43].

5.3 Equivalence of join dependency to a set of multivalued dependencies

Contents both of base relations instances and of the
overall universal relation instance are usually to satisfy
some semantic conditions (*constraints*) which have to be
permanently maintained; it needs their testing every time
when database update happens (like global consistency
testing). Constraints may often be formalized in form of
dependencies [7-9,50]; see also the paper of Thalheim B.
Semantical constraints for database models published in this
book.

One of well-known dependencies which attracted many
attention first of all in connection with *simplified
universal relation* concept [5] is so called *complete join
dependency* (CJD, [51,52]). Testing of CJD also testing of
global consistency is generally untractable [30,42] that is
why possibility to reduce it to testing more simple
dependencies is of high practice importance. It proved that
CJD is equivalent to a set of so called *multivalued
dependencies* (MVD) - which are in fact particular case of CJD
- iff a database is α-acyclic [5,20]; moreover in this case
CJD is equivalent to a set of *conflict-free* MVDs
[20,22,53,54] which facilitates the process of database
updating [39,53]. In any way replacing testing of CJD by
testing of MVDs set reduces the complexity from NP-complete
to polynomial of database scheme cardinality [44,55].

5.4 Semijoin programs and pairwise consistency

As it follows from previous considerations it is more
preferable from practical viewpoint to deal with pairwise
consistent databases. If a database is not pairwise
consistent then joining relations instances which "don't
coincide on intersections" we have some tuples of both
instances which are *passive* that is they don't take
participation in the join operation. This can cause wasting
resources in evaluating relational expressions in queries
processing particularly in distributed databases as a result
of transferring passive tuples. One of ways to avoid this
effect is making use of *semijoin* operation [56,57] which
allows to remove passive tuples from relations instances
beforehand. Consider it in more details.

Semijoin of relations η_{X_i} and η_{X_j} (designated by "α")is defined as follows:

$$\eta_{X_i} \propto \eta_{X_j} = \pi_{X_i} (\eta_{X_i} * \eta_{X_j})$$

the semijoin program is a sequence of semijoin operators of the kind:

$$\eta'_{X_i} := \eta_{X_i} \propto \eta_{X_j}$$

Informally the semijoin operation leaves in relation instance η'_{X_i} only the tuples which take participation in joining with η_{X_j}.

If a database is not pairwise consistent then its particular instance can not satisfy "coincidence on intersections" condition. Then executing a semijoin program on the database instance can result in very different results for example some relation instances can prove to be empty or resulting database instance will prove to be pairwise consistent; the semijoin program resulting in the last effect

is referred to as *full reducer* [20].

It proved that *full reducer* exists for any database instance iff the database scheme is α-acyclic [20,58,54] which gives an opportunity by pre-applying a full reducer to α-acyclic database, to deal only with pairwise consistznt instances.

5.5 Query processing in acyclic databases
Lossless joins

Let $\mathcal{R}=\{\eta_{X_1},\ldots,\eta_{X_m}\}$ be database instance having a scheme X, η_U be universal relation instance, $\mathcal{R}' \subset \mathcal{R}$ be a subset of database instance specified by a subscheme $X' \subset X$. The subset (*subdatabase*) $\mathcal{R}'$ is referred to as having *lossless join* property [51,52] iff it satisfies the condition

$$\underset{\mathcal{R}'}{*} \eta_{X_i} = \eta_U [\underset{X'}{\cup} X_i]$$

Methods of detecting such subsets play important role in queries processing in databases with universal relation interface. It turns out that provided a databases to be γ-acyclic and to have simplified universal relation [22,38,5] (this kind universal relation satisfies to CJD) any subdatabase specified by connected subhypergraph of the database hypergraph obeys lossless join property for any database instance [23]. This feature of γ-acyclic databases provides a simple and effective way of detecting lossless joinable subset. Remind that the same feature is hereditered by other Θ-acyclic databases with $\Theta \in \{B,3B,T,Z,S\}$.

On relationships among database attributes
Let $\mathcal{H}=\{U,X\}$ be the hypergraph of a database, $Y \subset U$ a nodes

subset of the hypergraph, $\mathcal{H}'=\{U',Y'\}$ be a minimal covering of this set. The relation instance $\eta_Y=\pi_Y\cdot(*\ \eta_{X_i})$ where η_{X_i} is base relation instance is refereed to as *relationship among attributes of the set* Y; this notion is directly related to queries processing problem. Generally η_Y depends on the cover Y'; if it is not the only one then η_Y - and hence evaluation of the query - can be ambiguous. But if we deal with γ-acyclic pairwise consistent database then the relationship among any subset of its attributes is unique [23].

Note that mentioned above feature is not stipulated by an unambiguity of coverings in γ-acyclic databases since in fact a covering can be ambiguous. As the example consider two hypergraphs represented on fig.9a,b and let $Y=\{c,d\}$. Each of the hypergraphs have the same two e-minimal coverings of Y - that is $Y'=\{X_1,X_2,X_4\}$ and $Y''=\{X_2,X_3,X_4\}$. The hypergraph on fig. 9a is γ-acyclic and it is easy to give an example of pairwise consistent database having this hypergraph in which the relationship among attributes c and d will depend on which namely of two covering will be chosen. As for the γ-acyclic hypergraph on fig. 9b, the relationship among attributes c and d in any pairwise consistent database doesn't depend on which of the coverings - Y' or Y'' - will be chosen.

Relational expressions over base relations
Query processing in RDB is eventually reduced to evaluating some relational expression on base relations. For the sake of saving resources in queries evaluating it is desirable that number of intermediate tuples would increase monotonely when the evaluating is going on which means in fact that no "excessive" tuples are created. Expressions having such the feature are referred to as *monotonous*. Since the monotony is important just in executing of multiple join operations we shall further discuss this property for expressions using only join operations.

It is proved that there exists a monotonous expression on all base relations of pairwise database if it is α-acyclic [20]; unfortunately this statement only ascertains the existence not giving ideas how to construct it. But if pairwise consistent database is γ-acyclic then any expression with brackets arranged in such a way that schemes of any two joined relations have not empty intersection is monotonous [24]; so this assertion indicates explicit way of arranging monotonous expressions in mentioned above kinds of databases.

6. TESTING HYPERGRAPHS FOR ACYCLICITY

Actuality of developing algorithms for testing hypergraphs for acyclicity follows from "desirability" of acyclic database properties. Most of the algorithms having been proposed in literature are in fact generalization of well-known *Graham algorithm* or (alternatively) GYO-algorithm proposed independently in [22] and [58] for testing hypergraphs for α-acyclicity. Let us begin with considering this algorithm.

General idea of the algorithm is consecutive removing from a hypergraph edges whose intersections with other edges are included in one of them; if this procedure will result in empty edges set, the original hypergraph is α-acyclic and α-acyclic otherwise. (GYO-algorithm is similar to testing graphs for acyclicity which removes step-by-step leaves of the graph).

Let $\mathcal{H} = \{U, \gamma\}$ be a hypergraph. The following is the formal description of GYO-algorithm.

Procedure GYO($\mathcal{H}$, RES);

begin RES:=FALSE;

A: $\gamma_1 := \gamma$; for each $x \in U$ if $\exists (X_i \in \gamma) \forall (X_j \in \gamma \setminus \{X_i\}) : x \in X_i \& x \notin X_j$

then begin $U := U \setminus \{x\}$ };

if $U = \emptyset$ then begin RES:= TRUE; STOP end;

for each $X \in \gamma$: if $\exists (Y \in \gamma, Y \neq X) : X \subseteq Y$ then $\gamma : \gamma \setminus \{X\}$;

if $\gamma \neq \gamma_1$ then goto A else STOP

end GYO

Variable "RES" serves in the procedure as indicator of the result of the testing: RES=TRUE iff $\mathcal{H}$ is α-acyclic and RES=FALSE otherwise. The complexity of the procedure is $o(|\gamma|^2 \cdot |U|)$, [20].

Alternative procedure solving the same problem for a time linear of $|\gamma|$ and $|U|$ is proposed.

As for testing other kinds of acyclicity, universal procedure REDUCE for testing Θ-acyclicity with $\Theta = \{B, H, T, S, \gamma, \beta\}$ is proposed in [16]; in [2,21] modified algorithm PRUNE for testing Θ-acyclicity with $\Theta = \{B, \gamma, \beta\}$ was proposed by the same authors. Both algorithms generalize GYO-algorithm in the sense that the testing procedure is reduced to recursive removing hypergraph edges satisfying some conditions. A kind of acyclicity or cyclity of a hypergraph under the testing is defined by particular predicate specifying mentioned above conditions and incorporated in the algorithm.

Let us consider here only PRUNE algorithm as more simple and "elegant". Let $\mathcal{H} = \{U, \gamma\}$ be a hypergraph.

Procedure PRUNE(γ, P_Θ);

comment: $P_\Theta(X, \gamma)$ is a predicate specifying condition for edge X to be removed; L is a set of edges being removed on each recursive step of the procedure.

```
begin RES:=TRUE;
    A: L:=∅;
    for each X∈𝒳 if  P_Θ(X,𝒳) then  begin  𝒳:=𝒳\{X};L:=L∪{X}
    end;
    if 𝒳=∅ then if L=∅ then RES:=FALSE else goto A
end PRUNE;
```

As an example let us give the predicate $P_\gamma(X,\mathcal{X})$ which can be used for testing γ-acyclicity:

$$P_\gamma(X,\mathcal{X}) = (\exists X_1 \forall X_2 : X \cap X_2 = X_1 \cap X_2) \bigvee (\forall X_1 \forall X_2 : X_1 \cap X = \emptyset \bigvee X_1 \cap X = X_2 \cap X)$$

A value of variable RES is here also an indicator of Θ-acyclicity or Θ-cyclicity of the hypergraph: the complexity of the procedure is $o(|\mathcal{X}|^2 \cdot |U|)$.

In [19] polynomial algorithm for testing β-acyclicity is independently proposed. It is based on direct definition of β-cycle and making use of the fact that 1st triple of a β-cycle edges (so called *triple initiating the cycle*) satisfies some particular conditions. The essence of the algorithm is to test all connected edges triples of the hypergraph for these conditions; if no triple satisfy these conditions the hypergraph is β-acyclic.

7. SUMMARY

In the paper a survey of issues related to acyclic hypergraphs and features of relational databases described by such hypergraphs is presented. In this context two following approaches ptoposed in literature were discussed.

The first one is based on cycle notion which comprehences cycles, by analogy with cycles in graphs, as closed paths, and percepts hypergraphs not having such paths as acyclic ones. In frameworks of this approach a wide variety of so called Θ-cycles was considered and harmonious classification of acyclic hypergraphs based on "negation" of the Θ-cycles was proposed. This classification is certainly valuable from the pure hypergraph-theoretical viewpoint. Besides a number of issues related to covering task in hypergraphs having important applications in query processing problem were achieved; since covering task is closely connected with navigating one (that is with seeking for paths in hypergraphs the approach based on path notion proved to be fruitful just in covering task solving.

The second approach is based on notion of connectivity *wet* nodes subsets and on comprehending acyclic hypergraphs as hypergraphs disconnected *wrt* intersections of edges pairs satisfying some special conditions. In frameworks of this approach the classification was as well proposed hypergraphs with different "degree of acyclicity" (α-β-γ- classification) and strong results related to α-β-γ- acyclic database features were obtained; these results are important both for data base theory and application viewpoints.

In conclusion a short survey of algorithms for testing acyclicity of hypergraphs is given.

ACKNOWLEDGEMENTS

The author thanks Hans Bruggemann for his valuable proposals on composition of the paper.

REFERENCES

1. Fagin R. Acyclic database schemes (of various degrees): a painless introduction in: Proceed. 8th Colloq. on Trees in Algebra and Programming. L'Aquila (Italy), March 1983; (Eds. Ausiello G., Protassi M.) LNCS, v.159, Springer Verlag, 1983, 65-89.
2. D'Atri A., Moscarini M.: Recognition algorithms and design methodologies for acyclic database schemes. Advances in Computing Research, v.3. (1986), 43-67.
3. Beeri C., Fagin R., Maier D., Mendelson A., Ullman J.D., Yannakakis M. Properties of acyclic database schemes. Proceed. 13th Ann. ACM Symp. on Theory of Computing, (Milwauker, Wisc., May 1981), ACM, New York, 1981, 355-362.
4. Ausiello G., D'Atri A., Moscarini M. Optimal acyclic coverings over hypergraphs, TAST-CNR Rep. #87. Rome 1984.
5. Faigin R., Mendelzon A., Ullman J.D.: A simplified universal relation and its properties. ACM Trans. on Database Systems, v.7, #3. (Sept. 1982), 343-360.
6. Paredaens J., Van Gucht D.: An application of the theory of graphs and hypergraphs to the decomposition of relational database schemas, TR #82-27, Universitaire Installing Antwerpen, August 1982.
7. Ullman J.D.: Principles of data base and knowledge base systems, V.1, Computer Science Press, Rockville MD 1983.
8. Paredaens J., De Bra P., Gyssens M., Van Gucht D.: The structure of the relational database model, Springer Verlag, London-Paris-Tokyo 1989.
9. Atzeni P., Batini C. and De Antonellis V.: Relational database theory, Addison-Wesley, Milano-Paris 1993.
10. Ullman J.D.: The U.R. strikes back, in Proceed. 1st ACM Symp. on Principles of Database Systems, (Los Angeles, Ca, March 1982), ACM, New-York 1982, 10-22.
11. Atzeni P., Parker D.S.: Assumptions in relational database theory, in: Proceed. 1st ACM Symp. on Principles of Database Systems (Los Angeles, Ca, March 1982) ACM, New-York 1982, 1-9.
12. Berge C.: Graphs and hypergraphs, North-Holland, New York 1976.
13. Berge C.: Hypergraphs, North-Holland, Amsterdam-New York-Oxford-Tokyo 1989.
14. Ausiello G., D'Atri A., Moscarini M.: Minimal coverings of acyclic database schemata, TAST-CNR Rep. #41, Rome 1982.

15. Ausiello G., D'Atri A., Moscarini M.: Minimal coverings of acyclic database schemata, in: Advances in Data Base Theory, v.2 (Eds. Gallaire H., Minker J., Nicolas J.-M.), Plenum Press, New York 1984, 27-51.
16. D'Atri A., Moscarini M.: Acyclic hypergraphs: their recognition and top-down vs bottom-up generation, IAST-CNR Rep. ≠29, Rome 1982.
17. F. Harary: Graph Theory, Addison-Wesley, Reading-Menlo Park-London 1969.
18. Oystein Ore: Theory of Graphs. Amer. Math. Soc., Rhode Island 1962.
19. Fagin R.: Degrees of acyclicity for hypergraphs and relational database schemes, J. of ACM, v.30. #3, (July 1983), 514-550.
20. Beeri C., Fagin R., Maier D., Yannakakis M. On the desirability of acyclic database schemes. J. of ACM, v.30, ≠3, (July 1983), 479-513.
21. D'Atri A., Moscarini M.: Recognition and design of acyclic databases, IAST-CNR Rep. #78, Rome: 1983.
22. Graham M.H.: On the universal relation, Tech. Rep. CSRG. of University of Toronto, Toronto 1979.
23. Zaniolo C.: Analysis and design of relational schemata for database systems. (PhD. Diss), Tech. Rep. UCLA-ENG-7669, UCLA 1976.
24. Fagin R.: Types of acyclicity for hypergraphs and relational database schemes. IBM Rep. RJ3330, IBM 1981.
25. Ausiello G.,D'Atri A., Moscarini M.: On the existence of acyclic views in a database scheme, IAST-CNR Rep. #86, Rome 1984.
26. Chase K.: Join graphs and acyclic databases schemes, in: Proceed. of 7th Intern. Conf. on VLDB (Cannes, France, Sept. 1981), ACM, New York 1981, 95-100.
27. Paredaens J., Van Gucht D.: An application of the theory of graphs and hypergraphs to the decomposition of relational database schemes, in: Proceed. 8th Colloqium on Trees in Algebra and Programming, L'Aquila (Italy), March 1983. (Eds. Ausiello G., Protassi M.), LNCS, v.159, Springer Verlag 1983, 351-366.
28. Goodman N., Shmueli O.: The tree property is fundamental for query processing, in: Proceed. 1st ACM Symp. on Principles of Database Systems (Los Angeles, Ca, March 1982), ACM, New York 1982, 40-48.
29. Goodman N., Schmueli O.: Transforming cyclic schemas into trees, in: Proceed. 1st ACM Symposium on Principles of Database Systems (Los Angeles Ca, March 1982), ACM, New York 1982, 40-48.
30. Hull R.: Acyclic join dependencies and database projections. J. Computer and Systems Science, v.27, ≠3, (1983), 331-349.
31. Maier D., Ullman J.D.: Connections in acyclic hypergraphs, in: Proceed. 1st ACM Symposium on Principles Database Systems. (Los Angeles Ca, March 1982), ACM, New York 1982, 34-39.

32. D'Atri A., Moscarini M., Spiratos N.: Answering queries
    in relational databases. in: Proceed. of Data Base Week
    (San Jose, May 1983), SIGMOD Record, v.13. #4 (1983),
    173-177.
33. Garey M.R. and Johnson D.: Computers and intractability,
    Freeman 1979.
34. Sacca D.: On the recognition of covering of acyclic
    database hypergraphs, in: Proceed. 2d ACM Sympos. on
    principles of DBS. (Atlanta, Georgia, March 1983), ACM
    1983, 297-304.
35. Maier D., Rosenstein D. and Warren D.S.: Windows on the
    World. SIGMOD Record, v.13, #4(Proceed. Ann. Meeting of
    SIGMOD, May 1983), 68-78.
36. Ausiello G., D'Atri A., Moscarini M.: On the existence of
    acyclic views in a database scheme, Theoretical Computer
    Science, v.35 (1985),165-177.
37. Paredaens J. and Van Gucht D.: Application of the theory
    of graphs and hypergraphs to the decomposition of
    relational database schemes, in: Proceed. 8th Colloqium
    on Trees in Algebra and Programming L'Aquila (Italy),
    1983), LNCS, v. 159. Springer Verlag, Berlin 1983,
    65-89.
38. Ullman J.D.: Universal relation interfaces for database
    systems, in: Proceed. of IFIP World Computer Congress,
    Paris 1983), 243-252.
39. Yannakakis M.: Algorithms for acyclic database schemes,
    in: Proceed. 7th Conf. on VLDB (Cannes, France, Sept.
    1981), ACM, New York 1981, 82-94.
40. Rissanen J.: Independent components of relations, ACM
    Trans. Database Syst, v.2, #4 (1977), 317-325.
41. Beeri C. and Rissanen J.: Faithful representation of
    relational database schemes, IBM Res. Lab., Res. Rep.
    RJ2722, San Jose 1980.
42. Honeyman P., Ladner R.E. and Yannakakis M.: Testing
    universal instance assumption, Inform. Proceed. Lettr,
    v.10, #1 (1980), 14-19.
43. Vardi M. On decomposition of relational databases, in:
    Proceed. 23th IEEE Symp. on Found. Computer Science
    (Chicago, Oct.1982), IEEE, New York 1982, 176-185.
44. Sciore S.: The universal instance and database design.
    (PhD. Dissert.) Prinston Univers., Prinston N.J. 1980.
45. Korth H.F. and Ullman J.D.: SYSTEM/U: A database system
    based on universal relation assumption, in: Proceed. XPT
    Workshop on Relational Database Theory, (Stony Brook,
    N.J. June 1980).
46. Lien Y.E.: Multivalued dependencies with null values in
    relational data bases, in: Proceed. 5th Int. Conf. on
    VLDB (Rio de Janeiro, Brasil, Oct., 1979), ACM, New York
    1979, 61-66.
47. Maier D.: Discarding the universal instance assumption:
    preliminary results, in: Proceed. XPT Workshop on
    Relational Database Theory, (Stony Brook. N.J., June
    1980).

48. Tarjan R.E. and Yannakakis M.: Simple linear-time
     algorithms to test hordality of graphs, test acyclicity
     of hypergraphs and selectively reduce acyclic
     hypergraphs. Bell Laboratories, Tech. Rep.,Murray Hill
     N.J. 1982.
49. Walker A.: Time and space in a lattice of universal
     relations with blank entries, in: Proceed. XPT Workshop
     on Relational Database Theory, (Stony Brook, N.J. June
     1980).
50. Thalheim B. Dependencies in Relational Databases, B.G.
     Teuber Verlagsgesellschaft, Stuttgart-Leipzig: 1991.
51. Aho A.V., Beeri C. and Ullman J.D.: The theory of joins
     in relational databases, ACM Trans. on Database Systems,
     v.4, #3 (1979), 297-314.
52. Rissanen J.: Theory of relations for databases - a
     tutorial survey, in: Proceed. 7th Symp. on Math. Found.
     of Computer Science, LNCS, v.64, Springer Verlag, New
     York 1978, 537-551.
53. Lien Y.E.: On the equivalence of database models, J. of
     ACM, v.29, #2, (1982), 333-362.
54. Honeyman P.: Functional dependencies and the universal
     instance property in relational model of database
     systems, (PhD. Diss.), Prinston University, Prinston,
     N.J. 1980.
55. Sciore S.: Some observations on real-world data
     dependencies, in: Proceed. XPT Workshop on Relational
     Database Theory, (Stony Brook, N.J. June 1980).
56. Bernstein P.A. and Chiu D.W.: Using semijoins to solve
     relational queries, J. of ACM, v.28, #1 (1981) 25-40.
57. Bernstein P.A. and Goodman N.: The power of natural
     joins, SIAM J. Comput., v.10, #4 (1981), 751-771.
58. Yu C.T. and Ozsoyoglu M.Z.: An algorithm for tree-query
     membership of a distributed query, in: Proceed. IEEE
     COMPSAC, (Chicago, Nov. 1979), IEEE, New York 1979,
     306-312.

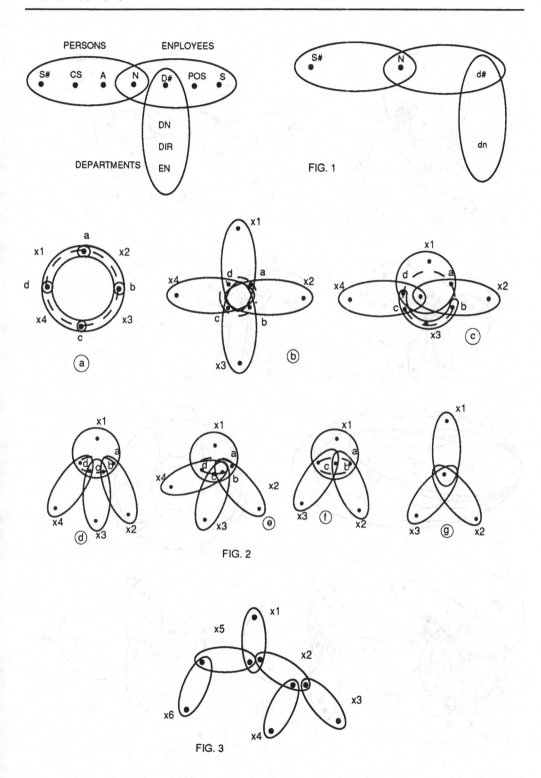

FIG. 1

FIG. 2

FIG. 3

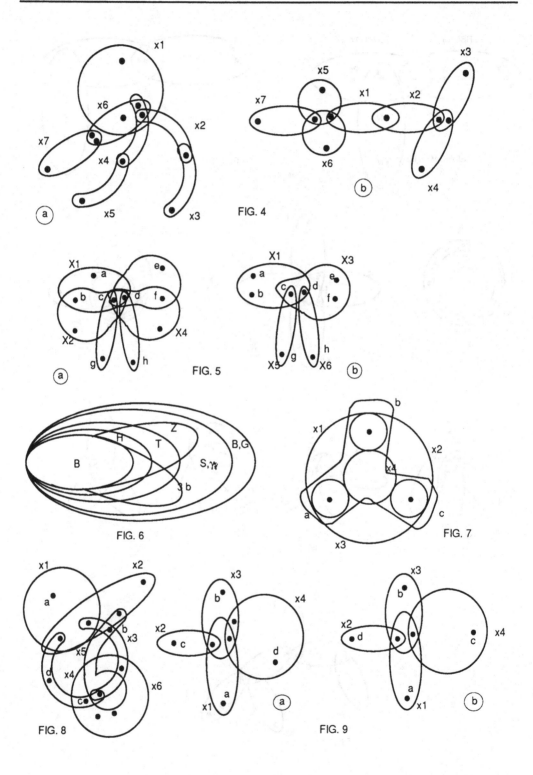

FIG. 4

FIG. 5

FIG. 6

FIG. 7

FIG. 8

FIG. 9

FOUNDATIONS OF DATABASE SYSTEMS:
AN INTRODUCTORY TUTORIAL

J. Paredaens

University of Antwerp, Antwerp, Belgium

and

Technical University of Eindhoven, Eindhoven, The Netherlands

Abstract

A very short overview is given of the principles of databases. The entity relationship model is used to define the conceptual base. Furthermore file management, the hierarchical model, the network model, the relational model and the object oriented model are discussed

During the second world war, computers were used for encoding and decoding messages of the English and German army. Only after the war the computers were used for more reasonable and economical reasons.

In the beginning of the fifties problems with typically a small amount of input data but for which complex calculations have to be made, were solved using computers. This was due to the small amount of memory and the long access time that was needed.

Typical programming languages for this kind of problems emerged: Fortran, Algol and later on Pascal, C and C++.

These languages however, were not user friendly enough, nor were they designed to handle huge amounts of complex data. So in the fifties we switched from simple file management to the use of a data structure that was more complex, but that enabled us to solve problems and answer questions that needed a huge quantity of data.

We will first introduce the concept of a database and then we will look to a number of different kinds of databases that have been used from 1960 until now.

1 What are databases?

A database is a set of software products that enable the user to handle, store and retrieve information. The total system is often called the database management system, DBMS. Sometimes the software can deduce new information from the stored information. Such software is called an information base or a knowledge base.

The DBMS is responsible for

- security of information
- privacy
- exact information
- integrity constraints
- synchronization
- crash protection
- recovery

We make a distinction between:

- the physical database, which describes how the information is stored;
- the conceptual database, which describes how we, human beings, look to the structure of the information;
- the views, which describe the structure of the information as it will be used by the languages in the DBMS.

Furthermore we call the instance of a database the content of the database. Clearly the instance of a database can change from time to time. It changes actually, every time an update is performed. The scheme of the database, however gives the structures of the conceptual model or of the view. We suppose that the scheme never changes.

To illustrate the difference between a scheme and an instance of a database, suppose we have a database of flowers. The conceptual scheme could include the entity types FLOWER and HABITAT, as well as other types of entities and it might include the relationship GROWS_IN between FLOWER and HABITAT, along with other relationships. The instance might include the entity rose and tulip of type FLOWER, with the information that tulip GROWS_IN Holland, while rose GROWS_IN Belgium and France, Holland, Belgium and France being instances of HABITAT. The scheme for the physical database might include that entities of type FLOWER and HABITAT are each character strings of length 10 and GROWS_IN is represented by a linked list of habitats for each flower, with the header of each list obtained by applying a particular hashing function to the name of the flower.

During the period we discuss here, mainly five kinds of databases have been used:
- file management
- hierarchical model
- network model
- relational model
- object oriented model.

We will discuss them now.

File management consists of the management of a number of sequential of direct or indirect access files. The program the have to be written by the users essentially read and write records on files. The total responsibility of the correctness of the software is with the users. The main disadvantages are:

- data redundancy and inconsistency
- difficulty in accessing data
- different formats of data
- concurrent access anomalies
- security problems
- integrity problems

The first two real DBMS's were the network and the hierarchical model.

In the hierarchical model the structure of the database was represented by a number of trees. The user has to navigate within these trees in order to find the record that has to be retrieved, updated or written. In the network model, the structure of the information is represented by a graph. Here too the user has to navigate.

The relational model was the first model in the user has not to navigate. He has not to say how the answer of his query has to be calculated, he only has to specify the information he wants.
At the end of the eighties it became clear that the relational model was too flat and was not convenient to handle information with a complex structure. Due to the impact of object orientation in programming languages the object oriented database model was introduced.

Two main languages are present in nearly every database system: the data definition language (DDL) and the data manipulation language (DML).

In the DDL one defines

- the structure of the entities
- the structure of the relations
- which constraints exist
- the representation of entities on physical level
- the representation of relationships on physical level
- the subschemes
- the granting authorizations
- when backup has to be taken

The DML contains

- the query language
- user friendly operations
- interfaces to host languages
- the transaction language
- granting authorizations

Database Administrator is responsible for

- scheme definition
- storage structure and access method definition
- scheme and physical organization modification
- granting of authorization for data access
- integrity constraint specification

Overall System Structure

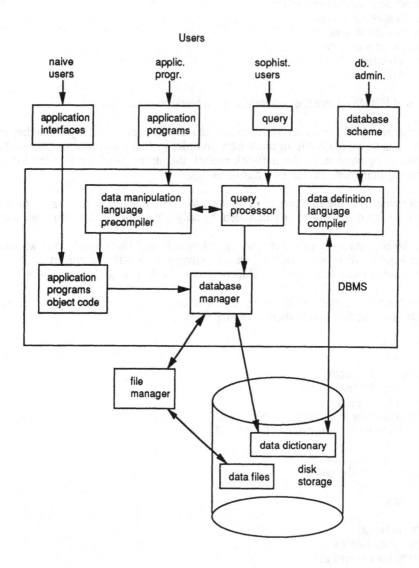

2 The Entity-Relationship Model

An Entity is an object

a house, a person, a number, a book, a town, ...

An Entity Set is a set of similar entities
    houses, persons, numbers, books, towns, ...

Each entity set has some attributes
    name, number, color, location, ...
      • an attribute is a function from an entity set into a domain
      • an entity is described by the value of its attributes
      • entity sets correspond to types

A relationship is an association among several entities.
    a person lives in a house, a book is in a library

A relationship set is a mathematical relation on $n \geq 2$ entity sets: let $E_1, ..., E_n$ be entity sets
then R, being a subset of $\{ (e_1, ... , e_n) \mid e_1 \in E_1, ... , e_n \in E_n \}$ is a relationship set.
    persons live in houses, books are in libraries

Note the difference between:
    • an entity set employees, with attribute phonenumber
    • two entity sets, employees and phonenumbers and a relationship set between them

Relationship set can be
    • one-to-one
    • many-to-one
    • one-to-many
    • many-to-many

Relationship set can have attributes
    People live in towns since date

A superkey is a set of one or more attributes which, taken collectively, allow us to identify uniquely an entity in the entity set.
    books with ISBN and title

A minimal superkey is a candidate key.
    Books have an ISBN number, a local lib. number, an author, a title. Here are several candidate keys

A primary key is the candidate key, chosen by the database administrator.

Strong entity set is a set with a primary key, else it is called a weak entity set.
    Strong : persons, books

A weak entity set has a discriminator and some existence dependencies.

An existence dependency: entity x is existence dependent on entity y, if the deletion of y implies the deletion of x. An existence dependency is binary and many-to-one.

A discriminator is a set of attributes that distinguishes all the entities existence dependent on a same entity.

registrations for courses

The primary key of a weak entity set is the discriminator + the primary key of the sets on which it is dependent.

Entity-Relationship diagrams

entity sets, relationship sets and attributes are represented as follows

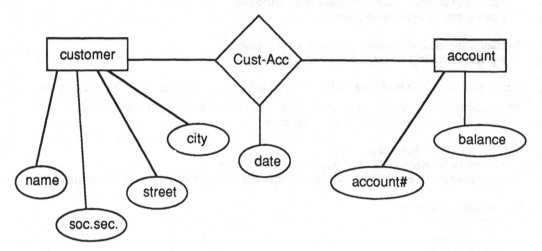

many-to-many relationships are represented by

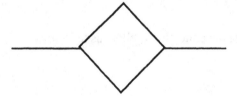

many-to-one relationships are represented by

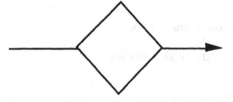

one-to-many relationships are represented by

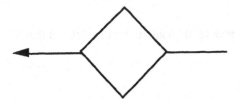

one-to-one relationships are represented by

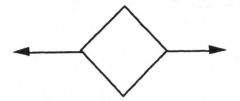

Role is a label on the edges.

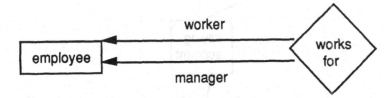

Primary keys for weak entity sets and strong entity sets are represented by

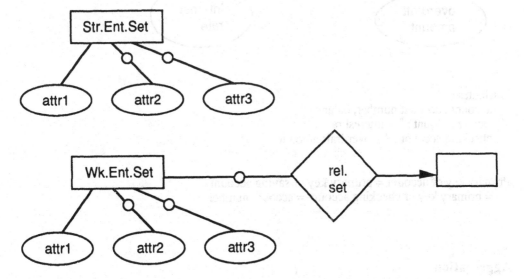

Generalization

Generalization indicates that an entity set is more general than another entity set and that it contains at least all the entities of the latter.

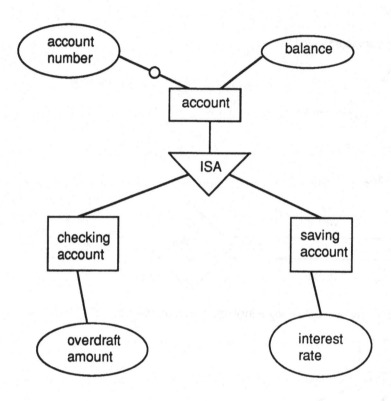

Attributes of
    account : account number, balance
    saving account : " + interest rate
    checking account : " + overdraft amount

Primary key of account = primary key of saving account
    = primary key of checking account = account number

Aggregation

Aggregation is a technique that puts a subdiagram together and considers it as a new entity.

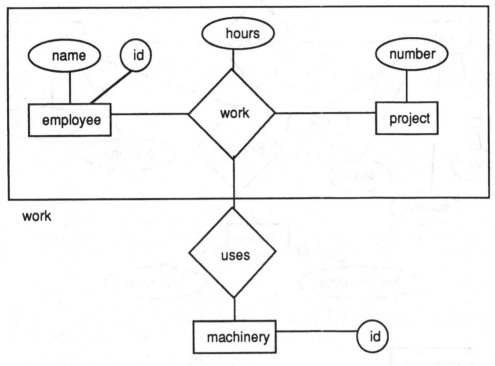

work

Design in the entity relationship model

The following are three entity relationship diagrams. The first diagram shows a ternary relation between customers, accounts and branches. In the second, the set of customers of a particular account in each of its branches has to be equal. In the third diagram every customer can only have at most one account in each branch.

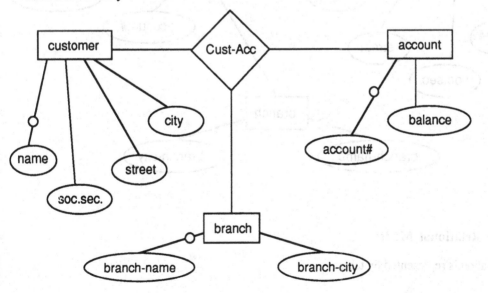

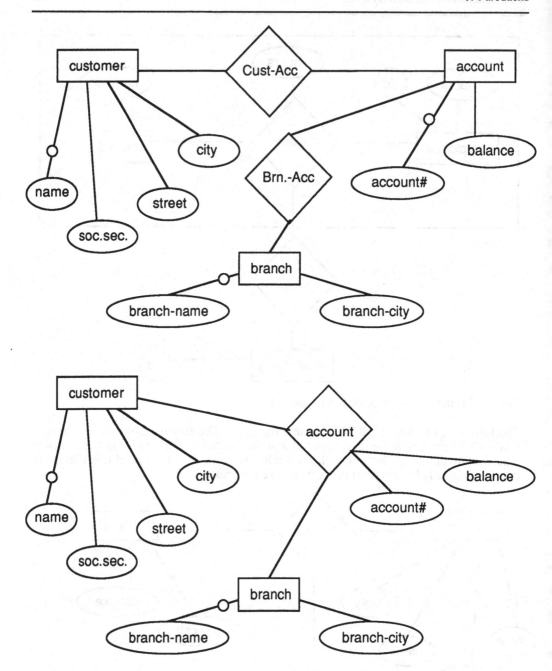

3 The Relational Model

Information is represented by tables

customer-name	street	city
John	Main	London
Mary	13th	Brussels
Tim	Alma	L.A
Harry	C-str.	S.F.

Relational Scheme

$(\Omega, \Delta, dom, M, SC)$

Ω, finite set of attributes, headings in table (here 3 attributes)

Δ, finite set of domains (here 3 domains - set of customer-names, set of street-names, set of city-names)

dom : Ω --> Δ, function associating the domain to every attribute
M : meaning in English
SC : set of constraints

Tuple is a row of the table
t : Ω--> $U_{\delta \in \Delta} \delta$, with $t(A) \in dom(A)$ for every $A \in \Omega$.

A relation instance is a set of tuples that fulfills all the constraints in SC.

A superkey is a subset SK of Ω with for every two tuples t and t', if $t(A) = t'(A)$ for every A of SK then $t = t'$.

Candidate key and primary key as before.

A database scheme is a set of relational schemes. A database instance of this database scheme is a set of associated relational instances.

Abstract Example
Let $\Omega = \{A,B,C\}$

$\Delta = \{$set of integers, set of prime numbers, set of minuscules$\}$
dom(A) is the set of minuscules, dom(B) is the set of integers, dom(C) is the set of primes.
SC contains the following constraints:

• for every tuple its B-value is smaller than its C-value;
• for every tuple its A-value is either the first letter of the English word for its B-value or the first letter of the English words for its C-value;
• there are no two different tuples with the same B-value;
• the sum of the B-value of all those tuples that have the same C-value is greater than that C-value.

An instance and a non-instance

A	B	C
s	6	7
s	3	7
t	20	43
s	11	17

A	B	C
f	14	17
t	2	19
t	21	19

t	2	43
s	7	17
f	22	43

Translation of the E-R Model to the Relational Model

• Translation of strong entity sets
    attribute per attribute
    keys

    customer, last example, Ω = {name,soc.sec.,street,city}

• Translation of weak entity sets
    attributes = attributes + primary keys of entity sets on which dependent
    primary key = primary key of entity sets on which
            dependent + discriminator

• Translation of relationship sets
    attributes = primary keys of related entity sets +
    attributes relationship set
    primary key = primary keys of related entity sets

• Translation of a generalization
    a relation for the high-level entity set and a relation for each low level entity set
    attributes = primary key high-level entity set +
    attributes low level entity set
    primary key = primary key high-level entity set

    account, Ω = {account number, balance}

    saving account, Ω = {account number, interest rate}

    checking account, Ω = {account number, overdraft amount}

4 The Network Model

In this model information is represented by graphs whose nodes are logical record types. The edges represent links that are many-to-one.

Logical record coincides with a tuple logical record has an address, so different logical records can have the same value.

A link is a pointer of a logical record to a logical record.

Example
Scheme

In a hotel database we have guests who stay in one or more rooms

Records
    Guests (Reg#, Name, Address)
    Rooms(Id#, NbOfBeds, Floor, Rate)
    Stay (FromDate, UntilDate)

Links

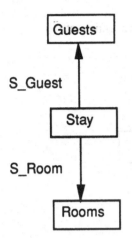

Instance

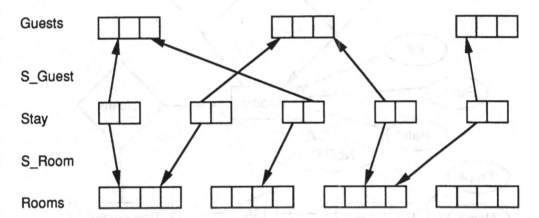

Guests

S_Guest

Stay

S_Room

Rooms

Translation of the E-R Model to the Network Model

• Translation of strong entity sets
   Logical record type

• Translation of weak entity sets
   logical record type + link to logical record type of entity sets on which
   dependent

• Translation of relationship sets
   binary and many-to-one => link
   many-to-one of E_1, ..., E_{k-1} to E_k, and E_k in no other relationship set =>
   logical record type with E_k as attribute
   others => logical record type + links to all logical record types of related entity sets

• Translation of a generalization
  logical record type for the high-level entity set
  logical record type with link to logical record above for each low level entity set

Example

Consider

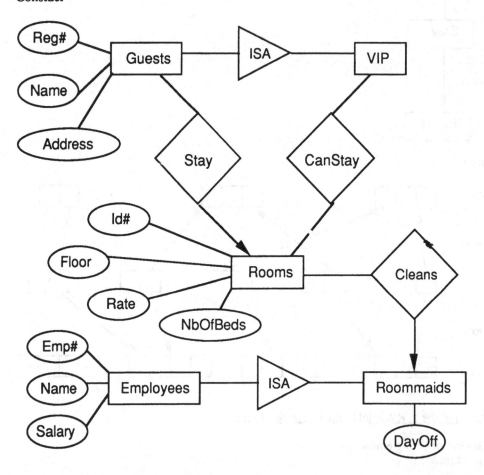

Network Model

Guests(Reg#, Name, Address)
Rooms(Id#, Floor, Rate, NbOfBeds)
Employees(Emp#, Name, Salary)
Roommaids(DayOff)
CanStay( )

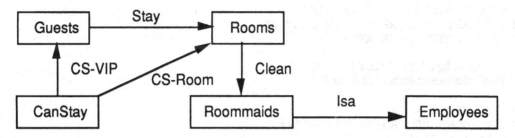

Data Definition Language

Many-to-one relation from R_2 to R_1 is called a DBTG-set (Data Base Task Group). Records of R_2 are the owners of the set, records of R_1 are the members.

```
RECORD GUESTS
  1 REG# INTEGER
  1 GNAME CHAR(20)
  1 ADDRESS CHAR(30);
RECORD ROOMS
  1 ID# INTEGER
  1 FLOOR INTEGER
  1 RATE REAL
  1 NBOFBEDS INTEGER;
RECORD EMPLOYEES
  1 EMP# INTEGER
  1 ENAME CHAR(10)
  1 SALARY REAL;
RECORD ROOMMAIDS
  1 DAYOFF CHAR(1);
RECORD CANSTAY;
```

```
DBTG SET STAY                   DBTG SET ISA
   OWNER IS ROOMS                  OWNER IS EMPLOYEES
   MEMBER IS GUESTS;               MEMBER IS ROOMMAIDS;
DBTG SET CS-VIP                 DBTG SET CLEAN
   OWNER IS GUESTS                 OWNER IS ROOMMAIDS
   MEMBER IS CANSTAY;              MEMBER IS ROOMS;
DBTG SET CS-ROOM
   OWNER IS ROOMS
   MEMBER IS CANSTAY;
```

Data Manipulation Language - Find-statement - Examples

Give the most recent accessed guests-record

```
XYZ = CURRENT OF GUESTS;
FIND GUESTS RECORD BY DATABASE KEY XYZ;
GET GUESTS;
```

Let ENAME be a CALC-KEY for EMPLOYEES (index)
Give the salary of Paredaens

```
EMPLOYEES.ENAME = "PAREDAENS";
FIND EMPLOYEES RECORD BY CALC-KEY;
GET EMPLOYEES; SALARY;
```

Let FLOOR be a CALC-KEY for ROOMS
Print all the roomnumbers of floor 4

```
ROOMS.FLOOR = 4;
FIND ROOMS RECORD BY CALC-KEY;
while not FAIL {
  GET ROOMS; ID#;
  printf("%d\n",ROOMS.ID#);
  FIND DUPLICATE ROOMS RECORD BY CALC-KEY;
}
```

Print the roomnumbers Clinton can stay in

```
GUESTS.GNAME = "CLINTON";
FIND GUESTS RECORD BY CALC-KEY;
FIND FIRST CANSTAY RECORD IN CURRENT CS-VIP SET;
while not FAIL {
  FIND FIRST ENTRIES RECORD IN CURRENT E_ORDERS SET;
  while not FAIL {
    FIND OWNER OF CURRENT CS-ROOM SET;
    GET ROOMS; ID#;
    printf("%d\n",ID#);
    FIND NEXT ROOMS RECORD IN CURRENT CS-ROOM SET;
  }
  FIND NEXT CANSTAY RECORD IN CURRENT CS-VIP SET;
}
```

Find all the employees with a salary above 100

```
DBTG SET ALLEMP
  OWNER IS SYSTEM
  MEMBER IS EMPLOYEES;

FIND FIRST EMPLOYEES RECORD IN CURRENT ALLEMP SET;
while not FAIL {
  GET EMPLOYEES;
  if (SALARY > 100) printf(" %s   %d\n",ENAME,SALARY);
  FIND NEXT EMPLOYEES RECORD IN CURRENT ALLEMP SET;
}
```

5 The Hierarchical Model

Scheme

A hierarchy is a network that is a collection of trees in which all links point in the direction from child to parent.

Network-Hierarchy Conversion Algorithm

```
void build(node n)
{
   make n selected;
   for (each link from some node m to n) {
        make m a child of n;
        if (m is not selected) build(m)
   }
}

void main(void)
{
   make all nodes unselected;
   while (not all nodes are selected) {
        pick an unselected node n;
        /* prefer a node n with no links to unselected nodes
        and prefer a node with many incoming links */
        build(n)
   }
}
```

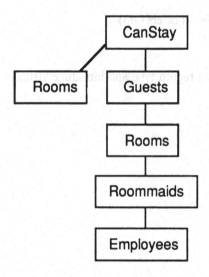

Instance

Collection of trees whose nodes are records

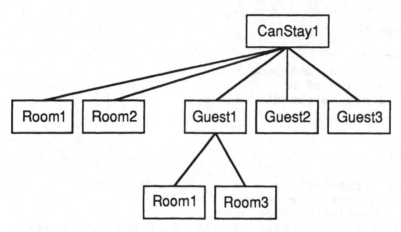

Duplicates
  • waste of space
  • potential inconsistency

In queries one can only go from parents to child
  • find all the offers of supplier Supp1
  • NOT find the supplier of Of3
        (solution is to check for every supplier whether it offers Of3)

Virtual Record Types

We insist to have one occurrence in the scheme of each record type and introduce virtual record types.

In the instance we use pointers.

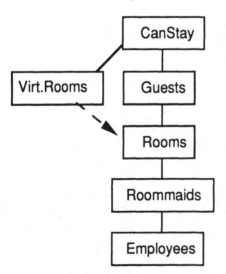

Conversion Algorithm becomes

```
void build(node n)
{
   make n selected;
   for (each link from some node m to n) {
        if (m is not selected) {
             make m a child of n;
             build(m)
        }
        else make virtual m be a child of n
   }
}
```

6 The Object Oriented Model

The main characteristics of the object oriented model in databases are the object identity, the use of complex objects, inheritance and encapsulation.

An elementary type (s.a. int, real, string, ...) is an object type;
If T is an object type then SET_OF(T) is an object type;
If T1, ..., Tn are object types then
RECORD_OF(id1:T1, ..., idn:Tn) is an object type.
If T1 is a subtype of T2 with supplementary fields <s.f.> we write
T1 = SUBTYPE_OF(T2; <s.f.>)
Example

GuestType = RECORD_OF(reg#:int, name: string, address: string,
                                        stay: RoomType)
VIPType = SUBTYPE_OF(GuestType)
RoomType = RECORD_OF(id#:int, floor: int, rate: real, nbofbeds: int,
              canstay: SET_OF(VIPType), cleans: RoommaidType)
or equivalently
SetOfVIPType = SET_OF(VIPType)
RoomType = RECORD_OF(id#:int, floor: int, rate: real, nbofbeds: int,
              canstay: SetOfVIPType, cleans: RoommaidType)
RoommaidType = SUBTYPE_OF(EmployeeType; dayoff: int)
EmployeeType = RECORD_OF(empl#: int, name: string, salary: real)

Methods
To each type (or class) methods are associated:

EmployeeType
GetName:
     return(name)
Raise(X:real):
     salary:=salary+X

Let T be a record-type. We define a subtype T' by adding components and methods to T. (Inheritance).

Methods may be redefined. (Overriding)

Bibliography

[1.] Date C.J. : *An Introduction to Database Systems*, Addison Wesley, 1990
[2.] Elmasri R., Navathe S.B.: *Fundamentals of Database Systems*, 1989
[3.] Korth H.K. , Silberschatz A.: *Database System Concepts,* WcGraw-Hill, 1991
[4.] Paredaens J., De Bra P., Gyssens M., Van Gucht D.: *The Structure of the Relational Database Model*, Springer-Verlag, 1989
[5.] Ullman J.D.: *Principles of Database and Knowledge-base Systems*, 1988

REQUIREMENTS AND DESIGN ISSUES
OF SPATIAL DATA HANDLING SYSTEMS

E. Apolloni
University "La Sapienza", Rome, Italy

F. Arcieri and L. Barella
Algotech s.r.l., Rome, Italy

M. Talamo
University "La Sapienza", Rome, Italy

Abstract.

In this paper we characterize the user profile of systems for spatial data handling. In particular, we characterize the user requirements of a spatial data handling systems dealing with planning and decision making problems. The basic features of these systems is the possibility to support incremental constraint definition and modeling activities.

Moreover, we show that a user requirement analysis in this field should not be performed simply factorizing the set of the operators related to the reference applications, but through an abstraction direct to characterize this reference applicative operations set in terms of "set-oriented" primitives.

We claim that the spatial join, together with few fundamental geometrical operations such as intersection and composition of sub-components, provides a sound platform to define applicative operations.

In particular we aim to point out which functionalities should be set at the system level, and which ones can be set at the application level. According to the present user profile, we also introduce a target architecture for a decision making system that is based on the view building mechanism; the related conceptual data model is also given. As an example, in the last section we introduce a real proposal.

Introduction.

The systems for the management of spatial data are a relevant example of complex applicative environments, due to the structural variety and plenty of relationships implicitly existing among data. These relationships are generally barely exploited, though they may be treated inside the well formalized theory of geometry.

Decisions in land management often determine strong effects on the human activities and natural resources and, in general, on the quality of life in the concerned areas. Information Technology (IT) may provide advanced support to strategic and tactical decision making, and to the assessment of the impact of land planning decisions on population, society, and environment.

In this framework the main interest of decision-makers and policy-makers in the user organisations is in the development of an IT-based environment capable - by means of the integration of the required subsystems and tools - to support the definition of methodologies for the building of plans for land resources and for the evaluation in terms of environmental and social impact of such plans.

The user of this environment is able to create and evaluate possible *scenarios* of the impact of strategic and tactical planning decisions in land resources management. The user, working on the basis of application-specific knowledge, is provided with the possibility of the interactive definition of hypotheses and, using suitable simulation models, testing their impact and consequences with respect to land resources in terms of social, economic and environmental aspects.

Scenarios are evaluated as a result of the interaction of mathematical models and textual/geographical databases and are presented to the user, in the form of thematic maps, by means of advanced graphical interfaces.

For example, a strategical planning activity can be carried out by (i) the characterization of the constraints to be applied to extract relevant spatial objects, (ii) the characterization of the territorial information describing a phenomenon, and (iii) the incremental application, led by an expert, of models constituting scenarios of land classifications according to compatibility and multiobjective optimality criteria.

In the past - before the advent of IT - the only way to answer *what if* questions and in general to make multiobjective planning was to manually combine maps using crayons and layers of acetate to achieve the goals. For this reasons the major requests to spatial data handling systems were:

- map drawing with the aim of the documentation;
- low rate of map redrawing;
- maps quality and reliability related to the skills of the cartographers.

Political borders maps, geological properties maps and other spatial data, had to satisfy the following requirements:

- the scale;
- the topological precision of some peculiar areas;
- the chosen georeferentiation system.

In the Sixties, with the advent of IT, new requirements and constraints were introduced in spatial data handling: the aim was to obtain digitalized maps starting from direct land analysis (or by conversion of existing maps), to store and retrieve the digitalized maps as documents, and finally to design new maps using specialised editors.

These requirements induced the development of the first real generation of cartographic systems, able to automatically support scale changes, to overlay special symbols, to overlay maps to other maps. In spite of that, these systems were essentially built as customisation of existing CAD systems without specific enhancements to the software architecture. For this reason we propose in section three a new architecture.

The applications available in user organizations are generally vertical applications built for specific problems, and are set on the top of a commercial system. Usually, the user does not have a real skill in structured methodologies for decision making and policy making in activities that involve spatial data. It is really impossible to run strategic planning on land resources in an unstructured way, without the possibility to obtain and to maintain the integration among the starting data and the results of the land management activity.

The main activity is actually to apply a set of geometrical transformations to an input data set (input maps) obtaining a new data set as a result: therefore, the emphasis is on geometrical transformations.

Nowadays, the topological properties of spatial data are considered more important than the pure geometrical aspects, the requirements are more focused on spatial data management, the users (who likely are engineers or commercial planners as well as geographers or planners) want extremely rapid responses to their queries; moreover, the users want to manipulate spatial data in order to obtain land scenarios to be evaluated in terms of multiobjective planning and decisions.

GIS applications are in practice very heterogeneous; for example, they may concern map management and composition, or automated land analysis directed to locate suitable sites for specific activities, or the integrated management of information coming from spatial simulation models of physical phenomena.

Common spatial data handling systems trend to be general-purpose, so that it is theoretically possible to implement a large variety, possibly the whole body, of GIS applications using the same system; nevertheless, this yields the uncontrollable growth of the command set, and of their options. It is often quite impossible to master the subsystems that compose a commercial general-purpose spatial data handling system, and sometimes the final user knows the acronyms of the subsystems, but actually does not exactly know what they are planned to do, or how they achieve the aimed targets.

Therefore, it is easy to observe that the common means of user requirement analysis are generally of no use with spatial data handling systems, since spatial applications are very different one another; besides, it is clear that the set of the required functionalities for a specific application is often exploitable only for that application, whereas the great part of these functionalities is useless in other applications.

We claim that a user requirement analysis should not be performed for each specific application; on the contrary, a crucial step in land management systems design is an abstraction process in application classes directed to characterize a reference operation subset that makes up the basement for new systems.

For example, a complete co-ordinate system transformation command, comprehensive of all kinds of geographic projections, may be absolutely necessary for a fixed application, whereas it may be cumbersome for the most part of applications.

On the other hand, the spatial join [1], together with few fundamental geometrical operations such as intersection, composition of sub-components and so on, provides a strong platform for a large class of applications. For example, consider the following typical query: *"extract all wheat fields whose distance is less than 500 m from the river R"*. Just in appearance a distance operator, to be applied to the whole database, is required; on the contrary, a *linebuffer* operator (that geometrically builds the locus of the points for which the distance from a line is less than a fixed value) may be applied to the river R; successively, a spatial join may be applied to the resulting region and to the wheat map to obtain the result of the query.

The achievement of this goal is subjected on a condition on the storage manager: the spatial data have to be represented in a raster format, namely the multivalue quadtree. CARTECH [2] is a working system that really implements the spatial join operation. From a physical point of view, the user works in a scale (e.g., 1:100'000) in which a raster representation is absolutely suitable. Incidentally, we observe that spatial operations are applied to *set-oriented* data representations (incorrectly named *raster*), rather than *shape-oriented* data representations (incorrectly named *vectorial*).

1. User profile.

It is possible to define at least two different GIS user profiles, related to two different uses of spatial data. We define them as *map processing user profile* and *land planning and decision maker user profile*.

1.1. Map processing user profile.

This kind of user is mainly involved in the following set of operations on spatial data:

- the search of the *interesting* data set;
- its selection;
- the application of a sequence of transformations on this data set;
- the utilization of the resulting data set for geometric composition with other data sets, using a suitable graphic editor;
- finally, the plotting of the result.

This set of operations assumes an user expert in cartographic problems and in the management of territorial data; the users perform the most of the abstraction and analysis operations.

The system that satisfies this kind of user must have the following characteristics:

- it has a command set allowing the realisation of all the transformations concerning the user;
- it permits the search and catalogation of data sets;
- it permits to overlay in a graphical way two data sets (georeferentiating them with respect to the same co-ordinate system), applying some geometric composition of the two maps; it builds and stores, if necessary, the new image.

In this sense, the best data type for this user profile is the vectorial data type. A geometric object is represented as a set of polygonal lines: the precision of the representation depends on the codification of the extreme points of the segments that make up the polygonal lines.

It is important to observe that transformations are the classical graphical operations on geometric elements, and that the user operates applying the transformations to the geometry of the spatial objects.

Considering these aspects, one of the best commercial systems supporting these operations is *Arc/Info*, because it presents a complex interface, which makes available more than 1000 commands, and manages many complex operations of geographic transformations requested for the drawing of the maps.

1.2. Land planning and decision maker user profile.

The actual typical user of GISs is more interested in performing different operations on spatial data that the previous one. The main activities of the user concern the planning, decision making and scenario building.

In particular, the user requirements may be so outlined:

- to obtain scenarios as results of complex queries representing a piece of geographic reality;
- to take decisions and to evaluate their consequences in a possibly multiobjective approach;
- to evaluate the impact of external events on the actual data (*data fusion* and *modeling*);
- to build working hypothesis and to compare them.

The main application fields where these characteristics are evident are the urban planning activities, the decision making field, the dynamic symbolization, the temporal analysis.

Then, the most usual operations that are carried out by the user can be summarised as follows:

- Definition of a view on the database. A set of spatial objects, presenting a geometric and descriptive part, which has some interest to the user is selected, while other cumbersome or deceiving objects are obscured.
- Building of the previously defined view: the selected objects are arranged so as to act as the basic datasets for the future handling, computing and transformation activities.
- On the user view, constraints are incrementally applied to extract spatial objects, both on the descriptive and geometric sides.
- Input data to mathematical models are extracted, computed or synthesized starting from the user view datasets. The user often has great difficulties in performing these operations, since neither formal nor practical tools have been developed.
- New spatial objects are created and introduced in the user view making queries, applying geometrical transformations (or functions), mathematical models and constraints.
- Lesser attention will be given to the input and output procedures (digitalizing, plotting, ...), since these can be easily modeled as standard activities that do not involve the typical spatial data elaboration issues. Actually, specific I/O modules may have interest if the system must have real-time capability, such as the elaboration of monitoring data on which a spatial simulation model is run.

A typical working session consists of two main steps:

- building a scenario, starting from the spatial object database, by means of queries on the database;
- customising the obtained scenario, by means of the application of constraints and transformations.

As a result, these operations produce a new scenario and a set of new spatial objects, satisfying the user needs.

Then, this kind of user wants to query the spatial objects with regard to their properties, eventually creating new objects as a result; the user is not interested in knowing (at least he could not know how to declare it) which transformation the production of new spatial objects needs.

This new user profile introduces a strong requirement for the GIS system; actually, the data cannot be considered like static information, but dynamic; the queries expressed by the user can induce some updates in the database, and these updates must be managed in a firm way, solving the problem of the consistency maintenance.

The origins and the nature of this problem is now discussed.

In general, a piece of geographical information has two components. The first one regards spatial aspects of the data item, like its shape and its position in the space; such elements implicitly define other relations among data, generally of topological and metric nature. The second one is concerned with values of descriptive properties associated to the data item, like - in the case of a city - its name, the number of inhabitants, the average income, and so on.

An efficient approach to the management of the two components of geographical information is to have different access methods at the physical level and an integrated view at the logical one. This also allows the user to interact with the system in a uniform and homogeneous way. Unfortunately, given the implicit spatial relations existing among geographical data, this does not guarantee the maintenance of the semantic consistency of information during user manipulations. Moreover, semantic relations existing among data as a consequence of the implicit relations are not adequately represented: the user can easily recognize some topological relations between spatial objects, but he cannot ask skilled queries to the system, since the only information it has about the object is, for example, that it is a polygon with the associated value for the field *mean population* is equal to 100; actually, the user does not need at all to know that his geographic objects are polygon, lines or points, since this distinction is forced merely by technical issues, and not by conceptual requirements.

The use of an application then requires the final user great integration and synthesis efforts. Therefore, the view building process has to be defined taking into account both aspects of geographical information. We now show with an example which consistency problems can arise during user interaction, even in very simple cases.

Suppose to have the following query: *"build the view representing river segments, with their average width, which cross the territory of 'A' region and have an average width larger than 10 meters"*.

The query can be solved using the implicit relation of spatial intersection among polylines representing rivers and the polygon representing 'A' region extent. Spatial processing of the query extracts river segments satisfying the intersection relation and this may result in breaking the thematic map[1] describing rivers. As a consequence it may not be possible to assign values of average width to river segments in a consistent way. See figure 1 as an example. On side (i) the case where line segment 'a' coincides with the part of the river crossing region 'A' is shown: in this case the average width of the river inside 'A' region territory coincides exactly with the average width of segment 'a'. On the side (ii) the line segment 'a' extends beyond the region 'A' boundaries, and the average width of the portion inside 'A' is not known.

We say that the thematism is *broken*, and new spatial elements must be computed, and the associated descriptive information must be in some way derived in a consistent way.

---

[1]A thematic map is a geometrical subdivision of a piece of land in areas homogeneous with respect to values of a set of attributes, together with a table which associate to each homogeneous area the given set of values for the attributes.

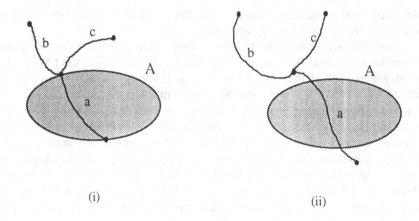

fig. 1.

Note that this example highlights a crucial point: what is difficult in GIS is the need of computing in a consistent way new geographical objects, that is new couples (spatial-datum, descriptive-datum), in consequence of queries involving implicit spatial relations. If querying never broke spatial components, relations could be explicitly stored in the system after having been pre-calculated. This would result in an overall system simpler to design and simpler to use. Under this hypothesis, in the situation used for the above example all couples (region, river-segment) which satisfy the spatial intersection relation could be explicitly stored in the database, and a query asking for "all rivers passing through 'X' region" would not need any spatial predicate to be computed.

2. Methodology issues in modeling.

The remarks previously made about the user profiles make evident the fact that the activity of the new kind of user of GIS is characterised by an higher level of abstraction from the implementation details than it was in the past.

Actually, when an application becomes even more complex, it is important to hide irrelevant details, focusing the attention of the user on the whole problem. It is possible to assert that many teams, involved in the research and modeling activities, focus up to 50% of their attention on computational issues that are irrelevant to the scope of the research or of the modeling [3]. It is clear that significant increases in efficiency are possible for applications where computation is a major activity. Since these users may then focus their resources on the solution of the whole problem, rather than on irrelevant computational issues, the efficiency should increase markedly. The geometric transformations of the data are important, but they do not constitute the real objective of the modeling.

Just as in the field of the programming languages with the passage from the procedural languages to the object oriented ones, or from the low level languages, where there are not control structures, to the structured languages, in the field of the spatial data management now it is important to know *what* we have to do, but we do not need to know *how*.

An analysis of the actual situation in the land resources management field was accomplished to understand the range of application areas, to gain knowledge of which activities are performed during the land management, to know the types of data required and/or used during these activities, to consider tools currently used to carry out land planning, their limitations and required improvements, to realize which are the most used methodologies in land management. This analysis involved the tools actually used by the users, the adopted methodology, the typical user profile, the data currently used and the high system functionalities available to the final user. The following areas were investigated: economic area (bank services, extractive activities, energy planning), network area (traffic, roads, technological networks, transportation, utilities location), social area (education, user information, leisure, telematic services), natural resources (waste, environmental monitoring, environmental planning, accident prevention), housing and built-up environment (urban improvement, town planning, heating plants).

The general results of this analysis can be summarized as follow:

- there are models for some planning activities; in practice, just simple models are used to aid land planning; the main problems opposing to the use of models are the lack of resources and the complexity of real world;
- no unified formal methodology is available; formal methodology use is closely related to the model availability for the planning activity; since there are several areas where no model exists, no formal methodology is used at all;
- however, there is a set of practical methodologies driven by heuristics tailored to each particular condition of one planning activity in one city;
- data required for carrying out planning activities seems to be more uniform across different planning activities and different cities. In general, cadastral, topological, statistical, descriptive and legislative data are required; the data usually come from public files of data which are available for other purposes;
- a graphic characterisation supported by maps is the most expressive representation used to present planning results to other people (decision makers, public, ...).

For each of the investigated points, we have defined the following requirements.

- Existing tools: for the planning area there are only *vertical applications* developed, in the best case, on the top of existing GISs.

- The methodology to be used in the planning activities includes the following steps:
    1) select a model
    2) build the view (Scenario)
    3) apply the model to the view
    4) evaluate results
    5) if not satisfied, restart from point 2
    6) use or validate the new spatial objects.
- The user profile is the profile of a system manager, skilled in IT, or a final user, that is a planner.
- The data used in the planning activities are urban objects having both geometrical and descriptive information: technological networks (gas, water, heating, electric, ...), roads, buildings, districts, offices, factories, shops, morphological constraints, area subjected to legal constraints; the information sources are very heterogeneous; there is a high spatial density of the descriptive side of the information at urban level; there is a high rate of updating.

The so defined user profile helps in the definition of a general methodology for the planning activities, which matches with the user adopted decision processes. The steps of this methodology are:

- build a scenario, define a view on the spatial objects;
- define the view schema, that is the new objects;
- apply constraints, both on the descriptive and geometric sides, to the object base, instantiating a new object;
- apply generic transformations (models, algorithms, ...);
- materialize the view.

In order to put these ideas in concrete form, we suppose that the user has to solve the following query: *"Find all the regions at distance less than 100 m from the regions that are covered (according to the result of a flood routing model execution) by water, in which the population density is greater than 1000 inhabitants per Km²"*.

The system designer can help the user in two ways: in the first, the designer makes available a flexible operator called *distance(x,y)*, where x and y are spatial objects; thus, the user can define a short sequence of commands to build the region near the flooded areas, and then intersect these with the population density map. This seems a good solution, but it is not the only one.

A better approach for a land planning user is to provide him with an environment in which he can define a predicate that selects all the regions of interest. In this case, the user is requested to define the result of the query according to the logical properties of the basic datasets. Supposing that *distance(x,d)* is now an operator that returns the areas at less than d from the spatial object x, the above query can be so expressed:

Select intersection(population, distance(flood,100))
where population.density > 1000.

This is due to the set-oriented nature of spatial data: therefore, it is straighforward to declare the properties of the desired geographical objects.

3. Target architecture for decision making.

The users solve complex territorial problems following a typically incremental and iterative way. In fact, many times the end-user interaction is mainly aiming to identify which classes of data are of interest and which relations exist (either explicitly or implicitly) among them; moreover, patterns of manipulations of data and relations cannot be defined a priori since they depend on the expert's working methodology. This means that the user interaction pattern is based on a identify-relate-apply cycle, where firstly the classes of data of interest are identified, then relations among them are established, and finally some expert-defined methodology is applied. Therefore, the user performs navigation actions through raw data and partially structured data, browsing through them to establish a schema of interest for his/her task: then he/she carries out experiments and processing actions required by the specific (user- and task- dependent) working methodology. This approach of deriving user views and refining them is common to a wide class of new applications, such as scientific, hypermedia, and financial applications [4].

The architecture for such a kind of systems is therefore centered around the module (view builder) supporting user interaction with the database by means of view building capabilities (figure 2).

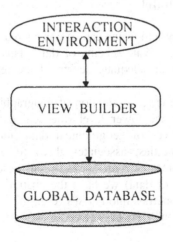

fig. 2.

As we have seen above, building a view may result in deriving new objects, that is extracting knowledge that before was implicitly contained in the data and it has been now materialized. Database is updated as a consequence of this process, which therefore needs to be defined in a way the ensures the maintenance of the overall data consistency. This requires the definition of an interaction model based on a suitable supporting mechanism to allow consistency maintenance. For geographical data such mechanism can be found in geometry which, thanks to the property of object identityness which characterises its instances (i.e. each spatial items), can act as a kind of fix-point during data manipulation and play the role of a universal key. Geometry allows to maintain those cross-reference links among different views which ensure consistency in the values of the descriptive part of those entities which are connected through implicit relations involving the spatial component. In this way it becomes possible to derive in a correct and consistent way not only the spatial component of new pieces of information and the relations which are involved, but also its descriptive counterpart.

Hence, geometry is the leverage allowing to work safely with implicit knowledge in geographical information. The implementation of such an approach requires the definition of primitive operators which allows to extract knowledge in an efficient and consistent way.

In order to give a profitable support to this kind of users, the system should allow a *high level* language to specify mixed topological and descriptive queries, and to create new spatial objects. This language ought to hide the topological relationship analysis and identification process induced by the query, realising the process of abstraction in the specification of the operations. It ought also to maintain the consistency of the spatial database.

4. The conceptual data model.

Our goal is to realize a system which can be considered as a view builder where each view is represented by a private schema of data. This approach needs in the phase of conceptual modeling an adequate design of the representation of data at different abstraction levels.

A reference schema for the representation of geographical data can be seen at two levels of abstraction. At the lower level (the schema of data) we have the abstraction that groups instances of geographical data into sets, *entities*, whose elements have common properties, associates them to an appropriate sets of geographic references and represents *relations* between these istances. At the next, higher, level (the metaschema of data) we have the abstraction that groups entities and relations with common properties into *classes* (e.g., the class *geographical entity* as abstraction of entities "Region", "Town", "River").

The general description of data is realized at the higher level of abstraction (the metaschema of data), since the first level is strictly bound to the particular context of the application (the view) on which the system operates.

In this context the view building process can be described as a particular instantiation of the metaschema. It is important to notice that this process does not modify the metaschema. In this way we are not bound to the particular context of the application which is represented by the schema, since the insertion of new data can involve the definition of new entities, but does not modify the schema of the classes (the metaschema).

A general description of geographical data maintained by the system at the metaschema level is sketched in the diagram of figure 3.

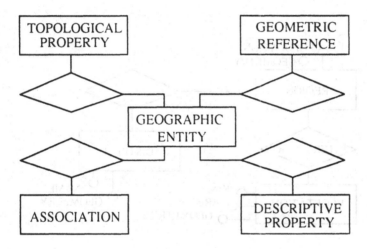

fig. 3.

The class GEOGRAPHICAL ENTITY represents the abstraction of all possible ways of classifying geographical data according to their descriptive nature (e.g., the element of the class "lake" represents the concept of the set of lakes in the territory of interest).

The class TOPOLOGICAL PROPERTY models the abstraction of all possible relations of topological type which can be associated to two instances of the class GEOGRAPHICAL ENTITY (e.g., relation of intersection, inclusion, and so on).

The class ASSOCIATION models the existence of this type of relation between the GEOGRAPHICAL ENTITY. The introduction of an association mechanism permits a structured organization of the data in the system.

The class GEOMETRIC REFERENCE models the sets of possible ways to represent spatial extension of GEOGRAPHICAL ENTITY in the territory of interest.

The class DESCRIPTIVE PROPERTY models the set of possible descriptive characteristics which can be associated to a GEOGRAPHICAL ENTITY.

In figure 4 a schema of data which represents a possible instance of metaschema previously described is sketched.

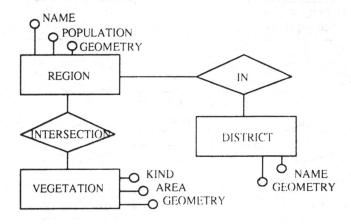

fig. 4.

From the previous discussion on the role of the geometry in the model, it follows that the geometry is a fundamental organising concept for maintaining consistence during manipulations and for the integration of both the geometric and descriptive components of the data. Therefore we need to be able to represent geometric elements, that is spatial extensions and their positions. We need also to be able to sustain the fundamental operations of intersection because they permit the extraction of implicit knowledge, and the operations of composition/decomposition (i.e. aggregation/disaggregation) because they permit the hierarchical structuring of the information.

Thus, the model of the data is defined taking the containment of objects as the fundamental principle for the structuring and taking the operation of intersection as the fundamental principle for the manipulation.

An *instance of a geographic database*, which we refer to also as a *database* for brevity, is a collection of geographical objects; a *geographical object* is an ordered pair (O,N) where O, the so-called *spatial element*, represents the form and position of the geographical object, and where N, the so-called *descriptive element*, is a set of values pertaining to the descriptive properties of the object.

In figure 5 an example of a geographical object is displayed demonstrating both the spatial component O and the descriptive element N consisting of the attributes A_1, A_2, A_3.

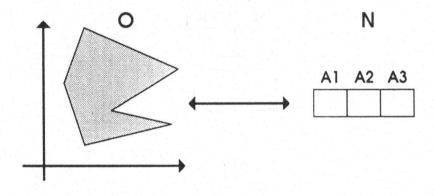

fig. 5.

One observes that the geographical objects are instances of the entities of the scheme, which are in turn instances of the class "Geographical entities" of the metascheme.

A precise formalization of this data model can be found in [3].

5. A concrete example.

In this section the top-level design of a spatial data handling system, carried out under the SWOP Project in co-operation of the *University of California, Santa Barbara* (UCSB) with us (i.e., the *Rome group*), is shown. The design was led by the ideas discussed in this paper.

5.1. Logical block architecture.

The system is designed on the basis of the formerly hypothesized land planning and decision maker user profile (see section 1.2).

A top-level architecture scheme is provided in figure 6.

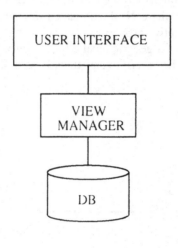

fig. 6.

The user interface is a typical software layer that constitutes a graphical operative environment in which menus, editing and browsing windows are supported in order to warrant an easy use of the modules below. A development system, for instance such as MOTIF, will be exploited in the code generation for graphical resources management.

The view manager is a set of modules whose main task is the creation of spatial objects, both making queries on the database and applying functions (transformations) on spatial objects.

The reference statement of the system has the following format:

transformation_type transformation_name(*parameter* p_1, ... , *parameter* p_n, *constraint* c),

where the name of the transformation is specified in transformation_name, p_1, ..., p_n are optional parameters, and the constraint c specifies the properties of the spatial object on which the transformation is applied. A constraint composed by spatial objects and recursion-less topological predicates. An object is either a global database object, or the result of a transformation. A transformation is applied to an only spatial object.

The view manager reference language is the MDBL [5,6] developed by the Santa Barbara group, extended to support all the planned functionalities.
A description of the view manager architecture is provided in figure 7.

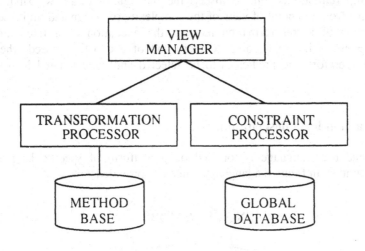

fig. 7.

Two submodules are contemplated. The transformation processor handles a method base, in which transformation and general purpose routines are stored. A transformation is meant to be the implementation of a complex algorithm, that moves from a single dataset to produce a single new dataset as a specialization of the input.

This module requires the constraint processor - via the view manager - to extract the input data (expressed as a constraint that defines the object properties) by means of a *select* statement, and to store the output data, i.e. the created spatial objects, by means of a *create* statement. It uses a transformation library. Moreover, the transformation processor permits the user to define a set of custom transformations that enhance the method base. The consistent updating of the database is delegated to the underlying DBMS.

The constraint processor permits the definition and the evaluation of spatial constraints by means of a specific topological rule definition language, that is directly translated into a set of spatial operations. Therefore, the constraint processor is planned to handle topological predicates over more than one dataset.

The constraint processor has access to a geometric engine (i.e., the CARTECH's geometric processor [2]) that performs a set of basic spatial operations. The resolution of spatial queries is a typical task of this module; for example, "*Select the areas for which the extractable material is iron and the extraction permission is given*" requires a topological join between the *materials* dataset and a *permission* dataset, and the intersection operator must be available. The constraint application result is a spatial object, that is passed to the view manager for further computing (i.e., transformations).

It is important at this point to observe that the creation of a new spatial object is a crucial issue from the point of view of the complexity of design and implementation. The evaluation of a transformation requires the execution of a fixed algorithm, whereas the evaluation of a complex query and of a constraint needs the use of topological operators and predicates to be selected and concatenated in execution time.

5.2. Abstraction level description.

The end user language is founded on a platform of specific languages for different activities. In figure 8 a language scheme is provided.

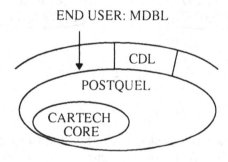

fig. 8.

The user reference language for modelling and database activities is the MDBL developed by the Santa Barbara group, for its capability to support definition and manipulation of a large variety of complex spatio-temporal objects and transformations.

As previously stated, the constraint processor is accessed by means of its own language. It is based on the CDL (Constraint Definition Language) [7] developed by the Rome group in the *ITU-Land* Esprit research project. In the reference statement:

$$\text{transformation}(p_1, \dots, p_n, c),$$

the constraint c is expressed in CDL. We make an assumption of spatial universality, for which the reference system is unique for the whole set of datasets.

The topological rule definition language is a fundamental characteristic of the system, since common expert systems for spatial resources management actually do not handle spatial data with a topological approach; on the contrary, they use a typically attribute-oriented approach. The Rome group might take advantage in the definition and implementation of the constraint processor language from the ITU-Land experience, and in the treatment of topological operator and predicates from the CARTECH development activities under the Multidata Project.

The underlying database, as suggested by the Santa Barbara group, is the extended relational system POSTGRES [8,9]; it seems to be very attractive because it is an open system that provides support for complex objects, provides user extendibility for data types and operators, and it is oriented towards rule supporting. POSTGRES fully plays the DBMS role: the whole data integrity and consistency management is delegated to this system.

The abstract data type Geometry, as it was defined by the Rome group in [10], might be defined as a POSTGRES class; the topological predicates and operators already developed by the Rome group in CARTECH might make up the methods of the class; spatial entities are objects of the Geometry class.

CARTECH core implements the geometry class, its owned methods, and indexing techniques on spatial data (extended quadtree storage manager). Hence, the class Geometry is the manager of the spatial data from the POSTQUEL point of view, which results enhanced to support spatial objects, upon which topological primitives are already available optimized and severely tested in the CARTECH experience.

The planned representation format of geometric data is multivalued-quadtree based in all the spatial operations supplied: nevertheless, procedure of conversion between different formats will be developed, so that at higher level of abstraction level operators will be available under whichever representational domain. Moreover, the uniqueness of spatial data type guarantees the consistency of spatial entities shared between different applications.

As pointed out in [8], adding a new data type in POSTGRES is quite easy, but designing and writing the related access methods is a very hard task; therefore, particular efforts are made to face this problem.

6. Conclusions.

In this paper we have characterized the profile of the typical user of spatial data handling systems for land planning and decision making. This user wants to query the spatial objects with regard to their properties and new objects are created as the result of the application of queries and constraints.

The main activities of the new user concern the planning, decision making and scenario building. So, the basic features of the future systems will be focused on constraint definition and modeling facilities. We noticed that there isn't a satisfactory alignment between the user needs and the real systems.

Moreover, we showed that a user requirement analysis should not be performed for each specific application, since it is of basic importance in land management systems design to perform an abstraction process in application classes directed to characterize a reference operation subset that makes up the basement for the new systems.

For example, we showed that the spatial join, together with few fundamental geometrical operations such as intersection and composition of sub-components, provides a sound platform for a large class of applications.

Acknowledgements.

We are indebted with many people who, at various times during the last month, were involved in fruitful discussions on the above described ideas; special thanks to Stefano Ercoli and Enrico Nardelli for their contribution in the development data model, and in the characterization of the target architecture.

References.

[1] M. Gargano, E. Nardelli, M. Talamo: "Abstract Data Types for the logical modeling of complex data", Information Systems, Vol. 16, n° 6, 1991.

[2] F. Arcieri, E. Nardelli, "An integration approach to the management of geographical information: CARTECH", 2nd ACM-IEEE International Conference on System Integration (ICSI'92), Morristown, New Jersey, USA, June 1992.

[3] E. Apolloni, F. Arcieri, S. Ercoli, E. Nardelli, M. Talamo, "Un modello di riferimento per l'interazione con sistemi per la gestione di dati geografici" (in italian), in Proc. of SEBD '93, June 1993, Gizzeria Lido, Italy.

[4] S.B.Zdonik, "Incremental database systems: databases from the ground up", Proc. of SIGMOD 93, Washington, D.C., USA, May 1993.

[5] T.R. Smith, J. Su, D. Agrawal, and A. El-Abbadi, "MDBS: a Modeling and Database System to support research in the earth sciences", Technical Report, Dept. of Computer Science, UCSB, 1993.

[6] T.R. Smith, J. Su, M.F. Worboys, "Supporting the Construction and Use of Spatio-Temporal Domains In Scientific Databases", July, 1993.

[7] E. Apolloni, G. Batini, M. Talamo, "Parallel alarm models: a logic framework for the assessment of flooding impact in the Tevere river basin", in Proc. of AM/FM European Conference IX "Spatial Management in a Europe without Borders", October 13-15, 1993, Strasbourg, France.

[8] M. Stonebraker, L.A. Rowe, and M. Hirohama, "The implementation of POSTGRES", IEEE Transaction on Knowledge and Data Engineering Vol. 2, n° 1, pg. 125-142, 1990.

[9] M. Stonebraker, and L.A. Rowe, "The design of POSTGRES", ACM SIGMOD Vol 15, n° 2, pg. 340-355, 1986.

[10] M. Gargano, E. Nardelli, M. Talamo: "A model for complex data: completeness and soundness properties", International Workshop on Database Management Systems for Geographical Applications, Capri, Maggio 1991, in G. Gambosi, M.Scholl, H.W.Six, (eds), Geographic Database Management Systems, Esprit Basic Research Series, Springer Verlag, June 1992.

HERMES: AN INTEGRATED APPROACH
TO MODELLING DATA BASE SYSTEMS DESIGN

F. Arcieri
Algotech s.r.l., Rome, Italy

E. Apolloni
University "La Sapienza", Rome, Italy

L. Barella
Algotech s.r.l., Rome, Italy

M. Talamo
University "La Sapienza", Rome, Italy

Abstract

Decisions in urban planning often determine strong effects on the social structure of urban areas and, in general, on the quality of life in such areas. Information technology may provide advanced support to strategic and tactical decision making and to assessing the impact of urban planning decisions on population and society.

The main goal of HERMES (ESPRIT Project 5405) was to define and show the capabilities of an environment for the creation and evaluation of possible scenarios of the impact of strategic and tactical planning decisions on urban areas. HERMES is an environment, based on a skeleton of a planning methodology, able to provide specific support to the activities related to the urban planning.

In this work we give a general description of the motivations and objectives of the projects, we describe the architecture of the HERMES prototype and of the underlying GIS, and we illustrate the models integrated in the final prototype, used with real data to solve effective problems of urban planning.

Introduction

Practice of urban administration and planning activities vary widely, particularly with regard to the role of central bureaux the use of consultants and service companies, and the nature of their own infrastructure. Thus the requirement for data and access to it will vary accordingly. Despite this, planning and administrative activities do follow a common pattern, in which one can distinguish day to day management from the analysis of options for change.

Despite the observed large variety of means and infrastructures, it is clear that methodologies of urban planning and planners do exist: for example, the use of statistical models for predictive purpose. But models themselves and the data and problems they relate to, are often unique to each urban authority. The HERMES project did not attempt to harmonise these models or data or to provide new ones, but intended to provide a uniform environment in which these differing models and data could be applied.

It was therefore envisaged that each local authority would already have its data, its methods, and its rules for evaluating decision, approved either for its own user or those of its consultants or contractors.

It was desirable that the information bases used for day to day management should in principle be available for evaluating the impact of or the options for change: in practice the large size of databases, and their differing infrastructures made this a challenge.

The main goal of HERMES was to define and show the capabilities of an environment for the creation and evaluation of possible scenarios of the impact of strategic and tactical planning decisions on urban areas. The user, working on the basis of application-specific knowledge, is provided with the possibility of interactively defining hypotheses and testing their impact and consequences with respect to urban areas, in terms of social, economic and environmental aspects.

Scenarios are built as a result of the interaction of mathematical models and textual/geographical databases and are presented to the user by means of advanced graphical interfaces, in the form of thematic maps and other suitable visual presentation metaphores (e.g. bar charts, graphs, space-time maps, ...).

Therefore, it was intended in this project to define and demonstrate solutions for the main issues, at the technical and the system levels, so as to make available to the user an environment which fully integrates subsystems for the management of geographic information, mathematical models, and specific knowledge.

1 - General overview

The ESPRIT Project 5405 HERMES (Highly interactive Environmental Resource Management Extendible System) is a 32 month project started in November 1990, and ended in June 1993 [1]. This project involves the following sites: Algotech Sistemi (Italy), main contractor; Azienda Servizi Municipalizzati of Brescia (Italy), user; Kommunedata (Denmark); University of Paisley (Scotland); Novosoft (Spain); Ayuntamento de Sevilla (Spain), user.

Azienda Servizi Municipalizzati di Brescia is the public utility company of Brescia. Its utility services are: electric power and district heating generation and distribution, water supply, natural gas distribution, city public transport, garbage collection and disposal, road clean up, street lighting, traffic lights and parking meters.

Ayuntamiento de Sevilla/LIPASAM is a public company of the Sevilla Municipality involved in street cleaning, waste collection and waste elimination. It is the biggest company in this area in Spain.

The main objectives of the project can be summarised as follows.
- To define an automated methodology for urban planning activities, by means of an abstraction process of the requirements coming from user driven case studies.
- To define an integrated environment to support strategic and tactical planning activities which combines mathematical models, heuristic knowledge and geographical data, with the intention of making it easier the evaluation of alternatives and options in the field of territorial planning.
- To generate the architecture of an environment for urban planning where decision makers can easily build and evaluate 'scenarios' of the impact of strategic and tactical planning decisions on urban areas, in terms of selected social, economical and environmental aspects. In this way, the system obtained is much more usable than current ones, whose technicalities very often make it difficult for decision makers to directly use them.

HERMES is an environment, based on a skeleton of a planning methodology, able to provide specific support to the activities related to the urban planning.

HERMES provides a framework integrating Descriptive Data (data managed by a DBMS) and Geometrical Data (data managed by a GIS/CAD), using a "logical" set of communication channels that makes the integration of this two kinds of data completely transparent to the users.

Moreover HERMES supports "logical" entry points for the developing (or porting) of mathematical models concerning urban territorial planning.

In particular in HERMES it is possible to individuate two different cycles of life:
a) Planning Activities. The related tasks are:
- Select the Data on which the planning should be carried out (Scenario Manager&Browser)
- Select the mathematical model suitable for the planning (Model Manager)
- Create the input data scenario for the model (Scenario Manager&Browser, Scenario Builder, Model Instantiator)
- Run the model and evaluate the results (Model executor, Model Analyser)
b) Development/Porting of Mathematical Models
- Describe the model to be inserted in the system (Model Manager)
- Describe an input scenario suitable for the model execution
- Insert the model in the system.

It is important to note that, during the planning activities, the results obtained by the execution of a model are directly integrated in the system; in fact, when a model is installed, the system gets the information about the output format of the model, and by means of this operation, the result of a model become re-usable as input for another model.

HERMES differs from other environments because it is an integrate framework for supporting urban planning activities. In HERMES the functionalities of the territorial management, of the alphanumeric data and of the mathematical models are indivisible and they give to the system user a unique conceptual view. For instance it is not possible, or at least it is not supported by the environment, to insert a new planning model without defining a minimum schema of the data necessary to the model and without having given the right control parameters for its execution.

The projectual chooses were oriented towards the reuse of already existing tools/environments possibly realised by the Consortium members in order to assure their optimal personalization towards the HERMES requirements. Moreover HERMES is able to port alphanumeric and geographic data for the territorial data management system of A.S.M. and, through the opportune export commands, from Arc/Info itself.

A particular regard must be given to the user analisys tests.

So far, people involved in urban planning, not only our users A.S.M. and Ayuntamento de Sevilla, did not have available an environment like HERMES - the other environments available on the market are generally vertical applications built for a specific problem and on the top of a commercial system - therefore, they do not have a real skill in structured methodologies for strategic planning. It is really impossible to run strategic planning in an unstructured way and without the possibility to obtain and to maintain a strict integration among the starting data and the results of the planning activity.

With reference to the above considerations, the goal pursued was to transform the planning methodology actually used, making it better defined and more specific in respect to the potentialities and prerogatives of the HERMES environment. The results of this activity themselves constitute an interesting result for the HERMES exploitation since their reachibility is granted by the existence of the tool. The use of a so defined methodology will allow a notable improvement of the services resulting from the planning activities.

In this framework, it is possible to support the urban planning at each level: the strategical planning, to define the guidelines for classifying urban areas with respect to the requested kind of decision and constraints; the tactical planning, to find out the pieces of urban area potentially suitable, with respect to the defined guidelines, to reach our planning objectives; the operational planning, to define actions, using both the actual data and the data coming from tactical activities.

A fundamental requirement directly coming from what written above is the need to maintain a strong link among alphanumeric and geographic data obtained by the strategical planning activity and the alphanumeric and geographic data already available in the planning environment in order to have a more complete use of them in the drafting of tactical/operative plans. The loss of such link makes it complex, if not impossible, the reuse of data in subsequent tactical/operative planning activities. In this case HERMES is different from many potential competitors on the market because such problems are solved thanks to the high level of integration among the different data typologies of the used data. This problem has been solved using a Geographical DBMS, CARTECH, described in the following, which permits to manage descriptive and spatial information, stored in two different ways, maintaining the consistency of the data and allowing, at the logical level, an integrated way to manage the information.

At the moment, the HERMES environment is available on a) HP risc series 700, XWindows 1.1 release 5, OSF Motif, DBMS Oracle, and on b) PCs 80486 running SCO ODT 3.0, XWindows 1.1 release 5, OSF Motif, DBMS Informix.

2 - The user-oriented architecture of HERMES

In figure 1 a schema of the HERMES functional modules is shown:

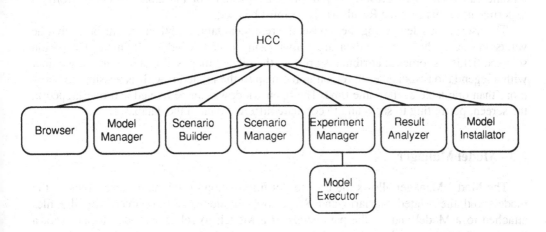

figure 1

2.1 - HCC: Hermes Control Centre

The HERMES Control Centre (HCC) was created to integrate the use of the separate modules of HERMES. It was designed to be both powerful and easy to use. The interface is well documented and all functions provided by it are covered in the On Line Help - accessed via the two help menus. The function of the HCC is to allow the use of the Browser, Model Manager, Model Instantiator, Scenario Manager, Result Analyzer, Model Installator, Scenario Builder to construct what-if scenarios to investigate proposed changes to an urban area in the context of land use planning. The use of the Results Analyser from within the HCC allows graphical quantification of the results of these model/scenario combinations. The Map component of the HCC is used to annotate experiments (model/scenario combinations). The HCC enables the user to draw new maps, in the internal format of HERMES, using some powerful drawing tools, allowing him to insert new spatial data in the system; it is also possible to create new map files as visual metaphors for the underlying data held in the Local Authority or Planning Department database.

2.2 - Browser

The browser permits to show the data contained in the database. In HERMES, the data are stored by means of relational tables, and therefore each piece of information can be retrieved by the user selecting the table and the attributes where it is contained. This module can be used to browse only the real tables and not the tables resulting from an experiment; in this case the Result Analyzer must be used.

The user must select, using the mouse, the relational table and then the attributes that he wants to show; the selected data are shown using a new window. If in the list of the selected fields a geometric attribute is present, the related map is also shown in the window with a legenda to associate each region in the map to the related row. It is possible to show more than one table at the same time. The open windows can be moved and overlapped in the screen, permitting to show and to compare different data in the database.

2.3 - Model Manager

The Model Manager allows the user to get information on the names and notes of the models and the related Scenario and Scenario Definition and Experiment, on the files attached to a Model and on the parameters of a Model; to select a Model, a Scenario, a Scenario Definition or all of them, making them available for other functions; to delete a Model; to edit the notes of a Model, the Scenario, the Scenario Definition or the Experiment related to that Model; to edit the parameters of a Model and the files which are attached to a Model.

2.4 - Scenario Builder

The Scenario Builder permits to create, select or delete a Scenario Definition or to create a Scenario.

In HERMES a Scenario Definition is a particular view on the real data present in the database. Each model, during an Experiment, interacts with the data contained in a Scenario Definition and with the real data: therefore a Scenario Definition must contain all the data needed for the execution of a model. Each Scenario Definition is related to one or more models: this means that these models can run on it, because all the data needed are present. This mechanism permits to run the models not only on the real data they are in the database, but these data can be selected and combined to have different views; in this way, the user has the possibilitiy to run the same model on different data. For each model the schema of the input tables must be defined, in order to build the Scenario Definition and to check if it contains all the data needed; also the output schema, that is the tables where the model will store the results, must be defined to analyze its results.

2.4.1 - Create Scenario Definition

This operation is invoked when the user wants to create a new Scenario Definition. The creation of the Scenario Definition and of the Scenario is necessary to define the data that will be used by the model during an Experiment.

The user must specify the name of the new Scenario Definition and the related models. The script that define the Scenario Definition is one or more statements SQL "create view ...", one for each table requested by the model; this script is built automatically, reading the input schema of the models and following the user inputs: the user can utilise the facilities offered by the program and he can take advantage of a set of complex widgets, by means of which the statement can be built using the mouse.

2.4.2 - Select Scenario Definition

This operation is invoked when the user wants to choose the "selected" Scenario Definition: this is the Scenario Definition that will be used in the following experiments, to create the view in which the model will operate. This option is also available in the Model Manager.

2.4.3 - Delete Scenario Definition

This operation is invoked when the user wants delete a Scenario Definition. A Scenario Definition cannot be cancelled if some Scenarios related with it are present in the database: it is necessary to previously delete these Scenarios using the Scenario Manager and, eventually, using the Experiments Manager.

2.4.4 - Make Scenario

This operation is invoked when the user wants to define a new Scenario (see section 2.5). The user must write the SQL instructions that define the Scenario in a text window, helping with the browser and the Scenario Definition Schema. This script can be also a NULL instruction.

2.5 - Scenario Manager

The Scenario Manager permits to modify, select or delete a Scenario.

In HERMES a Scenario is a particular instance of a Scenario Definition: it contains the instructions to modify the view defined by a Scenario Definition, in order to obtain the desired set of data on which a model will operate. This opportunity permits to evaluate the results of mathematical models when the input changes. For instance, considering a traffic model, for which a Scenario Definition has been defined, it is possible to evaluate the different traffic flows when the width of a particular road is modified; in this case, the Scenario script is an "update" instruction on the Scenario Definition.

The Scenario Definition mechanism permits to choose different real data as input for the different execution of a model, while the Scenario mechanism permits to modify these selected data.

2.5.1 - Select Scenario

This operation is invoked when the user wants to choose the "selected" Scenario: this is the Scenario that will be used in the following experiments, to modify the data for the model defined in the Scenario Definition. This option is also available in the Model Manager.

2.5.2 - Delete Scenario

This operation is invoked when the user wants to delete a Scenario. A Scenario cannot be cancelled if it is the "selected" one, otherwise it becomes impossible to run the selected model, or if it is related to some existing Experiments, otherwise it becomes impossible to analyse the Results of the related Experiments. To delete these Scenarios it is necessary to select a new one or cancel previously the Experiments using the Experiments Manager.

2.5.3 - Modify Scenario

This operation is invoked when the user wants to modify a Scenario; the system shows the actual script of the chosen Scenario and the user can edit this text to define the new one.

2.6 - Experiment Manager

This module performs two main functions. It manages records of experiments, and it instantiates models and scenarios for the running of new ones.

The HERMES environment may be used to analyse a scenario through the application of several models to the data. The grouping of the results tables into an Experiment allows convenient analysis at a subsequent stage of the results.

Several ways of using the HERMES environment are possible - the application of a single model to a series of scenarios in a series of experiments, or maybe an in-depth analysis of a single scenario or a small number of alternatives. The experiment concept ensures that the different sets of input and output of the hypothetical data pertaining to a series of different hypotheses do not interfere with each other, and remain conveniently aggregated for analysis and eventual deletion at a later date. It also allows a subsequent experiment to be based on the results of the previous ones.

Two options are provided to start new experiments. The first starts a new experiment in a new environment, with all details already set up for the experiment to use the selected model, the selected scenario and the results of any selected previous experiments; in this case a new instance of the module that manages the comminications with the database, the

Object Manager, is started. The second one uses the same Object Manager as it was used for an immediately preceding experiment, and the new experiment will run in this existing environment.

Experiments may be based on the results of previous experiments. These should never use the same model as any of the previous experiments as this will cause problems with access conflicts to the tables of data used by the models.

This facility allows extended sessions where the user may exit from the HERMES environment after an experiment, and continue later session using the resultant data. This decision should, however, be taken at an early stage to ensure all results are saved in a suitable form and the correct environment can be reconstructed.

The deletion of an experiment will delete the internal HERMES tables pertaining to this experiment, and also any results tables produced from the experiment.

2.7 - Model Executor

The Model Executor allows the user to drive the execution of the model code working on the alphanumeric and graphic data existing in the HERMES database, to control the execution flow, by activating the existing breakpoints or breakpoint variables and examine/change values of meaningful variables in a step of the execution of the model, to elaborate a trace of the evolution of the variables, to analyse the execution by examining the final variables values and applying analysis functions to the sequences of evolution of the values of variables.

The Model Executor is invoked by the Experiment Manager once the experiment environment has been prepared. The Model Executor main window presents all the controls to analyse the breakpoints, breakpoint variables and traceable variables that has been defined, to start/restart the model execution, to continue the execution of a stopped model, to invoke the analysis of the execution, to quit and return the control to the Experiment Manager and HCC.

2.8 - Result Analyzer

The Result Analyzer allows the user to browse the input, temporary and results tables associated to a recorded experiment of a model, to create and delete temporary data (user required "views" of the input/temporary/results tables of the experiment), to produce tabular data files that can be intensively analysed (statistics, distribution graphics, etc.) with any commercial spreadsheet. simple graphic operations (diagrams, etc.) with the input-data/result tabular data.

When the Results Analyzer is called from the HCC window and the user has chosen the model and one related experiment, the data associated to the model are shown and it is possible to analyse the input, output and temporary tables; these tables will have the original values that they had in the moment the experiment selected was executed, so different experiments will have associated tables with different values. It is also possible to analyse the values of one table with a commercial spreadsheet and create new temporary tables: there are database views of the existing input/temporary/result tables.

2.9 - Model Installator

The Model Installator permits to install a new model in HERMES. The user is asked to insert the data related to the model to be installed: the name, the name of the executable file that must be invoked to run the model, the information regarding itself, the notes to be associated with it, and the names of the files that contain the names of the tables and of the attributes of the model schemas, and the names of the files containing the description of the breakpoints groups, breakpoints, variables groups, variables, parameters groups, and parameters. These files must be written following a simple syntax. If the files contain some syntax errors, the program presents a text window showing the contents of the file, indicates the error and asks the user to correct it in the window.

All the models actually integrated in HERMES have been designed and developed during the project, but the architecture allows to integrate also external models, eventually providing a filter for the input and output if they do not use relational data; it is also necessary to indicate the input and output schema to build the Scenario Definitions. The most difficult step during this integration is the understanding of what data among those present in the database are really interesting for the user; for this reason this work must be done with a strong cooperation with the final users.

3 - The HERMES software architecture

The software architecture of the HERMES system can be represented as in figure 2.

The user interface is essentially the Hermes Control Centre and the Browser: it allows the user to access to the system. The scenarios management module consists of the Scenario Builder and the Scenario Manager; the models management module consists of the Model Manager and the Model Installator; the experiments management module includes the Model Instantiator, the Model Executor, the Result Analyzer.

The last modules interact with the client of the Object Manager: it is the manager of the relational tables, both the user tables and the HERMES system tables. The communication with the client side and the server side of the Object Manager is accomplished via TCP/IP protocol, using the socket mechanism to communicate. This solution permits to have more instances of HERMES running together, with only one direct interface with the underlying geographical and descriptive databases. The Object Manager permits to have different copies of the same real table, one for each instance of HERMES; in this way, each client can manage its own data, avoiding all the problems regarding the simoltaneous access to the data by different users. A specific instruction is provided to store permanently the modified tables in the database.

The OM-server provides the access to the relational database and to CARTECH, the geographical data management system.

This distribuited architecture permits to have the different modules of HERMES running in different machines.

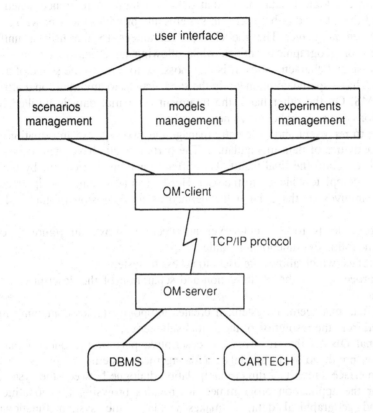

figure 2

3.1 - The Geographic Information System: CARTECH

As described before, the problem regarding the link among alphanumeric and geographic data has been solved with an high integration of the two data typologies, using the Geographical DBMS CARTECH, which permits to manage descriptive and spatial information maintaining the consistency of the data and allowing, at the logical level, an integrated way to manage the information. In this sense, this module of HERMES is a very significant characteristic of the system.

In [2,3,4] an analysis of advantages and drawbacks of different approaches to the realisation of geographical information systems was presented. The idea on which we have based our proposal is that the descriptive component and the spatial one of a given territorial datum have to be separated at the physical level, to obtain efficiency, but they have to be integrated at the logical level, so their representation and manipulation are simple and immediate. In the system integration approach we have adopted, it is therefore necessary to have a logical data model that defines a uniform reference schema for the specification of the integration between sub-systems and provides the user with a high level data manipulation language. The model thus guarantees to the user a uniform and integrated view of geographical entities while allowing an efficient access trough both descriptive and spatial characteristics. It is then possible to refer to the shape of a region or of an entity that has a spatial component, in the same way as to any traditional attribute of a relational DBMS. On the other hand, the treatment of spatial data is fulfilled by special purpose functions assuring higher efficiency.

The choice to represent and differently manage the two types of information generates two different activities of data manipulation. The partial results have then to be compared and integrated to obtain the final result. The different actions carried out by the different sub-systems are completely hidden to the user. He/she can access and manipulate data only through the primitives of the a language defined as an extension of the SQL, namely geoSQL.

This approach leads to a client-server architecture, shown in figure 3, consisting essentially of the following functional modules:
- a user interface which allows the users to access to system;
- a query processor for the identification and separation of the descriptive and spatial parts of the query;
- a spatial data management system; it creates temporary tables containing the partial results obtained from the resolution of the spatial subqueries;
- a relational DBMS that resolves the descriptive part of the query exploiting the temporary tables produced by the spatial data management system.

The user interface supports a direct-manipulation dialogue between the system and the human user or the application programmer; it provides browsing functionalities on the descriptive and geographical data, it makes available the system functionalities, it recognises the commands to be sent to the query processor, and displays the result of the operations, through browser functionalities. In HERMES this functionality is not activated, because the HERMES Control Centre and the other modules provide all the human-system interactions; only the connection of the query processor with the applications is active.

The query processor isolates spatial sub-expressions, involving exclusively spatial attributes, from non spatial ones, which refer to alphanumeric attributes. Spatial subexpressions can be found either in *select* clauses as spatial operators, or in *where* clauses as topological predicates. This functionality is carried out by a syntactical analyzer that successively sends the individuated subexpressions to the spatial management system for their evaluation. Temporary tables are destroyed by the query processor at the end of each "select" statement and at the end of a group of statements (begin-end sequence).

The query processor is also responsible for assuring the transparency of the geometrical information and the data consistency - via relational tables playing a role analogous to the system tables of the relational DBMS. In particular, a list of all extended tables (i.e. tables storing both descriptive and spatial data) is maintained in the relational DBMS, together with the additional information needed to link them in both directions with the special data structures which store spatial component of data.

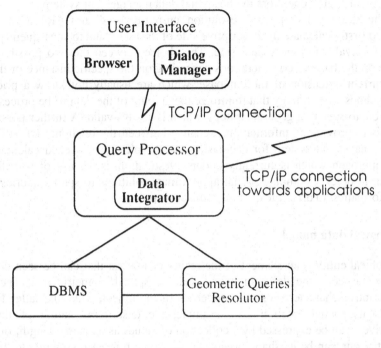

User Interface

Browser   Dialog Manager

TCP/IP connection

Query Processor

Data Integrator

TCP/IP connection towards applications

DBMS   Geometric Queries Resolutor

figure 3

The relational DBMS evaluates the queries concerning descriptive data and carries out the commands for table creation and modification produced by the spatial data management system.

The spatial data management system accepts as input spatial sub-expressions. Recall that these expressions have been recognised by the query processor in the *select/where* clauses. It carries out the computation of the temporary tables of the partial results, namely, the list of regions identifiers satisfying the imposed spatial conditions. Also, it has to compute the spatial functions. This latter activity produces spatial values if the spatial function is an operator of union or intersection, numeric values if the spatial data management system calculates the area of the specified regions.

In the evaluation of a query, the system verifies firstly the syntactic correctness of the input string. Spatial predicates are then processed: when one of these are recognised, the system creates a temporary relational table to store the results product by the spatial data management system. If spatial predicate involves the on-line creation of geometric values, then a single-tuple extended relation is temporary created to represent the given geometric value and the query is modified to make reference to this temporary table. The query being processed is modified by imposing in the *where* clause the belonging to these temporary tables; we eliminate also the references to spatial operators inserting only their operands in the *select* clause. This modified query is ready for being processed by the relational DBMS that memorises the results of this evaluation in a new relation. These data are necessary for the computation of spatial operators by the spatial data management system.

This is the strategy for queries resolution currently used in CARTECH. Another possibility is to firstly calculate the descriptive side of the query and to subsequently employ these results for evaluating the spatial side. The choice between the two possibilities can only be made on the basis of considerations depending on the specific instance of the query and on the current extension of the database, which are usually not know a priori. It is reasonable to choose the strategy that minimize the amount of the data to be processed: but it is not possible to specify a general strategy which is always valid. A further possibility of optimisation is to provide an information exchange between the relational DBMS and the spatial data management system for decreasing the complexity of needed calculation. To this end, an approach which is currently under investigation, is the use of so-called "on-line" approach to quickly compute partial approximate solutions to spatial queries [5] and to use this information to drive the query optimisation process.

3.1.1 - The logical data model

A geographical entity is an element of the reality of interest that can be seen under any one of its two aspects: the descriptive one and the spatial/geometric one. The former provides descriptive characteristics and properties of the object, while the latter furnishes its shape and its spatial location. For example, the descriptive nature of the entity "Mississippi river" can be expressed by a collection of values as its name, length, flow, etc., while the spatial one can be its shape, its location in some reference system, etc. From the point of view of the logical data modelling, the choice of a relational model leads to represent the logical structure of data in tables. In such a context, the descriptive nature of geographical entity (e.g. the flow of a river) can straightforward correspond to a single valued attribute whose underlying domain is traditional (e.g. alphanumeric). On the other side, attributed defined on traditional atomic domains cannot adequately represent the spatial nature of geographical objects. In fact, using traditional domains naturally leads to represent an object distributing its spatial/geometric characteristics on several relations as in [6,7,8]. In this way one obtains a fragmented logical data representation, far from the way the user looks at the reality of interest. In order that the logical structure of data reflects the way the user looks at data themselves, the logical model must therefore support non atomic domains, able to represent in a complete way the spatial/geometric component of an object. In the framework of the adopted system integration methodological approach to GIS realisation it is therefore desirable a logical model that:

- guarantees to the user a uniform and expressive view of geographical entities, still allowing to refer to them through both descriptive and/or spatial/geometric characteristics;

- supports the definition of high level data manipulation languages and the design of physical structures for the efficient answering of mixed queries;

- provides to the designer a formal methodology for the correct specification of geographical information at the logical level.

The relational data model has been suitably extended in order to represent in integrated way the descriptive and spatial components of geographical information. The possibility of treating in a relation geometric values as well as traditional alphanumeric attributes allows to extend the SQL language with new simple syntactic structures: topological predicates may be expressed on the geographical entities and it is possible to apply spatial operators on these.

Our proposal is based on the definition of a suitable logical data model that supports the representation, the manipulation and querying of geographical information. This model, which integrates descriptive and spatial/geometric data, defines a reference schema for the integration among different sub-system while providing the user with a high level data manipulation language and supporting the definition of physical data structures for the efficient answering of mixed queries.

The model guarantees to the user a uniform view of geographical entities, while allowing him/her to refer to them through both descriptive and/or spatial/geometric characteristics. Since the query language, by means of the logical model, does not rest on the physical level, the independence between integrated physical systems and query language can be guarantied and a more flexible overall system results.

Processing actions which are performed by the user on the selected data typically require to identify regions of the space where a certain set of descriptive properties holds at the same time. Therefore the basic primitive used during such processing is an intersection operation where all elementary zones homogeneous with respect to the given set of descriptive properties are identified and those satisfying the user defined constraints are selected. It is therefore clear that a logical data model which supports set-oriented manipulation both at the definition level of base item representing spatial information (which in our case is a finite subset of the integer-valued coordinate points of the plane) and at the level of operators (which in our case are composition/decomposition of sets and the basic boolean operators for sets - namely, union, intersection and complement) is a very effective base for the system definition activities. In fact, approaches using vectorial or polygonal elements as their base item incur in much higher computation costs for the basic manipulation operators and their performances are significantly reduced.

The model was formally defined in [3] and in [9] its formal properties were investigated and its completeness and soundness were proved. In the following we refer to the above cited references for a more complete and thorough treatment; for the aims of this work, it is sufficient to explain that in this data model a region, called SHAPE, is composed by one or more components; each component is a set of points in the plane.

3.1.2 - The query language geoSQL

The SQL language has been extended in order to include some operations on the spatial characteristics of the objects; this extension has been named geoSQL. It includes new relational operators, to be used in the *select* clause, and new topological predicate, to be used in the *where* clause.

The COMPOSE operator groups the values of one or more geometric attributes: the grouping is done on the basis of the equality of others attributes of the relation.

The MERGE operator groups the values of one or more geometric attributes applying to the grouped values a "fusion" function: also this grouping is done on the basis of the equality of others attributes of the relation. The difference between these two operators is that in the first case regions with more than one component may be given as output results, in the second one only regions with one component are produced. It follows, in the last case, that the resulting relation cannot be disaggregated in the original components.

The SEPARE operator perform the inverse function of the COMPOSE one. Each Shape of the geometric attribute on which the SEPARE is applied, is decomposed in its elementary components. Such an operation can be considered as a normalisation action on the relation.

Other geometric operators are the implementation of the correspondent operators introduced in the data model. In particular we have implemented the three binary operators which give a new region:

- INTERSECTION: applied to SHAPES A and B gives SHAPE intersection between A and B, that is the SHAPE whose components are given by the equality of a component of A with a component of B.

- INTERSECTION*: applied to SHAPES A and B gives the SHAPE whose components are the results of the intersection of every component of A with every component of B.

- UNION: applied to the SHAPE A and B furnishes the SHAPE C whose components are components of B or A.

A unary operator it is also introduced:

- AREA: it calculates the area of specified region surface.

The topological predicates provide a boolean result. In all cases the arguments are two geometric attributes, which may possibly belong to the same relation.

-    INTERSECT: it returns "true" when the regions represented by the two attributes have a non empty intersection; "false" if the two regions have an empty intersection.

-    INTERSECT*: it returns "true" when almost one component of region A intersect one component of region B ,"false" otherwise.

-    INCLUDE: it returns "true" if the region represented by the second attribute is included in the first one; "false" otherwise.

-    ADJACENT: it returns "true" if the two regions are adjacent; "false" if they are not.

-    EQUAL: it recognises when two regions are equal. That is, it returns "true" if the regions represented by the two attributes have the same shape and location in the plane; "false" otherwise.

We present now an example of application of geoSQL, supposing that the database schema is composed by two relations: the former describes the presence of minerals on the land, the latter describes the constraints presents on the land itself:

MINERALS_BY_QUANTITY(name, exploitation_quantity, shape);

CONSTRAINTS(type, shape);

During the interaction the user may be interested into the definition of exploitation plans by means of the construction of particular thematic maps, called exploitation maps, which describes the regions where the materials can be exploited, taking into account the constraints imposed on the land. Therefore it is interesting to evaluate which constraints can be relaxed in order to reach the objective of collecting a predefined amount of a given material. A possible methodological approach is described in what follows.

We start building a new relation, MINERALS, which groups the exploitation lands by type of mineral:

```
COMPOSE minerals_by_quantity.shape BY
minerals_by_quantity.name
FROM minerals_by_quantity;
```

The schema of the obtained relation is:
MINERALS(name, shape);
From the relation MINERALS and CONSTRAINTS, we can find the intersection between the pieces of land subject to constraints and the lands where there are minerals by issuing:

```
SELECT minerals.name, constraints.type
INTERSECT*(minerals.shape, constraints.shape) shape
    FROM MINERALS, CONSTRAINTS
    WHERE INTERSECT*(mineral.shape,constraints.shape);
```

The new relation MINERALS_BY_CONSTRAINTS with the schema
MINERALS_BY_CONSTRAINTS(name, type, shape):
is obtained, where the instances of the new geometric attribute 'shape' are the intersection between each land where is a mineral and each land subject to a constraint.

It is possible built other news maps to group all the lands where we can exploit a specific mineral and where the amount we can obtain is greater than a fixed threshold (say 500):

```
COMPOSE minerals_by_quantity.shape
    BY minerals_by_quantity.name
    FROM minerals_by_quantity
    WHERE (minerals_by_quantity.name = 'clay')
        AND (mineral_by_quantity.exploitation_quantity >
500);
```

4 - Physical data representation

To represent the elementary components of a region, the CARTECH library, employs a data structure, namely Multivalued Quadtrees [10]. Such a structure we do not need to explicitly represent all the couples of integer which belong to the component, but for each component only a limited amount of information is memorised, although each single point can be reached by means of the appropriate algorithm.

The multivalued quad-trees is a direct extension of quad-trees [11]. It is a hierarchical data structure, introduced and analysed in [10], for the representation of sets of regions overlapping on the plane. In the normal quadtree only regions which do not overlap are allowed. It is built starting from a regular decomposition of the plane in quadrants. The plane on which the queries are defined is represented as an array of $2^n \times 2^n$ elements. It is recursively split in quadrants and subquadrants until we arrive either at empty quadrants or at quadrants which entirely belong to a (set of) region(s). This decomposition may be represented with a tree, in which every internal node has four children. The leaves of this tree corresponding to homogeneous decomposition blocks are black: to allow the representation of overlapping regions, to every black node is associated a pointer to the list of all regions which share the block. Leaves corresponding to empty areas are marked white. All the other nodes, which are internal nodes, are marked grey. An example of a multivalued quad-tree is show in figure 4.

The simplest implementation of a quad tree is by means of a pointer data structure. This solution has the drawback since it requires a big quantity of memory.

For this reason the implementation has been based on a linearized view of the quadtree built by means of a depth first order visit of the quad tree and storing the order on which nodes are visited in an array. Such a structure has the advantage of resulting very compact e non restrictive, as any operation which can be realised on the tree can be realised on the linear data structure.

The correspondence among elementary components stored in the multivalued quad tree and the regions it is realised by means of a structure which furnishes the mechanism for associating to each component the region it belongs to. The strongest requirement of this association is the efficiency. The adopted solution uses arrays whose elements contains the references to regions. The array indexes, which are the identifiers of the elementary components, realises the association mechanism from the components to the belonging regions. A simple direct access to an array element establishes the link between elementary component and its region. Moreover, to each multivalued quad tree we can associate more regions arrays, each one of which can be considered as a particular view on the same geometry.

5 - Case studies

Some case studies were developed during the project: at the strategical level, the pollution control and reduction; - at the tactical multiobjective level, the parking plan; - at the tactical-operational level, the waste container placement. In all cases, ad hoc models were designed and implemented during the project with a strong collaboration between the developer partners and the users. All the models showed themselves effective for the resolution of the problems, confirming the goodness of the adopted approach in all the kinds of urban planning activities.

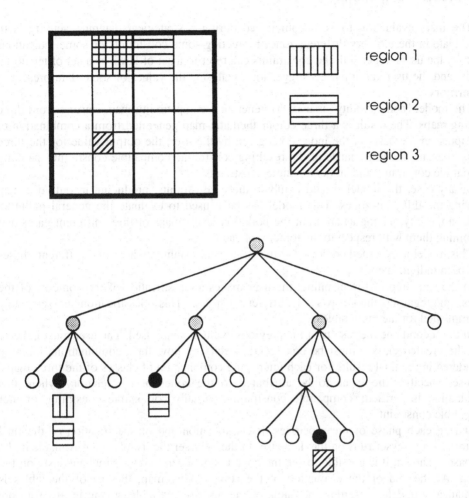

figure 4

Moreover, the reusability of the model results made it possible the realisation of a complete path for the planning: in fact, the result of a strategical model for the definition of the pollution levels in the city was used as an input for the tactical planning model regarding the definition of the zones suitable for the parking location.

All these models have been executed on real data coming from the Geographical Information System of the A.S.M. of Brescia.

In the following, the implemented models are briefly described.

5.1 - Model "compatibility"

The main evaluation to be accomplished during a strategical planning activity is to individuate in the territory different zones respecting some constraints or some indications given by the user. In general, the constraints can refer to a set of laws, or a set of territorial bonds, and the user can input his suggestions analysing the values of some data present in the territory.

The model "compatibility" is used to generate a compatibility map, starting from three existing maps. The result is a three colour thematic map generated from a combination of the inputs on the basis of the indications given by the user; the output value for the three zones indicates the importance of the resulting constraint: 'compatible constraint', 'partially compatible constraint' and 'not compatible constraint'.

In any case, the model should combine these constraints, producing in output a map showing the different zones. This model has been used to evaluate the general pollution levels in the city, having as an input the pollution levels maps of three different gases and combining them with respect to the toxicity of each gas.

This model uses a methodology for the strategical planning where two different phases have been individuated.

In the first step of the planning, the user makes a classification of the contents of the tables, aggregating their rows in different classes. This classification is separately accomplished for the input tables.

In the second one the results of the previous evaluation are used. The user must indicate how the created classes must be composed, specifying how their combinations must be considered in the final result. For each interesting combination of classes of the three maps, the user specifies the value to be attributed to the zones of the territory where this combination is verified: 'compatible constraint', 'partially compatible constraint' or 'not compatible constraint'.

During each phase of the processes of classification and of specification of the final constraints, a browser runs on the database. In the browser the list of tables available in the database is shown; it is possible to see the contents of several tables simultaneously on the screen. At the end of the evaluation of the compatibility map, the list of the tables is automatically updated inserting the name of the just created table, giving in this way the opportunity to immediately verify the obtained results.

5.2 - Model "function"

Often, during all the phases of the planning activities, it is necessary to make some evaluations on the thematic maps: this can happen when the user wants to build a new thematic map overlapping two existing maps and evaluating new thematic values, or when he wants to aggregate the instances of an existing map to obtain a simpler one. The model "function" can be used to generate a new map starting from one or two existing maps: the content of the resulting map is the result of an evaluation on the data contained in the input tables.

The model offers the possibility to calculate two different functions on the thematic maps during the various steps of the planning.

A first functionality is the possibility to combine two input maps presenting both a geometrical attribute and a numeric one: the model makes an overlapping of the input maps, and to each of the resulting regions associates a value obtained by the application of an input function specified by the user using as input the numeric values to the original regions.

The user must specify the operation to be made on the two maps. This operation can be a linear combination of the values of the numeric attribute. The result is a new table with two attributes: a geometric and a numeric one. The geometric field refers to the geometry of each region obtained from the intersection of the input maps, and the numeric one stores the result of the evaluation of the specified function on each of these regions.

The second function requires as an input only one relation showing a geometrical attribute and a numeric one; the rows in this relation are grouped according to the values assumed by the numeric attribute on the basis of specification defined by the user. The resulting map presents two attributes: a geometrical attribute and a numeric one.

Each of the resulting regions includes the set of regions in the input map that belong to the same aggregation; the value of the numeric attribute in each row of the resulting map is a value specified by the user.

5.3 - Model parking

The goal of the tactical planning is to individuate areas suitable for some purposes. A tipical example of this activity is the location of the areas of the city that can be included in a parking plan.

It uses two maps as input. The first one is a map which considers some possible constraints existing in the city; this map can show, for instance, the distribution of the pollution, or areas with different traffic density; it is possible, for instance, to use the map resulting from the model compatibility as input. The second map refers to the population of the city: this map is used, together with other data and with some user inputs, to evaluate the parking demand in the different areas of the city. These two maps are overlapped and the result is a new map showing the different zones: the areas with high parking demand and no constraints, that is the areas where it could be possible to build a parking, or the areas with constraints too strong and where it is impossible to build a parking, and so on.

The user, at the end of the evaluation, can either store permanently the resulting table or not.

5.4 - Model location

The particular problem that has been faced in the case study of HERMES is the placement of the waste containers in a city, a typical problem in the operational planning. For this aim, this model has been designed and implemented to find the number and the localisation of waste containers needed to adequately manage the waste collection in a town. This model has been designed starting from the requirements of the experts of waste collection of the city of Brescia, in Italy.

It uses as an input two tables containing the data regarding the geometry and the population of a city, and produces a new table containing the number of waste containers needed for each division of the city. The model has been used to find this number for each of the 322 electoral sections of Brescia.

The algorithms used to find the total number of containers are the algorithms used in the ASM of Brescia. The first of them evaluates the result starting from the total amount of waste produced in the year, some information regarding the size of the containers and the nature of waste: the result is evaluated in order to minimise the total number of containers. The second algorithm evaluates the total number of containers, minimising the distance that has to be covered by the user. The user can choose one of the two results, and the model shows the value of a great number of parameters the user is interested in: the total number of working hours in the year, the amount of hours spent for the washing of the trucks, etc. These values depend also on a set of parameters that can be changed by the user in order to evaluate the different solutions. The model distributes the total number of containers in the different sections proportionally to the respective inhabitants: the map showing the distribution of the containers in the different sections of the city is created and displayed. In this map, the user can select the different regions to extract the information on each of them.

The user, at the end of the evaluation and of the parameters tuning, can either store permanently the resulting table or not.

6 - Conclusions

In this paper an environment to support an integrated approach to decision making in urban planning field and to Modelling Data Base Systems design has been described. The proposed approach has been used with good results in some European cities and with different problems (urban planning, impacts evaluation). The adopted methodology proved itself suitable for the user requirements.

Future developments of the system architecture will concern the integration with object-oriented databases, the integration of vectorial and raster data, the integration with other kinds of transformations. The integration with other kind of models supporting decision making in various field of the planning (e.g., transport planning) will be also investigated.

References

[1]   ESPRIT Project HERMES 5405, Final Report, August 1993.

[2] M. Gargano, E. Nardelli: "A logical data model for integrated geographical databases", ACM-IEEE International Conference on Systems Integration, Morristown, NJ, April 1990.

[3] M. Gargano, E. Nardelli, M. Talamo: "Abstract Data Types for the logical modeling of complex data", Information Systems, 16, 6, 1991.

[4] F. Arcieri, E. Nardelli, "An integration approach to the management of geographical information: Cartech", 2nd ACM-IEEE International Conference on System Integration (ICSI '92), Morristown, New Jersey, USA, June 1992

[5] P.G. Franciosa, E. Nardelli: "A guaranteed approximation algorithm for on-line computing quad-tree border", International Workshop on Database Management Systems for Geographical Applications, Capri, Maggio 1991, in G.Gambosi, M.Scholl, H.-W.Six, (eds), Geographic Database Management Systems, Esprit Basic Research Series, Springer Verlag, June 1992.

[6] Chang N.S. and K.S. Fu, "A Relational Database System for Images". In: S.K. Chang and K.S. Fu (eds.), Pictorial Information Systems, Springer, 1980, 288-321.

[7] Chang N.S. and K.S. Fu, "Picture Query Languages for Pictorial Data-Base Systems". Computer 11, 1981, 23-33.

[8] Grosky W.I., "Toward a Data Model for Integrated Pictorial Databases", Computer Vision, Graphics, and Image Processing 25, 1984, 371-382 .

[9] M. Gargano, E. Nardelli, M. Talamo: "A model for complex data: completeness and soundness properties", International Workshop on Database Management Systems for Geographical Applications, Capri, Maggio 1991, in G.Gambosi, M.Scholl, H.W.Six, (eds), Geographic Database Management Systems, Esprit Basic Research Series, Springer Verlag, June 1992.

[10] F. Arcieri, P. Dell'Olmo, "A data structure for the efficient treatment of topological join", Fourth International Symposium on Computer and Information Sciences, Turkey, 1989.

[11] H. Samet, "The quadtree and other related hierarchical data structures", Computing Surveys, 16, 2, June 1984.

[12] F. Arcieri, L. Barella, E. Nardelli, "Multivalued quadtrees for the efficient processing of spatial data", manuscript, 1991.

THE WEAK INSTANCE MODEL

P. Atzeni
University "La Sapienza", Rome, Italy

R. Torlone
IASI-CNR, Rome, Italy

1 Introduction

It is common during the design of a database to decompose, for the sake of normalization, a relation scheme R into two or more relation schemes $R_1, \ldots, R_n$ that adequately represent R. However, the relation scheme R is the result of the modeling activity, and therefore it may represent the application requirements more closely than the normalized schemes. Also, the new database scheme may be more complex (at least because it includes more relation schemes), and queries would usually involve longer expressions, often based on the same sequences of joins. Therefore, in some cases it may be undesirable for users to have to know details of the decomposition: it would be useful to allow queries based on the relation scheme R (which does not really exist), thus liberating users from the need to know about the decomposition. Similarly, it may be reasonable to perform updates by inserting or deleting tuples (possibly defined on a proper subset of the attributes) without referring to the decomposition. The *weak instance approach* provides a framework that allows the user to refer to the original relation scheme and maps the external requests for queries or updates to the actual decomposed scheme. As often happens, the basic idea is quite natural, but some development is required to obtain a general and consistent framework.

This paper is devoted to the presentation of the approach and to the characterization of the main properties. For the sake of space, we present proof only for some of the major results. A complete development can be found in [4]. The paper is organized as follows. In Section 2 we review the needed background. In Section 3 we give the major definitions on dependency satisfaction, with the notions of weak instance and representative instance. In Section 4 we present the weak instance approach to query answering, with a definition and a characterization. In Section 5 we demonstrate how the information content of a database instance can be represented by the set of its weak instances, and discuss a notion of equivalence and a lattice on the partition induced by this equivalence. These notions are important for two reasons: (1) they clarify the semantics of the query-answering mechanism, and (2) they give the basis for subsequent notions related to updates. In Section 6 the weak instance approach to updates is presented, with its main properties. In Section 7 a formulation of the weak instance approach based on logical theories is shown that gives a good insight into its foundations.

2 Background Definitions and Notation

The *universe* U is a finite set of symbols $\{A_1 A_2...A_m\}$, called *attributes*. We assume that associated with each $A_i \in U$ there is a set of values called the *domain* of A_i and denoted with dom(A_i). Following common practice in relational database literature, we use the same notation A to indicate both the single attribute A and the singleton set $\{A\}$; also, we indicate the union of attributes (or sets thereof) by means of the juxtaposition of their names.

A *relation scheme* is an object $R(X)$, where R is the *name* of the relation scheme and X is a subset of U. A *database scheme* is a collection of relation schemes $\mathbf{R} = \{R_1(X_1), ..., R_n(X_n)\}$, with distinct relation names (which therefore can be used to identify the relation schemes) and such that the union of the X_i's is the universe U.

A *tuple* on a set of attributes X is a function t that associates with each attribute $A_i \in X$ a value of the domain dom(A_i). If t is a tuple on X, and $Y \subseteq X$, then $t[Y]$ denotes the restriction of the mapping t to Y, and is therefore a tuple on Y. With a little abuse of notation, if A is an attribute in X, then $t[A]$ indicates both a value and the restriction of a tuple.

A *relation* on a relation scheme $R(X)$ is a finite set of tuples on X. A *state* (or a *database*) of a database scheme $\mathbf{R}$ is a function $\mathbf{r}$ that maps each relation scheme $R_i(X_i) \in \mathbf{R}$ to a relation on $R_i(X_i)$; with a slight abuse of notation, given $\mathbf{R} = \{R_1, ..., R_n\}$, we write $\mathbf{r} = \{r_1, ..., r_n\}$.

Associated with a database scheme there is usually a set of *constraints*, that is, properties that are satisfied by the legal states. Various classes of constraints have been defined in the literature [4, 15]; here, we limit our attention to functional dependencies.

Let $YZ \subseteq X \subseteq U$; a relation r over a scheme $R(X)$ *(locally) satisfies* the *functional dependency (FD)* $Y \to Z$ if, for every pair of tuples $t_1, t_2 \in r$ such that $t_1[Y] = t_2[Y]$, it is the case that $t_1[Z] = t_2[Z]$. Without loss of generality, we will often assume that all FDs have the form $Y \to A$, where A is a single attribute.

3 The Weak Instance Model

3.1 Tableaux and Containment Mappings

A *tableau* is defined as a relation, except that it may contain other symbols, called *variables* (we assume that there are countably many of them: $v_1, v_2, ..., v_k, ...$), beside values from the domains. A tableau may be seen as a relation with unknown variables, which *represents* a relation (or a subset thereof). The notion of *containment mapping* will be introduced to

T	Player	Team	Coach
	Jim	v_1	v_2
	Sam	v_1	Clark
	Fred	v_3	v_4
	v_5	Bears	v_6
	Jack	Bears	v_7

r	Player	Team	Coach
	Jim	Lions	Clark
	Sam	Lions	Clark
	Fred	Hawks	White
	John	Bears	Carter
	Jack	Bears	Carter

Figure 1: A tableau and a relation

formalize this representation of relations by means of tableaux. Figure 1 shows a tableau and a relation obtained from it by replacing variables with constants.

Given a set of attributes X, a *row* over X is a mapping that associates with each attribute $A \in X$ either a value in dom(A) (a *constant*), or a variable. Clearly, a row is a generalization of the notion of *tuple*: a row with no variable is a tuple. We extend to rows the notations adopted to indicate values in tuples and subtuples ($t[A]$, etc.). If t is a row over X and $Y \subseteq X$, then t is Y-*total*, if $t[Y]$ does not involve variables (if $Y = X$ we simply say that t is *total*). A *tableau* T over a set of attributes X, sometimes denoted in the following by the notation $T(X)$, is a set of rows over X such that no variable appears as a value for two distinct attributes.[1] The reader can verify that what we have shown in Figure 1 is indeed a tableau.

Among the symbols that may appear as values for an attribute in a tableau, we define a partial order, indicated with $\preceq$, as follows: *(i)* constants are pairwise incomparable, and precede all variables; *(ii)* variables are totally ordered according to the order of their subscripts: $v_i \preceq v_j$ if and only if $i \leq j$. We write $s_1 \prec s_2$ if $s_1 \preceq s_2$ and $s_1 \neq s_2$.

Now, given two tableaux T_1 and T_2 over the same set of attributes X, a *containment mapping from T_1 to T_2* is a function ψ from symbols to symbols that satisfies the following conditions: (1) for every symbol s appearing in T_1, $\psi(s) \preceq s$, (2) if ψ is extended to rows and tableaux, then $\psi(T_1) \subseteq T_2$ (that is, for every row $t_1 \in T_1$, there is a row $t_2 \in T_2$ such that, for every $A \in X$, $\psi(t_1[A]) = t_2[A]$).

Let us expand the consequences of the condition $\psi(s) \preceq s$. A containment mapping ψ maps constants to themselves (therefore we also say that it is the identity on constants) and each variable either to a constant, or to a variable with a lower subscript. Recalling the intuitive notion of representation of relations by means of tableaux given before, we can say that a tableau T represents a (subset of) a relation r if there is a containment mapping from T to r. Given the tableau T and the relation r in Figure 1, a function ψ that is the identity on constants and is defined as follows on variables:

$$\psi(v_1) = \text{Lions} \quad \psi(v_2) = \text{Clark} \quad \psi(v_3) = \text{Hawks}$$
$$\psi(v_4) = \text{White} \quad \psi(v_5) = \text{John} \quad \psi(v_6) = \text{Carter}$$
$$\psi(v_7) = \text{Carter},$$

is a containment mapping from T to r. Similarly, if a function maps v_2 to Clark, v_7 to v_6, and is the identity on all the other symbols in the tableau T in Figure 1, then it is a containment

---

[1] In the literature, tableaux with this restriction are sometimes called *typed*.

T'	Player	Team	Coach
	Jim	v_1	Clark
	Sam	v_1	Clark
	Fred	v_3	v_4
	v_5	Bears	v_6
	Jack	Bears	v_6

Figure 2: A chased tableau

mapping from T to the tableau T' in Figure 2.

The notion of containment mapping is transitive: given tableaux T_1, T_2, T_3, if there is a containment mapping from T_1 to T_2 and a containment mapping from T_2 to T_3, then there is a containment mapping from T_1 to T_3.

Let us define satisfaction of FDs for tableaux in the same way as for relations, just referring to rows rather than tuples: a tableau T satisfies an FD $Y \to Z$ if for every pair of rows t_1 and t_2 in T such that $t_1[Y] = t_2[Y]$, it is the case that $t_1[Z] = t_2[Z]$.

3.2   The Chase Procedure

The chase [11] is a procedure that receives as input a tableau T and a set of FDs F, with the aim of transforming T into a tableau that satisfies F. We will often say that T *is chased with respect to F*, or, when F is irrelevant or understood, *the chase is applied to T*.

> **Algorithm 1**
> **input** a tableau T and a set of FDs F with singleton rhs's
> **output** a tableau $CHASE_F(T)$
> **begin**
> $T' := T$;
>   **while** there are $t_1, t_2 \in T'$ and $X \to A \in F$
>   such that $t_1[X] = t_2[X]$ and $t_1[A] \prec t_2[A]$
>   **do** change all the occurrences of the value $t_2[A]$ in T' to $t_1[A]$;
> $CHASE_F(T) := T'$
> **end**

The individual executions of the inner statement are called *steps* of the chase (or *chase steps*), and if the FD f and the rows t_1, t_2 are involved in a step, we say that there is an *application* of f (to t_1, t_2). Note that when the value of a row $t \in T$ for an attribute A is modified from s to s' in a step of the chase, then all the occurrences of s in the tableau are changed to s'; therefore, without referring explicitly to the involved rows, we can say that a *step changes s to s'*, and that *a sequence of steps changes s_1 to s_1', s_2 to s_2'*, and so on. We say that a sequence of steps *identifies s_1 and s_2*, if it changes both to a common value s, or if it changes s_1 to s_2 or s_2 to s_1.

Example 1 *Let us chase the tableau T in Figure 1 with respect to $F = \{P \to T, T \to C\}$. It is possible to apply $T \to C$ to the first and second rows, thus changing v_2 to "Clark," and then to the fourth and fifth rows, changing v_7 to v_8. No further applications are possible, and*

T'	Player	Team	Coach
	Jim	v_4	White
	Jim	Bears	Clark

Figure 3: A tableau for Example 2

T	Player	Team	Coach
	Jim	v_1	v_2
	Sam	v_1	Clark
	Jim	Bears	Carter

T'	Player	Team	Coach
	Jim	Bears	Clark
	Sam	Bears	Clark
	Jim	Bears	Carter

T"	Player	Team	Coach
	Jim	Bears	Carter
	Sam	Bears	Clark
	Jim	Bears	Carter

Figure 4: Tableaux for Example 3

therefore the algorithm exits the loop and terminates, producing the tableau in Figure 2. The sequence of steps has identified v_2 and "Clark," and v_7 and v_6.

Algorithm 1 always terminates if applied to a finite tableau. The number of symbols in a finite tableau is finite, and the value of each row for each attribute can be modified only a finite number of times (because for each symbol s, there is a finite set of symbols that precede s); therefore, the inner statement can be executed only a finite number of times. If applied to some tableaux, the chase detects violations of FDs, but cannot modify the involved values, because they are incomparable.

Example 2 *Let us consider the tableau T in Figure 3 and chase it with respect to $F = \{P \rightarrow T, T \rightarrow C\}$. It is possible to apply $P \rightarrow T$ and change v_4 to "Bears." The two rows then agree on T and disagree on C, but their C-values are incomparable, and therefore are not modified. The resulting tableau, which is indeed a relation, violates F.*

Also, in some cases, the algorithm is nondeterministic, because of the freedom in the choice of the FD and the choice of the rows in the predicate of the **while** loop and, therefore, in the modification performed.

Example 3 *Let us consider the tableau T in Figure 4 and chase it with respect to $F = \{P \rightarrow T, T \rightarrow C\}$. It is possible to apply $P \rightarrow T$ to the first and third rows, thus changing v_1 to "Bears," in both the first and second rows (note that the inner statement in the algorithm says that the value must be changed in all its occurrences). Then, $T \rightarrow C$ can be applied either to the first and second rows, or to the first and third rows. In the first case v_2 is changed to "Clark," in the second to "Carter." That is, either of the tableaux T' and T'' in Figure 4 can be obtained as a result. In both cases, the resulting tableau violates $T \rightarrow C$, and no further FD can be applied.*

The behavior demonstrated in Example 3 could jeopardize the practical applicability of Algorithm 1. Fortunately, it arises only in limited situations: nondeterminism always appears together with violations of FDs, as in Example 3. We devote our attention to the formalization of this claim, as follows: If one execution of the chase with T and F produces a tableau that satisfies F, then every execution of the chase produces the same tableau, and if one execution produces a tableau that violates F, then every execution produces a tableau that violates F (but not necessarily the same tableau).

THEOREM 1   Let T be a tableau and F a set of FDs. Consider the executions of Algorithm 1 with input T and F. Then: *(1)* if one execution generates a tableau that violates F, then every execution generates a tableau that violates F; *(2)* if one execution generates a tableau that satisfies F, then every execution generates the same tableau.

Theorem 1 (whose proof can be found in [4]) is fundamental in confirming the usefulness of the chase: If the result of the chase satisfies the dependencies, then it is unique.

We devote our attention now to the connections between the chase and containment mappings. First of all, note that, for every T and F, there is a containment mapping from T and $CHASE_F(T)$: it is the function ψ that maps every symbol s appearing in T, to the symbol s' to which it is changed by the chase. Also, since containment mappings enjoy the transitive property, we have that if for some T_1, T_2, and F, there is a containment mapping from $CHASE_F(T_1)$ to T_2, then there is a containment mapping from T_1 to T_2. The following lemma presents another important property of the chase, which will be used in the subsequent discussion.

LEMMA 1   Let T and T' be tableaux and F be a set of FDs. If there is a containment mapping ψ from T to T', and T' satisfies F, then ψ is also a containment mapping from $CHASE_F(T)$ to T', and $CHASE_F(T)$ satisfies F.

PROOF   Let $T_0, T_1, \ldots, T_k$, with $T = T_0$ and $T_k = CHASE_F(T)$, be the tableaux successively generated during the execution of Algorithm 1. For every $1 \leq i \leq k$, we show that (1) there is a mapping from T_i to T', and (2) T_i does not contain any violation of F.
(1) We proceed by induction on i. The basis holds trivially. Assume that there is a mapping from T_{i-1} to T', and let the ith step change some symbol s_1 to s_2 as the result of applying an FD $X \to A$ to rows t_1, t_2 (clearly, $t_1[A] = s_1$, $t_2[A] = s_2$). Now let $t'_1 = \psi(t_1)$ and $t'_2 = \psi(t_2)$; by definition of containment mapping, $t'_1, t'_2 \in T'$, and $t'_1[X] = t'_2[X]$. Then, since T' satisfies F, we have that $t'_1[A] = t'_2[A]$, and so $\psi(s_1) = \psi(s_2)$. Therefore, since the only difference between T_{i-1} and T_i is that all occurrences of s_1 are replaced by occurrences of s_2, it is the case that ψ is also a containment mapping from T_i to T'.
(2) Assume, by way of contradiction, that T contains a pair of rows t_1 and t_2 such that $t_1[A]$ and $t_2[A]$ are distinct constants and $t_1[X] = t_2[X]$. Let $t'_1 = \psi(t_1)$ and $t'_2 = \psi(t_2)$. Then, by definition of containment mapping, we have $t'_1[X] = t'_2[X]$ and $t'_1[A] = t_1[A] \neq t_2[A] = t'_2[A]$ against the hypothesis that T' satisfies F.   □

3.3   Weak Instances

One of the major motivations for studying dependencies is their relationship with normalization and therefore with the decomposition of relations (see for instance [4, 15]). When a relation (scheme) is decomposed, it is important to be able to enforce on the new database scheme the constraints defined on the original relation. This enforcement is not straightforward. Suppose that the constraints associated with a relation scheme $R(X)$ are a set of FDs F. If R is decomposed into a set of relation schemes $R_1(X_1), \ldots, R_k(X_k)$, we would like

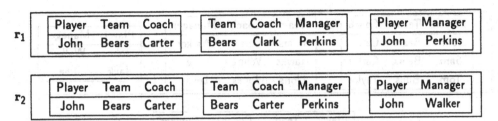

Figure 5: Database instances for the definition of interrelational FDs

to impose F as the set of constraints on $R_1, \ldots, R_k$. However, this is not trivial, because FDs are defined as intrarelational constraints, that is within individual relations, and cannot span over sets of relations. Therefore, there is a need for a definition of FD as an interrelational constraint: given a database scheme $\mathbf{R} = \{R_1(X_1), \ldots, R_k(X_k)\}$, when does one of its instances $\{r_1, \ldots, r_k\}$, satisfy an FD $Y \to Z$ such that $YZ \subseteq X_1 \ldots X_k$?

We argue for some desirable properties that the definition we are looking for should enjoy by discussing an example. Consider the database scheme

$$\mathbf{R} = \{R_1(PTC), R_2(TCM), R_3(PM)\}$$

obtained by decomposing a database scheme with one relation scheme $R_0(PTCM)$ (the attribute names are abbreviated and stand for *Player, Team, Coach, Manager*), and the FDs $F = \{P \to T, T \to C, T \to M\}$. Three database instances of $\mathbf{R}$ are shown in Figure 5.

Clearly, any reasonable definition should reject databases whose relations do not satisfy the embedded dependencies (let us say that $Y \to Z$ is *embedded* in $R(X)$ if $YZ \subseteq X$). This first requirement is not sufficient. Consider the database r_1: every relation trivially satisfies the embedded dependencies, including $T \to C$; nevertheless, the relationship between teams and coaches, as established by the first two relations taken together, is not functional, since "Bears" is associated with "Carter" in the first, and with "Clark" in the second. We would not expect our definition to classify this database as valid. Moreover, consider the database r_2; here neither of the above situations arise, yet, there is something undesirable. By reasoning on the intuitive meaning of FDs (and on their implication properties within relations), we have that each player plays for one team (by $P \to T$), and each team has one coach (by $T \to C$), and one manager (by $T \to M$). Therefore, each player has some relationship with one manager (as a matter of fact, $P \to M \in F^+$). On the other hand, our database associates with John two managers: Walker, directly, and Perkins, through his team. A reasonable definition of satisfaction should require composition of functional relationships to behave naturally, thus ruling out databases such as r_2. This requirement can be enforced by requiring the existence of a common "world" (that is, a relation over all the attributes) where functions cannot be defined independently of one another. Therefore, a suitable definition must consider the various relations as containing a (possibly proper) subset of the information globally expressed by our decomposed database; the fragments in the various relations should not be contradictory.

These considerations can be formalized as follows. Given a database instance r of a database scheme $\mathbf{R} = \{R_1(X_1), \ldots, R_k(X_k)\}$, a relation u over the set of attributes $X = X_1 \ldots X_k$ is a *containing instance* for a database instance $r = \{r_1, \ldots, r_k\}$ if its projections

Player	Team	Coach
John	Bears	Carter
Sam	Bears	Carter
Tom	Bulls	Taylor

Team	Coach	Manager
Bears	Carter	Walker
Hawks	White	Lee
Lions	Jones	Lewis

Player	Manager
John	Walker
Jack	Lee

Player	Team	Coach	Manager
John	Bears	Carter	Walker
Sam	Bears	Carter	Walker
Jim	Hawks	White	Lee
Jack	Sharks	Perkins	Lee
Tom	Bulls	Taylor	Green
Fred	Lions	Jones	Lewis

Figure 6: A database instance and one of its weak instances

over the relation schemes of R contain the respective relations in r (formally: $\pi_{X_i}(u) \supseteq r_i$, for $1 \leq i \leq n$). Given a set of dependencies F, a database r *(globally) satisfies* F if there is a relation w that (1) is a containing instance for r, and (2) satisfies F. Such a relation w is said to be a *weak instance* for r with respect to F. Since the definition refers only to containment, and we assume the domains to be infinite, if a database has a weak instance, then it has infinitely many finite weak instances. It follows from the respective definitions that global satisfaction implies local satisfaction, whereas the converse is not true, as confirmed by the database instances in Figure 5.

Example 4 *The databases in Figure 5 do not satisfy F: no weak instance can be found for them. Instead, the database in Figure 6 satisfies F: a weak instance for it is shown in the same figure.*

3.4   The State Tableau and the Representative Instance

The definition of *weak instance* is interesting, but not practical, since it does not say how weak instances can be computed. The concept can be made useful via the related notion of *representative instance*: For every database instance r, the representative instance is a tableau $RI(r)$ over U, defined as $CHASE_F(T_r)$, where T_r is the *state tableau* for r, formed by taking the union of all the relations in r extended to U by means of distinct variables.

Example 5 *The state tableaux for database in Figure 6 is shown in Figure 8 together with its representative instance. Note that both the database and its representative instance satisfy F.*

The next theorem shows the fundamental relationship between weak instances and representative instances, confirming that the situation in Example 5 is not coincidental. We show two lemmas before the theorem: the first one is in fact needed to prove the theorem, and the second is essentially its converse.

Player	Team	Coach	Manager
John	Bears	Carter	v_1
v_2	Bears	Carter	Perkins
John	v_3	v_4	Walker

Player	Team	Coach	Manager
John	Bears	Carter	Perkins
v_2	Bears	Carter	Perkins
John	Bears	Carter	Walker

Figure 7: A state tableau with its representative instance

Player	Team	Coach	Manager
John	Bears	Carter	v_1
Sam	Bears	Carter	v_2
Tom	Bulls	Taylor	v_3
v_4	Bears	Carter	Walker
v_5	Hawks	White	Lee
v_6	Lions	Jones	Lewis
John	v_7	v_8	Walker
Jack	v_9	v_{10}	Lee

Player	Team	Coach	Manager
John	Bears	Carter	Walker
Sam	Bears	Carter	Walker
Tom	Bulls	Taylor	v_3
v_4	Bears	Carter	Walker
v_5	Hawks	White	Lee
v_6	Lions	Jones	Lewis
Jack	v_9	v_{10}	Lee

Figure 8: Another state tableau with its representative instance

LEMMA 2 If a relation w over U is a weak instance for a database instance $\mathbf{r}$, then there is a containment mapping from the state tableau $T_{\mathbf{r}}$ to w.

PROOF By definition of *state tableau*, for each relation $r_i \in \mathbf{r}$ and each tuple $t_0 \in r_i$, there is a row t in $T_{\mathbf{r}}$ such that (1) $t_0 = t[X_i]$ and (2) $t[A]$ is a distinct variable for each attribute $A \in U - X_i$. By definition of *weak instance*, w is a containing instance. Therefore, for each t_0 as above there is (at least) a tuple $t' \in w$ such that $t_0 = t'[X_i]$. We can say that there is a function f that associates a row t' in the weak instance with each t_0 in the database instance. Now, we can define a function ψ that is the identity on constants and is defined as follows on variables. Let v be a variable that appears as a value for $t[A]$, where t is the row in $T_{\mathbf{r}}$ that originates form a tuple t_0 in a relation in the database instance. By the argument above, there is a tuple $t' \in w$ such that $t' = f(t_0)$. Then $\psi(v)$ is defined as the constant that appears as the value of t' on A. The definition is unambiguous, since each variable appears only once in $T_{\mathbf{r}}$. We claim that ψ is a containment mapping from $T_{\mathbf{r}}$ to w. In fact, for each s, we have that $\psi(s) \preceq s$, since constants are mapped to themselves, and variables are mapped to constants. Also, for each row $t \in T_{\mathbf{r}}$, there is a tuple $t' \in w$ such that, for every $A \in U$, $\psi(t[A]) = t'[A]$. If t_0 is the tuple (in relation r_i in $\mathbf{r}$) from which t originates, then the tuple $t' = f(t_0)$ satisfies the condition. In fact, $t[A]$ is a constant for every $A \in X_i$ and $t_0 = t'[X_i]$. Also, for every $A \in U - X_i$, $t[A]$ is a variable, and so $\psi(t[A])$ is defined as $t'[A]$.   □

LEMMA 3 Let w be a relation over the universe U and $\mathbf{r}$ a database instance. If *(a)* there is a containment mapping from $T_{\mathbf{r}}$ to w, and *(b)* w satisfies F, then w is a weak instance for $\mathbf{r}$.

PROOF We have to show that if w satisfies conditions *(a)* and *(b)*, then it is a weak instance for $\mathbf{r}$; that is, it satisfies conditions (1) and (2) in the definition of global satisfaction. Since (2) is the same as *(b)*, it suffices to show that *(a)* implies (1). We show that for every relation

$r_i \in \mathbf{r}$ and for every tuple $t_0 \in r_i$, there is a tuple $t \in w$ such that $t_0 = t[X_i]$, and so $t_0 \in \pi_{X_i}(w)$. By construction of $T_\mathbf{r}$, if $t_0 \in r_i$, there is a row $t' \in T_\mathbf{r}$ that is the extension of t_0 to U (that is $t_0 = t'[X_i]$). Then, since by condition *(a)* there is a containment mapping from $T_\mathbf{r}$ to w and (by definition) containment mappings map constants to themselves, w contains a tuple t such that $t[X_i] = t'[X_i]$. Therefore, $t_0 = t[X_i]$, and so $t_0 \in \pi_{X_i}(w)$.   □

THEOREM 2   A database instance $\mathbf{r}$ satisfies a set F of FDs if and only if the tableau $CHASE_F(T_\mathbf{r})$ satisfies F, where $T_\mathbf{r}$ is the state tableau for $\mathbf{r}$.

PROOF

If.   If we take the representative instance and replace all the variables with distinct constants, we obtain a relation that is a weak instance, since it satisfies F (because $CHASE_F(T_\mathbf{r})$ satisfies F) and it is a containing instance (by construction).

Only if.   Let w be a weak instance for $\mathbf{r}$ with respect to F, demonstrating that $\mathbf{r}$ satisfies F. By Lemma 2, there is a containment mapping ψ from $T_\mathbf{r}$ to w. Then, since w satisfies F, we have, by Lemma 1, that $CHASE_F(T_\mathbf{r})$ satisfies F.   □

It is clear from the definitions that local satisfaction is much easier to verify than global satisfaction: the latter requires the construction of the representative instance, whereas the former can consider individual relations separately. An interesting class of database schemes has been proposed and characterized for which the two notions of satisfaction coincide: a database scheme **R** with an associated set F of FDs is *independent* if every locally consistent instance of **R** is globally consistent [7]. Efficient characterizations exist for independent schemes, in various contexts [7, 10, 13].

4   Query Answering with Weak Instances

We introduce the approach by discussing an example.[2] Consider a database scheme $\mathbf{R} = \{[R(U), F]\}$ in which $U = PRTCLS$ (the attributes *Player, Role, Team, Coach, Level,* and *Salary* are abbreviated with the respective initials), and F contains the FDs $P \rightarrow LTCS$, $T \rightarrow C, C \rightarrow T, L \rightarrow S$. A decomposed, normalized scheme **S** contains four relation schemes:

$$[R_0(PR), \{\}]$$
$$[R_1(PLT), \{P \rightarrow LT\}]$$
$$[R_2(LS), \{L \rightarrow S\}]$$
$$[R_3(TC), \{T \rightarrow C, C \rightarrow T\}]$$

In fact, **S** is in BCNF and is an adequate representation of **R** since (1) it represents the FDs in F; (2) it is independent; and (3) it is a lossless decomposition of **R**.

Consider the instance **s** of **S** shown in Figure 9. It is legal and so globally consistent. Clearly, there is no instance of **R** that represents exactly the same information: the instance **r** obtained as $\bowtie_\mathbf{S}$ (**s**) (shown in Figure 10) does not embody the information represented by the dangling tuples.   However, if a query involves a proper subset of the given set of attributes U, then it is often reasonable to return also information that cannot be derived

---

[2]For the sake of simplicity, we assume that the original database scheme contains only one relation scheme. In general it contains more, and each of them can be decomposed, but the extension is straightforward.

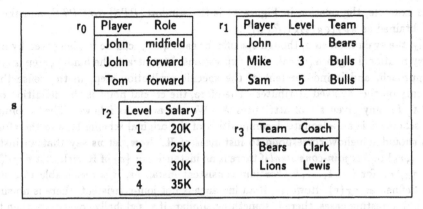

Figure 9: An instance for a decomposed scheme

Player	Role	Team	Coach	Level	Salary
John	midfield	Bears	Clark	1	20K
John	forward	Bears	Clark	1	20K

⋈s (s)

Figure 10: The join of the instance in Figure 9

from the join of all the relations in the current instance. For example, if the query is about players and their teams and salaries, for example, "List names and teams of the players that earn more than 22K," then it is reasonable to consider all the players whose salary and team are known and then select those that satisfy the condition (Figure 11). Clearly, the final result in Figure 11 cannot be obtained from the join of the relations in the database instance (Figure 10): it is the intermediate result in Figure 11 that allows us to include the tuple about Mike in the result.

The idea shown in the example is indeed general: more information is available if for each query we consider only the attributes actually involved and all the available tuples over them. The approach can be structured by saying that the answer to each query that virtually refers to the original relation can be generated by means of a two-step procedure:

1. *Binding*, which produces a relation x over the set of attributes X actually involved in the query; x is often called the *window* over X and is indicated with $[X](s)$. If the database instance is clear from the context, then we just write $[X]$.

2. *Evaluation*, which performs the specific operations involved in the query (often just a selection followed by a projection).

Player	Team	Salary
John	Bears	20K
Mike	Bulls	30K

Player	Team
Mike	Bulls

Figure 11: Intermediate and final results for a query

In the example, the relation in Figure 11 is the window $[PTS]$ over PTS, and the final result is obtained as $\pi_{PT}(\sigma_{S>22K}([PTS]))$.

Clearly, the evaluation step, though specific for each query, can be implemented by means of ordinary relational algebra (or calculus) expressions. In contrast, the binding step is typical of this approach, and is independent of the specific evaluation step, in the sense that it depends only on the involved attributes. Therefore, the crucial point is the definition of the window $[X]$ for any given set of attributes X. We can argue as follows. The decomposed database scheme $\mathbf{S}$ is an adequate decomposition of the original scheme $\mathbf{R}$, and therefore its instances should somehow correspond to instances of $\mathbf{R}$. Now, let us say that an instance $\mathbf{s} = \{r_1, \ldots, r_k\}$ of $\mathbf{S}$ is *join-consistent* if there is an instance $\mathbf{r} = \{r\}$ of $\mathbf{R}$ such that $\mathbf{r} = \bowtie_{i=1}^{k} r_i$ and $r_i = \pi_{X_i}(r)$, for $i = 1, \ldots, k$. For join-consistent instances, it is reasonable to consider $[X]$ to be defined as $\pi_X(r)$. However, if an instance is not join-consistent, there is no such r, but in most interesting cases, there is something similar: if $\mathbf{s}$ is globally consistent, then there is a weak instance for $\mathbf{s}$ (usually many more, and infinitely many if the domains are infinite). The argument does not apply for the instances that satisfy the local constraints but are not globally consistent. We believe that this is not a problem, since $\mathbf{S}$ is the decomposition of a database scheme with a single relation scheme, and so it is reasonable to consider the information embodied in its instances as a whole; also, if $\mathbf{S}$ is independent, then no instance falls in this category. As we know, if a database instance $\mathbf{s}$ is globally consistent, then there are many weak instances for it. Each of them embodies the information in $\mathbf{s}$, plus some more. In a sense, we may assume that the information in a database instance is represented by the set of all its weak instances.

Let us formalize this concept. We refer to a database scheme $\mathbf{S}$ with n relation schemes, $[R_i(X_i), F_i]$, for $i = 1, ..., n$, where F_i is a set of FDs over X_i. Also, $F = \cup_{i=1}^{n} F_i$, $U = \cup_{i=1}^{n} X_i$, and $W(\mathbf{S})$ is the set of globally consistent instances of $\mathbf{S}$, that is, the set of instances of $\mathbf{S}$ that have a weak instance with respect to F. Finally, for every instance $\mathbf{s} \in W(\mathbf{S})$, $WEAK(\mathbf{s})$ indicates the set of weak instances of $\mathbf{s}$, $T_{\mathbf{s}}$ the state tableau of $\mathbf{s}$, and $RI(\mathbf{s})$ the representative instance of $\mathbf{s}$, that is, the tableau obtained by chasing the state tableau: $RI(\mathbf{s}) = CHASE_F(T_{\mathbf{s}})$.

Then we can define the *window* $[X](\mathbf{s})$ over a set of attributes X, for a consistent instance $\mathbf{s}$ of $\mathbf{S}$, as the set of tuples on X that belong to every weak instance of $\mathbf{s}$:

$$[X] = \bigcap_{w \in WEAK(\mathbf{s})} (\pi_X(w))$$

It can be seen that the relation in Figure 11 is actually the set of tuples over PTS that belong to every weak instance of the database in Figure 9. At the same time, if we compute the representative instance $RI(\mathbf{s})$ of the database $\mathbf{s}$ in Figure 9, we obtain the tableau in Figure 12; we see that the PTS-total rows it contains correspond to the tuples in the relation on PTS in Figure 11. This is not a coincidence. In fact, it is always the case that the window over a set of attributes equals the *total projection* of the representative instance over those attributes, where the total projection $\pi^{\downarrow}_X(T)$ of a tableau T over a set of attributes X is defined as the set of total rows in the projection of T on X: $\pi^{\downarrow}_X(T) = \{t \mid t \in \pi_X(T) \text{ and } t \text{ is total}\}$. The following theorem states this claim.

THEOREM 3 For every $\mathbf{s} \in W(\mathbf{S})$, for every $X \subseteq U$, it is the case that

$$\bigcap_{w \in WEAK(\mathbf{s})} (\pi_X(w)) = \pi^{\downarrow}_X(RI(\mathbf{s}))$$

Player	Role	Team	Coach	Level	Salary
John	midfield	Bears	Clark	1	20K
John	forward	Bears	Clark	1	20K
Tom	forward	v_1	v_2	v_3	v_4
John	v_5	Bears	Clark	1	20K
Mike	v_6	Bulls	v_7	3	30K
Sam	v_8	Bulls	v_7	5	v_9
v_{10}	v_{11}	v_{12}	v_{13}	1	20K
v_{14}	v_{15}	v_{16}	v_{17}	2	25K
v_{18}	v_{19}	v_{20}	v_{21}	3	30K
v_{22}	v_{23}	v_{24}	v_{25}	4	35K
v_{26}	v_{27}	Bears	Clark	v_{28}	v_{29}
v_{30}	v_{31}	Lions	Lewis	v_{32}	v_{33}

Figure 12: The representative instance of the database in Figure 9

Theorem 3 establishes another relationship between weak and representative instances and confirms the robustness of the definition of the window. However, it does not provide an efficient procedure to compute the window over a set of attributes as it requires the chase of a tableau over the whole database. Since computing the chase of a tableau takes polynomial time in the number of the rows of the tableau [1], it should be highly desirable to have database schemes that allow to compute the total projection of the representative instance more efficiently. A scheme is said to be *bounded* if for any $X \supseteq U$ and for any tuple t in the X-total projection of the representative instance for a state s, t can be derived by T_s, by at most k chase steps, for some constant k. It has been shown that a scheme is bounded exactly when every X-total projection of the representative instance can be computed via a predefined relational algebra expression [12]. Boundedness of independent schemes and properties of the involved expressions were studied by Sagiv [13, 14]; Chan [6]; Ito, Iwasaki, and Kasami [10]; and Atzeni and Chan [2]. Other important classes of bounded schemes were studied by Wang and Graham [16] and Hernàndez and Chan [8].

5 Equivalence and Completeness of Databases

In this section we formalize and elaborate on the claim made in the previous section that the information in a database instance can be considered as represented by the set of its weak instances. A first observation to be made is that there may be database instances of the same scheme that have exactly the same weak instances; an example is given by the two instances s_1 and s_2 in Figure 13, which refer to a scheme S with two relation schemes, $[R_1(EPD), \{E \to D\}]$ and $[R_2(EPM), \{P \to M\}]$. We say that two database instances s_1, s_2 are *equivalent* (in symbols, $s_1 \sim s_2$) if they have the same set of weak instances; the property is clearly reflexive, symmetric, and transitive, and so it is actually an equivalence relation. Similarly, we say that s_1 is *weaker* than s_2 ($s_1 \preceq s_2$) if each weak instance of s_2 is also a weak instance of s_1. The following lemma and the subsequent theorem confirm the robustness of

	r_1	Employee	Project	Dept		r_2	Employee	Project	Manager
s_1		Jeff	A	CS			Jeff	B	Adams
		Rose	B	EE			Rose	A	Smith

	r_1	Employee	Project	Dept		r_2	Employee	Project	Manager
s_2		Jeff	B	CS			Jeff	A	Smith
		Rose	A	EE			Rose	B	Adams

Figure 13: A pair of equivalent database instances

Employee	Project	Dept	Manager
Jeff	A	CS	Smith
Rose	B	EE	Adams
Jeff	B	CS	Adams
Rose	A	EE	Smith

Figure 14: The representative instance for the database instances in Figure 13

these two notions, as they show their respective equivalence to other meaningful conditions.

LEMMA 4 If s_1 and s_2 are globally consistent instances of **S**, then the following conditions are equivalent. (1) $s_1 \preceq s_2$. (2) There is a containment mapping from $RI(s_1)$ to $RI(s_2)$. (3) $[X](s_1) \subseteq [X](s_2)$, for every $X \subseteq U$.

A couple of definitions are useful here. Two database instances are *query-equivalent* (in the weak instance approach) if for every $X \subseteq U$, their windows over X are equal. Two tableaux T_1 and T_2 are *tableau-equivalent* (or simply *equivalent*) if there exist both a containment mapping from T_1 to T_2 and a containment mapping from T_2 to T_1.

THEOREM 4 If s_1 and s_2 are globally consistent instances of **S**, then the following conditions are equivalent: (1) s_1 and s_2 are equivalent. (2) $RI(s_1)$ and $RI(s_2)$ are tableau-equivalent. (3) s_1 and s_2 are query-equivalent.

The two instances in Figure 13 have exactly the same representative instance, shown in Figure 14. This is a coincidence, due to the fact that in this case all variables are promoted to constants. It is interesting to note that if we perform the total projections of this representative instance on the relation schemes in **S** (by extending the notation π_S used in Chapter 5, we indicate it with $\pi^{\downarrow}_S$, and call it the *total projection on the database scheme*), we obtain the database instance s in Figure 15, whose relations are supersets of the corresponding relations in both s_1 and s_2. The instance s is equivalent to s_1 and s_2, and so its representative instance is the tableau in Figure 14. Therefore, s equals the total projection of its own representative instance on the database scheme. This property, which is not enjoyed by s_1 nor by s_2, is rather interesting, because it corresponds to the fact that each relation embodies all the relevant information: if a database instance does not satisfy it, then there is

r_1	Employee	Project	Dept	r_2	Employee	Project	Manager
s	Jeff	A	CS		Jeff	A	Smith
	Rose	B	EE		Rose	B	Adams
	Jeff	B	CS		Jeff	B	Adams
	Rose	A	EE		Rose	A	Smith

Figure 15: The total projection of the representative instance in Figure 14 on the database scheme

information corresponding to some relation scheme that can be derived from information in other relations. Therefore, we say that a database instance s is *complete* if $s = \pi^{\downarrow}s(RI(s))$. It turns out that for each instance $s \in W(\mathbf{S})$, there is one and only one complete equivalent instance s^*, which can be obtained as $s^* = \pi^{\downarrow}s(RI(s))$.

It is interesting to note that the relation $\preceq$ is not a partial order on the set of all consistent instances, because it is not antisymmetric. However, on the set of the complete instances, it is a partial order, as it is reflexive, antisymmetric, and transitive. With a technical modification, $\preceq$ can become a *complete lattice* on the set of complete instances. The next two lemmas show the existence of the greatest lower bound (glb) and least upper bound (lub), with respect to the partial order $\preceq$, on the set of complete instances extended with the complete inconsistent instance.

LEMMA 5 For each set $\mathcal{R}$ of complete instances there is a glb, which is equivalent to the instance obtained as the relationwise intersection of the instances in $\mathcal{R}$.

LEMMA 6 For each set $\mathcal{R}$ of complete instances there is a lub, which is equivalent to the instance obtained as the relationwise union of the instances in $\mathcal{R}$ or to the inconsistent instance.

6   Updates Through Weak Instances

In this section we show how it is possible to update decomposed databases without referring to the individual relation schemes, but only to (a subset of) the universe. We consider insertions and deletions of tuples, defined over any subset of the universe, in the same way that queries can be defined on any subset of the universe. The general idea is that the result of an insertion (a dual approach can be taken for deletions) of a tuple in a consistent instance is a consistent instance that contains (1) the information in the original instance and (2) the information embodied in the new tuple. Part (1) can be formalized by requiring the original instance to be weaker than the result; part (2), by requiring the new tuple to appear in the appropriate total projection of the representative instance of the result. In general, there are many *potential results*, with different modifications with respect to the original instance. For example, other tuples may be added to the relations besides those strictly needed to generate the new tuple as a result of queries.

Example 6 *If we want to insert in the instance in Figure 9 a tuple defined on PC, with values Mike for P and Green for C, we can consistently add a tuple to relation r_3, with* values Bulls *for* T *and* Green *for* C. *Because of the dependency* T → C, *the chase would combine the tuple* < Mike, 3, Bulls >, *already in* r_1, *with this tuple, thus generating a tuple in the representative instance with values* Mike *for* P *and* Green *for* C. *On the other hand, if we want to insert into the same instance another tuple defined on* PC, *but with values* David *for* P *and* Moore *for* C, *we obtain a potential result only if we add a tuple* < David, l, t > *to* r_1, *and a tuple* < t, Moore > *to* r_3, *whatever the values* l *and* t *may be (provided that the constraints are not violated). In this case, some further pieces of information (i.e., the level* l *and the team* t*) have to be added, and there are several possible choices.*

It makes sense to say that if there is a *minimum* potential result (that is, a result that precedes, in the partial order, all the others), then it is an "ideal" result, because it includes only information that is strictly needed. Unfortunately, the minimum result need not exist, as sometimes there may be several, incomparable "minimal" results. Therefore, we distinguish between *deterministic* and *nondeterministic* insertions, depending on the existence of the minimum result.

There are also cases where it is not possible to obtain a consistent result, because of inconsistency between the original instance and the new tuple or because of intrinsic weaknesses of the database scheme.

Example 7 *If the tuple to be inserted in Example 6 had values* John *for* P *and* Mason *for* C, *we could not find any consistent instance that would contain both the information in the original instance and that in the new tuple because, given the functional dependencies, they contradict each other, assigning two distinct coaches to a player.*

Example 8 *Given the universe* Professor, Student, Course, *and the database with the relation schemes* $R_1(PC)$, $R_2(SC)$, *with the empty set of constraints, no total tuple over the universe can belong to the representative instance of any instance, and therefore no result can be found for any insertion of a tuple over the three attributes.*

These concepts can be formalized as follows. We refer to a database scheme $\mathbf{S} = \{R_1(X_1), \ldots, R_n(X_n)\}$, with $U = X_1 X_2 \ldots X_k$, and consider an instance $\mathbf{s} \in W(\mathbf{S})$ and a tuple t over a set of attributes $X \subseteq U$, such that $t \notin [X](\mathbf{s})$. We consider the *insertion* of t into $\mathbf{s}$. An instance $\mathbf{s}_p \in I(\mathbf{S})$ is a *potential result* for the insertion of t into $\mathbf{s}$ if $\mathbf{s} \preceq \mathbf{s}_p$ and $t \in [X](\mathbf{s}_p)$.

For each instance and each tuple, there is a potential result; for example, the inconsistent instance is always a potential result. It is also possible that the inconsistent instance is the only potential result. As shown in the examples above, this may occur for very different reasons. In Example 8, the reason for the nonexistence of a consistent potential result is that the dependencies cannot generate any X-total row in the representative instance. In Example 7, the reason is a violation of the constraints. This gives rise to the following definitions: (1) The insertion of a tuple t in an instance $\mathbf{s}$ is *possible* if there is a consistent instance $\mathbf{s}'$ such that $t \in [X](\mathbf{s}')$. (2) A possible insertion is *consistent* if it has a consistent potential result. So, the insertion in Example 8 is impossible, whereas that in Example 7 is inconsistent.

The definition of *potential result* only requires the instance to contain the information in the original instance and that in the new tuple; any other piece of information may be included. It is interesting to consider the information that is common to all potential results: in the lattice framework described in Section 5, this is the glb of the potential results. It should be noted that this instance need not be a potential result. The glb of the potential results of the insertion of the tuple $<$ David, Moore $>$ in Example 6 is the original instance itself, which does not include the new tuple in its ED window. If the glb of the potential results is not a potential result, there are various minimal potential results (that is, potential results such that there is no properly weaker potential result), each of which represents a way to insert the new tuple by altering the instance as little as possible. Since each of them would have the same right to be considered as "the result" for the insertion, it is reasonable to talk of nondeterminism. We say that a possible and consistent insertion is *deterministic* if the glb of the potential results is a potential result.

Now, we give necessary and sufficient conditions for possibility, consistency, and determinism. We refer to our usual database scheme **S**, and consider a tuple t defined over a subset X of the universe U.

THEOREM 5 For every instance $s \in W(S)$, the insertion of t in s is possible if and only if there is a relation scheme $R_i(X_i) \in \mathbf{R}$ such that F implies the FD $X_i \rightarrow X$.

We now turn our attention to consistency, assuming that the insertion is possible. Let $RI(s)$ be the representative instance of s, and $T_{s,t}$ be the tableau obtained by adding to $RI(s)$ a row t_e obtained by extending t to the universe U by means of unique variables.

THEOREM 6 Let the insertion of t in s be possible. Then, it is consistent if and only if $CHASE_F(T_{s,t}) \neq T_\infty$.

We now turn our attention to the characterization of deterministic insertions. Let s_+ be the instance obtained by (totally) projecting $CHASE_F(T_{s,t})$ on the database scheme: $s_+ = \pi^\downarrow_S(CHASE_F(T_{s,t}))$.

LEMMA 7 Let the insertion of t in s be possible and consistent. Then s_+ is the glb of the potential results.

THEOREM 7 Let the insertion of t in s be possible and consistent. It is deterministic if and only if $CHASE_F(T_{s,t}) \equiv RI(s_+)$.

COROLLARY 1 Let the insertion of t in s be possible and consistent. It is deterministic if and only if $t \in \pi^\downarrow_X(RI(s_+))$.

Corollary 1 gives an effective characterization of insertibility: Given s and t, we can build $T_{s,t}$, chase it with respect to the given constraints, then generate s_+ and compute its representative instance $RI(s_+)$, and finally check whether the total projection $\pi^\downarrow_X(RI(s_+))$ contains t.

Example 9 *Consider again the insertion in Example 6. Following the definitions, we could build the tableau $T_{s,t}$, chase it, project the result on the database scheme, and thus obtain exactly the instance we suggested as a result.*

Let us now consider deletions. The definitions will be somehow symmetric with respect to those concerning insertions. However, the case will be easier, because no problems will arise regarding consistency and possibility. An instance s_p is a *potential result* for the deletion of a tuple t from an instance s if $s_p \preceq s$ and $t \notin [X](s_p)$.

The empty instance is a consistent potential result for every deletion, and so there is no need to define the notions of possible and consistent results for deletions. However, as for insertions, there may be several, incomparable potential results.

Example 10 *If we want to delete the tuple* $<$ John, Clark $>$ *on PT from the database in Figure 9, then it suffices to eliminate either the tuple* $<$ John, 1, Bears $>$ *from* r_1 *or the tuple* $<$ Bears, Clark $>$ *from* r_3*. The two instances obtained in these ways are incomparable and are both potential results and maximal among the potential results.*

It is therefore reasonable to introduce a notion of deterministic result, in a way that is dual with respect to that followed for insertions. A deletion is *deterministic* if the lub of the potential results is a potential result. It turns out that deletions are deterministic only in very restricted cases. Let s_- be the instance obtained by removing from each relation r_i such that $X \subseteq X_i$ each tuple t' such that $t'[X] = t[X]$.

THEOREM 8 Let s be a consistent instance and t be a tuple on X that belongs to $[X](s)$. The deletion of t from s is deterministic if and only if (1) there is a relation scheme $R_i(X_i)$ such that $X \subseteq X_i$ and (2) t does not belong to $[X](s_-)$.

7   The Weak Instance Model and First-Order Logic

There is an interesting way to look at the weak instance model, based on logical theories, which gives a good insight into its foundations. Given a fixed scheme S, there is a language that allows us to express predicates over all the possible sets of attributes, and for each instance s of S, there is a theory that enjoys a number of interesting properties. The theory contains (1) sentences that depend on the instance s, describing the tuples in the relations in s, and (2) sentences that depend on the scheme, referring to both the structure and to the dependencies.[3] The sentences in the second category essentially describe the semantics of the weak instance approach, namely the fact that the various relations are considered in a common framework, and that there is a virtual, although unknown, relation over the universe, from which the various relations are derived.

Let us now describe the logical theories in detail. In order to give examples, we refer to the database instance in Figure 9 and to its scheme.

Given a database scheme $S = \{[R_i(X_i), F_i] \mid i = 1, \ldots, n\}$, with $U = \cup_{i=1}^n X_i$, and $F = \cup_{i=1}^n F_i$, a *first-order language* is defined: its *constant symbols* are exactly the constants in the domain of the database, there are no *function symbols*, and there is a *predicate symbol* for each nonempty subset X of U.

With every database instance $s = \{r_1, r_2, \ldots, r_n\}$, a theory with five kinds of sentences is associated:

---

[3] A *sentence* is a formula with no free variables.

1. A set DB of atomic sentences describing the content of the relations in the database: for every relation $r_i \in s$ defined on the relation scheme $R_i(X_i)$, and for every tuple $t \in r_i$, there is the sentence $X_i(t)$.

2. A set INC of sentences saying that the relations in s are projections of the weak instance(s). These sentences are existentially quantified with respect to the attributes not appearing in the relation scheme: for every relation scheme R, if $Y = U - R$, there is the sentence $(\forall t)(\exists y)(R(t) \Rightarrow U(t, y))$.[4]

3. A set CON of sentences saying that for every tuple t over the universe, all of its subtuples are meaningful pieces of information over the involved attributes: for each $\emptyset \subset X \subset U$ there is the sentence $(\forall t)(U(t) \Rightarrow X(t[X]))$. If U contains m attributes, then CON includes $2^m - 2$ sentences. It is important to note that the sentences INC and CON, together, imply that each sentence $X(t)$ implies, for every $Y \subset X$, the sentence $Y(t[Y])$; in plain words, each tuple implies all its subtuples, and the weak instances implement this implication.

4. A set DIS of sentences stating that all constants are distinct. This a technical set of sentences.

5. A set DEP of first-order sentences representing the dependencies in F.

There are two important results that can be shown with respect to these theories, which confirm their actual correspondence to the weak instance approach. They are based on the notions of satisfiability and implication for theory, which we assume known.

THEOREM 9 Given S and F as above, a database instance s of S globally satisfies F if and only if the theory associated with s is satisfiable.

The second result shows the close correspondence that exists between the weak instance approach to query answering and the logical theories associated with it; again, this confirms the robustness of the approach.

THEOREM 10 For every consistent instance $s \in W(S)$, for every set X of attributes, the set of tuples t such that $X(t)$ is implied by the theory associated with s coincides with the window $[X](s)$ over X.

The logical theories that can be associated with database instances in the weak instance approach confirm that each tuple in each relation $r_i(X_i)$ is considered as a tuple over the universe whose values on the attributes in $U - X_i$ are not known, but do exist. However, since this point of view is not completely desirable, the definition of the weak instance approach can be modified in order to deal with applications where the missing values are not necessarily existent [3].

---

[4]The connective $\Rightarrow$ is shorthand: $f_1 \Rightarrow f_2$ stands for $\neg(f_1) \vee f_2$; its intuitive meaning is "if f_1, then f_2."

References

[1] A.V. Aho, C. Beeri, and J.D. Ullman. The theory of joins in relational databases. *ACM Trans. on Database Syst.*, 4(3):297–314, 1979.

[2] P. Atzeni and E.P.F. Chan. Efficient and optimal query answering on independent schemes. *Theoretical Computer Science*, 77(3):291–308, December 1990.

[3] P. Atzeni and M.C. De Bernardis. A new interpretation for null values in the weak instance model. *Journal of Comp. and System Sc.*, 41(1):25–43, August 1990.

[4] P. Atzeni and V. DeAntonellis. *Relational Database Theory: A Comprehensive Introduction.* Benjamin and Cummings Publ. Co., Menlo Park, California, 1993.

[5] P. Atzeni and R. Torlone. Updating relational databases through weak instance interfaces. *ACM Trans. on Database Syst.*, 17(4):718–746, December 1992.

[6] E.P.F. Chan. Optimal computation of total projections with unions of simple chase join expressions. In *ACM SIGMOD International Conf. on Management of Data*, pages 149–163, 1984.

[7] M.H. Graham and M. Yannakakis. Independent database schemas. *Journal of Comp. and System Sc.*, 28(1):121–141, 1984.

[8] H. Hernandez and E.P.F. Chan. Constant-time-maintainable BCNF database schemes. *ACM Trans. on Database Syst.*, 16(4):571–599, 1991.

[9] P. Honeyman. Testing satisfaction of functional dependencies. *Journal of the ACM*, 29(3):668–677, 1982.

[10] M. Ito, M. Iwasaki, and T. Kasami. Some results on the representative instance in relational databases. *SIAM Journal on Computing*, 14(2):334–354, 1985.

[11] D. Maier, A.O. Mendelzon, and Y. Sagiv. Testing implications of data dependencies. *ACM Trans. on Database Syst.*, 4(4):455–468, 1979.

[12] D. Maier, J.D. Ullman, and M. Vardi. On the foundations of the universal relation model. *ACM Trans. on Database Syst.*, 9(2):283–308, 1984.

[13] Y. Sagiv. A characterization of globally consistent databases and their correct access paths. *ACM Trans. on Database Syst.*, 8(2):266–286, 1983.

[14] Y. Sagiv. Evaluation of queries in independent database schemes. *Journal of the ACM*, 38(1):120–161, 1991.

[15] J.D. Ullman. *Principles of Database Systems.* Computer Science Press, Potomac, Maryland, second edition, 1982.

[16] K. Wang and M.H. Graham. Constant-time maintainability: a generalization of independence. *ACM Trans. on Database Syst.*, 17(2):201–246, 1992.

CONCEPTS FOR DATABASE PRIVACY

H.H. Brüggemann
University of Hildesheim, Hildesheim, Germany

ABSTRACT

Privacy is the individual's right of informational self-determination. Concepts for a privacy model of data are presented. A privacy view of data collects and encapsulates the personal data of one data subject. All kinds of individuals (e.g. users, data subjects) are uniformly represented in this model. Individual personal data is -of course- considered as private, but structural personal data is considered as public. Access rights are divided into structural and individual rights. Structural rights are authorities which can be used for a certain purpose only and refer to technical roles. Technical roles model the behavior pattern of social roles. The set of individuals which is concerned by a social role is modeled by individual rights.

1. INTRODUCTION

Privacy is the individual's right of **informational self-determination**. The right to privacy is a personal and fundamental right protected by the constitution of several countries (e.g USA [1], Germany [2]) or by conventions of supranational communities (e.g. Council of Europe [3]).

Undoubtfully privacy has to do with data and its dissemination. Nevertheless, up to now database systems are not well designed to technically support privacy.

Among the privacy goals are [3]: the personal data shall be
- obtained and processed fairly and lawfully,
- stored for specified and legitimate purposes and not used in a way incompatible with those purposes,
- adequate, relevant and not excessive in relation to the purposes for which they are stored,
- accurate and, where necessary, kept up to date,
- preserved in a form which permits identification of the data subjects for no longer than is required for the purpose for which those data are stored.

This paper aims at presenting some landmarks for a privacy model of data. It benefits from our experience within the DORIS project.

2. RELATIONAL VIEW AND PRIVACY VIEW OF DATA

In (relational) database systems the personal data of one **data subject** is scattered over several relations (like in the example below or even more scattered).

Example:

Fig. 1, Relational view of data

In this relational view the units to protect are basically topics (relations), i.e. finances, health, and business. The resulting addressing strategy is therefore: to retrieve data specify the topic (i.e. name the relation) first and subsequently specify the person (i.e. select the tuples).

In contrast, a **privacy view of data** [4] collects and encapsulates the personal data of one data subject. Thus the **knowledge** about this data subject is inside one unit and only the data subject itself persistently knows things about itself. Technically, we model the data subject as an object in the object-oriented sense. It is this object we call "**person**".

Nevertheless, we retain the idea that the knowledge of a person is structured into **attributes** which itself may be atomar or structured (e.g. sets, records).

Example:

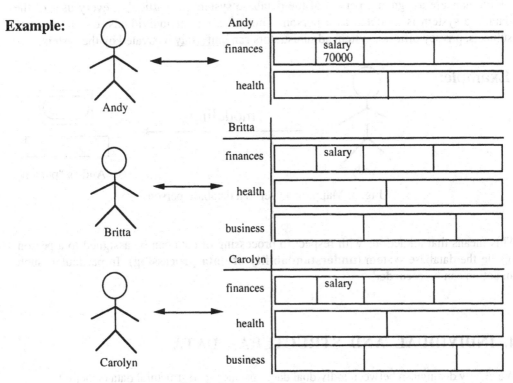

Fig. 2, Privacy view of data

In this privacy view the units to protect are basically persons, i.e. Andy, Britta, and Carolyn. The corresponding addressing strategy is: specify the person first, subsequently specify the topic.

This view has the following privacy benefits:

- The **provision of information to the data subject** concerning his own knowledge is easy to manage by giving every person the right to read its own attributes, and
- the **data must be collected from the data subject** itself because nobody else knows it.

3. MODELING ALL USERS INSIDE THE DATABASE SYSTEM

Each kind of data processing needs individuals who are responsible for it. All relevant individuals are assigned a person of the database system. In particular, every user of the database system is modeled as a person. Thus all kinds of individuals, e.g. users, data subjects, privacy officers, system administrators can <u>uniformly</u> be treated by the system.

Example:

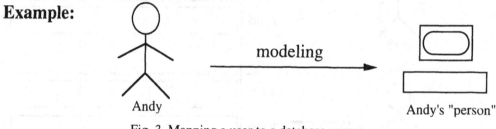

Andy   Andy's "person"

Fig. 3, Mapping a user to a database person

This means that all actions with respect to processing of data can be assigned to a person <u>inside</u> the database system (**understandability of data processing**). In particular, such an action can be **record**ed.

4. INDIVIDUAL AND STRUCTURAL DATA

We clearly distinguish between individual data (instance) and structural data (scheme).
We argue the following two rules should be enforced.

- **Individual** (personal) **data is private**, and thus must be kept secretly by the database system.

Example: Andy earns DM 70,000 a year. Then the database system contains a private entry like
Andy.KNOWS.finances = [..., salary=70000, ...]
Besides the knowledge of a person individual data are its acquaintances, the joint usable

rights (i.e. rights made available individually), and the recorded data.

- On the other hand, **structural** (personal) **data is public**, i.e. it may be read by everyone.

Example: The salary is given as yearly income in german currency. Then the database system contains a public entry like
Andy('s Class).ATTRIBUTES.finances =
[..., salary : INTEGER /* income in DM per year */, ...]
Besides type and interpretation of knowledge structural data are class-defined operations, authorities, and technical roles.

To distinguish between individual and structural data has several benefits: Technically, persons with the same structure can be grouped into **classes**. Then the structural data is maintained within class definitions, the individual data within class objects. From the designer's point of view, classes allow to describe the organization structures even if the assignment of persons to the organization units had not taken place. From the privacy point of view, this public information allows everyone to get information about which kind of data is stored in the database system and which kind of data processing is allowed. **(transparency of data processing)**

Moreover, a special class, called **Privacy Officer**, is assigned special rights for checking the recorded data.

5. CLASS HIERARCHY AND INHERITANCE

In the object-oriented world it is quite common to have partially ordered classes and to inherit structural data from the superclasses.

In the example below we show a very simple class hierarchy with two classes and the objects assigned to each class.

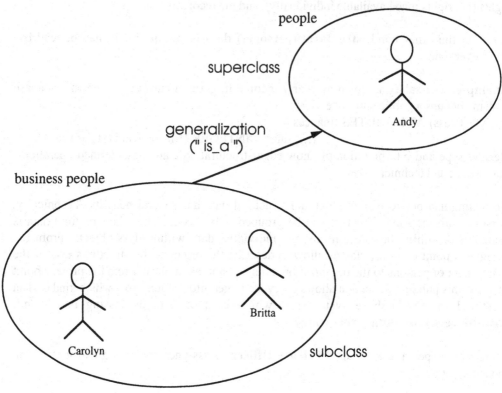

Fig. 4, An example class hierarchy

Class hierarchy in a privacy database system means that a class inherits not only attributes (the knowledge) and class-defined operations, but also authorities (purposes) ([5]) and technical roles (behavioral pattern).

6. RIGHTS

The basic idea is that the members of a class are allowed to perform certain operations with the members of (another) class. The necessary rights are divided into structural rights and individual rights.

6.1. Structural rights
The structural rights reflect the fact that individuals act in various **social roles**. A social role is defined by a pattern of behavior aiming at certain purposes and a set of individuals to which this behavior is exhibited.

Example:

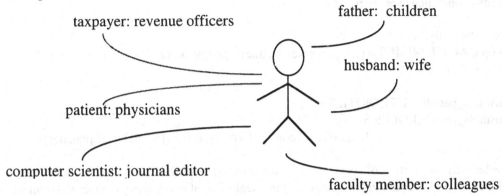

taxpayer: revenue officers

father: children

husband: wife

patient: physicians

computer scientist: journal editor

faculty member: colleagues

Fig. 5, An individual with some of its social roles

An individual should not be able to use the behavioral pattern provided for one social role in a different social role. Thus the idea is that (the class of) a person receives a right not in general but only for a certain **purpose**. This means that for one task a person cannot use several rights which this person was given for different purposes. In particular, such a policy supports the **separation of** social **roles**.

Purposes belong to the structural data and are therefore public. This means that the purposes of data processing and its possible data communications can be read off the structural data.

For practical reasons the structural rights are divided into two parts: A **technical role** describes the behavioral part of a social role and thus a piece of the behavioral pattern of (the persons of) a class by saying which operations are needed to practise this social role. Technical roles are defined in that class which is passive with respect to this technical role. On the other hand, an **authority** describes who is allowed to practise a technical role and what is the authorized purpose. Authorities are defined in that class which is active with respect to this technical role.

Example:
Andy('s class).AUTHORITIES = [..., purpose : Britta('s class) technical_role, ...]
Andy('s class).ROLES = ...

Britta('s class).AUTHORITIES = ...
Britta('s class).ROLES =
                 [..., technical_role = {operation[restriction], operation, operation}, ...]

The optional restriction contains e.g. attributes to which read (or write, insert, delete, modify) operations are restricted.

Less abstractly, we have:
people.AUTHORITIES = [..., purchase : business_people order, ...]
people.ROLES = ...

business_people.AUTHORITIES = ...
business_people.ROLES =
                        [..., order = {contract[article], deliver[article], cash[balance]}, ...]

Technically, separation of social roles is supported by requiring to address the authorities. This is done by mentioning the purpose at the beginning of every query or update statement [6]. A good schema design will try to identify purposes and authorities.

Separation of structural rights into technical roles and authorities makes the design process simpler: Generally, in the early design steps only the functionality of the system is fixed and thus the behavioral pattern of the classes. Independently, in later design steps it can be fixed which classes are allowed to practise these technical roles. Finally, it has to be determined which individuals are assigned to which classes.

Moreover, the division into technical roles and authorities makes the task of the following security checks easier:
What are the persons of a class (structurally) allowed at most?
What have the persons of a class (structurally) to suffer at most?
Are allowances and sufferings well-balanced?

Up to now we argued that persons are grouped into classes. As we have already pointed out a person can have several social roles. To cope with the complexity of the real world it is more desirable to model the social roles as classes. This avoids to be forced to define classes for any occurring combination of social roles. Technically, modeling social roles as classes requires to have **multiple inheritance** not only on class level but **on the instance level**. Then a person is an instance inheriting from several social roles.

6.2 Individual rights

A social role is not only defined by a certain pattern of behavior, but each social role determines a set of persons for which this role is applicable. Thus the structural rights given by authorities and technical roles in the class definitions are restricted to those persons to which a person is responsible for or **acquainted with**. These sets of persons (acquaintances) may vary not only from person to person but they also depends on the purpose and thus are usually different for every authority [6]. Only for these persons one gets the capability to communicate with.

Structural rights cannot be propagated (without changing the scheme), but they can be made available to other persons (e.g. to a substitute during vacations). This joint use permission is stored at the permitting person. If the joint user would like to use this right it has to refer to this permission and thus indirectly to the right it want to use. In this way an **owner retained control** ([4], [7]) is realized.

7. QUERIES AND INTENDED NON-FUNCTIONALITY

The query language is used not only for manipulation of the data but also for computing the set of addressees. Thus a query consists of the following four steps: First the purpose is explicitly mentioned by stating the corresponding authority, then the set of persons which are to be queried is determined, third the knowledge (attributes) in question is determined, and finally, the query states which result should be computed from the answers of the queried persons.

Results of queries cannot be stored permanently (within the system). Thus propagated data is erased immediately and update reports are never necessary. Privacy benefits are: **erasure deadlines** for propagated data and **deadlines for update reports** are trivially met.

8. DATA MODEL

The public structural data is given by class definitions. A **class definition** contains
- the name of the class,
- the position of the class in the class hierarchy,
- the structure of the knowledge of this class (the type and interpretation of its attributes),
- the operations which are defined for the class members,
- the authorities which can be used by the class members, and
- the technical roles, in which the class members can work.

Moreover, a class maintains the set of the class members belonging to the class.

The private individual data is stored in objects. An **object** contains
- its identity,
- the class(es) it belongs to,
- its knowledge according to the knowledge structure in its class definition,
- the acquaintances for each of its authorities,
- the rights which are made available to this person, and
- the recorded data with respect to this person.

9. FINAL REMARKS

We gave basic ideas for a privacy supporting database system. Of course, the system should be enriched for being able to deal with **non-personal data**, too. From the rights' point of view it is desirable to include not only **prohibitions** [5], but also **duties** and its opposite, the so-called **freedoms** [8].

REFERENCES

[1]   Congress, 93rd; 2nd Session: Privacy Act of 1974, Public Law 93-579.

[2]   Bundesverfassungsgericht: Urteil vom 15. Dez. 1983 zum Volkszählungsgesetz 1983, Bundesanzeiger 35, 241a (1983).

[3]   Council of Europe: Convention for the Protection of Individuals with Regard to Automatic Processing of Personal Data (Jan 28,1981), Bundesgesetzblatt, Teil II, 19.03.1985, 538-550.

[4]   Biskup, J., Brüggemann, H.H.: The personal model of data: towards a privacy-oriented information system, Computers & Security, Vol. 7, 1988, 575-597.

[5]   Brüggemann, H.H.: Object-oriented Authorization, in this volume.

[6]   Brüggemann, H.H.: Interaction of authorities and acquaintances in the DORIS privacy model of data, in: Proc. 2nd Symposium on Mathematical Fundamentals of Database Systems, June 1989, Visegrád, Hungary, LNCS 364, 1989, 85-99.

[7]   Graubart, R.: On the need for a third form of access control, in: Proc. 12th National Computer Security Conference, Baltimore, Oct. 1989.

[8]   Jonscher, D.: Extending access control with duties - realized by active mechanisms, in: Thuraisingham, B.M., Landwehr, C.E. (eds.), Database Security, VI: Status and Prospects, Elsevier, 1993, 91-112.

DATABASE SECURITY: POLICIES AND MECHANISMS

H.H. Brüggemann
University of Hildesheim, Hildesheim, Germany

ABSTRACT

An introduction into policies and mechanisms of database security is given. Three different policy classes for access control are distinguished: Owner driven access control (discretionary access control), organization driven access control (mandatory access control), and access control with security levels (multi-level access control). After giving intentions and characterizations for each policy class, we present mechanisms usually used with those policies. Thus the access control matrix is presented with their different views from a subject (capability list), from a granule (access control list), and from an operation (method control list). Further mechanisms which are considered in connection with owner driven access control are propagation of rights, database views, and query modification. Organization driven access control is studied with respect to classification and clearance, the relationship between confidentiality and integrity, and the appropriate granularity of classification. The dissemination control policy and -in more detail- the chinese wall policy are presented as examples for this class of policies. Mechanisms of the lattice-based access control with security levels include polyinstantiation (used for information hiding and cover stories) and trusted subjects. A final criticism points out the author's view of the strengths and weaknesses of each class of policies.

1. INTRODUCTION

Security mechanisms deeply depend on the security policy: Main security goals are to keep secrets (e.g. at military and secret services, administration (public or private)), to keep money or other possessions (e.g. at banks) [1], or to keep privacy (e.g. of citizen). In this paper we concentrate on the first goal. Privacy concerns are treated in [2]. Of the three basic security dimensions **availability**, **integrity**, and **confidentiality** ([3], [4], [5], [6]), policies and mechanisms for confidentiality are the best investigated ones.

Usually only **permissions** are considered. (For a more sophisticated approach see [7]). Permissions are given with respect to actions specifying which subject does which operation on which granule.

Each kind of access control relies on two essential prerequisites: First, not only user granules but also system granules must be protected to prevent unauthorized modification of data files which contain user rights. Second, reliable **identification** is needed to prevent **masquerading**: This includes
- user (subject) identification: No user should be in a position to obtain access rights of another subject. Usually this is tried to guarantee by authentication procedures (using knowledge like passwords, possessions like chip cards, or properties like fingerprints) during login.
- identification of operations, in particular for protection against **trojan horses** (which is a hidden piece of software which acts without the subject's knowledge but with the subject's identity and thus has all its permissions).
- identification of granules, in particular because of possible role shifts: procedures may become operations, programs may become processes (subjects).

2. OWNER DRIVEN ACCESS CONTROL (DISCRETIONARY ACCESS CONTROL)

2.1 Intentions and policy
The policy of the **owner driven access control** is a decentralized approach based on the concept of **ownership** and is common in multi-user operating systems (e.g. UNIX) and was taken over from most commercial database systems. Every user maintains the rights for those granules it owns.

The basic rules of this policy are the following:
- A granule is **own**ed by (at least) one subject.
- The **creator** of a granule becomes owner of this granule.
- An owner is implicitly allowed to do (nearly) all operations with respect to its granule, in particular to grant (or revoke) rights with respect to this granule. All other subjects may

perform only those operations which are explicitly granted to them.

The owner may grant access to its granules according to its own local strategies. From an organizational point of view the local user strategies may appear somewhat discretionary: that is why this policy often is called **discretionary access control**.

2.2 The rights matrix and its views

The **access control rights** state which actions are allowed to do. An **action** consists of three components: a **subject** s (an active unit like user, role of a user, or process), an **operation** o (an access type like read, insert, modify, append, create index, execute, create, drop, own, grant, revoke), and a **granule** g (a passive unit to protect like database area, relation, view, attribute, tuple, element). We can distinguish between the finite sets of existing subjects, operations and granules at a given time and the countably infinite sets of possible subjects, operations and granules (which are necessary to be able to create additional ones at any time).

From an abstract point of view all permissions can be thought as stored in a big matrix M, called **rights matrix** or **access control matrix**, which is a three-dimensional boolean matrix, saying "action allowed" or "action not allowed". (Of course, on the blackboard or here in the paper it is easier to draw a two-dimensional matrix, one row for each subject, and one column for each granule and each matrix element contains the set of all the allowed operations for this subject and this granule.)

Example:

$$M = \begin{bmatrix} \varnothing & \{\text{execute}\} & \{\text{read}\} & \varnothing \\ \varnothing & \varnothing & \{\text{read, write}\} & \{\text{read}\} \\ \varnothing & \varnothing & \varnothing & \varnothing \\ \varnothing & \varnothing & \varnothing & \varnothing \end{bmatrix} \begin{matrix} s1 \\ s2 \\ s3 \\ s4 \end{matrix}$$

$$[\, g1 \; g2 \qquad g3 \qquad\qquad g4 \,]$$

Fig. 1, A two-dimensional access control matrix

Note that the rights matrix can be changed not only in its content (if rights are granted or revoked) but also in its structure (the dimensions change if granules, operations or subjects are created or dropped).

From a practical point of view it is essential where these rights are physically stored. Thus we distinguish:
- the subject view of the rights matrix (called **capability list** C). All permissions of a subject are put together and stored with the subject (in everyday life: e.g. a bunch of keys).

Example: C(s1)={(execute, g2), (read, g3)}.
- the granule view of the rights matrix (called **access control list** A). All rights with respect to this granule are stored with this granule (in everyday life: e.g. access through magnet cards).
  Example: A(g3)={(s1, read), (s2, read), (s2, write)}.
- the operation view of the rights matrix (perhaps it should be called **method control list** B). All rights with respect to this operation are stored with this operation. This seems to be an appropriate view if in object-oriented systems access control should take place within the methods.
  Example: B(read)={(s1, g3), (s2, g3), (s2, g4)}.

Sometimes permissions are given only under certain conditions. In many cases this can be expressed by allowing a predicate specifying the condition to be an entry of the three-dimensional rights matrix. Typical conditions are
- content-dependent, i.e. a function of the values of the data which should be accessed (e.g. salary < 5000);
- time-dependent (e.g. access only between 9 a.m and 5 p.m.);
- context-dependent (e.g. a user is allowed to read either student names or student grades but not the combination of both);
- case history dependent (e.g. a process is not allowed to write into an unclassified file if it worked with classified data before).

2.3 Propagation of rights

While the owner is allowed to perform all operations with its granules, other subjects need the permissions to be granted to them before. In SQL syntax: GRANT operation-list ON granule-list TO subject-list. Now the grantee is allowed to perform the granted operation on the granted granule, but it is not allowed to grant this right to further subjects. If the grantee should be allowed to propagate the right, a grant option has to be added.

Typical units for the propagation of rights in commercial database systems are: in the case of subjects a user, a set of users or a user group, in the case of operations one or more operations, and in the case of granules relations and views (update operations can additionally be restricted to attributes).

The propagation of rights can be represented by a **rights propagation graph** for each granule. We use different symbols for the nodes (subjects) to indicate their different possibilities to propagate rights.

Example: Let subject s1 be the owner (represented by a triangle) of granule g1. s1 gives the select right and the update right to s2 including the option to propagate these rights (represented by a circle):

                s1: GRANT select, update ON g1 TO s2 WITH GRANT OPTION

Subsequently s2 gives the select right to s3.   s2: GRANT select ON g1 TO s3

s3 cannot propagate the right (represented by a square).

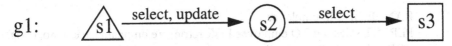

Fig. 2, A rights propagation graph

Note that the same subject can occur twice (as circle and as square) in a rights propagation graph.

Of course, rights can also be revoked. We distinguish between a **recursive revoke** and a non-recursive revoke. If in our example s1 revokes the select right from s2, s2 looses this right in any case. The difference is that a recursive revoke additionally revokes the select right from s3, because s3 received this right only from s2.

2.4 Database views
A database **view** is an imaginary relation which can be queried exactly as stored ones but does not exist physically. A view is precisely defined from stored relations using the usual query language.

The clue is to use views as granules. Subjects are given permissions usually only for views and not for stored relations.

Thus a view can be used in manifold ways, e.g.:
- to restrict access to attributes of a relation if a projection is used in its definition,
- to restrict access to tuples of a relation if a selection is used,
- to restrict access to a certain join if a join between relations is used,
- or any combination.

Example (in an SQL-like fashion):
        CREATE VIEW sales AS
        SELECT empname, empno, mgr FROM employee WHERE job='Salesman';
        GRANT select, update ON sales TO salesmgr;

Thus a subject having permission for the view gets the correct answer, a subject not having permission for the view only gets an error message.

2.5 Query modification
Query modification is another mechanism to implement owner driven access control. The rights of every subject are stored in a system relation in form of a restricting predicate (authorization condition). Then the selection condition of every query is conjunctively linked with the authorization condition of the querying subject.

Example (in an INGRES-like fashion):

RANGE OF e IS employee
PERMIT salesmgr TO employee FOR retrieve(e.empname, e.empno, e.mgr)
WHERE e.job='Salesman'

Then each subsequent query of salesmgr to the relation employee is restricted to the attributes empname, empno, mgr and to the tuples of the salesmen.

Thus two subjects with different access rights might get two different answers to the same query.

2.6 Criticism

The owner driven access control policy has been proven a flexible policy for many applications. Nevertheless with some justification it has been criticized for
- the lack of mechanisms to tie the owner policies to a global organization policy, especially in the case of rights propagation;
- not being able to arbitrarily change data via views without loss of integrity (if database views are substantially used);
- the lack of reliable identification of operations, in particular, lack of protection against trojan horses.

3. ORGANIZATION DRIVEN ACCESS CONTROL (MANDATORY ACCESS CONTROL)

3.1 Intention and general policy

Organization driven access control primarily reflects the needs of an organization (more than those of an individual). It introduces fixed limits for the maximum rights being granted. That is why here the damage due to trojan horses is limited. Often within these fixed limits owner driven access control is additionally used.

In many commercial database systems such limits are usually given for the different technically defined user roles: database system administrator, database administrator, database object creator, database user.

Organizations often prefer to distinguish between application defined **user groups** (at least for the last two roles).

A simple version of organization driven access control is the **compartment access control**: The enterprise is divided in several compartments and the subjects are restricted to the data of its own compartment. (In the moment we do not care about exceptions for the bosses.)

3.2 Classification and clearance

The basic mechanism to implement organization driven access control is to use **tags** as a container for the **security attributes** of the granules. These tags are part of the granules. The security attributes are usually set by the creator of a granule and used to implicitly fix the set of subjects which may have access to the granule. In the case of compartment access control the only security attribute is the name of the compartment the granule belongs to. Other examples for security attributes are the creating organization, the line of business, the citizenship, or the level of confidentiality. The security attributes of a granule in its entirety are called **classification**.

On the other hand the authorizing instance needs to check the corresponding properties of the subject, e.g. which compartment the subject belongs to. We call these properties **clearance**.

3.3 Confidentiality and integrity

Confidentiality has some drawbacks to database integrity: To maintain database integrity the database system should be able to check integrity constraints and to have access to some data which might not be directly requested (e.g. for reasons of data access or optimization). Thus, if we have data with different classifications e.g. the following questions may occur:
Is it allowed to check an integrity constraint (a read operation)?
Is it allowed to make a modification as a result of an integrity constraint (a write operation)?
Is it allowed to give an error message to the subject (from the view of the subject this is a read operation)?

Although the integrity problem and the problem of using the appropriate unit of classification (see section 3.4) are typical for organization driven access control up to now most of the investigations have been made for the special case of access control with security levels (see section 4).

The following integrity rules are widely accepted.
1. To ensure **entity integrity** no tuple may have null values in the primary key attributes. If we would allow different classifications for the primary key attributes there could be some user who sees null values in this tuple. Thus we need the rule: The classifications of the primary key attributes of one tuple must be the same.
2. Primary key attributes are used to access the tuple. Thus we must assure that if a classification allows the access to an attribute of a tuple the access to the primary key attributes of this tuple must be allowed, too. Otherwise the whole tuple cannot be accessed by the database system. This can be assured if there is some ordering on the classifications: Then the classifications of the element values of a tuple must be greater or equal than the classifications of the primary key attributes of this tuple.
3. The situation is rather similar with **referential integrity**: If $R[X] \subset S[Y]$ is an inclusion dependency the classifications of the X-values of the tuple from relation r must be greater or equal than the classifications of the corresponding Y-values of the corresponding tuple from the relation s. Otherwise a user could see a dangling tuple. Moreover, if X is a foreign key for S the entity integrity rule above has additionally to be taken into account.

4. For being able to use the data dictionary properly the classification of the relation scheme (in particular the relation name and the attribute types) must be smaller or equal than the classification of the tuples (usually this is the classification of its key attributes) of this relation.
5. The classification of a view must be greater or equal than the classification of the used basic relations, because otherwise the view cannot be computed.

3.4 Units of classification

In database systems the structure of data is modeled and structured data is stored. Thus we must answer the question: What is the appropriate **unit of classification**? The typical possibilities in the relational model are: data element, tuple, attribute, relation, view, database. This is an important design decision with the following trade-off: The smaller the units of classification the more the expressibility for the security, but the more the work-load for attaching classifications and the more the storage requirements for the tags and the time for authorization, too.

The approach of Hinke and Schäfer (1975) assigns a classification to every attribute. This approach uses integrity rules 1. and 2. Unfortunately it is rather complicated to modify a tuple with different classifications.

The IP Sharp model of Grohn (1976) assigns a classification only to every relation. This circumvents the update problems of the Hinke/Schäfer model. Nevertheless attribute-wise classification assignment can be simulated by vertical partitioning of the relation thus grouping together all non-key attributes with the same classification.

The naval dbms model of Graubart and Woodward [8] assigns a classification to every data element. Moreover, every tuple, attribute, relation, and database is viewed as a container and every container is assigned a so-called default classification. The actual classification is computed as the maximum of the classification of the data element and the classifications of all its surrounding containers.

The SeaView model of Denning et al. [9] assigns classifications to views. This allows a high level of flexibility. Depending on the definition of the view attributes, tuples, or even aggregations can be protected.

3.5 Special policies

3.5.1 Chinese Wall policy

The **chinese wall policy** [10] models commercial confidentiality interests, namely market analysis within a bank or the behavior of a consulting firm. The basic rule is that an analyst should not consult a company if he knows plans and/or the state of a competitor as an insider. But it is not a problem if he consults several companies which are not in competition.

There is one prerequisite: It is understood that each granule is relevant for only one company.

The data is grouped on three levels: On the bottom level there are the **granules**. Each **company** has a set of granules. The sets of those companies which are in competition are put into one class, called **line of business**.

Then the policy is that every subject is allowed to have access to granules of at most one company of each line of business. This means that in the beginning a subject has potential access to every granule, but subsequently every access restricts the possibilities of the subject.

Example: Let banks and oil companies be the lines of business. We have bank-1, oil company-1, and oil company-2. A new subject s may access any granule, because there is no data the subject has already read, so there is no conflict of interest. First subject s reads granules of oil company-1 and subsequently it wants to read granules of bank-1. In both cases access is granted, because both companies are in different lines of business. A subsequent access of s to granules of oil company-2 is prevented by the access control, because there is a conflict of interest between the two oil companies.

Thus the classification is rather simple, but the clearance changes with each access to data. Access is granted to data which is not in conflict with the data the subject already has, i.e. it depends on the previous knowledge of the subject.

The classification of a granule is the name of the company to which it is relevant; the clearance is the set of companies the subject already had access to. Moreover, we need a global mapping which yields the line of business of a company.

Data which is made accessible to the public (via newspapers, statistics etc.) can be modeled by introducing a further line of business (maybe called "public"), which contains one single "company". Then every subject is allowed to access to this set of granules.

3.5.2 Dissemination control

The **dissemination control** [11] aims at controlling who gets which documents. Typical security attributes are names or citizenships. If two documents are combined (partly or as a whole) the security attributes of the new document is computed as the intersection of the original ones.

Example: A first document is written for US and Canadian citizen. A second one is intended only for US citizen or (the British citizen) James Bond. If these two documents are combined into one the resulting document may be read only by US citizen.

3.6 Criticism
Introducing fixed right limits to application defined user groups is a good way to consider an organization's view of security.

Nevertheless, one problem with this approach is that for each new kind of security attribute, rules are needed for comparing these security attribute values. Moreover, specific rules for combining granules with different security attributes are needed. As a result the security attributes might become rather complex.

4. ACCESS CONTROL WITH SECURITY LEVELS (MULTI-LEVEL ACCESS CONTROL)

Access control with security levels is a specialization of organization driven access control. The only security attribute is the level of confidentiality (**security level**). The security level values are partially ordered and there are special rules for reading "down" and writing "up". Due to this behavior we would like to call this approach **semipermeable**.

In its more refined versions it is combined with compartment access control (using the powerset of the compartments, the so-called **categories**) and owner driven access control.

4.1 Intention and policy
The basic policy is linked with the name **Bell-LaPadula model** ([12]). It is mainly motivated by (in particular military) needs for security levels (like unclassified < confidential < secret < top secret). In this case both classification and clearance are security levels.

The basic policy has two rules:
- subjects with a "lower" security level are not allowed to read "secrets".
  More precisely, a subject may read a granule if the clearance of the subject is greater or equal than the classification of the granule.
- subjects with a "higher" security level are not allowed to disclose "secrets".
  More precisely, a subject may write into a granule if the classification of the granule is greater or equal than the clearance of the subject.

Otherwise, a subject could write its highly classified knowledge into a document which could be read by lower cleared subjects.

Immediately applied, this policy results in the absurd situation that a (highly cleared) chief is not allowed to give orders to his (lower cleared) subordinates, because the policy forces a one-way communication: The chief may read the reports of his subordinates, he may write reports to his superiors, but he is not allowed to write reports or to give orders to his subordinates.

That is why the security level assigned to the subject is understood as its **maximum security level**, e.g. each subject is given the interval [lowest security level of the system … maximum security level of the subject] (if the security levels are totally ordered) or the corresponding sublattice (if the security levels are partially ordered) and then the subject is allowed to choose a **current security level** within these restrictions.

Now a subject may choose the same security level as its subordinates and give orders. But in this situation the database gives it only the same view its subordinates have.

4.2 Polyinstantiation: information hiding and cover stories

Sometimes a subject may want to create a granule (or add some value to a granule) although the granule (or the value) already exists, but it is invisible to that subject. This means the classification of the granule (or of the value) is higher than the subject's clearance. Thus the invisible granule should not simply be overwritten. Moreover, if the subject should not know about the existence of the higher classified granule the database system has to maintain several versions of the granule (at most one version for each security level). In this case the granule identifiers (like primary keys) are unique only with respect to a security level, or to put it the other way round, the security level becomes part of the granule identifier which is invisible to the subjects. Thus **polyinstantiation** is a special kind of versions which are distinguished by the security level. A granule is **polyinstantiated** if several versions of this granule exist with different security levels.

In the relational database context we distinguish between polyinstantiated tuples and polyinstantiated elements. **Polyinstantiated tuples** are tuples which have the same primary key values, but the primary keys have different security levels. Polyinstantiated tuples are the result of inserting a tuple with the same primary key values and different security level as the existing tuples with this primary key. We have **polyinstantiated elements** if a non primary key attribute of a tuple has different values for different security levels. Polyinstantiated elements arise from inserting a value where a null value is shown, but in fact a value with a higher security level exists.

Thinking in the entity-relationship model tuples with polyinstantiated elements represent the same real world entity whereas polyinstantiated tuples represent different real world entities.

In relations without polyinstantiation for each primary key value K there exists only one value of a non primary key attribute A_i, i.e. the functional dependency $K \rightarrow A_i$ holds. In relations with polyinstantiation every non primary key attribute A_i functionally depends besides the key attribute value K on the security level of the key (C_k) and the security level of the non primary key attribute (C_i): $K\, C_k\, C_i \rightarrow A_i$.

Example:

	A1	A2	A3
	(mad, secret)	(17, secret)	(x, secret)
	(foo, secret)	(34, secret)	(w, top secret)
	(ark, top secret)	(5, top secret)	(y, top secret)

Fig. 3, A relation with element-wise security level assignment

	A1	A2	A3
	mad	17	x
	foo	34	null

Fig. 4, View to the example relation from a subject with security level secret

Inserting a tuple ((ark, secret), (22, secret), (z, secret)) creates a polyinstantiated tuple. If a subject cleared for security level secret complements the (foo,34,null)-tuple with an A3-value u then the system creates a polyinstantiated element.

To insert a further version of data (which is lower classified than the original version) not by accident but by intent (through a subject which usually has a higher maximum security level) is another technique to protect data from disclosure. Thus polyinstantiation can also be used for maintaining **cover stories**. Nevertheless it is not easy to support complex (i.e. if several tuples are involved or if some subjects have some pre-knowledge) cover stories consistently.

4.3 Trusted subjects
It may happen that a highly cleared subject would like to write into a lower classified document, e.g. to add some higher classified information or just for convenience to avoid changing the current security level. This is allowed according to the basic policy only if classification of the document is raised correspondingly. But then the system runs into the danger that the classifications of the documents get higher and higher: slowly but surely they creep to the highest security level. Because there is no significant difference between a security system in which all granules are classified as top secret and a "security" system in which all granules are unclassified (knowing one granule means knowing all), this level-reducing effect is not intended. For this reason so-called **trusted subjects** are introduced which are allowed to reduce the classifications of the granules without having to obey the basic policy rules.

4.4 Criticism
This policy supports a clear ordering of security attributes. But the right of free choosing the

current security level gives the subjects with a high clearance a substantial freedom of choice. This freedom works against the original limitation for write operations. Moreover, it is some kind of ironic that those access control policies whose origin is driven by the lack of trust in its subjects need at least into some of its subjects exactly this trust.

Especially if the number of security levels is large (e.g. if the classification is a combination of the level of confidentiality and the powerset of compartments) polyinstantiation may lead to database instances in which nearly all data is wrong from the view of the highest clearance.

5. FINAL REMARKS

We gave an introduction into policies and mechanisms in the area of database security. Although some mechanisms can be used in connection with several policies we introduced them together with that policy we felt it was most deeply linked. Due to space limitations we restrict ourselves to the basic policies and mechanisms of access control and of (what is usually called) information flow control. We did not cover the area of data encryption (the data can be accessed, but not interpreted) nor the area of inference control (e.g. statistical database queries with its methods based on linear algebra). More detailed descriptions can be found in [13], [14], and [15]. For further reading we suggest to include [16], [17], and [18].

ACKNOWLEDGEMENT
Valuable comments came from Joachim Biskup, Gerrit Bleumer, Christian Eckert, Ralph Jacobs, and Bernd Teßmer.

REFERENCES

[1]   Clark, D.D., Wilson, D.R.: A Comparison of Commercial and Military Computer Security Policies, in: IEEE Symposium on Security and Privacy, 1987, 184-194.

[2]   Brüggemann, H. H.: Concepts for Database Privacy, in this volume.

[3]   Department of Defense: Trusted Computer System Evaluation Criteria (Orange Book), Aug 1983 (revised 1985).

[4]   Commission of the European Communities, XIII-F: Information Technology Security Evaluation Criteria (ITSEC), Version 1.2, June 1991.

[5]   Canadian System Security Centre: The Canadian Trusted Computer Product Evaluation Criteria, Version 3.0, April 1992.

[6]   National Institute of Standards and Technology & National Security Agency: Federal Criteria for Information Technology Security, Version 1.0, December 1992.

[7]   Brüggemann, H. H.: Object-oriented Authorization, in this volume.

[8]   Graubart, R.D., Woodward, J.P.L.: A preliminary naval surveillance dbms security model, in: IEEE Symposium on Security and Privacy, 1982, 21-37.

[9]   Denning, D., Akl, S.G., Morgenstern, M., Neumann, P.G., Schell, R.R., Heckman, M.: Views for multilevel database security, in: IEEE Symposium. on Security and Privacy, 1986, 156-172.

[10] Brewer, D.F.C., Nash, M.J.: The Chinese Wall Security Policy, in: IEEE Symposium on Security and Privacy, 1989, 206-214.

[11] Jensen McCollum, C., Messing, J.R., Notargiacomo, L.: Beyond the Pale of MAC and DAC - Defining New Forms of Access Control, in: IEEE Symposium on Research in Security and Privacy, 1990, 190-200.

[12] Bell, D.E., LaPadula, L.J.: Secure Computer Systems: Unified Exposition and Multics Interpretation, MTR-2997, The MITRE Corporation, Bedford, MA, July 1975 (ESD-TR-75-306).

[13] Denning, D.E.R.: Cryptography and Data Security, Addison-Wesley, Reading, MA, 1982.

[14] Fernandez, E.B., Summers, R.C., Wood, C.: Database Security and Integrity, Addison-Wesley, Reading, MA, 1981.

[15] Millen, J.K.: Models of Multilevel Computer Security, in: Advances in Computers, Vol. 29, 1989, 1-45.

[16] Bell, D. E.: Putting Policy Commonalities to Work, in: Proc. 14th National Computer Security Conference, 1991, 456-471.

[17] Biskup, J.: A general framework for database security, in: Proc. European Symposium on Research in Computer Security, Toulouse, Oct. 1990, 35-41.

[18] Lunt, T.F., Fernandez, E.B.: Database Security, SIGMOD Record, Vol. 19, No. 4, (Dec 1990), 90-97.

OBJECT-ORIENTED AUTHORIZATION

H.H. Brüggemann
University of Hildesheim, Hildesheim, Germany

ABSTRACT

In this paper we introduce an intuitive approach to the semantics of an authorization system based on a clear object-oriented modeling of the (application) world. The authorization system consists of rights which permit or prohibit actions. Actions consist of subjects, operations (access types), and granules (objects to protect) specifying who does which operation on whom. Each of these constituents of actions may be grouped into classes. Moreover, for each of these constituents we have a separate class hierarchy. A right can be given for either one object or for all objects of a class. All rights (permissions and prohibitions) must be specified explicitly. This allows the easy specification of general rules and of exceptions to such a rule. For distinguishing between a general rule and the exception we use priorities, which allow exceptions on an arbitrary level. Moreover, we can use priorities for resolving rights conflicts. We distinguish between specified rights which may contain class names and explicit rights in which only objects are allowed and in which the priority is dropped because of it is understood that only the right with the highest priority for one action is mentioned. Since the number of explicit rights is drastically larger than the number of specified rights we need and give efficient strategies to query the authorization system. In our approach we assume that there are one or more authorization administrators for setting and changing the rights. For reducing unintended side effects if several administrators can independently modify the rights we propose partially ordered priorities.

Preliminary versions of parts of this paper appeared as [1] and [2].

1. INTRODUCTION

The need for authorization in computer systems came up with the multi-user time-sharing operating systems in the mid sixties. So in the beginning of the seventies the UNIX operating system [3] had an authorization system in which rights could be given relative to a file distinguishing between three kinds of operations (read, write, execute) and three classes of users (owner, owner's group, others). In the database area authorization systems are discussed since the mid seventies (cf. [4], [5]). [6] introduced implicit authorization to reduce the storage requirements for the authorization system.

In the area of advanced/object-oriented database systems there has been a big discussion (cf. [7], [8], [9]), but in this controversy less or nothing is said about authorization. Moreover the situation in this area is discrepant: On the one hand the units to protect often are small but there are very many of these units; this makes the task more difficult. On the other hand the availability of the object-class and class-superclass relationships in object-oriented systems gives a chance for a more structured authorization system. Up to now only few authorization models for object-oriented database systems have been proposed ([10], [11]/[12], [13]/[14], [15]). We generalize the work of [11] in several directions: The approach of [11] uses the object-class structure for implicit authorization. We additionally make use of the class-superclass structure. Moreover [11] introduces negative authorization to explicitly distinguish between a prohibition and the absence of authorization. In their approach prohibitions are directly linked to operations. Our approach links a prohibition to an action. This leads to a sophisticated usage of the class hierarchy. [11] distinguishes between strong and weak authorization to have the possibility of overriding authorizations. We generalize this two-value-based approach by introducing a general, at least linearly ordered priority system. Thus in some sense we introduce several levels of exceptions. If a maximum and/or minimum priority is desired our methods are also valid for this situation.

In the authorization literature rights are usually given in terms of subjects (or more restrictive: users), operations (or access types), and objects. To avoid confusion with the terminology from the object-oriented area (see e.g. [16], [17]), we use the term 'object' in the usual object-oriented sense and take the term 'granule' for the passive component of a right. Moreover we use the term 'item' to denote either an object or a class.

The paper is organized as follows: In section 2 we demonstrate how to specify the world to be modeled. We introduce actions which are the units that can be permitted or prohibited. We use the object-class and the class-superclass relationships for separately modeling the constituents of actions, namely subjects, operations, and granules. In section 3 we informally introduce the elements of a language for specifying rights. In particular, we allow class names to denote sets of objects, introduce right tags to distinguish between permissions and prohibitions, and introduce priority specifications as an overriding mechanism. In section 4 we demonstrate how the specified rights can be translated into explicit rights. We show that the class hierarchy must be used differently for permissions and prohibitions. Although we introduced priorities as a tool for removing conflicts, we must take care of design errors. We discuss two different notions of the (remaining) conflicts. Section 5 shows how a user can get information about which rights hold and which not. For that reason we introduce two slightly different semantics: The pure abbreviation semantics is deeply linked to the transformation process of the previous section. Queries are processed in an "expand and look up"-manner. The dynamic class semantics is a little bit different if class names are used in the query. Using this semantics we do not derive a right with respect to a class if the rights with respect to all its class members are valid. In this sense the right with respect to a class is stronger than the corresponding rights with respect to all its class members. The advantage is that when querying classes the result of a query is constant, if the rights are unchanged but the class membership is changing. In section 6 efficient strategies for evaluating queries and detecting conflicts are given. In section 7 we deal with priority scopes, thus achieving partially ordered priorities. We show the two basic application areas for priority scopes and explore a new kind of conflict.

A running example from the medical area will make the situation more descriptive.

2. SPECIFICATION OF THE WORLD TO BE MODELED: ACTIONS

Before we can specify the rights we must specify what actions are possible in our world to model. An action is the unit which can be permitted or prohibited, and consists of three components: a subject, an operation, and a granule.

Thus to model a world we start with specifying its possible subjects, granules and operations. We treat these components totally independently, thus there is no restriction e.g. for the set of subjects and the set of granules to be disjoint, so one item can act as a subject in one right and as a granule in another (or even the same) one.

Furthermore we allow classes for either subjects, granules or operations to model objects with a similar behavior. To securely distinguish between classes and their objects we require that the class names are syntactically disjoint from the object names of the same category (categories in this context are subject, granule, and operation). That is why in this paper class names start with a capital letter and object names with a lower one. In general we do not require an object to have at most one class membership.

Formally: Let S be the set of **subjects**, O be the set of **operations**, and G be the set of **granules**. Furthermore let SC be the set of **subject classes**, OC be the set of **operation classes**, and GC be the set of **granule classes**. We require $S \cap SC = \emptyset$, $O \cap OC = \emptyset$, and $G \cap GC = \emptyset$.

Class memberships are modelled by functions which map a class name to its set of class members:

$$msc : SC \rightarrow \wp(S),$$
$$moc : OC \rightarrow \wp(O),$$
$$mgc : GC \rightarrow \wp(G).$$

We use the following abbreviation for dealing with (multiple) class memberships (and the analogous ones for granules and operations): $class(s) := \{sc \in SC \mid s \in msc(sc)\}$ $s \in S$.

We have different **class hierarchies** depending on whether we consider classes of subjects, granules, or operations. The meaning of the hierarchy is "**is allowed more to do**" in case of subject classes, "**is not so sensitive as**" in case of operation classes, and "**is part of**" in case of granule classes. We allow a class to have more than one superclass.

We model these three class hierarchies by acyclic, reflexive, transitive relations, specifying the (class, superclass)-pairs:

$$\leq_S \subset SC \times SC,$$
$$\leq_O \subset OC \times OC,$$
$$\leq_G \subset GC \times GC.$$

The reflexive part models the existence of a class, the irreflexive part the class hierarchy. We denote the set of subclasses resp. of superclasses of a class c by

$$subclasses_S(c) := \{c' \mid c' \leq_S c\}, \text{ and}$$
$$superclasses_S(c) := \{c' \mid c' \geq_S c\} \text{ (and analogously for granules and operations)}.$$

If there is no ambiguity we omit the index.

Then an **elementary action** simply is a triple $ea \in S \times O \times G$.
The set of all elementary action is denoted by EA.
More generally, a (**specified**) **action** is a triple $a = (s,o,g) \in S \cup SC \times O \cup OC \times G \cup GC$.
Its components are a subject item, an operation item, and a granule item. The set of all (specified) actions is denoted by A.

Example: For convenience classes and their hierarchies are given by directed graphs. We specify an extract from the medical field:

subject classes and its hierarchy

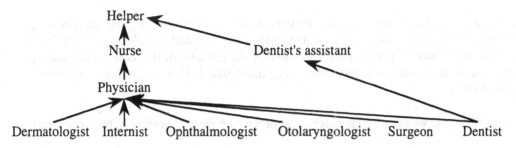

operation classes and its hierarchy   granule classes and its hierarchy

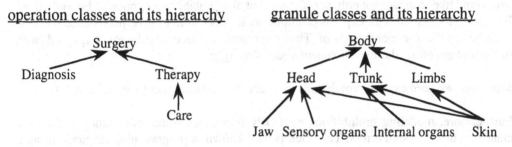

Fig. 1, The three class hierarchies for actions

Class membership is given for:

msc(Physician)={john, jane}   mgc(Body)=Ø
msc(Dermatologist)={catherine}   mgc(Head)=Ø
msc(Ophthalmologist)={ruth}   mgc(Trunk)=Ø
msc(Otolaryngologist)=Ø   mgc(Limbs)={arm, leg}
msc(Surgeon)={hendrik, anne}   mgc(Skin)={skin}
msc(Internist)={anne, raffael}   mgc(Internal organs)=
msc(Dentist)={sabine}   {heart, stomach, kidney, lung, liver, appendix}
msc(Dentist's assistant)={willy}   mgc(Sensory organs)={eye, ear, nose}
msc(Nurse)={karin}   mgc(Jaw)={teeth}
msc(Helper)={thomas}

moc(Diagnosis)={examine, x-ray}
moc(Therapy)={prescribe, administer, inject}
moc(Surgery)={surgery, transplant, anaesthetize, amputate}
moc(Care)={bandage, wash}

Additional world objects (besides those already given in the class membership relations) are:
mike∈ S, first_aid∈ O, and bone∈ G.

3. SYNTAX: SPECIFICATION OF RIGHTS

Often there is no syntactic distinction between actions and permissions. Then an access right usually consists of the three components subject, operation, and granule; expressing that the subject is allowed to perform the operation on the granule. In this case prohibitions are implicit (usually with the meaning "everything which is not explicitly permitted is prohibited").

In the following we describe language constructs which allow to specify rights more clearly.

3.1 Explicit prohibitions

We would like to model not only permissions but also prohibitions explicitly. For only if we have a rights system with explicit prohibitions it is possible to give persistence to those prohibitions the designer thought of. Thus these prohibitions cannot be easily ignored (with or without intention) during subsequent updates of rights.

Moreover, we need explicit prohibitions to be able to state exceptions (see section 3.3).

Furthermore, modeling prohibitions explicitly introduces some redundancy and thus a chance to detect design errors. This trick is well-known in programming language design. Thus we have a chance to detect whether there are either no or several conflicting rights specifications for one action.

We achieve this goal by augmenting an action with a Boolean valued **right tag**.
E.g. (a,permission) allows the action a, whereas (a,prohibition) forbids the action a. For clarity we use TAG={prohibition, permission} instead of BOOLEAN={false, true}, but we use boolean operations, e.g. not prohibition=permission.

Thus an **explicit right** is a tuple xr=(ea,t)=(es,eo,eg,t)∈ EA×TAG.
Let XR be the set of all explicit rights. We usually write (s,o,g,t) instead of ((s,o,g),t).

The set of all explicit rights should immediately answer the question "Who is (not) allowed to do which operation on whom?"

3.2 Class names within rights

Explicit rights are easy to understand but not very convenient to specify. Instead there should be several possibilities for abbreviation.
One source of abbreviation stems from the integration of object-class and class-superclass relationships. Syntactically, we allow not only elementary actions but specified actions (and thus class names) in the first right component:

Using a **class name** in a right means this right is valid for all its **class members**.
We distinguish between two slightly different semantics: A **pure abbreviation semantics** in which a class stands for the set of all class members at the moment, and a **dynamic class semantics** which also reflects possible future changes of this set. (See section 5 for details.)

Furthermore a class name has to reflect the **class hierarchy.** Using a class name in a right means this right is valid for either its superclasses or its subclasses, too, depending on whether we operate on the normal or on the inverted class hierarchy. (See section 4.1 for details.)

Sets of objects are evaluated elementwise, i.e. after having evaluated the class hierarchies the action (Dermatologist, Diagnosis, Skin) means ({catherine}, {examine, x-ray}, {skin}) which eventually stands for {(catherine, examine, skin), (catherine, x-ray, skin)}.
Other sets than sets of all class members (e.g. set with explicitly enumerated elements or sets implicitly described by set expressions with set operations) can be handled by the same semantical rules of our pure abbreviation semantics.

3.3 Modeling exceptions explicitly using priorities
Another source of abbreviation stems from the specification of **exception**s:
Many applications can be described more clearly (and briefly) using a general rule and few exceptions. The use of the object-class and the class-superclass relationships allows us to state general rules very easily. If we allow to specify exceptions it is necessary to have a mechanism to make clear what the general rule is and what the more specific exception to this rule.

Whenever we want to handle exceptions, we are forced to introduce a priority system. Several variants of implicit priorities are likely:
- Prohibitions always dominate permissions (e.g. [14]). But then it is impossible to specify exceptions where the general right is a prohibition and the specialized right is a permission!
- The more specialized right dominates the more general right: This immediately models the exception mechanism implicitly. But then the result of right updates become very complicated and not easy to survey. Moreover, in our approach there are several possibilities to determine the meaning of "more specialized": A more specialized right could be e.g. the right with the more specialized subject (and if the subjects are equal, that one with the more specialized operation, and if the operations are equal, that one with the more specialized granule). Such a decision would destroy the orthogonality of subjects, operations, and granules.
- A more recent right takes priority over older rights: This would require an additional time component. Moreover, deleting and subsequently inserting the same right could have severe semantical effects.

We argue that not only prohibitions but also the priority system should be explicit. Then there is a chance to detect inconsistencies which are due to design imperfections (e.g. wrong priority assignments) on the conceptual level.

The approach to distinguish between strong and weak rights [11], some kind of Boolean valued priorities, allows one-level exception handling. We decided to use more general priorities to allow multi-level exception handling.

For this reason a further component of a right is introduced, a **priority specification**. The idea is that for one action a the right with the maximum priority wins, e.g. a right (a,permission,7) suppresses (a,prohibition,5). Up to chapter 6 we assume that priority specifications are linearly ordered and we use integers in our examples. In chapter 7 we investigate partially ordered priorities.

Thus a **specified right** is a tuple sr=(sa,t,p)∈ A×TAG×PRIO.
Its components are an action, a right tag, and a priority specification. Let SR be the set of all specified rights (of an application).

Now we can model exceptions: We describe a general rule by using a low priority and rather general classes to denote a big set of objects and exceptions to this rule by using a higher priority, the inverted right tag and a more restrictive notion for the set of objects.
Thus {(Nurse, Therapy, Body, prohibition, 20), (Nurse, inject, Limbs, permission, 30)} states that a nurse is not allowed to therapy in general, but she may perform injections into a limb.

Example: We assume the following rights being specified:

SR$_1$ = { (Surgeon,	Surgery,	Internal organs,	permission,	50),
(hendrik,	Surgery,	heart,	prohibition,	60),
(Physician,	transplant,	Body,	prohibition,	20),
(Physician,	Therapy,	Body,	permission,	10),
(Dentist,	Therapy,	Limbs,	prohibition,	20),
(Dentist,	Therapy,	Trunk,	prohibition,	20),
(Nurse,	Care,	Body,	permission,	10),
(Nurse,	Therapy,	Body,	prohibition,	20),
(Nurse,	inject,	Limbs,	permission,	30) }

In the next section we give a precise semantics of a set of specified rights. This includes a solution of the problem what exactly should be the meaning of a set of specified rights when the denoted sets of objects overlap as in {(Physician, transplant, Body, prohibition, 20), (Surgeon, Surgery, Internal organs, permission, 50)}.

4. SEMANTICS: TRANSLATION INTO EXPLICIT RIGHTS

The semantics of a set of specified rights is specified by a translation into explicit rights. This translation process essentially consists of three steps:
- process the class-superclass relationship,
- process the object-class relationship,
- evaluate the priorities.

Furthermore we have to detect possible inconsistencies.
The first two steps compute the set of elementary actions which are covered by one action.

Explicit rights are mainly thought as a tool for having a clear semantics for the specified rights. Since generally the number of explicit rights is drastically larger than the number of specified rights we do not propose to really compute the explicit rights (maybe with the exception of planning games of the authorization administrator) or to answer queries of the access control system through using explicit rights.

4.1 Evaluation of the class-superclass relationship
We try to keep to the intuitive semantics as near as possible. That is why we use the following strategy:

The **class hierarchy of granules** can be treated simply:
A right specified for a granule class is valid for all its subclasses. E.g. a right (permission or prohibition) given for the class Head is also valid for the class Jaw.

Thus for modeling the "is part of"-relationship we use the normal class hierarchy.

Both **class hierarchies of subjects and operations** are evaluated in different ways depending on whether the specified right is a permission or a prohibition:
A permission specified for a subject class is valid for all its subclasses. E.g. a permission given for the class Nurse is also valid for the class Physician.
A prohibition specified for a subject class is valid for all its superclasses. E.g. a prohibition given for the class Physician is also valid for the class Nurse.
A permission specified for an operation class is valid for all its subclasses. E.g. a permission given for the class Surgery is also valid for the class Diagnosis.
A prohibition specified for an operation class is valid for all its superclasses. E.g. a prohibition given for the class Diagnosis is also valid for the class Surgery.

This means that the "is allowed more to do"- and "is not so sensitive as"-relationships behave like "is a"-relationships only in case of permissions. In case of prohibitions we have to use the inverted hierarchies.

The effect of expanding the class hierarchies is formally modeled through the covered_classes functions:
Let $ss \in SC$, $so \in OC$, $sg \in GC$, $t \in TAG$.

covered_classes(ss,t) := if t=permission then subclasses(ss) else superclasses(ss)
covered_classes(so,t) := if t=permission then subclasses(so) else superclasses(so)
covered_classes(sg,t) := subclasses(sg)

Example:
covered_classes(Physician, permission) =
{Physician, Dermatologist, Internist, Ophthalmologist, Otolaryngologist, Surgeon, Dentist},
covered_classes(Physician, prohibition) = {Physician, Nurse, Helper}.

4.2 Evaluation of the object-class relationship

The next step is to substitute the class names by their sets of class members and to evaluate the result elementwise. This is straightforward due to our clear modeling of the world.

The goal is to receive a set ER of **elementary rights**, i.e. tuples er=(ea,t,p)∈ EA×TAG×PRIO.
Here the first component is an elementary action (and thus contains no class names).

Let ss∈ S∪SC, so∈ O∪OC, sg∈ G∪GC, t∈ TAG, p∈ PRIO.
The Boolean function is_object checks whether its parameter is a class or an object.
Then the covered_objects functions yield the set of objects covered by one item:

covered_objects(ss,t) := if is_object(ss) then {ss} else $\bigcup_{sc\in covered\_classes(ss,t)} msc(sc)$

covered_objects(so,t) := if is_object(so) then {so} else $\bigcup_{oc\in covered\_classes(so,t)} moc(oc)$

covered_objects(sg,t) := if is_object(sg) then {sg} else $\bigcup_{gc\in covered\_classes(sg,t)} mgc(gc)$

Example: covered_objects(Physician, prohibition) = msc(Physician) ∪ msc(Nurse) ∪ msc(Helper) =
{john, jane, karin, thomas}

Subjects, operations, and granules are evaluated orthogonally:
covered_actions(ss,so,sg,t) :=   {(es,eo,eg)∈ EA | es∈ covered_objects(ss,t) and
                                                       eo∈ covered_objects(so,t) and
                                                       eg∈ covered_objects(sg,t) }

covered_rights(sa,t,p) := {(ea,t,p)∈ ER | ea∈ covered_actions(sa,t)}

Thus elementary_rights(SR) := $\bigcup_{sr\in SR}$ covered_rights(sr)   is the set of all elementary rights produced from the set SR of specified rights.

4.3 Evaluation of the priorities

We compute the set of explicit rights from the set of all elementary rights by choosing for each elementary action ea that right with the highest priority. (If there are different such rights we have a conflict, see chapter 4.4.) Its right tag tells us whether it is an explicit permission or an explicit prohibition.

maximal_priority(ER) := {(ea,t,p)∈ ER | ∀ er'∈ ER: er'=(ea,t',p') ⇒ p'≤p}

forget_priority(ER) := {(ea,t)∈ XR | (ea,t,p)∈ ER}

With these definitions we can state which explicit rights are generated from a set of specified rights:
explicit_rights(SR) := forget_priority(maximal_priority(elementary_rights(SR)))

Example: Now we can check e.g. that only hendrik and anne are allowed to do transplantations of the lung.

4.4 Conflicts between rights
It is not very desirable to have a specification in which the same thing is both allowed and prohibited. This obviously is a **conflict**. Allowing to specify both permissions and prohibitions has the consequence, of course, that there can be such conflicts. Thus we have (during rights initialization and after rights changes) to detect these conflicts and, if any, to supply the authorization administrator with an understandable error message.

Different priorities resolve conflicts. Nevertheless the phenomenon of conflicting rights remains: Obviously a rights conflict may only arise if two (elementary) rights have the same elementary action ea but have different right tags. Furthermore there only can be a conflict between rights of the same priority, for otherwise the priority itself removes the conflict.

We distinguish between two different notions of conflict. **Actual conflicts** are those conflicts which are immediately effective, whereas the notion of **basic conflict** additionally includes those conflicts which are suppressed by another right with a higher priority. A **latent conflict** then is a basic, non-actual conflict.

Actual conflicts are related to explicit rights.
Let xr=(ea,t) and xr'=(ea',t') be two explicit rights:
actual_x_conflict(xr,xr') :=   ea=ea' and t=not t'

Basic conflicts are related to elementary rights. This notion is more closely related to design decisions.
More formally, let er=(ea,t,p) and er'=(ea',t',p') be two elementary rights.
basic_e_conflict(er,er') :=   ea=ea' and t=not t' and p=p'.

For efficiency reason we are interested in characterizations of conflicts between specified rights. These are given in section 6.2.

Example: Specification of the two rights sr_1=(hendrik, transplant, heart, prohibition, 60), and sr_2=(Surgeon, transplant, heart, permission, 60) results in an actual conflict between (hendrik, transplant, heart, prohibition) and (hendrik, transplant, heart, permission). If additionally a third right sr_3=(Surgeon, Surgery, heart, permission, 70) has been specified, the actual conflict disappears, but the basic conflict between (hendrik, transplant, heart, prohibition, 60) and (hendrik, transplant, heart, permission, 60) remains. This latent conflict will become actual when sr_3 will be deleted.

Of course we must decide, whether we want to detect actual conflicts only or latent conflicts, too. Although it is sufficient for the evaluation of rights to limit yourself to the detection of actual rights conflicts, it is very desirable to have consistent designed rights and therefore to find all basic conflicts. Perhaps a mixed strategy is most useful: Actual conflicts result in an error, latent conflicts in a warning, so the authorization administrator is notified, but not forced to solve latent conflicts immediately.

5. QUERYING THE RIGHTS

Our rights database may be queried for the purpose of access control. Furthermore we propose facilities to support the authorization administrator and to inform a user about what is allowed or prohibited.

Syntactically, a **simple query** is an explicit right. A **query** additionally allows classes instead of objects. More formally, a simple query is a tuple $sq=(ea,t)\in EA\times TAG$, and a query is a tuple $q=(sa,t)\in A\times TAG$. The result of a query q with respect to a set of specified rights SR is given by the predicate is_valid(q,SR).

Below we introduce two kinds of semantics. The first one corresponds exactly to the semantics introduced in section 4, the second one is slightly modified for efficiency reasons, but for simple queries there is no difference.

5.1 Pure abbreviation semantics
In the **pure abbreviation semantics** the class name stands exactly for the current set of its class members. As far as class names are involved in the query this semantics answers the question: "Which rights are valid for all objects of this class?"

A simple query sq can be very easily processed by looking up the set of explicit rights: The result of a simple query sq is just $\qquad$ $is\_valid_{pas}(sq,SR) :\Leftrightarrow sq\in explicit\_rights(SR)$.

Allowing classes in queries is slightly more complicated. We process class hierarchies and class memberships in the same way as stated in sections 4.1 and 4.2 yielding a set of simple queries with a uniform right tag. Let $q=(sa,t)$ be a query and $Q(sa,t) := \{(ea,t)\ |\ ea\in covered\_actions(sa,t)\} = covered\_actions(q)\times\{t\}$ be the set of simple queries generated from the class hierarchy expansion and class substitution procedures. Then we test whether the generated set is included in the set explicit_rights(SR):

$$\text{is\_valid}_{pas}(q,SR) :\Leftrightarrow Q(q) \subseteq \text{explicit\_rights}(SR).$$

In order not to confuse the querier (the answer "no" would have the meaning "set of simple queries is <u>not fully</u> included in the set of explicit rights" and an unpunctilious user could mix up "not fully allowed" with "fully prohibited") and to give a more expressive answer we return a numerical result: the ratio of the number of the simple queries which are really in the set of the explicit rights to the number of generated simple queries. Thus "100%" means "yes" and all other figures are different versions of "no". Then the result is $|Q(q) \cap \text{explicit\_rights}(SR)| / |Q(q)|$.

5.2 Dynamic class semantics

The dynamic class semantics is a modification of the pure abbreviation semantics. The main goal was to achieve a more efficient query processing. The key idea is to allow to check the rights one by one and to immediately decide whether this right is important for the query or not.

Nevertheless there is some intuitive justification for this semantics. Using pure abbreviation semantics the result of a query may change if only the class memberships (but no rights!) change, too. That is why in the dynamic class semantics we do not allow to conclude from a right that is valid for the set of all class members to a right valid for its class.

The dynamic class semantics is especially useful with the following design philosophy: use classes for modeling the structural roles of an application and assign objects to these classes in a second, postponed step.

As far as class names are involved in the query dynamic class semantics answer the question: "What are the (structural) rights an object gets when it becomes a member of this class?".

There are two differences to the pure abbreviation semantics:

1. A class name in a specified right stands for more than all its (actual) class members. Especially this means that we can not conclude that a right is valid for a class even if it is valid for all its class members.

   Example: Assume the specified rights SR={(s, examine, g, permission, 20), (s, x-ray, g, permission, 20)} and the query q=(s, Diagnosis, g, permission). Using pure abbreviation semantics $\text{is\_valid}_{pas}(q,SR)$ yields true because of moc(Diagnosis)={examine, x-ray}. The dynamic class semantics reflects the fact that class membership may change and the specified rights cannot assure the validity of (s, Diagnosis, g, permission) over time (e.g. if the class Diagnosis gets additional class members). Thus $\text{is\_valid}_{dcs}(q,SR)$ yields false.

The point that a class name in a right stands for more than its class members can technically be realized by initially assigning a special placeholder member to each class. These **placeholder objects** cannot be given any rights individually.

Example: The placeholder object is denoted by _classname. Thus we have
_Physician∈ msc(Physician), _Diagnosis∈ moc(Diagnosis), _Body∈ mgc(Body).

2. Exceptions will not be considered (even if the exception has a higher priority!) unless the exception covers their queried class (or object) totally.

Example: Assume that an exception for a class member has been specified: SR = {(Surgeon, Surgery, Internal organs, permission, 50), (hendrik, Surgery, heart, prohibition, 60)}). For the query q=(Surgeon, Surgery, Internal organs, permission) is_valid$_{dcs}$(q,SR) yields true, but surgeon hendrik does not have the full rights.

We propose dynamic class semantics. We take the position that if a querier uses a class name he usually wants to know whether the right being asked for is given for the class itself as a part of the structure of the institution rather than to the (accidental) actual members of the class.

6. EFFICIENCY

For simplicity we assume in all theorems below that each object belongs to exactly one class and there are no empty classes. The last assumption is immediately satisfied in the case of the dynamic class semantics.

6.1 Efficient Query Processing

Using pure abbreviation semantics it is not easy to shorten the "expand and look up" way of calculation. E.g. if a query contains a class name it is not sufficient to consider only those specified rights which include classes (cf. example in section 5.2).

From the computational point of view the main advantage of dynamic class semantics is that we can immediately decide whether one specified right affects the query or not. There are no specified rights which affect a query only partially (this could be the case with pure abbreviation semantics).

Computation of dynamic class semantics can be done in the following steps:
- compute the set of specified rights which affect the action sa' of the query,
- from this set select those rights with the maximum priority, (then the absence of actual conflicts assures that all these rights have the same right tag t !),
- compare the right tag t' of the query with the right tag t of the set above.

Let q=(sa',t') be a query, SR be the set of specified rights which is queried.

A specified right affects a query if the action sa' of the query is subsumed by the action of the specified right:

affects(q,SR) := {(sa,t,p)∈ SR | covered_actions(sa',t) ⊂ covered_actions(sa,t)}

Note that affects(q,SR) does not depend on t'.

The function maxpriority selects those specified rights with the highest priority:

maxpriority(SR) := {(sa,t,p)∈ SR | ∀(sa',t',p')∈ SR: p'≤p}

The predicate tag returns the right tag of a set, if all elements have the same one:

$$\text{tag(SR)} := \begin{cases} \text{permission} & \text{if SR≠∅ and ∀sr∈ SR: sr=(sa,t,p) ⇒ t=permission} \\ \text{prohibition} & \text{if SR≠∅ and ∀sr∈ SR: sr=(sa,t,p) ⇒ t=prohibition} \\ \text{undefined} & \text{else} \end{cases}$$

Then the result of a query using dynamic class semantics is defined by

is_valid$_{dcs}$(q,SR) :⇔ tag(maxpriority(affects(q,SR)))=t'

For computing the rights which affect the query we have the following

Theorem: Let q=(ss',so',sg',t') be a query, SR be a set of specified rights free of actual conflicts. Then

affects(q,SR) =   { (ss,so,sg,t,p)∈ SR |
           if is_object(ss')
               then if t=permission then ss∈ {ss'}∪ superclasses(class(ss'))
                    else ss∈ {ss'}∪ subclasses(class(ss'))
                    else if t=permission then ss∈ superclasses(ss') else ss∈ subclasses(ss')
           and
           if is_object(so')
               then if t=permission then so∈ {so'} ∪ superclasses(class(so'))
                    else so∈ {so'} ∪ subclasses(class(so'))
                    else if t=permission then so∈ superclasses(so') else so∈ subclasses(so')
           and
           if is_object(sg')
               then sg∈ {sg'} ∪ superclasses(class(sg'))
               else sg∈ superclasses(sg') }

Note that for computing the affects function every specified right has only to be checked once. Within this check each of the first three components of such a right must be compared only with a set of items the cardinality of which is bounded by the height of the hierarchy forest plus one (in case of one superclass per class and one class per object) or by the number of nodes in the hierarchy forest plus one (in the general case). The class of an object can be computed very easily. The sets of superclasses and subclasses can be precomputed at startup time.

Example: We query q=(Dentist, inject, Limbs, permission). Thus we have to compute:
affects (Dentist, inject, Limbs, SR_1) =
{(ss,so,sg,t,p)∈ SR_1 | (t=permission

     and ss∈ {Dentist, Physician, Nurse, Helper, Dentist's assistant}
     and so∈ {inject, Therapy, Surgery} and sg∈ {Limbs, Body})
   or (t=prohibition and ss∈ {Dentist} and so∈ {inject, Therapy, Care}
     and sg∈ {Limbs, Body})}
= { (Physician, Therapy, Body, permission, 10),
  (Dentist, Therapy, Limbs, prohibition, 20),
  (Nurse, inject, Limbs, permission, 30) } =: SR_1'

maxpriority(SR_1') = {(Nurse, inject, Limbs, permission, 30)} =: SR_1''
is_valid(q,SR_1) ⇔ tag(SR_1'') = t' ⇔ permission=permission ⇔ true
Thus the queried right is allowed.

6.2 Efficient conflict detection

For efficiency reasons we prefer conflict notions on the level of specified rights.
Semantically, a set of specified rights contains a conflict if the generated set of elementary
rights resp. explicit rights do.

Below we state equivalent definitions for actual conflicts on elementary rights resp. specified
rights:
actual_e_conflict(er,er',ER) :⇔
er,er'∈ maximal_priority(ER) and actual_x_conflict(forget_priority(er), forget_priority(er'))

actual_s_conflict(sr,sr',SR) :⇔
∃ er∈ covered_rights(sr): ∃ er'∈ covered_rights(sr'):
  actual_e_conflict(er,er',elementary_rights(SR))

Then actual conflicts can be checked using the following
Lemma:
Let sr=(sa,t,p) and sr'=(sa',t',p') be two elements of the set of specified rights SR.
actual_s_conflict(sr,sr',SR) ⇔ t= not t' and p=p' and
  ∃ ea∈ covered_actions(sa,t) ∩ covered_actions(sa',t') :
   ∀ sr''∈ SR : sr''=(sa'',t'',p'')∈ SR and ea∈ covered_actions(sa'',t'') ⇒ p''≤p

Basic conflicts are conceptually simpler and therefore easier to detect:
basic_s_conflict(sr,sr') :⇔
∃ er∈ covered_rights(sr): ∃ er'∈ covered_rights(sr'): basic_e_conflict(er,er')
basic_s_conflict(sr',SR) := {sr∈ SR | basic_s_conflict(sr,sr')}

Lemma: Let sr=(sa,t,p) and sr'=(sa',t',p') be specified rights.
basic_s_conflict(sr,sr') ⇔ t= not t' and p=p' and
    covered_actions(sa,t) ∩ covered_actions(sa',t') ≠ ∅

Basic conflicts can be efficiently characterized by the following

Theorem: Let sr'=(ss',so',sg',t',p') be a specified right, SR be a set of specified rights.

basic_s_conflict(sr',SR) ⇔ {(ss,so,sg,t,p)∈ SR | t=not t' and p=p' and

       if is_object(ss')

         then if is_object(ss) then ss'=ss

             else (if t'=permission then class(ss')≥ss else class(ss')≤ss)

         else if is_object(ss)

             then (if t'=permission then ss'≥class(ss) else ss'≤class(ss))

             else (if t'=permission then ss'≥ss else ss'≤ss)

       and

       if is_object(so')

         then if is_object(so) then so'=so

             else (if t'=permission then class(so')≥so else class(so')≤so)

         else if is_object(so)

             then (if t'=permission then so'≥class(so) else so'≤class(so))

             else (if t'=permission then so'≥so else so'≤so)

       and

       if is_object(sg')

         then if is_object(sg) then sg'=sg else class(sg')≤sg

         else   if is_object(sg) then sg'≥class(sg)

           else   ∃ sg"∈ GC : sg"≤sg and sg"≤sg'}

Example: Assume the set SR_1 of specified rights as given in section 3. We would like to add sr'= (catherine, Diagnosis, Skin, permission, 20).

basic_s_conflict(sr',SR_1)

= {(ss,so,sg,t,p)∈ SR_1 | t = prohibition and p=20 and

        if is_object(ss) then ss=catherine else class(catherine)≥ss

        and if is_object(so) then Diagnosis≥class(so) else Diagnosis≥so

        and if is_object(sg) then Skin≥class(sg)

             else (∃ sg"∈ GC : sg"≤sg and sg"≤Skin) }

= {(ss,so,sg,t,p)∈ SR_1 | t = prohibition and p=20 and

        if is_object(ss) then ss=catherine else Dermatologist≥ss

        and if is_object(so) then Diagnosis=class(so) else Diagnosis=so

        and if is_object(sg) then Skin=class(sg) else Skin≤sg }

= {(ss,so,sg,t,p)∈ SR_1 | t = prohibition and p=20 and

             [ss=catherine or ss∈ {Dermatologist}]

       and   [class(so)∈ {Diagnosis} or so∈ {Diagnosis}]

       and   [class(sg)∈ {Skin} or sg∈ {Skin,Head,Trunk,Limbs,Body}]]}

= ∅

Thus no conflict will arise during insertion of sr'.

7. PARTIALLY ORDERED PRIORITIES, PRIORITY SCOPES

Priorities allow the specification of exceptions and thus help to reduce the number of specified rights. The difficulty with linearly ordered priorities stems from their global impact, i.e. the priority of one new inserted right can influence all other rights. This is even more a problem if a system has several authorization administrators for updating the rights.

What we need is a new mechanism for reducing the impact of priorities: priority scopes.

Therefore we divide the priority component into two subcomponents, the first one is the **priority scope**, the second one the **local priority**, which describes the priority between rights within the same priority scope.

We assume that the priority scopes are partially ordered, the local priorities are linearly ordered as before.

Formally, let PS be a set of priority scopes. PS is partially ordered w.r.t. $<_{PS}$ with the meaning "**has a weaker priority scope**".
A priority is a pair $p=(ps, l) \in PS \times INTEGER$.

Priorities are ordered w.r.t. $(ps_1,l_1) \leq_P (ps_2,l_2) :\Leftrightarrow ps_1 <_{PS} ps_2 \lor (ps_1 =_{PS} ps_2 \land l_1 \leq l_2)$, i.e. the lower priority has a weaker priority scope or the same priority scope and the lower local priority.

The local priority now removes conflicts only within one priority scope.

7.1. Priority scopes for independent working of several authorization administrators

In many applications there are several authorization administrators, and every administrator is able to change the rights. Especially in distributed systems it is an advantage if every node has an own administrator. In such situations it is often appropriate to identify a priority scope with an authorization administrator and to use the **creator of a right** as name of the priority scope.

Example: A corresponding priority situation can also be found in the juristical domain: There we can distinguish between international law (e.g. intergovernmental treaties or the law of supranational communities), federal law, and state law. Each law is also valid in all smaller units, the rights setting unit contains.

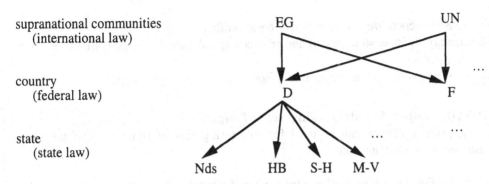

Fig. 2, A hierarchy of priority scopes

Especially, we have (Nds,7) $\leq_P$ (D,5), which is a correct description of the rule "Federal law takes precedence over State law".

7.2. Priority scope induced conflicts

Introducing partially ordered priorities has its price: The maximal priority is not necessarily unique any longer. We did rely on this fact during evaluation of the priorities (in chapter 4.3). Instead we now have a new kind of conflict.

For describing this conflict we need the notion of validity scope, which is the set of all smaller priority scopes.
A right with priority scope ps is **valid** only within its **validity scope**
valid(ps) := {ps' | ps'$\leq_{PS}$ps}.

If the validity scopes of two incomparable priority scopes have a non-empty intersection then **priority scope induced conflicts** between rights may appear within this intersection priority scope.

This means that such a conflict can only arise if two priority scopes have a common subscope.

Example: The rights sr_1=(hendrik, heart, transplant, prohibition, (EG,3)) and sr_2=(Surgeon, heart, transplant, permission, (UN,4)) generate for Germany (=D) a priority scope induced conflict, because of both priority scopes are incomparable and from sr_1 we can deduce (hendrik, heart, transplant, prohibition) and from sr_2 (hendrik, heart, transplant, permission).

Formally: Two elementary rights er=(ea,t,(ps,l)) and er'=(ea',t',(ps',l')) are in a priority

scope induced (basic) conflict   if
ea=ea' ∧ t= not t' ∧ (ps,ps' incomparable ∧ ∃ps*: (ps*$<_{PS}$ps ∧ ps*$<_{PS}$ps')).

It makes sense to generalize our definition of basic conflict:
Two elementary rights er=(ea,t,(ps,l)) and er'=(ea',t',(ps',l')) are in a basic conflict   if
ea=ea' ∧ t= not t' ∧
((ps$=_{PS}$ps' ∧ l=l') ∨ (ps,ps' incomparable ∧ ∃ps*: (ps*$<_{PS}$ps ∧ ps*$<_{PS}$ps'))).

7.3. Priority scopes for structuring sets of rights
Moreover, priority scopes can be used for structuring sets of rights even if they are administrated by one administrator.

Example [2]: For describing traffic rules we can distinguish between general rules (like "Cars must drive on the right lane of the road."), rules for overtake, and rules for right of way. For each corresponding set of rights we use one priority scope with the following ordering: GENERAL $<_{PS}$ OVERTAKE $<_{PS}$ RIGHT OF WAY. Within these priority scopes the local priorities are used for distinguishing between e.g. right_of_way-signs, traffic lights, and traffic control by policemen.

The main advantage is that there are less possibilities of errors when updating the rights because usually only one set of rights has to be considered.

8. CONCLUSION

Our approach to an authorization system uses implicit rights for class members, but requires explicitly specified prohibitions and priorities. The object-oriented modeling of the (application) world enables us to specify rights briefly and clearly. With the help of priorities we can specify general rules and multi-level exceptions very compactly.

The linearly ordered priorities are a good solution if only one administrator is responsible for the consistency of rights. If there are more, priority scopes should be introduced and each administrator should be restricted to its validity scope. Moreover, priority scopes can be used for structuring the sets of rights in any case.

ACKNOWLEDGEMENT
Valuable comments came from Bernd Teßmer.

REFERENCES

[1]   Brüggemann, H.H.: Rights in an Object-Oriented Environment, in: Landwehr, C.E.,
        Jajodia, S. (eds.), Database Security, V: Status and Prospects, North-Holland,
        Amsterdam, 1992, 99-115.

[2]   Brüggemann, H.H.: Priorities for a Distributed, Object-Oriented Access Control (in
        German), in: Proc. Verläßliche Informationssysteme VIS'93, Munich, May 93,
        Vieweg, 51-66.

[3]   Ritchie, D.M., Thompson, K.: The UNIX Time-Sharing System, Communications
        of the ACM, Vol. 17, July 1974, 365-375.

[4]   Griffiths, P.P., Wade, B.W.: An Authorization Mechanism for a Relational Database
        System, ACM Transaction on Database Systems, Vol. 1, 1976, 242-255.

[5]   Fernandez, E.B., Summers, R.C., Wood, C.: Database Security and Integrity,
        Addison-Wesley, 1981.

[6]   Fernandez, E.B., Summers, R.C., Lang, T.: Definition and Evaluation of Access
        Rules in Data Management Systems, in: Proc. 1st Int. Conf. on Very Large Data
        Bases, Boston, 1975, 268-285.

[7]   Atkinson, M., Bancilhon, F., DeWitt, D., Dittrich, K., Maier, D., Zdonik, S.: The
        Object-Oriented Database System Manifesto, in: Proc. First International Conference
        on Deductive and Object-Oriented Databases, Kyoto, Dec. 1989, 40-57.

[8]   Stonebraker, M., Rowe, L.A., Lindsay, B., Gray, J., Carey, M., Brodie, M.,
        Bernstein, P., Beech, D.: Third-Generation Data Base System Manifesto, TR
        UCB/ERL M90/28, College of Engineering, University of California, Berkeley,
        April 1990.

[9]   Kim, W.: Research Directions in Object-Oriented Database Systems, in: Proc. 9th
        Symposium on Principles of Database Systems, 1990, 1-15.

[10]   Dittrich, K.R., Härtig, M., Pfefferle, H.: Discretionary Access Control in
        Structurally Object-Oriented Database Systems, in: Landwehr, C. (Ed.), Database
        Security II: Status and Prospects, North-Holland, 1989, 105-121.

[11]   Rabitti, F., Woelk, D., Kim, W.: A model of Authorization for object-oriented and
        semantic databases, in: Proc. Int. Conf. on Extending Database Technology, Venice,
        March 1988, LNCS 303, Springer, 1988, 231-250.

[12]   Rabitti, F., Bertino, E., Kim, W., Woelk, D.: A Model of Authorization for Next-

Generation Database Systems, ACM Transactions on Database Systems, Vol. 16, March 1991, 88-131.

[13]   Fernandez, E.B., Gudes, E., Song, H.: A security model for object-oriented databases, in: Proc. IEEE Symposium on Security and Privacy, Oakland, 1989, 110-115.

[14]   Larrondo-Petrie, M. M., Gudes, E., Song, H., Fernandez, E.B.: Security Policies in Object-oriented Databases, in: Spooner, D.L., Landwehr, C. (Eds.), Database Security III: Status and Prospects, North-Holland, 1990, 257-268.

[15]   Kelter, U.: Group-oriented discretionary access controls for distributed structurally object-oriented database systems, in: Proc. European Symposium on Research in Computer Security (ESORICS), Toulouse, Oct. 1990, 23-33.

[16]   Goldberg, A., Robson, D.: Smalltalk-80: The Language and its Implementation, Addison-Wesley, Reading, 1983.

[17]   Zdonik, S.B., Maier, D.: Fundamentals of Object-Oriented Databases, in: Zdonik, S.B., Maier, D. (Eds.), Readings in Object-Oriented Database Systems, Morgan Kaufmann, 1990, 1-32.

A BROWSING THEORY AND ITS APPLICATION
TO DATABASE NAVIGATION

A. D'Atri and L. Tarantino
University of L'Aquila, L'Aquila, Italy

ABSTRACT

A formal model and a set of primitives are introduced to represent the process of displaying and browsing in a database represented by means of a graph, or a network. Several kinds of navigational processes with an increasing level of complexity are formalized, and some desirable properties for browsers are also investigated. It is shown, by simple examples, how this formalism can be used as an abstract tool to describe and implement this interaction style with databases.

This work has been partially supported by the MURST (projects "Formal Methodologies and Tools for Advanced Databases" and "Graph theory and algorithms"), and the CNR (project "MULTIDATA").

1   Introduction

Browsing is an easy data retrieval technique, based on an exploratory search in which the user examines related concepts and their neighborhood, successively disclosing new portions of the database. Thus, a browsing environment requires the definition and the management of a *structure* which gives the "adjacency" between the database concepts (according to a data representation model), *points of view* on this structure, and a set of *navigation primitives* to change the point of view, i.e., to move a "visibility window" on the structure during a simple man-machine dialogue.

This technique has received a great research and development effort in a variety of contexts, like database systems (see, e.g., [4,11,12,15,16,20]), hypertext systems (see, e.g., [3,9,17,18,21]), programming environments (see, e.g., [1,2,8,10,13]), and also in the general context of graphical tools and dialogue models for human-computer interaction (see, e.g., [5,14,19]).

A main reason for this interest, from both the scientific and the industrial point of view, is that a browser provides an effective solution to some usability problems that users meet with formal languages (as those used to formulate queries against a database). In particular, in database systems a browser can be considered *complementary* to a query processor with respect to:

- *Requirements.* It does not assume user experience about the application, the data model and/or a query language.
- *Goals.* The user may have an imprecise idea about the information that can be obtained from the system.
- *Interaction mode.* A browser provides a "viewing" environment and not a "query" language (where the user formulates his/her needs in procedural, functional or logical terms).
- *Ease.* Browsing is simpler to learn and more friendly to use than a formal language.
- *Use of graphics.* The data and interaction structures of a browser are generally geared towards immediate display and easy graphical manipulation, while is harder to obtain the same property for a query language.

The complementarity of the browsing style with respect to a querying formalism (as relational algebra and calculus) refers also to the way in which the research community approached these two interaction styles. In fact, while querying paradigms have been deeply studied from both the theoretical and the practical point of view, on the other side, browsers are mainly informally described in the literature as "software tools" and a limited number of proposals exist to formalize their desirable properties (e.g., [14,21]).

The aims of this paper are:

- to isolate the behavior aspects of browsers that are independent of both the interpretation of the explored structure and of the graphical aspects that support the display and the dialogue;
- to formalize simple kinds of browsing processes with step-by-step navigation features and an increasing level of complexity;
- to investigate limits and desirable properties of these browsers, and requirements for their implementation.

To formalize browsing processes independently of a particular data representation model, in the following we will assume that:

- the database is represented by means of a directed labeled graph (or a network) that gives the adjacency between objects according to the *internal data model*. In this context each vertex has an internal identifier that is known to the system, but is never shown to the user;
- the *interaction model* is based on a set of "local views", where each view corresponds to a visibility window on the database from an observation point (i.e., a vertex); these windows show local information in terms of vertex labels (which are the only visible parts of the graph).

Since a view shows local information, after a number of navigation steps the user may "get lost" (i.e., s/he is not able to realize the position of the window in the network), and the problem of identifying the observation point in a browsing state (i.e., of identifying the current vertex from the content of the local view) arises. Hence, the concept of *vertex identification*, which here is studied with respect to browsing processes (a more general discussion of this topic can be found in [7]), plays a central role to increase usability and power of browsers and to give their formal definition. Since this technique is oriented to non expert users, "simple" and "natural" identifiers are required to understand the position in the network.

Rephrasing and summarizing these considerations in graph terms, the *object identification problem* for a browsing window in an interaction state may be informally expressed in the following way:

> Given a labeled graph and a vertex in it, find a "simple and local structure of labels" that can be used in a state of the browser to identify such a vertex in an unambiguous way.

The rest of the paper is structured as follows. Section 2 presents the browsing formalization in the simple case of label identifiable graphs (i.e., graphs in which the node labelling function is injective), by providing the concepts of *interaction state* and *interaction primitive*, and by defining a basic set of *browsing primitives.* In Section 3 we analyze the vertex identification problems in networks and introduce a first type of composite identifier, whose inclusion in the browsing formalization is done in Section 4. In Section 5, after having discussed two more classes of composite identifiers whose structures reflect the *breadth* and the *depth* aspects of the navigation, we sketch the problem of their inclusion in more complex browsing models. Finally, conclusions are drawn in Section 6.

2 Elementary graph browsers

More or less standard terminology on graphs is used in the paper. In particular a (labeled directed) *graph* G is a 4-tuple $\langle V, A, \Lambda, \lambda \rangle$, where V is a finite set of *vertices*, $A \subseteq V \times V$ is a set of *arcs* ($out(v)$ denotes the vertices directly connected from $v \in V$, and $in(v)$ is similarly defined), Λ is a countable set of *labels* that can be associated to vertices, and λ is a *labeling function* that associates to each vertex $v \in V$ a label $\lambda(v) \in \Lambda$. We will extend the domain of the labeling function to sets of vertices and other substructures of the graph: for example, $\lambda(V')$ will denote the (multi-) set of labels of a set of vertices $V' \subseteq V$ (in the following we will enclose multisets in square brackets).

In this section we refer to a simple kind of graphs, in which all vertices are *label identifiable*, i.e., they can be unambiguously selected by means of their label (in other words, the labeling function is injective). We will use *label identifiable graphs* as the starting point in the definition of the concept of navigation and of the desirable features of a browsing system.

Definition 1 Let $G = \langle V, \Lambda, \lambda, A \rangle$ be a label identifiable graph:

- A *local view* of G from a vertex $v \in V$ is a pair $L = \langle \lambda(v), s \rangle$ where s is a subset of $\lambda(out(v))$;
- a *view* of G is a non empty collection $W = [L_1, \ldots, L_n]$ of local views from some of its vertices;
- a *(interaction) state* is a triple $S = \langle W, L, j \rangle$, where W is a view, $L \in W$ is the *current local view* $\langle l, s \rangle$, and $j \in \{l\} \cup s$ is the *current label*. Furthermore, $\mathcal{S}(G)$ denotes the set of all possible states for G, including a conventional *empty* state $\triangleright$ that occurs, for instance, when the system starts.

☐

The above definition of local view captures the simple nature of a browsing process that explores the neighborhood of an object. The concept of state provides a simple formal model to denote the set of objects that the system is handling in a given moment, and, among them, the object selected as current.

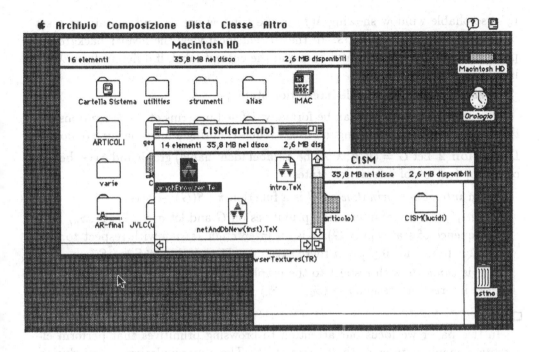

Figure 1: *An example of interaction state*

In terms of the I/O devices, each local view is supposed to be represented on the screen by means of a suitable display technique (e.g., a labeled scrollable menu in a graphical window) and the current local view and the current label in it are identified by a marker (e.g., the cursor position in the screen). The definition of a "display model", as well as the mapping of the above concepts in it, may be considered a successive phase in the design of the user interface as discussed, e.g., in [6].

Example 1 To illustrate the above concepts in a real environment, let us consider the representation of the file system in the popular Macintosh interface. In this case the data structure is a tree T with internal nodes representing directories (or *folders* according to the terminology of the Macintosh desktop metaphor) and leaves representing files (or *documents*)[1].

In this scenario, a local view of T from a folder f is a pair $L = \langle \lambda(f), s \rangle$ where s is a subset of $\lambda(out(f))$. Each local view is represented on the screen

---

[1] To conform to Definition 1 we have to assume the tree label identifiable. This is not realistic, and we will show in the following sections how to remove such restrictive hypothesis.

by a scrollable window showing $\lambda(f)$ in the window header and containing a set of labeled icons representing s. In the current local view the header background presents a number of horizontal lines and the current label, if different from $\lambda(f)$, is in reverse screen[2].

Figure 1 depicts a possible interaction state. $\square$

Navigational primitives can be formally defined in terms of the transitions between pairs of states, occurring, on user's request, during a man-machine dialogue.

Definition 2 Let $G = \langle V, \Lambda, \lambda, A \rangle$ be a (label identifiable) graph and $\mathcal{S}(G)$ be the correspondent set of interaction states.

- An *interaction primitive* on G is a function $\pi : \mathcal{S}(G) \rightarrow \mathcal{S}(G)$.
- Let $\prod$ be a set of interaction primitives on G and let $\sigma = \langle S_0, \ldots, S_n \rangle$ be a sequence of states in $\mathcal{S}(G)$; σ is an *interaction session* with respect to $\prod$ if $S_0 = \triangleright$ and for $0 \leq i < n$ there exists $\pi \in \prod$ such that $\pi(S_i) = S_{i+1}$.
- $\prod$ is *complete* with respect to the graph G if for each $S \in \mathcal{S}(G)$ there exists an interaction session $\sigma = \langle S_0, \ldots, S_n \rangle$ with $S_n = S$.

$\square$

In this paper we focus our attention to browsing primitives that perform elementary manipulations of the system state. These manipulations occur during a navigation process in which the user examines an object and its neighborhood, in such a neighborhood he/she selects another object that becomes current, and so on, iteratively. We consider, in particular, the following set $\prod_{base}$ of *browsing primitives*, each of them corresponding to an atomic navigation step:

open(S_i) adds a new local view, associated to the current vertex (if any), to S_i. More precisely, if we consider a non empty state $S_i = \langle W_i, L_i, j_i \rangle$, where j_i is the label of the current vertex v, the new state is $S_{i+1} = \langle W_i \cup \{L\}, L_i, j_i \rangle$, where $L = \langle \lambda(v), \lambda(out(v)) \rangle$. If the current state S_i is empty (i.e., $i = 0$), the *open* primitive returns an *initial state* $S_1 = \langle W_1, L_1, j_1 \rangle$, where W_1, L_1 and j_1 are selected according to default criteria. For the sake of simplicity, we will suppose that this default view W_1 is a singleton $\{L_1\} = \{\langle j_1, s_1 \rangle\}$, where j_1 is the label of a predefined vertex v in G (called the *starting vertex*) and $s_1 = \lambda(out(v))$;

select(S_i, L, j) changes the current local view and/or the current label within the view associated to the state S_i. More precisely, if $S_i = \langle W_i, L_i, j_i \rangle$ and j is a label in a local view $L \in W_i$, the new state is $S_{i+1} = \langle W_i, L, j \rangle$;

---

[2]As a matter of fact, in the Macintosh interface it is also possible that none of the windows is current (when the users clicks on the screen background). The inconsistency with our model is only apparent and due to the fact that a complete formalization of the Macintosh interface (not presented here for the sake of brevity) should include also the special folder *desktop*.

$close(S_i)$ either reduces the current local view, by removing the current label, or deletes the current local view from S_i. More precisely, let $S_i = \langle W_i, L_i, j_i \rangle$ and $L_i = \langle l, s \rangle$:

- if $j_i \in s$, the new state is $S_{i+1} = \langle W_{i+1}, L, j \rangle$, where $L = \langle l, s - \{j_i\} \rangle$, $W_{i+1} = W_i - \{L_i\} \cup \{L\}$, and the current label j is either (according to some criterium) selected in $s - \{j_i\}$ (if there are other labels in s), or $j = l$ (otherwise);

- if $j_i = l$, two cases are possible:

  - if there is more than one local view in W_i the current local view is deleted from S_i. More precisely, the new state is $S_{i+1} = \langle W_{i+1}, L, j \rangle$ where $W_{i+1} = W_i - L_i$ and the new current local view L (and the current label j within it) is selected, according to some criteria, among those remaining in W_{i+1};

  - if L_i is the only local view in W_i the empty state is obtained.

This set of primitives allows us to state a desirable property for graphs with respect to browsing completeness.

Proposition 1 *The set* $\prod_{base}$ *of browsing primitives is complete with respect to a graph G if and only if there exists a direct path from the starting vertex to each vertex in G.*

Sketch of the proof When the above property is satisfied, it is possible to produce any state $S = \langle W, L, j \rangle$. In a first phase, a sequence of *open* and *select* primitives allows to generate each local view in W or a larger local view containing it. In a second phase, a sequences of *close* primitives can be used to remove, from the obtained state, all local views and/or label that are not in W. The only-if part is trivially proved by contradiction. $\square$

3   The adjacency structure of a database

Because of their simplicity, label identifiable graphs, although adequate to formally introduce the concepts related to the navigation, have a limited representation power, insufficient to represent general and powerful data models. For this reason, in this section we study the problems that arise when extending the browsing primitives from graphs to *networks*, which are the basis of several data models (e.g., semantic networks, object-oriented data models).

A network is a multigraph with labels associated to both vertices and arcs. Formally, a *network* N is a 7-tuple $\langle V, A, s, t, \Lambda, \lambda_a, \lambda_v \rangle$ where V is a finite set of

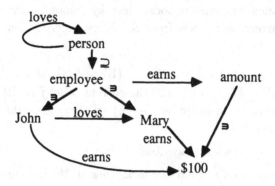

Figure 2: *An example of semantic network.*

vertices labeled by means of the vertex labeling function $\lambda_v : V \to \Lambda$ (as in the definition of graph); A is a set of *arcs* between pairs of vertices, determined by a *source* function $s : A \to V$ and a *target* function $t : A \to V$ that specify, for each arc, the source vertex and the destination one, respectively; λ_a is an *arc labeling* function that associates to each arc $a \in A$ a label $\lambda_a(a) \in \Lambda$ (we suppose that $\lambda_a(A) \cap \lambda_v(V) = \phi$).

In the following we will only consider *simple* networks, i.e., networks without identical pairs of arcs (two arcs $a, a' \in A$ are *identical* if $s(a) = s(a')$, $t(a) = t(a')$, and $\lambda_a(a) = \lambda_a(a')$).

Example 2 A *semantic network* (e.g., as the one described in detail in [16]) is composed by *objects*, and different kinds of binary *relationships* between pairs of them (an example is graphically given in Figure 2). A possible definition of semantic network is the following one. Objects have distinct names and are either *classes* (e.g., `employee` and `amount`) or *tokens* (e.g., `John` and `$100`); relationships are *memberships* (e.g., `John` ∈ `employee`), *specialization* (e.g., `employee is_a` person), *generic* relationships, which describe intensional properties of classes (e.g., `employee earns amount`), and *specific* relationships, which describe extensional properties of tokens (e.g., `John earns $100`). □

In order to exploit the results of the previous section and extend to networks the browsing model defined for graphs, we define a mapping of networks into graphs.

Definition 3 Let $N = \langle V, A, s, t, \Lambda, \lambda_a, \lambda_v \rangle$ be a network. The graph *associated to N* is the bipartite graph $G_N = \langle V', \Lambda, \lambda, A' \rangle$, where:

- V' is partitioned into the set V and a new set W containing a vertex v_l for each $v \in V$ having at least one outgoing arc $a \in A$ with $\lambda_a(a) = l$ (see Figure 3);

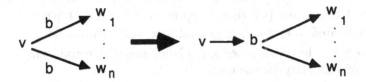

Figure 3: *The basic step of the mapping procedure.*

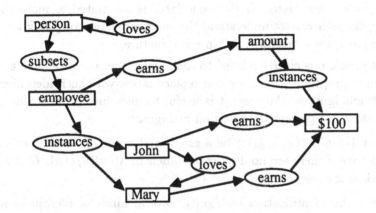

Figure 4: *The graph associated to the network in Figure 2.*

- for each $v \in V$, $label(v) = \lambda_v(v)$, and for each $v_l \in W$, $label(v_l) = l$;
- $A' = A_1 \cup A_2$ where $A_1 = \{(v, v_l)|v \in V$ and v_l is one of the above defined vertices in W associated to $v\}$ and $A_2 = \{(v_l, t(a))|a \in A$, $s(a) = v$, $alabel(a) = l$, and v_l is the corresponding vertex in $W\}$.

□

It is easy to see that this mapping is injective, i.e., it is possible to recover the network from its associated graph, and that there are graphs that do not correspond to any network (e.g., a non bipartite graph).

Example 3 In Figure 4 the bipartite graph associated to the semantic network of Figure 2 is shown, where the vertices belonging to the two components of the partition have distinct shapes (rectangular for vertices in V, and oval for vertices in W). □

Generally (as we can see also in the previous example), the graph associated to a network representing a database is not label identifiable. In fact, while it could be reasonable that database objects are required to have distinct names (although this constraint is not always present in the data model), the same property does not hold for the labels of arcs (which may represent the relationship names). Hence the vertices associated to arcs are, in general, not label identifiable.

In the context of a browsing process, not label identifiable graphs may give rise to some kinds of ambiguity for the user:

- *Selection ambiguity.* If there are duplicated labels in $out(v)$, associated to distinct vertices of the graph, the user cannot unambiguously select the new direction to follow in the exploratory process.
- *Identification ambiguity.* If the same label is associated to more than one vertex, the user cannot understand the current position by just knowing the vertex label, thus "getting lost" in the structure.

The first problem is clearly related to the second one: once we have a way for uniquely identifying the vertices, we can replace labels with such identifiers, thus solving both ambiguities. Anyway, it is useful to introduce a particular class of graphs that does not present the selection ambiguity.

Definition 4 Let $G = \langle V, \Lambda, \lambda, A \rangle$ be a graph and v one of its vertices. We say that v is *selective* if there are no duplicated labels in $\lambda(out(v) \cup v)$. G is *selective* if all its vertices are selective. $\square$

As regards the identification ambiguity, several kinds of identifiers may be introduced, and their use leads to extensions of the browsing model we have defined in Section 2. In this section we consider a simple "external" identifier that is obtained by selecting a pair of labels (associated to an arc of the graph) instead of the vertex label.

Definition 5 Let $G = \langle V, \Lambda, \lambda, A \rangle$ be a graph, $\langle u, v \rangle$ be one of its arcs and $\lambda(\langle u, v \rangle)$ be the correspondent ordered pair of labels. $\lambda(\langle u, v \rangle)$ is an *arc-in-identifier* (shortly *arc identifier*) of v if for all $\langle u', v' \rangle \in A$ with $\lambda(\langle u, v \rangle) = \lambda(\langle u', v' \rangle)$ we have $v' = v$; G is *arc identifiable* if all its vertices have a label identifier or an arc identifier (similar definitions might be given with respect to outcoming arcs giving rise to the concept of *arc-out-identifiability*). $\square$

We notice that, in general, more than one arc identifier may be associated to the same vertex (for example, in Figure 5, $\langle B, A \rangle$ and $\langle C, A \rangle$ identify the same vertex). Since this *identifier multiplicity* may result in complications for the browser and in ambiguity for the user, we introduce the concept of *identifier singleness* for vertices, which is a desirable property for a graph to browse.

Definition 6 A vertex of a graph is *s-identifiable* if it has a label identifier or a unique arc identifier. A non label identifiable node is *m-identifiable* if it admits more than one arc-identifier. $\square$

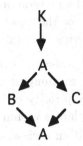

Figure 5: *An arc identifiable graph with an m-identifiable vertex.*

The introduction of arc identifiers gives a relevant improvement to the possibility of identifying vertices in general kind of graphs and networks. In fact we note that if the vertices in a network have distinct labels (e.g., in semantic networks as introduced in Example 3), then its associated graph has several important properties, as stated in the following proposition.

Proposition 2 *If a (simple) network has a label identifiable vertex set, then its associated graph is selective, arc identifiable, and with all vertices s-identifiable.*

Sketch of the proof Let $N = \langle V, A, s, t, \Lambda, \lambda_a, \lambda_v \rangle$ be a network with label identifiable vertices, and $G_N = \langle V', \Lambda, \lambda, A' \rangle$ be its associated graph. All vertices in $V' - V$ either are label identifiable, or admit only one arc identifier, since (by construction) they have only one incoming arc from a label identifiable vertex. ☐

4   Browsing in networks

The introduction of arc identifiers allows us to extend the concept of browser state to arc-identifiable graphs (and hence to networks with arc-identifiable associated graphs).

Definition 7 Let $G = \langle V, \Lambda, \lambda, A \rangle$ be an arc-identifiable graph. A *local view* of G from a vertex $v \in V$ is a pair $L = \langle i, s \rangle$ where if v is label identifiable then i is its label, else i is one of its arc identifiers; similarly s is a family of (label or arc) identifiers associated to some vertices in $out(v)$. The definitions of *view*, *state*, $\mathcal{S}(G)$, *interaction primitive*, *interaction session*, and *completeness* are similarly obtained from Definition 1 and Definition 2 by considering identifiers instead of vertex labels. ☐

If the graph has no identifier multiplicity, no additional concept is needed; otherwise, since more than one identifier may be associated to an m-identifiable vertex

v, if v appears in several local views of an interaction state, distinct identifiers may refer to v (resulting in an ambiguity for the user). In this case two identification approaches may be followed for removing the ambiguity:

- The *local meaningfulness* of identifiers. Since browsing is a local process, in order to make identifiers as meaningful as possible with respect to the local view they appear in, this priority criterion assigns arc identifiers to m-identifiable vertices by using labels within the local view;

- The *uniqueness* of identifiers within a view. In this case the renaming (and hence the ambiguities) for vertex identifiers in the view is not allowed. In this way it is possible that a vertex is "externally" identified even if it admits an identifier within the local view it appears.

Example 4 Let us consider, the graph in Figure 5 and the interaction state composed by the local views $\langle B, \{\langle B, A \rangle\} \rangle$ and $\langle \langle K, A \rangle, \{C\} \rangle$ with the current label C. We have that a new local view $\langle C, \{\langle C, A \rangle\} \rangle$ satisfies the local meaningfulness, yet has an ambiguity between $\langle B, A \rangle$ and $\langle C, A \rangle$, which identify the same vertex. On the other side, a new local view $\langle C, \{\langle B, A \rangle\} \rangle$ satisfies the uniqueness, yet contains the non-local identifier $\langle B, A \rangle$. $\square$

Let us extend to arc-identifiable graphs, and hence to the corresponding networks, the set Π_{base} of browsing primitives by considering vertex identifiers instead of vertex labels within the local views and by giving an assignment criterion (that takes into account the uniqueness and/or the local meaningfulness) when more identifiers are available. We note that *select* and *close* are trivially extended (they do not require the assignment of new identifiers), while assignment problems arise for the *open* primitive, which may be extended in two distinct ways (denoted $l-open$ and $u-open$) by adopting either local meaningfulness or uniqueness. In particular:

$l-open(S_i)$ works like $open(S_i)$ and assigns identifiers according to the local meaningfulness criterion. More precisely, the identifier of an m-identifiable vertex w in a local view $\langle l, s \rangle$ from the vertex v is assigned in the following way:

1. If $j = \langle label(v), label(w) \rangle$ is an arc-identifier, then the identifier is j;

2. else if one (or more) arc-identifier has already been assigned to w (in a distinct local view within the current view), the identifier is selected among these;

3. otherwise, a new identifier is selected among the possible ones.

$u-open(S_i)$ works like $open(S_i)$ and assigns identifiers according to the uniqueness criterion. More precisely, the above rules 1. and 2. are exchanged in order to avoid multiple identifiers for a vertex in a view.

We denote with $\prod_{l-base}$ and $\prod_{u-base}$ the sets of primitives based on $l - open$ and $u - open$, respectively. It is easy to see that, if the graph has identifier multiplicity, neither $\prod_{l-base}$ nor $\prod_{u-base}$ can guarantee completeness. Then we consider a weaker completeness concept, by restricting $\mathcal{S}(G)$ to either $\mathcal{S}_{\mathcal{L}}(G)$ or $\mathcal{S}_{\mathcal{U}}(G)$, composed by the states that satisfy the local meaningfulness or uniqueness criterion, respectively.

Definition 8 Let G be an arc-identifiable graph. $\prod_{l-base}$ is *l-complete* if for each $S \in \mathcal{S}_{\mathcal{L}}(G)$ there exists a browsing session $\sigma = \langle S_0, \ldots, S_n \rangle$ with $S_n = S$, such that $S_i \in \mathcal{S}_{\mathcal{L}}(G)$ for $0 \leq i \leq n$. A similar definition can be given for *u-completeness*. $\square$

The following proposition extends to arc identifiable graph the result stated in Proposition 1:

Proposition 3 *The set $\prod_{l-base}$ ($\prod_{u-base}$) of browsing primitives is l-complete (u-complete) with respect to an arc-identifiable graph G if and only if the starting vertex v is s-identifiable and there exists a direct path from v to each vertex in G.*

Sketch of the proof To prove the l-completeness we notice that the difference from states in graph browsers and in this case is that in a state $S \in \mathcal{S}_{\mathcal{L}}(G)$ a vertex w may be m-identifiable; then the identifier of w in S depends on the interaction history, i.e., on the sequence performed to reach S. If there exists a direct path from v to each vertex in G, w is reachable from any vertex in $in(w)$. Hence it is possible to generate all its admissible arc identifiers. The only if part is proved by contradiction. An analogous proof can be followed for u-completeness. $\square$

As immediate consequence of the property proved in Proposition 2, we have that the two above identification criteria provide the same result for graphs associated to networks with label identifiable vertices (as those described in Example 2), since all browser states satisfy both the local meaningfulness and the uniqueness properties.

Finally, we note that a different way to handle identifier multiplicity is to show in local views the set of all identifiers of an m-identifiable vertex (instead of a preselected one). In this way the browser must handle more information, but this set can be considered as a unique vertex identifier.

5 More sophisticated browsers

As we saw in the previous section, the identification ambiguity in networks does not affect the browsing model given for graphs, but for the assignment of identifiers. Thus, as a measure of the applicability of a browser, we can take the "identification power" of the kind of identifier it adopts: the introduction of identifiers more

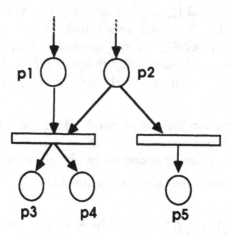

Figure 6: *An example of Petri net*

complex than arc identifiers allows us to define unambiguous browsing process for more general networks.

We note that in several networks the concept of arc identifiers is not powerful enough to distinguish all vertices. Let us consider, for example, a Petri net, which is an interesting formalism for integrating dynamic aspects in a data model.

Example 5 A (simple) *Petri net* $N = \langle S, T, F \rangle$ is composed by a finite set S of *places*, and a set T of *transitions*, where each transition is an ordered pair of sets of places (*preset* and *postset*). This formalism can be represented by a bipartite graph whose vertices are either places or transitions and arcs are used to connect a transition from its preset to its postset. It is easy to see that vertices associated to transitions between sets of places may be not arc identifiable (while a transition can be identified by considering the related pair of sets of places).

For example, in Figure 6 the transition on the right is not arc identifiable (the place p_2 has an outgoing arc to both transitions) whereas the pair $< preset, postset >$ clearly uniquely identifies the transition. □

In order to define other identifiers meaningful in the context of a browsing process, let us observe that browsing is a process aimed at viewing the neighborhood of vertices, while exploring the structure following paths that traverse the graph. We can then single out a "horizontal" (breadth) and a "vertical" (depth) aspect in the navigation, and, correspondingly, define classes of identifiers whose structure privileges either aspect.

5.1   Breadth identifiers

This first extension of the arc identifiability concept is based on the horizontal aspect of the navigation, and it is achieved by considering the collection of labels in an object's neighborhood.

Definition 9 Let v be a vertex of the graph G, let $\mathcal{N}(v) = \langle in(v), v, out(v) \rangle$ be its *neighborhood* and $\lambda(\mathcal{N}(v))$ be the associated families of labels. We say that:

- $\lambda(\mathcal{N}(v))$ is the *neighborhood identifier* of v in G if there is no other vertex v' in G with $\lambda(\mathcal{N}(v)) = \lambda(\mathcal{N}(v'))$;
- G is *neighborhood identifiable* if all its vertices have the neighborhood identifier.

□

We note that the above definition allows to solve the identification problems in bipartite graphs associated to Petri nets introduced in Example 5 (when they are neighborhood identifiable).

The neighborhood of a vertex may be very large in complex graphs (as those associated to databases), where it may happen that some labels in $\lambda(\mathcal{N}(v))$ might be unnecessary for uniquely identifying v. Hence the concept of neighborhood identifier can be extended by allowing the identification of a vertex v by using a portion of $\lambda(\mathcal{N}(v))$.

Definition 10 Let $G = \langle V, \Lambda, \lambda, A \rangle$ be a graph, v be one of its vertices and let $loc(v) = \langle \Lambda_1, \lambda(v), \Lambda_2 \rangle$ be either $\lambda(\mathcal{N}(v))$ or a portion of $\mathcal{N}(v))$ obtained by eliminating some labels from it. We say that:

- $loc(v)$ is a *local identifier* of v in G if there is no $loc(v')$ associated to another vertex v' in G such that $loc(v) = loc(v')$;
- G is *locally identifiable* if all its vertices have a local identifier.

□

We observe that label and arc identifiers can also be regarded as special cases of local identifiers.

5.2   Depth identifiers

The second approach for the extension of the arc identifiers privileges the vertical aspect of the navigation. It is based on the assumption that the user may consider as a natural way for identifying a vertex v one of the sequences of labels of vertices that have been visited to reach v, i.e., its "browsing history". If the system prevents the navigation process to cross vertices more than once, we have that the browsing history is limited to a path and the following definitions arise.

Definition 11 Let v be a vertex of the graph G, let $h(v) = \langle v_1, \ldots, v_n \rangle$ be a sequence of vertices in G, where $v_n = v$ and, for each $1 \leq i < n$, $\langle v_i, v_{i+1} \rangle$ is an arc in G. Let $\lambda(h(v))$ be the correspondent sequence of labels. We say that:

- $\lambda(h(v))$ is an *history identifier* for v in G if there is no other vertex in G with the same history identifier;
- $\lambda(h(v))$ is a *path identifier* for v in G if $h(v)$ is a direct path in G (no vertex is duplicated in the sequence) and if there is no other vertex in G with the same path identifier;
- v is *history identifiable* if it has a history identifier in G; G is *history identifiable* if all its vertices are history identifiable. Similar definitions hold for path identifiability.

□

We note that several data models have a hierarchical structure that, e.g., specifies complex objects in terms of their components, with, possibly, a unique maximal element. If the internal nodes are selective (i.e., if within a complex object it is possible to distinguish its components from their names) it is easy to see that an object identifier can be found by taking the labels in a path starting from the hierarchy root (whenthe root is label identifiable). Other examples of path identification can be found also in different fields: for example, in a programming language to select a component of a complex data, or in a hierarchical file system to identify any (internal or leaf) node (which may represent a file or a directory).

As regards the history identifier, we notice that increases the identification power of path identifiers, by taking into account the existence cycles. Examples of history identifiers are less frequent and may be introduced, e.g., in the context of finite state automata, where a state may be identified by means of one of the possible strings that leads to it. For a more detailed discussion we refer to [7].

5.3   Including complex identifiers in browsers

More complex browsers may be based on neighborhood, local, history and path identifiers. In this way it is also possible to deal with graphs and networks that represent object oriented databases, as, for instance, those described in [4,6].

A first extension of the concepts of browsing state and of browsing primitives to neighborhood and to locally identifiable graphs leads to consider the local view from the vertex v composed by the identifier of v and the identifiers of vertices adjacent to v. Hence a local view contains the whole set (or a portion of it) of labels with distance not greater than two from the current vertex.

When such local views are too complex, the problem of reducing the amount of information displayed in the local view arises. This problem may be solved by displaying labels with distance two on request[3]. In this case, the display of a local view from a vertex v can be based on $\lambda(\mathcal{N}(v))$ for a neighborhood identifiable graph, whereas, for a local identifiable graph, the display of the local view can be based on a subset of $\lambda(\mathcal{N}(v))$ that contains at least one local identifier. In both cases the information contained in display of the local view may be not sufficient to guarantee an unambiguous selection of a new current vertex in a select-open step of the browsing process. In fact, the identification of a new vertex is delayed at the moment in which such a vertex is opened, and an additional close operation may become necessary when a wrong label is selected in the local view.

Similar extensions may be defined for browsers based on depth identifiers and for general browsers that utilizes the different kinds of identifiers, depending upon the characteristics of the objects.

6   Conclusion and future work

We presented a formal model for browsing processes in information systems. The introduced primitives (*open*, *select*, *close*) correspond to the atomic steps in which an elementary navigation can be decomposed. We notice that, because of its simplicity, such an elementary browsing may suffer from some limitations:

- *Short-sighted navigation.* Only concepts adjacent to the current one can be seen and visited. Since no global view on the whole structure is available, some consequences are: the user can get lost, already performed navigations may be repeated, relevant portions of the structure may remain unexplored.
- *Limited power.* Since no summarization tool is available (due to the lack of distinction between schema and instances) and no shortcuts are available (to reach distant concepts without long navigations) the system shows extremely detailed information that may confuse the user, and after a while the step-by-step process becomes tedious, unless the system provides some tools for "automating" the process.
- *Weak integration.* The browsing and the querying environments are often distinct, thus separating learning and querying activities.

We are now investigating possible extensions of the model presented here, in order to formally define more sophisticated styles of browsing which allow to overcome the above limitations, according to the approach suggested in [5] for reducing the gap between browsing and querying.

---

[3]It may be also opportune to consider non redundant and minimal local identifiers (we refer to [7] for a detailed discussion of minimality problems and their complexity).

References

1. Bachman, C.: The Programmer as a Navigator. Communication of the ACM, 16(11), 1973.

2. Bell, J.L. : Reuse and Browsing: Survey of Program Developers, in: Object Frameworks, (Ed. D. Tsichritzis), Technical Report, Universite de Geneve, 1992, 197–220.

3. Botafogo, R.A., Rivlin, E. and Shneiderman, B. : Structural Analysis of Hypertexts: Identifying Hierarchies and Useful Metrics. ACM Transactions on Information Systems, 10:2, (1992), 142–180.

4. D'Atri, A., Laenens, E., Paoluzzi, A., Tarantino, L. and Vermeir, D.: A Graphical Browser to Object-oriented Knowledge Bases. Database Technology, Pergamon Press, 4(1), (1991), 45–55.

5. D'Atri, A. and Tarantino, L.: From Browsing to Querying. Data Engineering, IEEE Computer Society, 12(2), (1989), 46–55.

6. D'Atri, A. and Tarantino, L.: A Friendly Graphical Environment for Interacting with Data and Knowledge Bases. in: Designing and Using Human-Computer Interfaces and Knowledge Based Systems, (Eds. G. Salvendy and J. Smith), Advances in Human Factors/Ergonomics 12B, Elsevier, 1989, 195–202.

7. D'Atri, A. and Tarantino, L.: The vertex identification problem in graph and network databases. Unpublished manuscript, 1993.

8. Goldberg, A.: Smalltalk 80: the Interactive Programming Environment. Addison-Wesley, 1984.

9. Halasz, F.: Reflections on Notecards: Seven Issues for the Next Generation of Hypermedia Systems. Communication of the ACM, 31(7), (1988), 836–852.

10. Helm, R. and Maarek, Y.: Integrating Information Retrieval and Domain Specific Approaches for Browsing and Retrieval in Object-Oriented Class Libraries. in: Proceedings of OOPSLA '91, Phoenix, 1991, 47–61.

11. Herot, C.: Spatial Management of Data. ACM Transactions on Database Systems, 5(4), (1980), 493–513.

12. Mander, R., Salomon,G. and Wong, Y.Y. : A 'Pile' Metaphor for Supporting Casual Organization of Information. in: Proceedings of the ACM Conference on Human Factors in Computing Systems, CHI'92, May 3–7, 1992, Monterey, CA, ACM Press, 627–634.

13. Meyer, B.: Lessons from the Design of the Eiffel Libraries. Communications of the ACM, 33(9), (1990), 69–88.

14. Motro, A. : Browsing in a Loosely Structured Database. in: Proceedings of ACM-SIGMOD International Conference on Management of Data, ACM, New York, New York, 1984, 197–207.

15. Motro, A. : BAROQUE: an Exploratory Interface to Relational Databases. ACM Transactions on Office Information Systems, 4(2), (1986), 164–181.

16. Motro, A., D'Atri, A. and Tarantino, L.: KIVIEW: The Design of an Object-Oriented Browser. in: Proceedings of 2nd International Conference on Expert Database Systems, Vienna, VA., (Ed. L. Kerschberg), Benjamin/Cummings Publishing Company, 1988, 107–133.

17. Nielsen, J.: The Art of Navigating through Hypertext. Communication of the ACM, 33(3), (1990), 296–310.

18. Nielsen, J.: Hypertext & Hypermedia, Academic Press, New York, 1990.

19. Pintado, X. and Tsichritzis, D.: SaTellite: Hypermedia Exploration by Affinity. in: Hypertext: Perspectives, Concepts and Applications, ACM, Cambridge University Press, 1990, 278–288.

20. Stonebraker, M. and Kalash, J.: Timber: a Sophisticated Database Browser. in: Proceedings of the Eighth International Conference on Very Large Data Bases, VLDB Endowment (available from Morgan-Kaufmann, Los Altos, California), 1982, 1–10.

21. Stotts, P.D. and Furuta, R. : Petri-net-based Hypertext: Document Structure with Browsing Semantics. ACM Transactions on Information Systems, 7(1), (1989), 3–29.

AN APPLICATION OF THE MILORD SYSTEM TO HANDLE RADIOLOGICAL DATA

G. Di Stefano
University of L'Aquila, L'Aquila, Italy

M.V. Marabello
Itaca S.r.l., Rome, Italy

A. D'Atri
University of L'Aquila, L'Aquila, Italy

Abstract

The spreading of diagnostic and therapeutic procedures, brought to a large amount of information that should be handled by the physicians without loosing interaction easiness. In such a situation there is a growing demand for multimedia integrated environment. The MILORD project has been designed to give an effective answer to this requirement providing a developing system for multimedia databases devoted to manage all the information arising from daily hospital activities. MILORD is a project supported by the EC in the context of the AIM R&D programme on Telematic Systems in Areas of General Interest. In this paper we describe the main features of the project, and we show an application (CLINICA) developed to test the capabilities of the MILORD system with respect to the storage manipulation, retrieval and sharing of clinical and radiological data.

1   Introduction

In current medical practice, we can observe an increasing number of specialists involved in the care of the patients and a spreading of diagnostic and therapeutic procedures. Consequently, a very large amount of information are daily exchanged among different hospital departments: to collect all available clinical data is a difficult and time consuming activity that produce negative results on the effectiveness of large size health care organizations. Data handled by physicians are intrinsically heterogeneous: anamnestic and physical findings, laboratory data, radiological and endoscopic images, biomedical signals, diagnostic reports, etc.. Therefore there is a growing demand for Multi-Media Workstations and for Integrated Hospital Information Systems. The MILORD project is aimed at the design and implementation of a system (the MILORD system) which is an integrated environment to develop multimedia medical applications in which the medical staff can manage directly, for diagnostic and therapeutic purposes, all the information involved in a specific hospital department, as well as access to the information provided from other departments. The aim of this paper is to give a description of the MILORD system, and of an application, CLINICA, developed by means of this system: in Section 2 we describe the goals of the MILORD project, and the architecture of the MILORD system; in Section 3 we give a detailed description of the CLINICA application analyzing its main features from the user point of view. A discussion on the future developments is finally given in Section 4.

2   The MILORD project

MILORD (*Multimedia Interaction with Large Object-oriented Radiological and clinical Databases*) is a three years project on multimedia medical workstations (coordinated by the University of L'Aquila) carried on by a consortium composed by eleven organizations (industries, health care providers, academic and public research centers) located in five European countries. The Commission of the European Union launched (starting from January 1992) a R&D programme on Telematic Systems in Areas of General Interest. One of the main areas in this programme (denoted *AIM - Advanced Informatics in Medicine*) aims at coordinating and supporting the European research efforts on the application of the information and telecommunication technologies to health care [1]. MILORD [2] is an AIM project whose goals and architecture are described in the following sections.

2.1   MILORD objectives

In order to develop systems integrating information processing activities in hospital departments, different problems arise:

- the design of an Integrated Hospital Information System (HIS) imposes strong requirements to the design of the global system architecture and to the definition of the human computer interaction environment, and involves predefined and coherent resource choices.

- multimedia data, as diagnostic digital images, represent a heavy workload both for hardware and connecting network of HIS. Therefore, in most cases, the design of a fully integrated HIS had to be postponed and research groups focused their attention to study the possibility of obtaining an integration mainly at departmental level.

- the hospital organization is intrinsically characterized by several substructures which cooperate each other and evolve in different ways towards an highly integrated structure. Moreover, a fully integrated system has to be avoided since failures originated in a part of the system may affect the entire hospital, thus causing a "failure propagation";

Hence the main goal of the MILORD project is to overcome the present insufficient hospital departmental integration (of data, workstations and information sources) by exploiting and extending the most advanced database technology. MILORD system has been developed with the aim of giving an answer to the following medical requirements [9]:

- an integrated knowledge representation and user interaction environment to represent and to handle multimedia data;

- a fast image and multimedia data storage, retrieval, and processing;

- a flexible environment to integrate multiple information sources and to communicate and cooperate among medical staffs.

For the first requirement, the MILORD system provides a powerful object-oriented data model for implementing a true multimedia knowledge representation. In particular, to satisfy the modeling requirements the system offers the knowledge representation and manipulation language LOCO+ (LOgic for Complex Objects) [17], based on a tight integration between the object-oriented and the logic programming paradigms. This language plays a double role of data definition and manipulation language, and programming language for the development of applications (like CLINICA). In this way, it is equally easy to program both the user

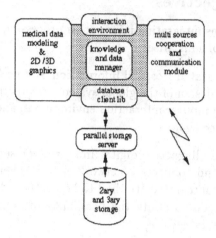

Figure 1: *MILORD gross architecture*

interface and the database layers of a program. LOCO+ also offers multimedia capabilities, which extends the X-interface of LOCO [13] (the language from which
LOCO+ is originated) to encompass new media (such as pictures and sounds).

The second requirement has an answer in a parallel hardware to implement a
database parallel server and a graphic parallel server. On such a machine runs
very efficient parallel algorithms, that are able to improve both tasks related to
multimedia data retrieval and image handling and displaying.

The third point is faced by two integrated modules of the MILORD system: the
teleconferencing module and the multi-source cooperation module. The first one
gives the possibility of connecting clinicians in locally different places for expert
consultation, the second one allows to connect different MILORD workstations in a
federated database in order to exchange data by local and remote databases access
as well as accessing external information sources (e.g. medical equipment, existing
databases) by obtaining an open system.

In the following section we give a more detailed description of the MILORD
system architecture, while a deeper view of some modules will be shown during the
description of the CLINICA application.

2.2   MILORD Architecture

The MILORD environment [10, 16] supports a federation of autonomous MILORD
systems, each system is composed by at least one storage server, a number of client
workstations, and interfaces to external information sources. MILORD users can
cooperate and share the same patient data in a real time cooperative work mode

supported by a teleconference module. The MILORD environment is not based on conventional computer equipment and communication networks, that are not suitable for efficient storage, processing, retrieval and transfer of very large amounts of multimedia data. The system uses a parallel hardware to implement a database parallel server and a graphics parallel server, both interfaced to Unix workstations (the usage of T9000 transputers is planned). The bandwidth problems are also solved (whilst keeping cost down) by the adoption, for image transmission, of both FDDI and specialized point to point connections (using transputer asynchronous communication on optical fiber links).

The interaction environment and the knowledge and data manager are not separated (see figure 1) but they strict cooperate and can be considered as a unique module: the Medical Application Development System (or the MILORD Toolkit). This module offers the developer (a user interface designer, or a knowledge engineer) an effective and flexible environment for building applications meeting to the health care requirements. It is mainly devoted to the high-level description of the objects stored in the database (using the LOCO+ language) and it provides the User Interface Development System (UIDS) to define and maintain a full application environment covering tasks related to the data and knowledge representation, and static and dynamic aspects of the visual user interface.

One of the major objectives of the MILORD project is the management of diagnostic images together with other kinds of medical data. The graphic module provides an environment to display 2D and 3D images, and to work on images (e.g. filtering, measuring distances, angles, areas etc.) [5].

The parallel server [6, 7, 8] is a powerful multimedia object storage server whose main characteristics are:

- the efficient storage and retrieval of all kinds of objects, including multimedia data (images, texts, biosignals, voices, animations);

- the support of all the currently emerging storage means (optical disks, magnetic storage, jukeboxes);

- the multi-user support.

It is interfaced to the system through the Database Client Library which is directly handled by the LOCO+ language.

The Multi-Source Cooperation and Communication Module (MSCM) [3] implements the MILORD architecture for a federated hospital information environment, with the objective to provide a unified framework integrating functions for database management and teleconferencing services in a distributed MILORD system. To achieve this result, the principle and the techniques of federated databases and information system have been chosen. The motivation for this choice is that a hospital environment is characterized by a large number of distributed information sources and different user categories with different information needs. The federated system is thus a solution which can provide information exchange between a number of autonomous but interconnected sub-systems. This module also allows to incorporate the teleconference functionality by connecting clinicians in locally different places and providing facilities for experts consultation.

3 The CLINICA application

CLINICA is a first level prototype application that implements some of the functionality of the MILORD environment. CLINICA is able to give the end-user, that is supposed to be a physician, a testing environment for the multimedia data management and processing. The application has been developed in strong cooperation with the medical partners of the project, in order to get useful feedback even during the development phase. The following description of the applicationis given from an operational point of view. This means that by showing and explaining the user interface functionality and the views on medical records collected in CLINICA, we describe the lower level layers the application is based on, and we give the reader a global vision on the MILORD system.

3.1 Data modeling and management

Figure 2 shows a start-up view on the CLINICA user-interface that can be considered as the control panel of the application, from which it is possible to activate most of the functionalities that have been implemented until now. The list of patients locally available on the workstation contains, according to the physicians' needs, the work of a week in the department. Clinical cases that are here shown comes from a real medical situation. This means that medical data in the application have been analyzed, managed and then provided by the medical partners of the project.

In an HIS (Hospital Information System) the data from individual patients play a central role. The information has to be complete, problem oriented, clearly organized and displayed, easily gathered for routine tasks. While some data are fairly structured (e.g. administrative data) others may be very complex and irregular, thus implying the need of a not rigid data model, able to follow the individual evolution of objects. The model developed in CLINICA is based on the so called Medical Information Category (MIC) and Medical Information Element (MIE) [4]. The MIE is defined as an item that has a medical meaning and belongs to the patient folder: examples of MIEs are " thyroid ecography" or "Red Blood Cells Counts (RBC)", whereas a MIC is a cluster that groups homogeneous MIEs, in this case respectively "ecography" and "laboratory examinations". In some words, every MIC

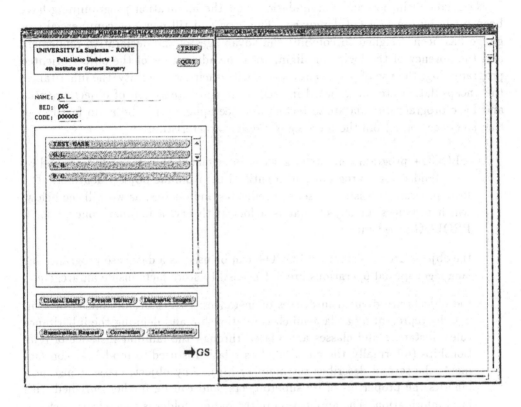

Figure 2: First view on CLINICA application

represents a set of medical concepts, which must be specialized into MIEs in order to be instantiated. Using this model it is possible to describe and manage medical information expressed by single values, graphics, images or even sounds, and then to create database objects locally available at a single MILORD system but which can also be shared among the various connected MILORD systems that constitute the MILORD system network.

The data definition and manipulation, and the application programming have been made by the LOCO+ language. This new and till now not commercial language has been designed to combine the advantages of the declarative refinement and the potency of the logic paradigm, with the advantages of the object oriented programming: the use of persistent objects with their own identity, the inheritance, the encapsulation etc. It is based in fact on a tight integration of object oriented and logic programming database techniques (see appendix). The main features of this language come from the merging of these characteristics:

- a LOCO+ program consists of a set of interrelated objects, each described by an extended logic program and identified by a unique object identifier. The logic program consists of a set of predicates and clauses, as we will see below, which produces an object that is a logical theory, a familiar concept for a PROLOG programmer.

- the objects are persistent, so LOCO+ can be used as a database programming language; special operations are not needed to store facts inside an archive.

- the objects are divided in classes or instances; classes are organized in a hierarchy representing a class-subclass relationship and defining the inheritance rules; instances and classes are related through the familiar instance-of relationships (informally, the class-subclass relation is used to model set containment, the second describes set membership). Any object, class or instance, inherits the properties of its superobjects, and can be further enriched with local information. The application in the patient folder is then clear: each patient has a standard subset of clinical data, necessary for the inter-specialists communications and for statistical and epidemiological analysis; at the same time it is possible to model individuality.

- LOCO+ provides convenient and object oriented access to all of X's facilities. The interface is largely widget-independent, currently it supports the OpenLook and the MOTIF widget sets.

The LOCO+ system provides also powerful facilities for integrating external software into a LOCO+ program. In particular, it is now possible to develop predicates written in C language, but that can be used transparently within LOCO+ programs,

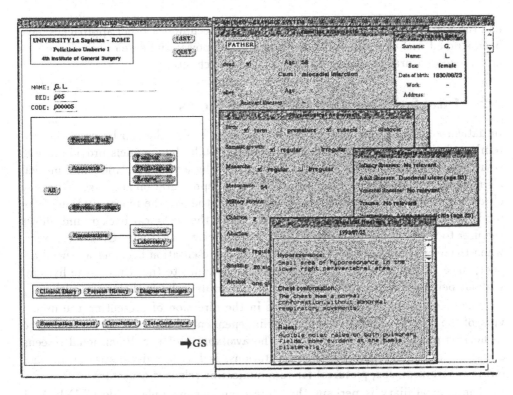

Figure 3: Medical data from the selected patient folder

just like normal predicates. Future goals are the integration of LOCO+ with other languages like FORTRAN and PASCAL.

From the view shown in figure 2 the user, after selecting the patient from the list and clicking on the button TREE, can get information about personal data, anamnesis or physiological status before the patient admission at the hospital (see figure 3). The system provides also a list of the examinations performed by the patient; the images related to the instrumental exams are classified by type (e.g. ecographies, magnetic resonances, computerized tomographies) using different icons. Figure 2 also shows other buttons which activate various kinds of views and functionalities on data that will be described in the following paragraphs.

The interaction paradigm offered by the CLINICA application is the browsing among stored data; this is a different approach with respect to the traditional one, the "formal querying", where the user presents his queries using a formal query language. The reason of this choice is to provide an easy access to all the potential users of the medical records. In fact, the browsing doesn't require, like the query, a preliminary knowledge about the query language, the knowledge of data organization and the goals. Between the mentioned interaction techniques, other approaches have been studied with the aim of balancing expressive power and ease of use. Examples are: pseudo-natural language, by examples approach, etc.

3.2   Interface functionalities and views

In database systems the problem to be faced is to bridge the gap between the system's and the user's perception of the reality. While data models provide formal structuring mechanisms, in order to be perceived by a user such modeling mechanisms have, in turn, to be expressed in terms of a representation language. One may observe that the more the user is a system expert, the less the representation of the model is required to be close to the reality, since the technical background allows the user to learn with a reasonable effort new abstract constructs. On the contrary, when the user is not a computer scientist, the representation becomes a crucial aspect, since s/he should interact with something similar to the reality s/he lives in, without being acquainted with the existence of an underlying abstract model.

The recent visual representations are in the direction of presenting the user a view of the objects of interest apparently independent of the data model (and close to her/his perception of the reality). The availability of two-dimensional screens allows us to exploit such visual representations, and to use visual structures (e.g., forms, diagrams, icons, pictures) for communicating relevant concepts.

The clinical diary is perhaps the more complete example inside CLINICA of the possible visual representations offered by the MILORD system. Keeping in mind the MILORD data model described above, a view on medical information can be defined as aggregations of MICs and MIEs along the time. The clinical diary (figure 4) regards the single patient day by day status during his admission in the hospital. It provides the physician to know the today's patient conditions and everything concerns his clinical case: examinations done or to be done, diagnoses, therapies, surgical interventions and so on. The view enables him to look at the same time the information of the previous days, in order to have a complete picture of the patient clinical situation. In particular, the physician can see a graph of temperature variation, a list of values regarding the metabolism of the patient, and the images related to his examinations. The browsing paradigm, which allows the access to different data representations, is based on the Medical Application Development System (MADS) to satisfy the modeling requirements and to meet the different users demands [11].

The MADS is based on a knowledge handler (LOCO+) and it includes the UIDS. The MADS consists of a number of layers which incrementally add functionalities to the system: the User Interface Description Objects (UIDOs), the Display Model and the Interaction Paradigm (see Figure 5).

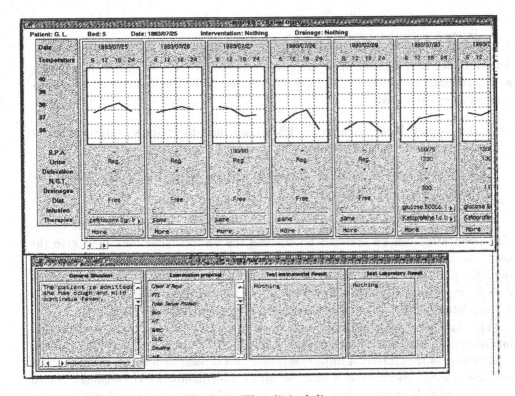

Figure 4: The clinical diary

- The UIDOs layer provides convenient and object-oriented access to all of the X's facilities;

- the Display Model associates with each object in the database an appropriate visual representation;

- the Interaction Paradigms are a collection of different ways in which one can interact with the database.

Two interactive tools, aimed at graphically supporting the developer in tailoring and customization activities, had been developed to be used jointly with the programming environment:

- the Display Model Generator (DMG) which is basically an interface to the Display Model layer of the MADS;

- the Customized Presentation Builder (CPB) which can be regarded as an interface to the UIDOs layer [18].

CORRELATION is another useful interface functionality available in the CLINICA application can be accessed by clicking the button. The idea is to give the user a contemporaneous temporal view on some medical data (for example the patient temperature and the action of antibiotics). Showing on a graph the desired data during a selected range of time, the physician can verify a supposed correlation among data, having then a more complete view on the patient's situation.

The data processing till now implemented is limited to the normalization, the future idea of making also a statistical study on their time correlation stresses another aspect of the CLINICA implementation; this is possible because LOCO+, that is below mainly described as a data definition and manipulation language, is also a programming language able to give the application more complex functionalities than those, like the browsing on data, normally requested to work with database objects.

3.3   Integration with other modules

Figure 2 shows the button EXAMINATIONS, the user can use to access the instrumental and laboratory exams of the patient s/he is interested to; the instrumental exams consist of schedules containing the corresponding values, while the laboratory ones are equipped (see figure 6) with forms containing date, report and images belonging to them.

As told previously, one of the main goals of the MILORD project is to implement and evaluate 2D and 3D functions for graphical processing and manipulation of

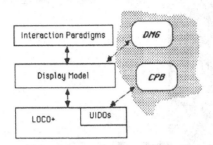

Figure 5: Medical Application Development System

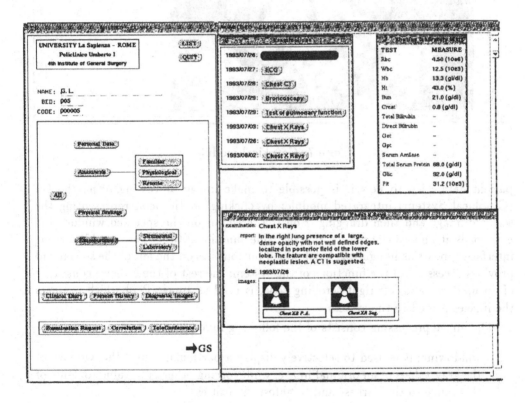

Figure 6: Examinations forms

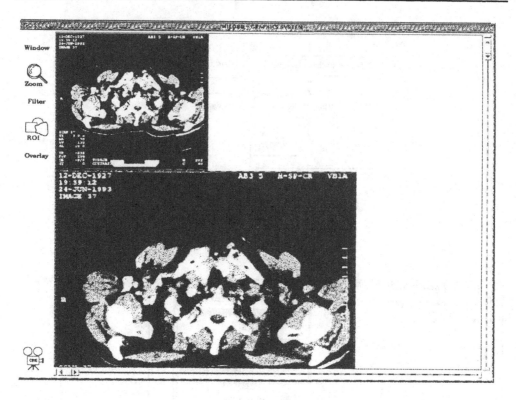

Figure 7: Graphical module

patient data. Up to now it is possible to make image processing using the GS (Graphical System) integrated module; by clicking on the icon representing the selected image and then dragging it on the screen or on the specified window, the user loads it and can access to the available functionalities. The graphical user-interface appears as in figure 7: a column of buttons lies on the left of the screen and provides access to all the functions of the system; the rest of the screen , consisting of an up-down and left-right scrolling zone, is used as Image Pool which presents the images loaded to the system.

The image processing consists of the following functions:

- windowing; it is used to selectively display a particular range, the window, of the gray values of an original image, while forcing other gray values outside of this range to the darkest and brightest intensities.

- filter; it allows the user to select four kinds of filters to apply to the images. The inverse filter can be used to display the image with its inverted pixel values, i.e. to make the negative film effect on it; the smoothing filter generates a low passered filtered copy of the original image and gives rise to a smoothed effect; the sharpening filter generates a detail-enhanced copy of an original image by enhancing the edges; the Laplacian filter produces a resultant image which is basically an edge map of the original.

- zoom; this function generates a new image which is the zoomed copy of the original selected image. It allows both the x2, x3 enlargement and x1/2 reduction. It is also possible to rotate 180 degrees and to mirror against its vertical and horizontal central axis the original image.

- Region Of Interest (ROI); this function allows the user to interactively define or edit regions of interest of rectangular, circular or polygonal forms. The user can also duplicate an existing ROI to another image in the same relative position to the upper left corner of the first image. The function performs also a statistical measurement within a given ROI; the following statistical parameters are measured and displayed: the histogram distribution in a logarithmic scale, the mean gray value and the standard deviation, the size of the ROI (in pixels).

- overlay; under this name some other subfunctions are collected. By clicking on one of the items of the submenu, it is possible to interactively draw a line or an angle, and in addition the system displays its length or measure in degrees (Distance, Angle). It is then possible to interactively define marks on the image, which are displayed as arrows on the screen, (Marker), and also to input some annotation texts on it (Text).

The graphical module also offers the user another functionality: the cine display. If the selected patient folder contains a complete medical imaging examination, i.e. the whole set of images belonging to it, it is possible to successively display the sequence of these images, like a video display. The user can also select only a fragment of successive frames from a complete scan for the cine display, by simply specifying the first and the last frame.

The image processing module is up to now at its first implementation. Functional improvement and extension of it in the visual image enhancement, interactive image manipulation and measurement will be included in the next revised version which will be mainly devoted to more efficiently support to the clinical diagnosis.

After having described the capabilities of the graphical system, it is possible now to introduce another module just available in the present application to support the communication between the nodes of the federation plays a primary rule in the day-by-day work of hospital physicians.

The actual prototype offers (by clicking on the button TELECONFERENCE) the connection of clinicians in locally different places. The power of the teleconference communication mode is in the on-line exchanging of image information between the connected nodes. If one of the users wants to show the other a particular image of the exam under consideration, to have for example a consultation about it, he has only to select it from the patient folder, as just described below for the images of the graphical module, and then to drag it on the teleconference window; the image will be straight after shown on the corresponding window in the monitor of the other workstation. Actually, it is also possible to use the graphical module on the just selected image, in order to make an on-line image processing on it; near future plans consider also the availability of a teleconference voice communication functionality.

4   Conclusion

Summarizing, the application has shown the capability in:

- providing tools to build and interact with medical folders in order to give an integrated view of the patients data. In particular the application proved the suitability of LOCO+ as medical data representation language, and the effectiveness of the MILORD UIDS for the development of customized user interfaces;

- providing a smooth integration of the different modules of the MILORD system.

It has to be noticed that the present implementation of CLINICA is based on the first integrated prototype of MILORD, dated June 1993. Future work will be devoted to achieve full exploitation of the MILORD prototype system on one hand, and to include new high level functionality in the Clinical User Module on the other hand. The final implementation, which will benefit from the progresses done in the MILORD modules, will include "smart" navigation capabilities, data entry support and a full exploitation of the Remote Sources Interface. This last functionality is particularly useful to make CLINICA smoothly integrate with other information systems possibly already present in the clinical environment. From a properly medical point of view, CLINICA is expected to give the physician also a support in making the correct diagnoses and in deciding the consequent therapies. A medical knowledge layer will be then implemented, in order to give the clinician a useful instrument able to better help him in his daily work.

Acknowledgments

We wish to thank L.Beolchi and C.Daskalakis (CEC DGXIII-AIM) and all the remaining members of the MILORD Team: S. Cabasino, F. Danza, F. Mandolini

A.Suatoni (Itaca s.r.l., Italy); S. Christodoulakis, N. Ailamaki, D. Anestopoulos, S. Argyropoulos (MUSIC-FORTH, Greece); G. Peise, C. Spahn, L. Tassakos, (Parsytec Computer Gmbh, Germany); M. Alshen, J. Ljungberg, M. Persson, G. Udderborg (The Swedish Institute for Systems Development - SISU); Y. Bao, D. Faulkner, A. Gehring, U. Jackisch, H. Lemke, M. Rudolph, G. Faulkner (Technical University of Berlin, Germany) D. Vermeir, F. Staes, J. Naudts (university of Antwerp, Belgium); A. Bernabei, B. Zobel (University of L'Aquila, Italy); C. Catalano, F. Drudi, F. Consorti, R. Passariello (University of Roma "La Sapienza", Italy); D. Pisanelli, F. Ricci (ISRSDS-CNR, Italy).

References

[1] *Research and Technology development on telematic systems in healthcare, AIM 93 annual status report,* CEC DGXIII/C/3, Office for the official publications of the European Cummunities, Luxemburg, 1993.

[2] A. D'Atri, et al., "MILORD: Advanced Database Technology for Implementing a Multimedia Medical Workstation", *Proc. of IMAC93,* IEEE Computer Society Press, 46–54, 1993.

[3] M. Ahlsen, J. Ljungberg, G. Uddeborg, M. Persson, "Specification of the architecture of the Multi-Source Cooperation Module", *Milord Report E3,* 1992.

[4] M. Ahlsen, et. al. "Multimedia Patient Folder: Computerized Support for Clinical Activities in a Federated Information System". *Proc of MIE93.* In press, 1993.

[5] Y.Bao, U.Jackisch, F.Danza, A.Suatoni, "Detailed Specification of the Graphical Functionality", *Milord Report G3,* 1992.

[6] S. Christodoulakis, A. Ailamaki, M. Fragonikolakis, Y. Kapetanakis and L. Koveos, "An Object Oriented Architecture for Multimedia Information Systems", *IEEE Data Engineering Bulletin,* September 1991.

[7] S. Christodoulakis, N. Ailamaki, D. Anestopoulos, S. Argyropoylos, "The Device Layer of MILORD", *MILORD Report D2,* 1992.

[8] S. Christodoulakis, D. Anestopoulos, S. Argyropoulos, "Data Organization and Storage Hierarchies in a Multimedia Server", *IEEE COMPCON'93 Proceedings,* February 1993.

[9] F.Consorti et al., "Specification of the medical Requirements", *MILORD Report A3,* 1992

[10] A. D'Atri, G. Di Stefano, L.Tarantino, "On the Representation and Management of Medical Records in a Knowledge Based System," *Expert Systems with Applications*, Vol. 6, 469–482, 1993.

[11] F. Staes, L. Tarantino, D. Vermeir, *Rapid prototyping of user interfaces in the MILORD system*, Proc. of the Software Engineering and Knowledge Engineering International Conference, SEKE93, 355–359, 1993.

[12] W. Kim, *Introduction to Object Oriented Databases*, MIT Press, 1990

[13] E. Laenens, B. Verdonk, D. Vermeir, D. Saccà. "The LOCO Language: Towards an Integration of Logic and Object-Oriented Programming", *Proc. Workshop on Logic Programming and Non-Monotonic Reasoning*, Austin, Texas, pp. 62–72, 1990.

[14] A. MacLean, et al., "User-Tailorable Systems: Pressing the Issues with Buttons", in *Proc. of CHI'90*, Seattle, WA, April 1-5, pp.175-182, 1990.

[15] M. Tsangaris and J. Naughton, "On the Performance of Object Clustering Techniques", *ACM SIGMOD*, 1992

[16] D.Vermeir et al., " Description of the MILORD Architecture", *Milord Report A2/A4*, 1992.

[17] D. Vermeir, et. al., "Design of the LOCO+ Language", *MILORD Report B3*, 1992

[18] Tarantino, L., et. al., "The Design of the Multimedia User Interaction Environment", *MILORD Report B/C5*, 1993

Appendix

An example of LOCO+ statements to create a MIE element.

```
#include         "system.H"
#include         "commonSchema.H"
#include         "commSchview.H"
```

```
%---------------------- Structure of a MIE --------------
%--------------------(Medical Information Element)--------
```

```
% Every object mie(X) is defined as
% a subclass of the class "db"

(db)mie(X)=

{

%
%    Attributes of every object "mie(X)"
%
        ubase(name(key(str))).
        ubase(patient(str)).
        ubase(notes(str)).


%
%The method by which it is possible to create a new object
%"mie(X)" and to define its properties
%

        create(Mie,Name,Patient,Notes):-
               mie(Y).new,
               mie(Y).assert(name(Name)),
               mie(Y).assert(patient(Patient)),
               mie(Y).assert(notes(Notes)).
}
```

```
%
%the object "main" contains the rule 'main' ; the default
%action of the LOCO+ runtime system is to solve this rule.
%


main=

{
main:-               % The rule 'main'
     create(_,'Abdominal Pain','Donald Duck','Terrible Pain!'),
     mie(X).patient(Patient),
     printf('Our poor patient is %s\n', [Patient]).
 }




%This fragment of code creates the MIE "Abdominal Pain" of
%the patient "Donald Duck" that suffers for a "Terrible Pain!".
```

OBJECT-ORIENTED DESIGN OF INFORMATION SYSTEMS: THEORETICAL FOUNDATIONS

H-D. Ehrich, R. Jungclaus and G. Denker
Technical University of Braunschweig, Braunschweig, Germany

A. Sernadas
INESC, Lisbon, Portugal

Abstract

Information systems are reactive systems with a database. For their specification and design, concepts from conceptual data modeling and concurrent processes are relevant. In this paper, we outline a unifying theory borrowing ideas from these approaches and from abstract data type theory. Our approach utilizes a variant of temporal logic. It has been used to give a formal semantics for TROLL, the object-oriented information systems specification language developed at TU Braunschweig.

1   Introduction

Conventional information systems design starts with separating data from operations, designing each with its own collection of concepts, methods, tools – and people: conceptual modeling for the information structure, and program design for the application programs. The separation carries through until the final implementation: data are collected in databases and managed with database management systems, and application programs accessing the database are implemented in programming languages.

This approach tends to suffer from a problem known as *impedance mismatch*: the basic paradigms underlying databases and programs – modeling, design, languages

*This work was partly supported by the EC under ESPRIT BRA WG 3023/6071 IS-CORE and WG 3264/6112 COMPASS, by DFG under Sa 465/1-3, and by JNICT under PMCT/C/TIT/178/90 FAC3 contract.

and systems – do not fit: there are incompatible type systems, data formats, operation modes, etc. Recent 4th-generation systems encapsulate and hide the problem to some extent, but do not really remedy the situation.

The object-oriented paradigm promises to overcome the problem: a system is viewed as a community of interacting objects, each incorporating data and operations. While we still have object-oriented programming languages incompatible with object-oriented database systems, ideas and approaches seem to converge towards homogeneous software systems dealing with both data and operations in a unified way.

Viewing the system as a community of interacting objects doesn't solve all problems. Beyond the object concept, abstraction and structuring principles are needed, together with languages and methods to work with them. And we need a sound theoretical underpinning that allows for giving formal semantics and proof systems to languages so that relevant system properties can be formally stated and verified.

The ideas put forward in this paper have been mainly developed in the ESPRIT Working Group IS-CORE: employing objects as a unifying concept and aiming at a conceptually seamless methodology from requirements to implementation [1, 2, 3, 4, 5, 6, 7, 8, 9].

The TROLL language developed at TU Braunschweig [10, 11, 12] aims at specifying information systems, providing appropriate abstractions and structuring mechanisms for design and implementation.

The project is based on OBLOG, a language project started by INESC in Lisbon back in 1986. The resulting language is described in [13]. The underlying concepts and semantic issues were investigated before in cooperation with TU Braunschweig [14], and elaborated later on [8, 6, 1, 2, 3, 4, 9, 15]. In 1989, commercial interest appeared in OBLOG and a graphical version, OBLOG89, was developed [16, 17, 18]. Meanwhile TU Braunschweig, cooperating with INESC, started work on an improved versions of the language leading to the development of TROLL and, later on, an operational dialect called TROLL *light* [19, 20].

These activities have been greatly influenced by related work on specification languages and theoretical foundations [21, 7, 22, 23, 24, 25, 26, 27]. We took great benefit from work on conceptual modeling, concurrency theory, and the theory of abstract data types. As for the latter, there are two lines of development, the algebraic approach and the model based approach. [28] gives an introduction to both. Theoretical treatments of the algebraic approach can be found in [29, 30]. Relevant textbooks for diverse approaches to process theory are [31, 32, 33, 34]. As for conceptual modeling, we refer to [35, 36, 37, 38, 39, 40, 41, 7].

An ad-hoc integration of approaches which has become popular is OMT [40]. While OMT offers useful concepts accepted by many practitioners in the field, there are problems with its lack of formalization. As a consequence, concepts and constructs are not smoothly integrated, and their meaning is not always clear.

In this paper, we outline a theory of object-oriented information systems specification and design, focussing on a formal semantics for TROLL. In his recent dissertation

[42], the second author offered a close to complete formal semantics adopting OSL [43] which is based on temporal logic. We extend this approach in order to allow for a complete semantic description, including also dynamic object roles and phases as well as object creation and deletion.

2 Basic Concepts

In order to facilitate reading this paper, we provide an informal explanation of the basic concepts made precise in subsequent sections. We feel this is necessary because their is no generally agreed ontology of object-oriented concepts.

An *information system* is a reactive system with a database and application programs, establishing a simulation model of the real (or virtual) world. In object-oriented view, an information system is a community of interacting objects where an object is a unit with an immutable identity, encapsulating structure and behavior. In more technical terms, an object is a process endowed with data.

The specification of an information system is called a *schema*. A major part of the schema consists of templates for objects and classes, and many kinds of relationships between templates expressing specialization, generalization, aggregation, interaction, interfaces, etc. The intended semantics of a schema describes the structure and behavior of its permissible populations. By a population, we mean a collection if interacting object instances. An object (instance) has states, and it can move from state to state by means of transitions. The current state of an object consists of its current situation and the execution state of its process.

In this paper, we concentrate on schema specification, i.e., we are mainly concerned with templates and relationships between templates. A schema also has to deal with identification or naming issues for objects and classes, but we do not elaborate on this point here.

A *template* is a generic pattern of structure and behavior for objects. An object may have several templates, describing its aspects. A template is like a type, it defines an invariant property that an object instance may or may not have. Its templates give criteria for an object to be *permissible* in a certain context, e.g., as a member of a class. The invariant properties of a template consist of the presence of specific attributes which can take values, and specific actions which can occur in the course of time. Typically, an action changes one or more of the attribute values when it occurs. Depending on the current situation, an action may be *enabled* or not. An action can only occur if it is enabled. We put forward that, at any time, only a part of an object's template should be visible, i.e., *in scope*.

The semantics of a template specification is given by the permissible situations an object may be in, and a generic process describing the permissible behavior patterns for instances. A *situation* contains information about the current values of attributes, the actions currently in scope, the actions currently enabled, and the actions currently occurring. For modeling behavior, we adopt a simple process model: a process is a set of life cycles where a life cycle is a finite or infinite sequence of situations.

An object *class* is not the same as a template! A class defines a time-varying population. In a class specification, a member template is given together with a naming mechanism for the members of the class. The member template defines the property an object must have in order to qualify for membership. Thus, at any time, all members of the class must have this same member template. However, not all objects with a fitting template are members, membership is only defined by explicit insertion and deletion. Our class concept coincides with that used in object-oriented databases. In object-oriented programming, the term "class" is used for what we call a template.

The schema of an information system has to specify not only templates, but also *relationships* between templates. Such relationships comprise several kinds of interaction (action calling or sharing, synchronously or asynchronously), ways of how objects can be put together to build complex objects (aggregation of parts), ways of how to encapsulate different views of the same object (specialization, roles) or a unified abstract view of different objects specified before (generalization), and ways of abstracting and encapsulate only part of the features specified (interfacing).

The relationships between template specifications are formalized by *template specification morphisms*, i.e., property preserving maps between template specifications. An important special case is that of inclusion: one example is the embedding of a role template into the entire template, another example is the embedding of a component template into a composite template. The semantics of template specification morphisms is given by *process morphisms* which are structure and behavior preserving maps among situations and processes in the reverse direction. For example, the semantics of a template inclusion is the projection of the whole onto the part.

For specifying templates and their relationships in subsequent sections, we use a TROLL-like pseudocode, omitting technical details. As in [42], the semantics is given by translation into an appropriate logic. We use an extension of OSL [43].

3 Templates

Example 3.1 : We give an example of a PERSON template, describing persons with names, capable of entering and leaving the scene, working, eating, getting hungry, etc. After a person entered, she has the name given on entry, and she is not hungry. From work, she gets hungry. She has the choice of eating fish or meat. After eating fish, she didn't have enough. After eating meat, she is full. She may eat only if she is hungry, and she may leave the scene only if she is not hungry. If she is hungry, she must eat some time.

```
template PERSON
    data types ...;
    attributes
        name:  string;
        hungry:  {yes,no};
```

```
actions
    birth enter(n:string);
    eat(f:{fish,meat});
    work;
    death leave;
valuation ...;
    [enter(n)]name=n;
    [enter(n)]hungry=no;
    [work]hungry=yes;
    [eat(fish)]hungry=yes;
    [eat(meat)]hungry=no;
    ...
behavior
    permissions;
        variables f:{fish,meat}; ...;
        {hungry=yes}eat(f);
        {hungry=no}leave;
        ...
    obligations ...;
        {hungry=yes} => eat(meat);
        ...
end template PERSON.
```

For describing specifications like this formally, we assume that an appropriate system of data types is given. Data type specifications are omitted from the examples in this paper, so we do not go into this issue here. The interested reader is referred to [29, 30]. Syntactically, data types are described by a *data signature* DSIG $= (S, \text{OP})$ where S is a set of data sorts, and OP is a system of data operations. DSIG defines the set of data terms $T_{\text{DSIG}}(X)$ over given variables X. We assume that the given data signature has a fixed interpretation which is a many-sorted data algebra.

In contrast to the data part describing the constants, the following items describe the variables. That is, the interpretation is intended to be situation-dependent.

Definition 3.2 : An *attribute signature* ATT $= \{\text{ATT}_{x,s}\}_{x \in S^*, s \in S}$ is an $S^* \times S$-indexed family of *attribute generators*. The set of *attribute terms* over a given set X of variables is $T_{\text{ATT}}(X)$. An *attribute a* of sort s is a constant term $a = b(t_1, \ldots, t_n)$ where $b \in \text{ATT}_{s_1, \ldots, s_n, s}$ and $t_i \in T_{\text{DSIG}}(\emptyset)_{s_i}$ for $1 \leq i \leq n$.

Instead of writing $a \in \text{ATT}_{s_1, \ldots, s_n, s_0}$, we use the more convenient notation $a(s_1, \ldots, s_n) : s_0$. In example 3.1, we only have parameterless attribute generators, i.e., $n = 0$. name:text is an example denoting an attribute generator. name is an example of a constant attribute term, i.e., an attribute.

Definition 3.3 : An *action signature* ACT $= \{\text{ACT}_x\}_{x \in S^*}$ is an S^*-indexed family of *action generators*. An *action α* is an constant term $\alpha = \beta(t_1, \ldots, t_n)$ where $\beta \in \text{ACT}_{s_1, \ldots, s_n}$ and $t_i \in T_{\text{DSIG}}(\emptyset)_{s_i}$ for $1 \leq i \leq n$.

As for attributes, we use the notation $\alpha(s_1, \ldots, s_n)$ instead of $\alpha \in \text{ACT}_{s_1, \ldots, s_n}$. In example 3.1, `eat(f:{fish,meat})` denotes the action generator $eat(s)$ where sort s is interpreted by the set $\{fish, meat\}$. Corresponding actions are $eat(fish)$ and $eat(meat)$. The action generator denoted by `enter(n:text)` generates infinitely many actions, one for each actual text parameter.

For each attribute a and each data value v of the same sort, we assume special actions $r_a(v)$ for reading the value v from a, and $w_a(v)$ for writing the value v into a. Additionally, we assume a predicate $a = v$ saying that a currently has the value v.

Definition 3.4 : A *template signature* is a pair TSIG $=$ (ATT, ACT) where ATT is an attribute signature, and ACT is an action signature.

The ATT and ACT parts of a template signature correspond to the `attribute` and `action` sections in template specifications.

Template situation logic is a first-order predicate logic with $a = t$, $\sqrt{\alpha}$, $\triangleright\alpha$ and $\odot\alpha$ as atomic formulae where a is an attribute, t is an attribute term, and α is an action. $\sqrt{\alpha}$ means that α is visible, i.e., in scope; $\triangleright\alpha$ means that α is enabled; $\odot\alpha$ means that α occurs. The enabling predicate was introduced in OSL in order to capture nondeterminism. The in-scope predicate is introduced here to capture visibility of actions as required by roles. In combination with the implicit read actions it also captures visibility of attributes.

A *situation* is a theory of template situation logic, describing current values of attributes, actions in scope, enabled and occurring actions, etc. That is, we model situations by uninterpreted sets of formulae closed with respect to logical consequence, rather than modeling situations by interpretations. The latter would be too restrictive when extending the concept towards deductive capabilities – which we do not do in this paper. Within each situation σ, we assume fixed frame rules expressing causality $\odot\alpha\epsilon\sigma \Rightarrow (\triangleright\alpha\epsilon\sigma \wedge \sqrt{\alpha}\epsilon\sigma)$, etc.

Template specification logic is a temporal extension of template situation logic using the temporal operators $\square$(always), $\Diamond$(sometime), O(next), and $\cup$(until). For brevity, we speak of template logic if we mean template specification logic.

The interpretation structures of template logic are *life cycles*, i.e., sequences of situations $\lambda =< \sigma_1, \sigma_2, \ldots >$. We refrain from working out in detail how *satisfaction* $\lambda \models \varphi$ is defined, i.e., when a life cycle satisfies a template logic formula. This is temporal logic standard. As for situations, we assume general frame rules for life cycles expressing causality of attribute change, etc. We do not go into detail here.

The model class of a given set of template logic formulae is the set of life cycles satisfying all given formulae. Adopting the life cycle model, a *process* is precisely this: a set $\Lambda = \{\lambda_1, \lambda_2, \ldots\}$ of life cycles. Thus, by employing loose semantics, the semantics of a set of formulae is a process.

Definition 3.5 : A *template specification* TSPEC $=$ (TSIG, AX) consists of a template signature TSIG and a set of axioms AX in template logic.

The semantics [TSPEC] of a template specification TSPEC is given by translation into template logic. By the semantics of the latter, the permissible situations and life cycles specified by a template specification are characterized.

Thus, the semantics of a template specification is the most liberal behavior permitted by the axioms.

Example 3.6 : Referring to example 3.1, the attribute and action sections of the PERSON template determine the template signature in an obvious way. In the valuation section, clauses of the form $[\alpha]a = t$ are translated to formulae $\odot \alpha \wedge t = v \Rightarrow Oa = v$ where v is a value of appropriate sort. Permission clauses of the form $\{b\}\alpha$ are translated to $\triangleright\alpha \Rightarrow b$. Obligation clauses of the form $\{b\} \Rightarrow \alpha$ are translated to $b \Rightarrow \Diamond\odot\alpha$. More elaborate templates need more translation rules, we refer to [42] for further details.

4 Specialization, Generalization and Roles

Specialization means to add properties, i.e., attributes and actions. In TROLL, dynamic specialization can be expressed, i.e., *roles* that an object can temporarily play. The life cycle segment between entering and leaving a role is called a *phase*. During a life cycle, an object may enter and leave several phases of the same role.

Referring to example 3.1, we specify the patient concept as a role of person.

Example 4.1 : At times, a person can be a patient. A PATIENT has a temperature as a local attribute which is only visible when she is a patient. Similarly, there is a local massage action. The local fall-ill and recover actions serve as entry into and exit from the phase, respectively; they correspond to birth and death actions of objects.

```
object class PATIENT
    role of PERSON
    attributes
        temp:   [35..42];
    actions
        birth fall-ill;
        massage;
        death recover;
        ...
end template PATIENT.
```

We note in passing that a conventional specialization is a special case of a role, namely a permanent role entered with birth and left with death. TROLL offers special language expressions for permanent specialization.

The semantics of roles is straightforward. For example, the `birth fall-ill` clause in the above example is translated to

$$\odot\texttt{fall-ill} \Rightarrow O(\sqrt{}\texttt{massage} \wedge \sqrt{}\texttt{recover} \wedge \forall t \epsilon\, [35..42] : (\sqrt{}r(\texttt{temp}, t) \wedge \sqrt{}w(\texttt{temp}, t))$$

$$\wedge(\neg\triangleright\texttt{fall-ill} \cup \odot\texttt{recover})).$$

Please note that the birth event of a role has to be visible outside that role: it must be possible for it to occur there. So `fall-ill` is in fact a PERSON action.

Definition 5.4 : For $i \in \{1,2\}$, let $\text{TSPEC}_i = (\text{TSIG}_i, \text{AX}_i)$ be template spec-ifications. A *template specification morphism* $h : \text{TSPEC}_1 \rightarrow \text{TSPEC}_2$ is a tem-plate signature morphism $h : \text{TSIG}_1 \rightarrow \text{TSIG}_2$ preserving the axioms, i.e., satisfying $\text{AX}_2 \models \ll h \gg (\text{AX}_1)$.

The semantics of a template specification morphism is a corresponding projection in the reverse direction. In the person-patient example, the projection reduces patient situations and life cycles to person situations and life cycles: from each patient situation in each patient life cycle, we omit the special patient items, retaining only the items visible for persons. This projection map makes the idea of *ISA inheritance* precise: a patient "is a" person at the same time.

Let $h : \text{TSPEC}_1 \rightarrow \text{TSPEC}_2$ be a template signature morphism. The corresponding projection is the semantic map $[\![h]\!] : [\![\text{TSPEC}_2]\!] \rightarrow [\![\text{TSPEC}_1]\!]$ projecting each situation σ_2 in each life cycle in $[\![\text{TSPEC}_2]\!]$ onto $\ll h \gg^{-1} (\sigma_2)$. If h is a template *specification* morphism, then $[\![h]\!]([\![\text{TSPEC}_2]\!]) \subseteq [\![\text{TSPEC}_1]\!]$ holds, and vice versa. Referring to ex-amples 3.1 and 4.1, this means that the reduction of each permissible patient life cycle is a permissible person life cycle, but not all permissible person life cycles need to be obtained this way. This reflects the fact that a person's behavior might be restricted when being a patient.

Also the semantics of generalization can be made precise with template specification morphisms and their semantic reduction maps. In example 4.1, the customer template can be considered to be embedded into the person and company templates. The two template signature morphisms are given by the renaming clause. Since axioms are meant to be preserved, we have template specification morphisms $h_p : \text{CUSTOMER} \rightarrow \text{PERSON}$, and $h_c : \text{CUSTOMER} \rightarrow \text{COMPANY}$. The common source indicates that persons and companies *share* the property of being a customer.

In fact, template specification morphisms and corresponding reduction functors are a very powerful mathematical tool for describing semantics of TROLL language features. Not only specialization and generalization as well as their dynamic versions can be captured but also aggregation and interfacing. We will elaborate on these issues in the next sections.

We note in passing that template specifications and template specification mor-phisms constitute a category which is small cocomplete. Colimits reflect the composi-tion of template specifications with shared templates. On the semantic side, processes over situations and their reduction maps constitute a semantic category which is small complete. Limits reflect parallel composition of processes. The syntactic map $\ll . \gg$ is a continuous functor, and the semantic map $[\![.]\!]$ is a cocontinuous functor. Our template specification logic with its syntax and semantics constitute an *institution* [44].

6   Aggregation and Interaction

Template specification morphisms and corresponding reduction functors are an appro-priate mathematical tool for giving semantics to aggregation of templates into complex templates, too. Complex templates characterize complex objects having other objects as components.

In this section, we also give a brief account of the TROLL approach to *interaction*. The reason why we describe interaction here is that objects which interact have to be considered together with their environment in which the communication takes place, the "medium" so to speak. This environment constitutes a complex object with the interacting objects as components.

We give a simple example of an aggregated template for complex TEAM objects.

Example 6.1 : A TEAM consists of a COACH and PLAYERS. The COACH is a person, and the PLAYERS are a list of persons. For the latter, we assume a complex template LIST(PERSON) built from PERSON by including list operations like insertion, deletion, etc.

```
template TEAM
    components
        coach:   PERSON;
        players:  LIST(PERSON);
        ...
end template TEAM.
```

The inclusions of components into a complex template constitute obvious examples of template specification morphisms. In example 6.1 above, we have inclusions coach : PERSON $\hookrightarrow$ TEAM and players : LIST(PERSON) $\hookrightarrow$ TEAM. These are other instances of *substitution inheritance*: wherever a person is expected as a parameter, we may submit a coach of a team via his inclusion as fitting morphism, etc.

On the semantic side, we have corresponding projections to the parts, e.g., [coach] : [TEAM] $\to$ [PERSON] and [players] : [TEAM] $\to$ [LIST(PERSON)], respectively. This is very much like *ISA inheritance*, but the relationship is between templates for *different* objects rather than aspects of the same object. Therefore, we suggest to speak of *HASA inheritance*: a team "has a" coach, etc.

As mentioned above, interaction is best viewed as happening between the components of complex objects, with the complex object as "communication medium". In TROLL, the basic interaction mechanism is *action calling* which is a synchronous and directed mode of communication.

Example 6.2 : The following template specification fragment adds interaction clauses to the TEAM template in example 6.1.

```
        ...
    interactions
        coach.calls-players(i) >> players(i).hears-coach;
        players(i).scores >> coach.cheers;
        players(i).fouls >> coach.curses;
        ...
```

The intended meaning should be obvious. The semantics of interaction clauses is given by translation into appropriate axioms in template logic. A clause of the form $c.\alpha >> d.\beta$ is translated to $\Box(\odot c.\alpha \Rightarrow \odot d.\beta)$. Of course, if $\odot c.\alpha$ happens in a situation, then $\triangleright d.\beta \land \sqrt{d.\beta}$ must hold true. That means that $d.\beta$ must be visible and enabled, otherwise it cannot occur.

These translations contribute to establish the formal template specification associated with a TROLL specification text.

TROLL also allows for a symmetric mode of interaction, namely *action sharing*. For all intents and purposes, action sharing is equivalent to mutual calling. Thus, the semantics is easily captured by replacing $\Rightarrow$ by $\Leftrightarrow$ in the above semantic clause.

7   Interfaces

Template specification morphisms and corresponding reduction functors are also useful for formalizing the semantics of *interfaces*. However, we have one more complication here: interfacing may introduce spontaneous attribute changes and other nondeterministic behavior – and it usually will!

As an example, consider read-only database views: many changes to the database state are observable but not explainable from local actions – they appear to be spontaneous.

Example 7.1 : In the following example of an automatic teller machine (ATM) template, the bank's full access to all services is restricted by the customer interface, hiding, say, the amount of money available in the machine as well as the refill action. This introduces nondeterminism: after the same manipulation sequences, say, to withdraw money, the customer may observe different reactions. Only the bank knows why: sometimes the amount available is sufficient, sometimes not.

```
template ATM-CUSTM
   encapsulating ATM-BANK
      ...
   attributes ...;
      READY: bool;
      ...
   actions ...;
      read-card(card:cardtype);
      accept-card;
      reject-card;
      deliver(amount:money);
      ...
      ...
end template ATM-CUSTM.
```

The ATM-BANK template contains the ATM-CUSTM template given above, together with the amount-available:money attribute and the refill(amount:money) action. Thus, we

have a template inclusion ATM-CUSTM ↪ ATM-BANK which is a template specification morphism. The semantics is given by the interface restriction [ATM-BANK] → [ATM-CUSTM]
defining the restricted view of the customer on the machine's services and behavior.

The template inclusion ATM-CUSTM ↪ ATM-BANK is another instance of *substitution inheritance*: wherever the customer view of an ATM is expected as a parameter, the bank view can serve the purpose via the inclusion as fitting morphism. On the semantic level, we have the corresponding *ISA inheritance*: the bank "is a" customer of its own ATMs since it has access to all customer services.

TROLL also supports join interfaces to several templates simultaneously. This is equivalent to an interface to the aggregation of the templates in question. Another feature, however, is to *share* an interface among several templates. This is currently not supported by TROLL. Sharing interfaces can be viewed as a generalization of action sharing: whatever happens or is visible in the shared interface occurs simultaneously in all templates sharing it. In a sense, shared interfaces are like "channels" combining the participating templates in a strictly synchronous way.

8   Concluding Remarks

In this paper, we give precise explanations for basic object-oriented features, focussing on the semantic concepts underlying TROLL. We demonstrate that our template specifi-
cation logic is a powerful enough tool to give complete semantic descriptions of TROLL, TROLL *light*, and similar languages. In particular, the dynamic parts of object creation and deletion, as well as role entry and exit, can conveniently be dealt with.

Of course, this paper does not give a complete description of TROLL, we concentrate on particular aspects and simple examples. A more comprehensive introduction into TROLL features is given in the companion paper in this volume [12]. Moreover, the interested reader is referred to the language reports [10, 19].

The TROLL languages are based on concepts from semantic modeling, algebraic specification and specification of reactive systems, combining the advantages of these approaches. They offer a variety of structuring mechanisms for specification so that system specifications can be constructed from components that can be analysed locally. Language features not discussed in this paper give support for data type specification for attribute values, derived attributes, derived actions, derived components, integrity constraints, initiative, explicit process description, etc. New language features are under discussion including in-the-large concepts like reification, parameterization, mod-
ules and libraries, supporting reuse by modularizing the system architecture.

One fundamental concept which has hardly been mentioned is *instances*. The idea is that objects are named instances of (role clusters of) templates, but the picture has to be detailed carefully. An object instance runs through states. The state tells what the current values of attributes are, which actions are enabled and in scope, which actions are occurring, and what the object's "rest" process is which it can pursue from the current state on. The *operational semantics* of a schema should tell precisely how

Similarly, the `death recover` clause in the above example is translated to

$$\odot\text{recover} \Rightarrow O(\neg\sqrt{}\text{massage}\wedge\neg\sqrt{}\text{recover}\wedge\forall t\,\epsilon\,[35..42] : (\neg\sqrt{}r(\text{temp},t)\wedge\neg\sqrt{}w(\text{temp},t))$$
$$\wedge(\triangleright\text{fall-ill})).$$

It might not be obvious, but a local role attribute a keeps its last value v until the next phase of the same role. All the time between the phases, $a = v$ holds true, i.e., this formula is in the situations. But $r_a(v)$ and $w_a(v)$ are not in scope. So a is "not accessible" between the phases. But it is possible to reason with $a = v$. As soon as $r_a(v)$ and $w_a(v)$ become visible again, a can be accessed displaying its last value v.

Generalization is the inverse of specialization: we want to specify an aspect that several templates specified so far have in common.

Example 4.2 : Persons and companies can both be customers of a bank. Given templates PERSON and COMPANY, we can specify the bank CUSTOMER concept as follows.

```
template CUSTOMER
    generalization of PERSON, COMPANY
        data types ...
    attributes
        name:  string;
        address:  string;
        account-no:  nat;
        ...
    actions
        open-account(account-no:  nat);
        close-account(account-no:  nat);
        ...
    renaming ...
        ...
end template CUSTOMER.
```

The attributes and actions listed here are assumed to occur in PERSON and COMPANY as well. Since the latter have been specified before, it is not certain that "the same" attributes and actions have the same names, they may have been chosen independently by different specifiers. That is why the **renaming** clause is necessary: it allows for chosing arbitrary names in CUSTOMER and relating them to the corresponding local names in PERSON and COMPANY.

TROLL favors only static generalization, though one can imagine temporary generalized roles like persons and companies being customers only from time to time, not permanently. Forthcoming language versions will probably include dynamic generalization.

The semantics of static generalization can be defined very simply, namely by textual inclusion of the constituent templates, applying appropriate renaming. This semantics, however, is not satisfactory: it is "flat". It doesn't reflect the fact that, for instance,

PERSON, COMPANY and CUSTOMER are separate pieces of specification text. Each should have a meaning of its own, obtaining the meaning of the whole by appropriate composition of the meanings of the parts.

This idea is elaborated in the next section.

5   Template Relationships

The PATIENT template in example 4.1 doesn't stand alone, it refers to the PERSON template in example 3.1. In PATIENT, all items of PERSON are visible as if PERSON were a textual part of PATIENT.

Similarly, the CUSTOMER template in example 4.2 can be regarded as a textual part of both the PERSON and the COMPANY templates, albeit modulo renaming: the former specifies a common visible part of the latter.

Textual embedding of template specifications, possibly with renaming, is a general kind of relationship which occurs in many constructions. The embedding preserves the specification structure, it is an example of a *template specification morphism* to be defined below. Specification morphisms make *substitution inheritance* precise: wherever a PERSON template is expected as a parameter, a PATIENT template can be submitted, to be adapted via the fitting morphism PERSON↪PATIENT. And wherever a CUSTOMER template is expected, a PERSON as well as a COMPANY template can be submitted, to be adapted via the fitting morphism CUSTOMER↪PERSON or CUSTOMER↪COMPANY, respectively.

For simplicity, we assume that the underlying data signature is the same for all templates. We refer to the concept of data signature morphism well known from abstract data type theory [29, 30]. Attribute and action signature morphisms are defined in very much the same way.

Definition 5.1 : For $i \in \{1, 2\}$, let $\text{ATT}_i = \{\text{ATT}_{i;x,s}\}_{x \in S^*, s \in S}$ be attribut signatures. An *attribute signature morphism* $f : \text{ATT}_1 \to \text{ATT}_2$ is a family of maps $f = \{f_{x,s} : \text{ATT}_{1;x,s} \to \text{ATT}_{2;x,s}\}_{x \in S^*, s \in S}$.

Definition 5.2 : For $i \in \{1, 2\}$, let $\text{ACT}_i = \{\text{ACT}_{i;x}\}_{x \in S^*}$ be action signatures. An *action signature morphism* $g : \text{ACT}_1 \to \text{ACT}_2$ is a family of maps $g = \{g_x : \text{ACT}_{1;x} \to \text{ACT}_{2;x}\}_{x \in S^*}$.

Combining these morphisms in an obvious way, we arrive at the definition of a template signature morphism.

Definition 5.3 : For $i \in \{1, 2\}$, let $\text{TSIG}_i = (\text{ATT}_i, \text{ACT}_i)$ be template signatures. A *template signature morphism* $h : \text{TSIG}_1 \to \text{TSIG}_2$ is a pair $h = (f, g)$ where $f : \text{ATT}_1 \to \text{ATT}_2$ is an attribute signature morphism, and $g : \text{ACT}_1 \to \text{ACT}_2$ is an action signature morphism.

As is usual (and obvious), a template signature morphism h defines a translation, i.e., a map, from TSIG_1 formulae to TSIG_2 formulae. We denote this map by $\ll h \gg$. Taking the axioms into account, we obtain the notion of template specification morphism.

the states of objects look like and how they change. In particular, it should make precise how the states of aggregated objects are composed from those of the parts. Ultimately, the state of the entire object population is characterized as an aggregation of the states of its members.

However, the concept of (central) state is not always adequate, for instance if the system is truly distributed, i.e., without some central coordination. Here we come to the limits of our object model: as it is, it does not capture truly distributed cases. It is good practice to identify large portions of the system where a central state makes sense, for instance the sites of the distributed system, so here we can use our approach. Giving a logics and semantics for an entire truly distributed system, however, would require to substitute our process model by another one, involving true concurrency and distributed states. Petri nets may be a good idea. We are confident that it is possible to substitute other process models into our approach.

There is another fundamental issue of object-orientation which is not treated in this paper, namely *reification*. Reification means to give a more detailed description on a lower abstraction level, for attributes as well as for actions. For instance, actions have to be reified by transactions which have to maintain atomicity on the abstract level while being not really atomic on the lower level. It remains to be investigated what an appropriate semantic concept for reification is, how reification can be described by suitable language features, and what an appropriate notion of correctness is in this framework. Naturally, the issue of (hierarchic) transaction management comes in here, among others.

It should be pointed out that the reification relationship we have in mind is between objects and objects, not to be confused with satisfaction of specifications by objects, and not with specification refinement either. That is, what we have in mind is software layers sitting on top of each other within running systems.

It is commonplace that *modularization* is of paramount importance to software construction and reconstruction. The object concept itself is a sort of modularization principle, but a rather in-the-small one. For effective software reuse, we need an in-the-large concept which makes it possible to put building blocks into a library, find the ones we need and put them together effectively.

Such software modules should have standardized interfaces by which they easily fit together – like LEGO bricks. At least two interfaces are indispensible: a "downward" one for accepting lower-level services, and an "upward" one for providing higher-level services. Hidden in its body, the module should have correctly implemented the latter on top of the former. Often, it is necessary to have more than one "upward" interface, like databases with multiple views.

That is, reification as explained above is one of the essential concepts for software modules.

Situations are becoming rare where we have to build *new* software. Reusing and adapting old software is greatly supported by a module concept which tells how to encapsulate *existing* software and put it together with other software.

Software is rarely designed for one specific purpose, and it is rarely reused in exactly the same way as it was once implemented. What is needed is a way to make modules *generic* and being able to *instantiate* them with different actual parameters. This way, a module can fit flexibly into many environments, reducing the need for costly ad-hoc redesign and reimplementation.

Therefore, what is needed is a concept for parameterization and instantiation of software modules.

Reification, modularization and parameterization are currently not supported by TROLL. Appropriate language features are under discussion, together with foundational work on appropriate semantic models to formalize these concepts.

Acknowledgements

We gratefully acknowledge inspirations, discussions, suggestions and criticisms that we have received within the ISCORE project, the TU Braunschweig information systems group, and the INESC Lisbon computer science group. Especially, we appreciate contributions by Gunter Saake and Martin Gogolla who are in charge of the TROLL and TROLL *light* projects, respectively.

References

1. H.-D. Ehrich, J. A. Goguen, and A. Sernadas. A Categorial Theory of Objects as Observed Processes. In J.W. deBakker, W.P. deRoever, and G. Rozenberg, editors, *Proc. REX/FOOL Workshop*, pages 203–228, Noordwijkerhood (NL), 1990. LNCS 489, Springer, Berlin.

2. H.-D. Ehrich, M. Gogolla, and A. Sernadas. Objects and their Specification. In M. Bidoit and C. Choppy, editors, *Proc. 8th Workshop on Abstract Data Types (ADT'91)*, pages 40–65. Springer, Berlin, LNCS 655, 1992.

3. H.-D. Ehrich and A. Sernadas. Fundamental Object Concepts and Constructions. In G. Saake and A. Sernadas, editors, *Information Systems – Correctness and Reusability*, pages 1–24. TU Braunschweig, Informatik Bericht 91-03, 1991.

4. H.-D. Ehrich, G. Saake, and A. Sernadas. Concepts of Object-Orientation. In *Proc. of the 2nd Workshop of "Informationssysteme und Künstliche Intelligenz: Modellierung", Ulm (Germany)*, pages 1–19. Springer IFB 303, 1992.

5. J. Fiadeiro, C. Sernadas, T. Maibaum, and G. Saake. Proof-Theoretic Semantics of Object-Oriented Specification Constructs. In R. Meersman, W. Kent, and S. Khosla, editors, *Object-Oriented Databases: Analysis, Design and Construction (Proc. 4th IFIP WG 2.6 Working Conference DS-4, Windermere (UK))*, pages 243–284, Amsterdam, 1991. North-Holland.

6. A. Sernadas and H.-D. Ehrich. What Is an Object, After All? In R. Meersman, W. Kent, and S. Khosla, editors, *Object-Oriented Databases: Analysis, Design and Construction*

(Proc. 4th IFIP WG 2.6 Working Conference DS-4, Windermere (UK)), pages 39–70, Amsterdam, 1991. North-Holland.

7. C. Sernadas and J. Fiadeiro. Towards Object-Oriented Conceptual Modelling. *Data & Knowledge Engineering*, 6:479–508, 1991.

8. A. Sernadas, J. Fiadeiro, C. Sernadas, and H.-D. Ehrich. The Basic Building Blocks of Information Systems. In E. Falkenberg and P. Lindgreen, editors, *Information System Concepts: An In-Depth Analysis*, pages 225–246, Namur (B), 1989. North-Holland, Amsterdam, 1989.

9. G. Saake, R. Jungclaus, and H.-D. Ehrich. Object-Oriented Specification and Stepwise Refinement. In J. de Meer, V. Heymer, and R. Roth, editors, *Proc. Open Distributed Processing, Berlin (D), 8.-11. Okt. 1991 (IFIP Transactions C: Communication Systems, Vol. 1)*, pages 99–121. North-Holland, 1992.

10. R. Jungclaus, G. Saake, T. Hartmann, and C. Sernadas. Object-Oriented Specification of Information Systems: The TROLL Language. Informatik-Bericht 91-04, TU Braunschweig, 1991.

11. G. Saake. *Objektorientierte Spezifikation von Informationssystemen*. Teubner, Leipzig, 1993.

12. G. Saake, T. Hartmann, R. Jungclaus, and H.-D. Ehrich. Object-oriented design of information systems: TROLL language features. This volume.

13. J. Costa, A. Sernadas, and C. Sernadas. OBL-87: Manual do Utilizador. INESC, Lisbon, 1988.

14. A. Sernadas, C. Sernadas, and H.-D. Ehrich. Object-Oriented Specification of Databases: An Algebraic Approach. In P.M. Stoecker and W. Kent, editors, *Proc. 13th Int. Conf. on Very Large Databases VLDB'87*, pages 107–116. VLDB Endowment Press, Saratoga (CA), 1987.

15. H.-D. Ehrich, G. Denker, and A. Sernadas. Constructing Systems as Object Communities. In M.-C. Gaudel and J.-P. Jouannaud, editors, *Proc. TAPSOFT'93: Theory and Practice of Software Development*, pages 453–467. LNCS 668, Springer, Berlin, 1993.

16. A. Sernadas, C. Sernadas, P. Gouveia, P. Resende, and J. Gouveia. OBLOG—Object-Oriented Logic: An Informal Introduction. Internal report, INESC, Lisbon, 1991.

17. C. Sernadas, P. Resende, P. Gouveia, and A. Sernadas. In-The-Large Object-Oriented Design of Information Systems. In E. Falkenberg, C. Rolland, and E. N. El-Sayed, editors, *Information Systems Concepts: Improving the Understanding*, Alexandria, 1992. IFIP Transactions A, North-Holland, Amsterdam, 1992.

18. C. Sernadas, P. Gouveia, J. Gouveia, A. Sernadas, and P. Resende. The Reification Dimension in Object-Oriented Data Base Design. In D. Harper and M. Norrie, editors, *Specification of Data Base Systems*, pages 275–299. Springer-Verlag, London, 1992.

19. S. Conrad, M. Gogolla, and R. Herzig. TROLL *light*: A Core Language for Specifying Objects. Informatik-Bericht 92-02, TU Braunschweig, 1992.

20. N. Vlachantonis, R. Herzig, M. Gogolla, G. Denker, S. Conrad, and H.-D. Ehrich. Towards Reliable Information Systems: The KORSO Approach. In C. Rolland, F. Bodart, and C. Cauvet, editors, *Proc. 5th Int. Conf. on Advanced Information Systems Engineering (CAiSE'93)*, pages 463–482. Springer, Berlin, LNCS 685, 1993.

21. A. Sernadas. Temporal Aspects of Logical Procedure Definition. *Information Systems*, 5:167–187, 1980.

22. J. Fiadeiro and T. Maibaum. Temporal Theories as Modularisation Units for Concurrent System Specification. *Formal Aspects of Computing*, 4(3):239–272, 1992.

23. J. A. Goguen and J. Meseguer. Unifying Functional, Object-Oriented and Relational Programming with Logical Semantics. In B. Shriver and P. Wegner, editors, *Research Directions in Object-Oriented Programming*, pages 417–477. MIT Press, 1987.

24. J. Goguen and D. Wolfram. On types and foops. In R. Meersman, W. Kent, and S. Khosla, editors, *Object-Oriented Databases: Analysis, Design and Construction (Proc. IFIP WG 2.6 Working Conference DS-4)*, Windermere (UK), 1990. North-Holland, Amsterdam, 1991.

25. L. Rapanotti and A. Socorro. Introducing foops. Report PRG-TR-28-92, Programming Research Group, Oxford University Computing Lab, 1992.

26. E. Astesiano, A. Giovini, G. Reggio, and E. Zucca. An integrated algebraic approach to the specification of data types, processes, and objects. In *Algebraic Methods – Tools and Applications*, pages 91–116. LNCS 394, Springer-Verlag, Berlin, 1989.

27. J. Meseguer and X. Qian. A logical semantics for object-oriented databases. In *Proc. of the 1993 ACM SIGMOD Int. Conf. on Management of Data*, pages 89–98. SIGMOD Record Vol. 22, Issue 2, 1993.

28. B. Cohen, W. T. Harwood, and M. I. Jackson. *The Specification of Complex Systems.* Addison-Wesley, Reading, MA, 1986.

29. H.-D. Ehrich, M. Gogolla, and U.W. Lipeck. *Algebraische Spezifikation abstrakter Datentypen.* Teubner, Stuttgart, 1989.

30. H. Ehrig and B. Mahr. *Fundamentals of Algebraic Specification I: Equations and Initial Semantics.* Springer-Verlag, Berlin, 1985.

31. M. Hennessy. *Algebraic Theory of Processes.* The MIT Press, Cambridge, 1988.

32. C. A. R. Hoare. *Communicating Sequential Processes.* Prentice-Hall, Englewood Cliffs, NJ, 1985.

33. R. Milner. *Communication and Concurrency.* Prentice-Hall, Englewood Cliffs, 1989.

34. W. Reisig. *Petri Nets.* Springer-Verlag, Berlin, 1985.

35. G. Booch. *Object-Oriented Design.* Benjamin/Cummings, Menlo Park, CA, 1990.

36. P. Coad and E. Yourdon. *Object-Oriented Analysis.* Yourdon Press/Prentice Hall, Englewood Cliffs, NJ, 1989.

37. P.M.D. Gray, K.G. Kulkarni, and N.W. Paton. *Object-Oriented Databases: A Semantic Data Model Approach.* Prentice Hall, Englewood Cliffs, NJ, 1992.

38. I. Graham. *Object-Oriented Methods*. Addison Wesley, Reading, MA, 1991.

39. R. Hull and R. King. Semantic Database Modeling: Survey, Applications, and Research Issues. *ACM Computing Surveys*, 19(3):201–260, 1987.

40. J. Rumbaugh, M. Blaha, W. Premerlani, F. Eddy, and W. Lorensen. *Object-Oriented Modeling and Design*. Prentice-Hall, Englewood Cliffs, NJ, 1991.

41. C. Rolland and C. Cauvet. Trends and Perspectives in Conceptual Modeling. In P. Loucopoulos and R. Zicari, editors, *Conceptual Modeling, Databases, and Case*, pages 27–48. John Wiley & Sons, New York, 1992.

42. R. Jungclaus. *Modeling of Dynamic Object Systems—A Logic-Based Approach*. Advanced Studies in Computer Science. Vieweg Verlag, Braunschweig/Wiesbaden, 1993.

43. A. Sernadas, C. Sernadas, and J. F. Costa. Object Specification Logic. Research report, INESC/DMIST, Lisbon (P), 1992. *To appear in Journal of Logic and Computation*.

44. J.A. Goguen and R. Burstall. Institutions: Abstract Model Theory for Specification and Programming. *Journal of the ACM*, 39:95–146, 1992.

OBJECT-ORIENTED DESIGN OF INFORMATION SYSTEMS: TROLL LANGUAGE FEATURES

G. Saake, T. Hartmann, R. Jungclaus and H-D. Ehrich
Technical University of Braunschweig, Braunschweig, Germany

Abstract

We present features of the language TROLL for the abstract specification of information systems. Information systems are regarded to be reactive systems with a large database. Before we present the constructs of TROLL, we briefly explain the basic ideas on which the language relies. The Universe of Discourse is regarded to be a collection of interacting objects. An object is modeled as a process with an observable state. The language TROLL allows for the integrated description of structure and behavior of objects. We explain the abstraction mechanisms provided by TROLL, namely roles, specialization, and aggregation. To support the description of systems composed from objects, the concepts of relationships and interfaces may be used.

1 Introduction

Information systems represent the relevant aspects of a portion of the real world (referred to as the Universe of Discourse (*UoD*) in the sequel) that are to be computerized. As such, an information system is capable of storing, processing and producing data about the UoD and thus is embedded in the UoD. The stored information changes over time according to interactions with the environment or predefined internal functions. Thus, information systems are *dynamic* in the sense that they may be regarded to be

---

*This work was partially supported by CEC under ESPRIT-II Basic Research Working Group 6071 IS-CORE II (Information Systems – COrrectness and REusability). The work of Ralf Jungclaus and Thorsten Hartmann is supported by Deutsche Forschungsgemeinschaft under Sa 465/1-3.

reactive systems [1] (note that we do not address the evolution of the schema). That is, an information system subsumes data, behavior and knowledge about both data and behavior. Recent trends in information systems research concern the distribution of information over (heterogeneous) systems and interoperability between cooperative systems, as information systems are increasingly used in a decentralized manner.

Information systems represent increasingly large and complex UoD's. Thus, adequate means to support the *design* are becoming more and more important. The design starts with collecting and representing *knowledge* about the UoD, which covers the relevant static and dynamic aspects [2]. In this phase, it is highly irrelevant to know *how* these aspects are implemented, thus a modeling approach should support a *declarative* description. As in engineering, the design process should produce *models* of solutions that can be assessed formally before any concrete system is implemented. Thus, formal specifications of mathematical models should be made as early as possible in the development process of information systems.

In this paper, we give an introduction to the language TROLL. TROLL is a specification language suitable for the description of the UoD and the information system on a high level of abstraction. TROLL is a logic-based language to describe properties and behavior of dynamic (cooperative) systems in an object-oriented way. That is, the specification is structured in objects. As far as possible, knowledge is localized in objects. Objects may interact by synchronous communications. Thus, a system is regarded as a collection of interacting objects. In these objects, the description of structure (by means of properties and components) and behavior over time (by means of processes over abstract events) is integrated. Collections of objects are further structured using the concepts of classification, specialization, generalization, and aggregation. Interactions and global assertions can be specified apart from object specifications to describe system properties and the overall behavior of systems.

The approach evolved from integrating work on algebraic specification of data types [3, 4] and databases [5, 6], process specification [7, 8], the specification of reactive systems [9, 1, 10], conceptual modeling [11, 12, 13, 14, 15] and knowledge representation [16, 17, 18]. The concept of object used as a basis for TROLL has been developed in [19, 20, 21] accompanied by work on a categorical semantics [22, 23]. Based on this formal concept, work has been done towards a logical framework of structured theories over a suitable logical calculus [24, 25]. First versions of the language introduced in this paper have appeared in [26, 27, 28, 29]. A complete description can be found in [30].

The paper is structured as follows: In the next section, we explain the basic ideas behind TROLL. We give a motivation for using an object-oriented approach and introduce informally the concept of object that underlies our language. In section 3, we show how objects as the basic system components can be specified. In section 4, we introduce abstraction mechanisms to construct objects from objects. In section 5, mechanisms to relate objects to build systems are presented. In the last section, we summarize and briefly discuss further research issues.

2   Basic Ideas behind TROLL

TROLL tries to integrate ideas from conceptual modeling (in the tradition of the ER-approach) and the specification of reactive systems with the object-oriented paradigm. This paradigm has been attracted a lot attention in different fields of computer science. In the software engineering community, object-orientation has taken the way up from programming (e.g. [31, 32]) to design (for a survey see [33]) and has already entered analysis (e.g. [34, 35]). In the database community, object-oriented databases have been very popular in recent years [36, 37, 38, 39, 40]. According to traditional research issues, each community puts special emphasis on certain aspects of object-orientation [41]

Traditionally, many notations for conceptual modeling have been *entity-based* in the sense that they look at the world consisting of interrelated entities [11]. Whereas entity-based notations emphasize *structural* aggregation, abstraction and inheritance, most object-oriented notations being around currently emphasize *behavioral* aggregation and inheritance. In conceptual modeling, *both* structural and behavioral aspects should be paid equal attention. Additionally, *temporal* aspects like precedence relationships between state transitions or possible life cycles and global aspects are of interest [42]. Temporal aspects in system specification have been addressed by approaches to use *temporal logic* (see e.g. [1]) in conceptual modeling of databases and information systems [9, 43, 10].

The basic idea is to integrate all static and dynamic aspects local to an entity (or object) in an *object description*. Object descriptions are thus encapsulated units of structure and behavior description. An object instance has an internal state that can be observed and changed exclusively through an object *interface*. In contrast to object-oriented programming languages that emphasize a functional manipulation interface (i.e. *methods*), object-oriented databases put emphasis on the observable structure of objects (through *attributes*). We propose to support both views in an equal manner, i.e. the structural properties of objects may be observed through attributes and the behavior of objects may be manipulated through *events* which are abstractions of state changing operations.

The encapsulation of all local aspects in object descriptions implies that object descriptions are the *units of design*. Following this perspective, we may model the system *and* its environment in a uniform way. We achieve in having clean interfaces between components that are part of the environment and components that are to be computerized later on. This approach results in having higher levels of modularity and abstraction in the early phases of system design.

An object description usually is regarded as a description of possible instances of the same kind which is similar to the notion of *type* in semantic data modeling. In object-oriented programming, the notion of type is closely related to (and sometimes even mixed up with) the notion of *class*. In our view, a class defines a *collection* of instances of the same type. Objects can be composed from other objects (*aggregation*).

Aggregation of objects imposes a *part-of* relation on a collection of object-descriptions. This kind of inheritance is known from semantic data models where it is used to model objects that appear in several roles in an application. Object descriptions may also be embedded in a *specialization* hierarchy. Usually, specialization implies reuse of specification code and allows to treat instances both as instances of the base class and the specialization class. A related concept is *generalization* that allows to treat conceptually different instances uniformly as instances of the generalization class.

Besides the structuring mechanisms mentioned above, a means to describe the *interaction* of object instances is needed to specify system dynamics. For conceptual modeling, we have to abstract from implementation-related details that arise from using message-passing and process communication. Communication is modeled conceptually by *calling* or *identifying* events of interrelated objects.

We do not present a detailed discussion of the basic ideas and their formalization here but refer instead to the accompanying paper by Hans-Dieter Ehrich, Ralf Jungclaus, Grit Denker and Amílcar Sernadas in this volume [44].

3   Specification of Objects

Throughout the rest of this paper, we use fragments of the following example taken from commercial applications. A bank maintains a number of accounts for customers. It also owns a number of automatic teller machines (ATMs) that are operated remotely. Accounts have the usual properties such that they may not be overdrawn etc. Associated with a checking account is a number of cash cards that can be used to withdraw money at an ATM. An ATM accepts a cash card, communicates with the user and the bank to carry out the transaction and dispenses cash if the transaction was successful and the ATM is not empty. The bank coordinates the card verification requests and the bank transactions issued concurrently from the ATMs.

In this section, we introduce object descriptions. The body of an object description is called *template*. In a template, the *signature* (the interface) as well as the structure and behavior of an object is described. A simple template may include the following sections:

template [*template name*]
   data types *import of data type signatures*
   attributes *attribute name and type declarations*
   events *event name and parameter declaration*
   constraints *static and dynamic constraints on attribute values*
   derivation *rules for the derivation of attributes and events*
   valuation *effects of events on attributes*
   behavior
      permissions *enabling conditions for event occurrences*
      obligations *completeness requirements for life cycles*

    patterns *transactions and scripts*
[**end template** *template name*]

A single object is defined by a proper name and a template. An object class is defined by a class name, a template and an identification mechanism. In TROLL, we declare *external identifiers*. External identifiers are elements of the carrier set of an abstract data type. Similar to primary keys in databases, external identifiers are tuples of atomic data values. The set of external identifiers and the template make up the *class type*. An external identifier along with the class name defines a unique identification for instances of that class. The set of identifiers for a class is called the *id space*. An id space is an isomorphic copy of the set of external identifiers of the associated class type. As a notational convention, we denote the id space of a class C with |C|. Please note that |C| is a data type. Associated with an id space is an operation that maps an external identifier to the corresponding element of the id space. As a convention, the name of this operation is the class name: C: *type of external identifier* -> |C|.

Consider now an example for the description of a class in TROLL, the specification of the class Account. For this and the following examples, we assume a simple enumeration data type UpdateType={deposit,withdraw} to be defined elsewhere. We assume data types in general to be specified independently from object specifications in a suitable algebraic framework (e.g. [3]). The signature of such datatypes is explicitly imported in each template.

The attribute and event declarations defined make up the *local signature* which is the alphabet for the template. For our account example, the signature is specified as follows:

attributes
    constant Holder:|BankCustomer|;
    constant Type:{checking,saving};
    Balance:money;
    Red:bool;
    CreditLimit:money;
    derived MaxWithdrawal:money;
events
    birth open(**in** Holder:|BankCustomer|,**in** Type:{checking,saving});
    death close;
    new_credit_limit(**in** Amount:money);
    accept_update(**in** Type:UpdateType, **in** Amount:money);
    withdrawal(**in** Amount:money);
    deposit(**in** Amount:money);
    update_failed;

The local signature defines the *interface* of instances since it introduces the names and parameters of all visible properties of an instance. In the Account-example, we declared the attributes `Holder`, `Type`, `Balance`, `Red`, `CreditLimit` and `MaxWithdrawal` along with their codomains, i.e. attributes in T$_{ROLL}$ are typed. `Holder` is a *constant* attribute, i.e. it will be instantiated at creation time of an instance and may not be altered throughout the lifetime of that instance. The value of the attribute `Holder` is an identifier of an instance of class `BankCustomer`, i.e. it is a reference to another object (which is, however, *not a component*). The attribute `Type` denotes whether the account is used as checking account or savings account. The value of the attribute `MaxWithdrawal` is derived from the values of the other attributes according to the rules given in the **derivation**-section of a template.

In the **events**-section, the event names and parameters are declared. At least one **birth**-event is required that denotes the creation of an instance. Optionally, we may declare **death**-events that denote the destruction of an instance but we may declare objects that live "forever". All other events denote a noteworthy change in the state of instances. Events may have formal parameters which allow to define the effects of events on attribute values or for data to be exchanged during communication. The keywords **in** and **out** are used to decide about the data-flow direction during communication.

In the **constraints**-section, we may impose restrictions on the observable states. For accounts, we state the following:

constraints
    initially Red = **false**;
    initially CreditLimit = 0;
    initially Balance = 0;
    initially (**sometime** (Balance > 100) **before** Red);
    Red => (Balance <= CreditLimit);
    Red => **sometimef**(**not** Red);
derivation
    { Red } ==> MaxWithdrawal = CreditLimit - Balance;
    { **not** Red } ==> MaxWithdrawal = Balance + CreditLimit;

Constraints with the keyword **initially** state conditions to be fulfilled with respect to the initial state after the **birth**-event occurred. For initial and ordinary constraints we admit *dynamic* constraints stated in future tense temporal logic [9, 43, 10]. Dynamic constraints describe how the values of attributes may evolve in the future. Consider the initial constraint

    initially ((**sometime** (Balance > 100) **before** Red);

which says that after an account has been opened, the balance must have been more that 100 before it can be overdrawn. The formula

    Red => **sometimef**(**not** Red);

states that if an account is in 'red condition', sometime in the future it has to leave this condition. Implicitly, constraints restrict the possible state transitions.

In the **derivation**-section, rules to compute the values of the derived attributes may be stated. For the Account-template, we have conditional expressions to compute the maximal amount of money that can be withdrawn in the current state depending on the value of the attribute Red.

The values of attributes may change with the occurrence of events. Thus, to describe the change of objects over time, we have to describe how the occurrence of events affect the values of attributes. *Valuation formulae* stated in the **valuation**-section of a template are based on a positional logic [45]. The **valuation**-section of our account example looks as follows:

```
valuation
   variables m:money;
   [new_credit_limit(m)]CreditLimit = m;
   { not Red and (m <= Balance)} ==> [withdrawal(m)]Balance = Balance-m;
   { not Red } ==> [deposit(m)]Balance = Balance+m;
   { not Red and (m > Balance)} ==>
      [withdrawal(m)](Balance = m-Balance), (Red = true);
   { Red } ==> [withdrawal(m)]Balance = Balance+m;
   { Red and (m >= Balance)} ==>
      [deposit(m)](Balance = m-Balance), (Red = false);
   { Red and (m < Balance)} ==> [deposit(m)]Balance = Balance-m;
```

Valuation formulae may be conditional like the following one:

```
{ not Red and (m <= Balance)} ==> [withdrawal(m)]Balance = Balance-m;
```

The rule will only be applied if the condition evaluates to **true**. The rule states that after the occurrence of the event withdrawal instantiated by a value m the attribute Balance will have the value of (Balance-m). The term on the right side of the equals sign is evaluated in the state *before* the event occurred. In the following rule, we state that the occurrence of an event has an effect on more than one attribute. In that case, we may use a list of effects:

```
{ not Red and (m > Balance)} ==>
      [withdrawal(m)](Balance = m-Balance), (Red = true);
```

We implicitly use a *frame rule* saying that attributes for which no effects of event occurrences are specified do not change their value after occurrences of such events.

A major part of an object description is the description of the behavior of instances. Let us first give the **behavior**-section of the Account template:

behavior
  permissions
    variables t,t1:UpdateType; m,m1,m2:money;
    { Balance = 0 } close;
    { **not sometime**(after(accept_update(t,m1)))
      since last(after(update_failed) **or**
              after(deposit(m2)) **or**
              after(withdrawal(m2)))} accept_update(t1,m);
    { **sometime**(after(accept_update(t,m)))
      since last after(accept_update(t1,m1)) **and**
      t = **withdraw and** (m > MaxWithdrawal)} update_failed;
    { **sometime**(after(accept_update(t,m)))
      since last after(accept_update(t1,m1)) **and**
      t = **deposit** } deposit(m);
    { **sometime**(after(accept_update(t,m)))
      since last after(accept_update(t1,m1)) **and**
      t = **withdraw and** (m <= MaxWithdrawal)} withdrawal(m);

Basically, we provide three sections. In the **permissions**-section, we may state enabling conditions for event occurrences. Events may only occur if the enabling condition is fulfilled. Thus, permissions state that something bad may never happen. The general form of permissions is

    { *(temporal) condition* } *event_term*;

Permissions may refer to the current observable state (*simple permissions*) or to the history of events that occurred in the life of an instance so far (*temporal permissions*). As an example for a simple permission look at the following rule that requires an account to be empty before it can be closed:

    { Balance = 0 } close;

For temporal permissions, we may state preconditions being formulae of a past tense temporal logic. It is defined analogously to the future tense temporal logic of [10, 46]. Besides the temporal quantifiers **sometime**, **always** and **previous** we may also use the bounded quantifiers **sometime ... since last ...** and **always ... since last ....** The following rule for example states that after a transaction has been completed with the occurrence of one of the events update_failed or deposit(m1) or withdrawal(m1), at most one event accept_update may occur (i.e. we do not allow to handle interleaved updates in an account):

{ **not sometime**(after(accept_update(t,m1)))
    since last(after(update_failed) **or**
            after(deposit(m2)) **or**
            after(withdrawal(m2))) } accept_update(t1,m);

In the **obligations**-section, we state completeness requirements for life cycles. These requirements must be fulfilled before the object is allowed to die. Usually, obligations depend on the history of the object. The following requirement states that once an event `accept_update(t,m)` occurs, this update must be completed eventually by an occurrence of one of the events `update_failed` or `deposit(m)` or `withdrawal(m)`:

```
{ after(accept_update(t,m)) } ==>
      deposit(m) or withdrawal(m) or update_failed;
```

A template makes up the body of a *class type definition*. A class then can be seen as a container for instances of the associated type. In a class type specification we define an *identification mechanism* along with the template. An identification mechanism describes the set of possible external identifiers of instances. Each external identifier will be mapped to an immutable internal surrogate.

Let us now give the specification of the class `Account` as a whole:

```
object class Account
  identification
    data types nat;
    No:  nat
  template
    data types |BankCustomer|,money,bool,UpdateType;
    attributes
      constant Holder:|BankCustomer|;
      constant Type:{checking, saving};
      Balance:money;
      Red:bool;
      CreditLimit:money;
      derived MaxWithdrawal:  money;
    events
      birth open(in Holder:|BankCustomer|,in Type:checking,saving);
      death close;
      new_credit_limit(in Amount:money);
      accept_update(in Type:UpdateType, in Amount:money);
      withdrawal(in Amount:money);
      deposit(in Amount:money);
      update_failed;
    constraints
      initially Red = false;
      initially CreditLimit = 0;
      initially Balance = 0;
      initially ((Balance > 100) before Red);
      Red => (Balance <= CreditLimit);
```

```
    Red => sometimef(not Red);
  derivation
    { Red } ==> MaxWithdrawal = CreditLimit - Balance;
    { not Red } ==> MaxWithdrawal = Balance + CreditLimit;
  valuation
    variables m:money;
    [new_credit_limit(m)]CreditLimit = m;
    { not Red and (m <= Balance)} ==>
      [withdrawal(m)]Balance = Balance-m;
    { not Red } ==> [deposit(m)]Balance = Balance+m;
    { not Red and (m > Balance)} ==>
      [withdrawal(m)](Balance = m-Balance), (Red = true);
    { Red } ==> [withdrawal(m)]Balance = Balance+m;
    { Red and (m >= Balance)} ==>
      [deposit(m)](Balance = m-Balance), (Red = false);
    { Red and (m < Balance)} ==> [deposit(m)]Balance = Balance-m;
  behavior
  permissions
    variables t,t1:UpdateType; m,m1,m2:money;
    { Balance = 0 } close;
    { not sometime(after(accept_update(t1,m1)))
      since last(after(update_failed) or
                 after(deposit(m2)) or
                 after(withdrawal(m2)))} accept_update(t,m);
    { sometime(after(accept_update(t,m)))
      since last after(accept_update(t1,m1)) and
      t = withdraw and (m > MaxWithdrawal)} update_failed;
    { sometime(after(accept_update(t,m)))
      since last after(accept_update(t1,m1)) and
      t = deposit } deposit(m);
    { sometime(after(accept_update(t,m)))
      since last after(accept_update(t1,m1)) and
      t = withdraw and (m <= MaxWithdrawal)} withdrawal(m);
end object class Account;
```

There is another means to describe the behavior of objects. Parts of life cycles (behavior *patterns*) may be described using a process language that draws on CSP [7] and LOTOS [47]. Examples for the use of this process language can be found in [30].

The last remaining basic language construct is the declaration of event synchronization by *event calling*. When events e_1 and e_2 are related by calling $(e_1 >> e_2)$, then the occurrence of e_1 forces e_2 to occur simultaneously. Thus, calling can be characterized as synchronous communication between the components of a complex object. Calling declarations are marked with the keyword **interaction**. For examples see the next section. Using parameters, we may specify the exchange of values during interactions (*communication*). The unification of uninstantiated variables with instantiated ones constitutes the flow of information. Calling is further discussed in [48, 49, 50] and [51, Section 7.2].

Templates are the building blocks of system specifications. As a first concept to structure system descriptions, we introduced classification. In the following section we want to introduce more concepts for the structuring of specifications.

4 Abstractions

System descriptions in TROLL can be structured in several ways. The mechanisms presented in this section are *roles*, *specialization*, and *aggregation*.

4.1 Roles and Specialization

Both concepts are related in the sense that they describe *is_a* relationships between object descriptions, i.e. each instance of a role / specialization class may be referred to as an instance of the base class, too.

4.1.1 Roles

The concept of *role* describes a dynamic (temporary) specialization of objects, i.e. a special view of objects [52]. As an example consider the roles customer or employee of persons. When looking at an object playing a role, we may want to know things that are not relevant for the base object. Thus, a role has additional properties, it is a more detailed description of the base object from a certain point of view.

Consider now an example. Suppose we have specified a template describing persons, called `Person`. The `Person` template is assumed to have the usual attributes like `Name`, `FirstName`, `Address`, `Birthdate` etc. The dynamics only cover attribute updates. In our bank world, let us now look at persons being customers:

```
object class BankCustomer
  role of Person
  template
    data types nat,set(nat);
    attributes
      Accts:set(nat);
    events
      birth bc_bank_customer;
      death cancel;
      active open_account(out Acct:nat);
      active close_account(in Acct:nat);
```

```
valuation
  variables n:nat;
  [bc_bank_customer]Accts = emptyset();
  [open_account(n)]Accts = insert(n,Accts);
  { in(n,Accts) } ==> [close_account(n)]Accts = remove(n,Accts);
behavior
  permissions
    variables n:nat;
    { sometime(after(open_account(n))) } close_account(n);
end object class BankCustomer;
```

In the template, we introduce new attribute and event symbols that extend the
Person signature. Here, we have an additional attribute Accts that clearly makes
sense only for bank customers.

A birth event for a role corresponds to an ordinary event of the base object and
denotes the start of playing a role. Each object may play a role several times. A
death-event of a role denotes that an object ceases to play a role (at least for that
moment).

In the BankCustomer-template, two other events are declared. Both are marked
active, which denotes that they may occur on the initiative of the BankCustomer
whenever they are permitted to.

Semantically, we have to deal with both syntactical and semantical inheritance.
Syntactically, the base template is included in the role template. The local specifications extend the base template. Semantically, each role instance includes the corresponding base instance. In our example this means that an instance of BankCustomer
includes the instance of Person of which it is a role. This way, a role instance may
access the base instance's attributes and may call the base instance's events.

4.1.2 Specialization

A special case of a role is the definition of a *specialization*. We decided to introduce
extra language features for this concept because it arises frequently in a system specification. Specialization describes that an object plays a role throughout its entire
lifetime. In conceptual modeling, this concept is known under the term *is-a* or *kind-of*.
A specialization hierarchy describes a *taxonomy* on objects.

For specializations, we do not have to describe the birth of a specialized object
explicitly since it corresponds to the birth event of the base instance. Thus, we do
not have to specify a birth event for a specialization. In case of a specialization, we
must provide a specialization condition, stating which objects belong to the specialized
object class.

As an example, consider two specializations of our Account: A savings account
(SavingsAccount) and a checking account (CheckingAccount). Both have special
properties in addition to their common ones which are described in the base template

Account. A special aspect of savings accounts is that the bank (usually) pays interest for it. Furthermore, the balance of a savings account is always non-negative, i.e. the credit limit is 0. Every once in a while, interest is paid (computed by some interesting function) and is added to the balance. Please note that we may not update directly the attribute Balance of the Account – we have to *call* explicitly the event deposit of the Account to update the Balance. The specialization class SavingsAccount is specified as follows:

```
object class SavingsAccount
  specializing Account where Type = saving;
    template
      data types real,date;
      attributes
        constant interest_rate:real;
        last_interest_paid:date;
      events
        pay_interest(in date:date);
      constraints
        alwaysf (CreditLimit = 0);
        alwaysf not Red;
      valuation
        variables d:date;
        [pay_interest(d)]last_interest_paid = d;
      behavior
        permissions
          variables d:date;
          { days_between(d,last_interest_paid) > 30 } pay_interest(d);
        interactions
          variables d:date;
          pay_interest(d) >>
                  deposit((days_between(d,last_interest_paid)/360) *
                    (Balance * interest_rate / 100)
                  );
end object class SavingsAccount;
```

Consider now the specialization class CheckingAccount. In our small UoD, we may assign cashcards to checking accounts. With each checking account, a constant personal identification number (PIN) is associated:

```
object class CheckingAccount
  specializing Account where Type = checking;
    template
      data types nat,|CashCard|,money;
```

```
    attributes
       constant PIN:nat;
       Cards:set(|CashCard|);
    events
       assign_card(in C:|CashCard|);
       cancel_card(in C:|CashCard|);
    constraints
       initially Cards = emptyset();
    valuation
       variables C:|CashCard|;
       [assign_card(C)]Cards = insert(C,Cards);
       { in(C,Cards)} ==> [cancel_card(C)]Cards = remove(C,Cards);
end object class CheckingAccount;
```

Note that we do not impose further restriction on the life cycles – cashcards may be assigned anytime, and for example the credit limit may be updated anytime due to the occurrence of the event new_credit_limit inherited from the base object (although this is not done on the initiative of a CheckingAccount-instance itself).

4.2   Composite Objects

Using the aggregation concept, we may construct objects from components. In the database community, this is also known as constructing *composite objects*. Basically, we can identify two kinds of composite objects [53]:

- *Disjoint* composite objects do not share any components. This implies that components cannot exist outside the composite object, they are strongly dependent and the components are *local* to the composite object. The composition is always static. Language features for defining disjoint composite objects in TROLL can be found in [30, 48, 50].

- *Non-disjoint* composite objects may share components. Thus, components are autonomous objects. In TROLL, we distinguish two kinds of non-disjoint composite objects: Dynamic composite objects may alter their composition through events whereas the composition of static composite objects is described through static predicates.

For disjoint and non-disjoint composite objects the components are encapsulated in the sense that their state may only be altered by events local to the components. Their attribute values, however, are visible. The coordination and synchronization between the composite object and its components or between the components must be done by communication. Let us now continue with the concepts of non-disjoint composite objects, that is static and dynamic aggregation.

4.2.1 Static Aggregation

The aggregation of static composite objects is described using predicates over identifiers and constants. In contrast to dynamic aggregation where the structure of the composite object may vary over time, the structure of a static composite object never changes. Specificationwise we describe the *possible* object composition not violating the constraints for aggregation. Possibly there are components belonging to the composite object that are not yet born.

For example let us consider the specification of an object Bank1. Suppose that we want to describe this Bank1 object including all possible Account objects. The specification may look as follows:

```
object Bank
  template
    including Account;
    data types |Account|,set(|Account|),nat;
    attributes
      TheAccounts:set(|Account|);
    events
      birth establish;
      death close_down;
      open_account(in No:nat);
      close_account(in No:nat); ...
    valuation
      variables n:nat;
      [open_account(n)]TheAccounts = insert(Account(n),TheAccounts);
      [close_account(n)]TheAccounts = remove(Account(n),TheAccounts);
    behavior
    permissions
      variables n,p,p1:nat; m,m1:money; t,t1:UpdateType;
      { not in(Account(n)) } open_account(n);
      { sometime after(open_account(n)) } close_account(n);
    interactions
      variables t:UpdateType; m:money; n:nat;
      open_account(n) >> Account(n).open;
      close_account(n) >> Account(n).close; ...
end object Bank;
```

In the interaction section communication between the composite object Bank and its components – the Accounts – is specified. Since the aggregated object is constructed from a set of accounts, we must use an operation Account : nat $\rightarrow$ |Account| to generate identifiers for included objects.

Identifiers are only *references* to objects, thus a second operation taking an object identifier and yielding the object itself is needed. Since there is no ambiguity – the accounts are *subobjects* of the bank – we could leave out the second operation, assuming that `Account(n)` delivers an object instance:

> `open_account(n) >> Account(n).open;`

In this case for example the `Bank` event `open_account(n)` calls the `Account` event `open` in component object `Account(n)`. Thus the creation and destruction of `Account` instances is triggered by the `Bank` object. Note that the conditional calling (intuitively) only occurs if the condition evaluates to true in the current state.

Let us now give a few words on the semantics. The signature of the `Bank` object is obtained by disjoint union of the (local) signatures of the `Bank` and the `accounts`. Since we included a set of objects we have to deal with indexed symbols. Indexing is denoted using the dot notation (for example `Account(n).open`). For the life cycle of the composite object we state that if we constrain a life cycle to the events of a component object, we have to obtain a valid life cycle of this component.

4.2.2 Dynamic Aggregation

The use of dynamic composite objects allows for a high level description of object composition. Components may be specified as *single components* as well as *sets* or *lists* of components. Again, properties of components must not be violated. Components have a life of their own and may be shared by other objects as well.

With the specification of a dynamic composite object denoted with the keyword **components** we have implicitly defined events to update the composition. Additionally we have implicit attributes to observe the composite object. For example for a *set* of component objects we have events to insert and delete objects and an attribute to observe set-membership. For *lists* of objects we have events to append and to remove objects and for *single* objects there are events to add and remove them as well as an attribute to test if the component is assigned. A complete list of implicitly generated events and attributes for each composite object construction can be found in the TROLL language report [30].

This view of composite objects is operational instead of declarative like the concept of static aggregation. Before we will say how dynamic aggregation fits in our semantic framework we will give an example :

object AnotherBank
  template
    data types nat,|ATM|,UpdateType,money,|CashCard|;
    components
      Depts:**LIST**(Department);
    events
      birth establish; **death** close_down;
      open_dept(**in** No:nat);
      close_dept(**in** No:nat);

```
behavior
  permissions
    variables n,p,p1:nat;
    { not Depts.IN(Department(n)) } open_dept(n);
    { sometime after(open_dept(n)) } close_dept(n);
    ...
  interaction
    variables ...,n:nat;
    open_dept(n) >> Depts.INSERT(Department(n));
    open_dept(n) >> Department(n).open;
    close_dept(n) >> Depts.REMOVE(Department(n));
    close_dept(n) >> Department(n).close;
    ...
end object AnotherBank;
```

In this example, we partially model AnotherBank object with a component list of Department objects. Initially, AnotherBank has no component. To manipulate the set of component accounts, the events Depts.INSERT(|Department|) and Depts.DELETE(|Department|) are automatically added to the signature of the AnotherBank object. For set components a parameterized, bool-valued attribute, in this example Depts.IN(|Department|):bool, is included.

For the behavior of the composite object the communication inside the composite object must be specified. Communication can take place between the component objects and between the composite object and the component objects. In this example only the latter case is used. See for example the clauses

```
open_dept(n) >> Department(n).open;
open_dept(n) >> Depts.INSERT(Department(n));
```

which state, that every time a department identified by the natural number n is opened, the event open is called in the corresponding object Department(n) and it becomes a member of the set of components. Note that the event open_dept in the Bank object may only occur if the expression not Depts.IN(|Department|) evaluates to true.

Let us now briefly look at the semantics of dynamic object aggregation. Since our concept of object only allows for static object composition, i.e. embedding the components into the composite object, we need to simulate dynamic composition using the concept of static aggregation. This is done in the following way: for each possible composition the corresponding template is obtained by including the object signatures of all objects that are part of this composite object. Whenever the composition changes, a new composite object is created in the same way and the old one is destroyed. The observable properties of the unchanged components remain the same in the new instance.

5   Specification of Systems

When it comes to describing systems of interacting objects, it is not sufficient to provide only the structuring mechanisms described in the previous section. In system specification, we have to deal with static and dynamic *relationships* between objects, with *interfaces*, and with *object societies*.

5.1   Relationships

Relationships connect objects that are specified independently. Basically, relationships are language constructs to describe how system components are connected in order to describe the whole system.

In TROLL, two types of relationships are supported:

- (global) *interactions* and

- (global) *constraints*.

5.1.1   Global Interactions

Global interactions describe communication between objects. We use the syntax for interactions inside complex objects. Global interactions along with the specifications of the connected objects describe patterns of communication between the connected objects (these patterns are called *scripts* elsewhere [12]). As usual, communication is described using event calling.

From a process point of view, relationships describe how the involved processes *synchronize*. In interaction specifications, we may want to refer to the history of events in the connected objects. Consider the interaction between an ATM and the Bank that maintains it. Here, we must put precedence rules into conditions for interactions to model the process of communication:

```
relationship RemoteTransaction between Bank,ATM
   interaction
      /* -- Card checking business */
      ATM(n).check_w_bank(a,p) >> Bank.check_card(a,p);
      {after(ATM(n).check_w_bank(a,p))} ==>
          Bank.card_OK >> ATM(n).card_OK;
      {after(ATM(n).check_w_bank(a,p))} ==>
          Bank.card_NOK >> ATM(n).card_not_OK;
      /* -- Bank transaction business */
      ATM(n).issue_TA(n,m) >> Bank.process_TA(n,m);
      {after(ATM(n).process_TA(a,m))} ==>
          Bank.TA_OK >> ATM(n).TA_ok;
      {after(ATM(n).process_TA(a,m))} ==>
```

```
     Bank.TA_failed >> ATM(n).TA_failed;
  end relationship RemoteTransaction;
```

For precedence rules, we may use the **after** predicate, which holds in a state immediately after the event being the argument occurred. The following clause e.g. states that an interaction induced by the calling of the TA_failed event in an ATM by the TA_failed event in the Bank may only take place if the event process_TA(a,m) occured immediatley before that in the ATM:

```
  {after(ATM(n).process_TA(a,m))} ==>
      Bank.TA_failed >> ATM(n).TA_failed;
```

Please note that we use a very simple execution model. A chain of calls may only be carried out if all called events are permitted to occur (atomicity principle) [49]. We are aware of the limitations of our approach with respect to exceptions and long transactions and plan to work on a more sophisticated model of execution.

5.1.2 Global Constraints

When we model systems by putting together objects, we sometimes have to state constraints that are to be fulfilled by related but independently specified objects. Such *global constraints* set up a relationship between objects. Consider the following example. When modeling our banking world, there may be a regulation that one particular bank customer may only be holder of at most one checking account. Please note that this is an example for a relationship since it cannot be specified to be local to *one* instance of the class CheckingAccount. In TROLL, this would be specified as follows:

```
relationship IB1 between CheckingAccount C1,CheckingAccount C2;
  data types |BankCustomer|,nat;
  constraints
     (C1.Holder=C2.Holder) => (C1.No=C2.No);
end relationship IB1;
```

Global constraints are specified using the same syntax as local constraints.

If a relationship between object classes contains both interactions and constraints, both sections may be specified together.

5.2 Interfaces

An object interface or object class interface is first of all a mechanism to describe access control to objects. Interfaces in TROLL support the explicit encapsulation of object properties. Access control is achieved by projecting the attribute and event symbols to external visible symbols. Interfaces may be defined for single objects as well as for object classes. For object classes, we may additionally define selection interfaces, thus restricting the visible population of the class to some proper subset. Selection interfaces resemble the well known views from relational databases [28].

The first example shows a simple class interface for ATM's seen by a customer:

```
interface class ATMToCustomer
  encapsulating ATM:
    data types bool,|CashCard|,nat,money;
    attributes
      dispensed:bool;
    events
      active ready;
      active read_card(in C:|CashCard|);
      card_accepted; bad_PIN_msg; bad_account_msg;
      active issue_TA(in Acct:nat,in Amount:money);
      active cancel;
      TA_failed_msg; eject_card;
      dispense_cash(in Amount:money);
end interface class ATMToCustomer;
```

The only observation for customers is the status of the ATM in terms of the bool-valued attribute dispensed. Information about the amount of money available inside the machine should (for obvious reason) not be public. An interface to dynamic objects must define also the possible operations visible at this level of system description. Here a customer should only be able to talk to the ATM at 'user level', i.e. (s)he must be able to insert cards, issue transactions, cancel the transaction and not at least dispense money. Customers must not be able to refill a machine or even remove it. Also they should not see details of the internal operations, for example the event check_card_w_bank is not relevant at 'user level'. The semantics of this simple kind of interface is just a signature restriction to the explicit noted event and attribute symbols.

Another kind of access restriction in contrast to the above mentioned projection interface is the selection interface. Suppose we only want customers to use ATM's identified by a natural number between 100 and 199:

```
interface class ATMToCustomer2
  encapsulating ATM
  selection
    where IdentNo >= 100 and IdentNo <= 199
  data types bool,...;
  attributes
    dispensed:bool;
  events
    ...
end interface class ATMToCustomer2;
```

Here the actual visible population is limited using a predicate over the external key. The semantics of this kind of interface definition is given by an object class specialization followed by a projection interface. The predicate used for the definition of the specialized class can be seen as a filter allowing only those instances to pass, that satisfy the selection condition evaluated locally to the object instances.

In general we do not only want to restrict the external object interface to some subset of events and attributes, but also be able to present derived properties of objects. We may specify views of an object where some information is explicitly computed from existing attributes. An example interface for the ATM class may be used for service personnel only. Suppose that we want to indicate machines that must be refilled to avoid a dispensed condition. Therefore this view defines a derived bool-valued attribute please_refill to be true for ATM's with CashOnHand below a threshold value of 1000:

```
interface class ATMToService
  encapsulating ATM
  data types bool,money;
  attributes
    please_refill:bool;
    dispensed:bool;
  events
    refill(in Amount:money);
    ...
  derivation
    please_refill = (CashOnHand <= 1000);
end interface class ATMToService;
```

Note that the derivation part is generally hidden from the view users. Technically, an interface with derived properties consists of a formal implementation step [21, 54] and an explicit projection interface. More general we can also look at specialized operations as a view on the dynamic part of objects. For example we may have users of the ATM that have to pay an extra charge for each bank transaction. Suppose that the ATM has an additional (may be constant) attribute extraCharge:money, denoting the amount of money to be withdrawn from the account:

```
interface class ATMToExtraUser
  encapsulating ATM
  data types money,bool,money;
  attributes
    extraCharge:money;
    dispensed:bool;
  events
    issue_TA_Extra(nat,money);
    ...
```

derivation
  calling
    variables n:nat, m:money;
    issue_TA_Extra(n,m) >> issue_TA(n,m+extraCharge)
end interface class ATMToExtraUser;

The attribute `extraCharge` is seen from the specialized user, since he should know about the extra charge. Each time this user issues an `issue_TA_Extra(n,m)` at this ATM, an additional extra charge is withdrawn.

Object interfaces have nothing to do with object copies. Interfaces are just a means to specify different views on objects, that is, to select special object populations out of the existing set of instances and to restrict the use of objects with respect to their observation and operation interface.

6 Conclusions and Outlook

In this paper, we have introduced an abstract specification language for information systems. Specifications are structured in objects. An object description includes the specification of structural properties and the specification of behavioral properties. For simple objects, attributes are used to describe static aspects of the object's state and events are used to describe the basic state transitions. The admissible temporal ordering of events is described using (temporal) enabling conditions (permissions), conditions to be guaranteed by objects (obligations), and explicit patterns of behavior. The evolution of the object's state depending on the actual behavior over time is described by valuation rules that specify the effects of event occurrences on attribute values.

Object descriptions are the basic units of structure. In TROLL, we may apply a number of abstraction mechanisms to object descriptions. Roles describe temporal (dynamic) specializations of objects. An object may play several roles concurrently and may play each role more than once. Specializations are roles which are fixed for the lifetime of an object. Using generalization, we may collect different objects under a common (virtual) class. Furthermore, we may describe objects that are constructed from components. Disjoint complex objects have components that are strongly dependent on the base object – such components may be described using subtemplates. Static and dynamic aggregation describe objects with components that may be shared between objects.

Object descriptions and their abstractions are the components of systems. They have to be connected in order to provide the services of a system. For this purpose, TROLL provides the features of relationships and interfaces. Relationships describe constraints and interactions between objects that are specified independently. Interfaces describe explicit views on objects and may be used to control access to system components.

TROLL offers a large number of constructs that are especially suited for the conceptual modeling of information systems at a very high level of abstraction. It combines features of conceptual modeling approaches and object-oriented approaches with formal approaches to data and process modeling. Providing objects as units of design, TROLL allows to achieve higher levels of modularity with clean but complete interface descriptions. Thus, the boundaries between the information system and the environment as well as the boundaries between data and processes become transparent.

Further work on TROLL will cover in-the-large issues like reuse, modularization above the object level, and parameterization. We plan to put another language level above TROLL with constructs that enable the construction of system descriptions from components of various grain.

In another direction, we are working on a language kernel which include those TROLL concepts that are suitable to describe (distributed) implementation platforms like operating systems and databases in an abstract way. This kernel language is regarded as an interface to an implementation platform. We then want to investigate the transformation of TROLL specifications into this kernel language. In our group, a dialect called TROLL*light* [55] has been developed as a simplified language especially suited for verification purposes.

Acknowledgements

For many fruitful discussions on the language we are grateful to all members of IS-CORE, especially to Amílcar Sernadas, Cristina Sernadas, José Fiadeiro, and Roel Wieringa.

References

1. Z. Manna and A. Pnueli. The Anchored Version of the Temporal Framework. In J. de Bakker, W. de Roever, and G. Rozenberg, editors, *Linear Time, Branching Tome and Partial Order in Logics and Models for Concurrency*, pages 201–284. LNCS 354, Springer-Verlag, Berlin, 1989.

2. J. J. van Griethuysen. Concepts and Terminology for the Conceptual Schema and the Information Base. Report N695, ISO/TC97/SC5, 1982.

3. H. Ehrig and B. Mahr. *Fundamentals of Algebraic Specification I: Equations and Initial Semantics*. Springer-Verlag, Berlin, 1985.

4. H.-D. Ehrich, M. Gogolla, and U.W. Lipeck. *Algebraische Spezifikation abstrakter Datentypen*. Teubner, Stuttgart, 1989.

5. H.-D. Ehrich. Key Extensions of Abstract Data Types, Final Algebras, and Database Semantics. In D. Pitt et al., editors, *Proc. Workshop on Category Theory and Computer Programming*, pages 412–433. Springer, Berlin, LNCS series, 1986.

6. H.-D. Ehrich, K. Drosten, and M. Gogolla. Towards an Algebraic Semantics for Database Specification. In R.A. Meersmann and A. Sernadas, editors, *Proc. 2nd IFIP WG 2.6 Working Conf. on Database Semantics "Data and Knowledge" (DS-2)*, pages 119–135, Albufeira (Portugal), 1988. North-Holland, Amsterdam.

7. C. A. R. Hoare. *Communicating Sequential Processes.* Prentice-Hall, Englewood Cliffs, NJ, 1985.

8. R. Milner. *Communication and Concurrency.* Prentice-Hall, Englewood Cliffs, 1989.

9. A. Sernadas. Temporal Aspects of Logical Procedure Definition. *Information Systems*, 5:167–187, 1980.

10. G. Saake. Conceptual Modeling of Database Applications. In D. Karagiannis, editor, *Proc. 1st IS/KI Workshop, Ulm (Germany), 1990*, pages 213–232. Springer, Berlin, LNCS 474, 1991.

11. P. P. Chen. The Entity-Relationship Model—Toward a Unified View of Data. *ACM Transactions on Database Systems*, 1(1):9–36, 1976.

12. J. Mylopoulos, P. A. Bernstein, and H. K. T. Wong. A Language Facility for Designing Interactive Database-Intensive Applications. *ACM Transactions on Database Systems*, 5(2):185–207, 1980.

13. M. Brodie, J. Mylopoulos, and J. W. Schmidt. *On Conceptual Modelling— Perspectives from Artificial Intelligence, Databases, and Programming Languages.* Springer-Verlag, Berlin, 1984.

14. A. Borgida. Features of Languages for the Development of Information Systems at the Conceptual Level. *IEEE Software*, 2(1):63–73, 1985.

15. G. Engels, M. Gogolla, U. Hohenstein, K. Hülsmann, P. Löhr-Richter, G. Saake, and H.-D. Ehrich. Conceptual modelling of database applications using an extended ER model. *Data & Knowledge Engineering, North-Holland*, 9(2):157–204, 1992.

16. M. L. Brodie and J. Mylopoulos, editors. *On Knowledge Management Systems.* Springer-Verlag, Berlin, 1986.

17. J. W. Schmidt and C. Thanos, editors. *Foundations of Knowledge Base Management.* Springer-Verlag, Berlin, 1989.

18. J. Mylopoulos and M. Brodie, editors. *Readings in Artificial Intelligence & Databases.* Morgan Kaufmann Publ. San Mateo, 1989.

19. A. Sernadas, C. Sernadas, and H.-D. Ehrich. Object-Oriented Specification of Databases: An Algebraic Approach. In P.M. Stoecker and W. Kent, editors, *Proc. 13th Int. Conf. on Very Large Databases VLDB'87*, pages 107–116. VLDB Endowment Press, Saratoga (CA), 1987.

20. A. Sernadas, J. Fiadeiro, C. Sernadas, and H.-D. Ehrich. The Basic Building Blocks of Information Systems. In E. Falkenberg and P. Lindgreen, editors, *Information*

System Concepts: An In-Depth Analysis, pages 225–246, Namur (B), 1989. North-Holland, Amsterdam, 1989.

21. A. Sernadas and H.-D. Ehrich. What Is an Object, After All? In R. Meersman, W. Kent, and S. Khosla, editors, *Object-Oriented Databases: Analysis, Design and Construction (Proc. 4th IFIP WG 2.6 Working Conference DS-4, Windermere (UK))*, pages 39–70, Amsterdam, 1991. North-Holland.

22. H.-D. Ehrich, J. A. Goguen, and A. Sernadas. A Categorial Theory of Objects as Observed Processes. In J.W. deBakker, W.P. deRoever, and G. Rozenberg, editors, *Proc. REX/FOOL Workshop*, pages 203–228, Noordwijkerhood (NL), 1990. LNCS 489, Springer, Berlin.

23. H.-D. Ehrich and A. Sernadas. Fundamental Object Concepts and Constructions. In G. Saake and A. Sernadas, editors, *Information Systems – Correctness and Reusability*, pages 1–24. TU Braunschweig, Informatik Bericht 91-03, 1991.

24. J. Fiadeiro, C. Sernadas, T. Maibaum, and G. Saake. Proof-Theoretic Semantics of Object-Oriented Specification Constructs. In R. Meersman, W. Kent, and S. Khosla, editors, *Object-Oriented Databases: Analysis, Design and Construction (Proc. 4th IFIP WG 2.6 Working Conference DS-4, Windermere (UK))*, pages 243–284, Amsterdam, 1991. North-Holland.

25. J. Fiadeiro and T. Maibaum. Temporal Reasoning over Deontic Specifications. *Journal of Logic and Computation*, 1(3):357–395, 1991.

26. R. Jungclaus, G. Saake, and C. Sernadas. Formal Specification of Object Systems. In S. Abramsky and T. Maibaum, editors, *Proc. TAPSOFT'91, Brighton*, pages 60–82. Springer, Berlin, LNCS 494, 1991.

27. G. Saake and R. Jungclaus. Konzeptioneller Entwurf von Objektgesellschaften. In H.-J. Appelrath, editor, *Proc. Datenbanksysteme in Büro, Technik und Wissenschaft BTW'91*, pages 327–343. Informatik-Fachberichte IFB 270, Springer, Berlin, 1991.

28. G. Saake and R. Jungclaus. Specification of Database Applications in the TROLL-Language. In D. Harper and M. Norrie, editors, *Proc. Int. Workshop Specification of Database Systems, Glasgow, July 1991*, pages 228–245. Springer, London, 1992.

29. R. Jungclaus, G. Saake, and T. Hartmann. Language Features for Object-Oriented Conceptual Modeling. In T.J. Teory, editor, *Proc. 10th Int. Conf. on the ER-approach*, pages 309–324, San Mateo, 1991.

30. R. Jungclaus, G. Saake, T. Hartmann, and C. Sernadas. Object-Oriented Specification of Information Systems: The TROLL Language. Informatik-Bericht 91-04, TU Braunschweig, 1991.

31. A. Goldberg and D. Robson. *Smalltalk-80: The Language and Its Implementation*. Addison-Wesley, Reading, MA, 1983.

32. B. Meyer. *Object-Oriented Software Construction*. Prentice-Hall, Englewood Cliffs, NJ, 1988.

33. J. D. McGregor and T. (Guest editors) Korson. Special Issue on Object-Oriented Design. *Communications of the ACM*, 33(9), 1990.

34. P. Coad and E. Yourdon. *Object-Oriented Analysis*. Yourdon Press/Prentice Hall, Englewood Cliffs, NJ, 1989.

35. J. Rumbaugh, M. Blaha, W. Premerlani, F. Eddy, and W. Lorensen. *Object-Oriented Modeling and Design*. Prentice-Hall, Englewood Cliffs, NJ, 1991.

36. K. R. Dittrich and U. Dayal, editors. *Proceedings of the 1986 International Workshop on Object-Oriented Database Systems*, Pacific Grove, CA, 1986. IEEE Computer Society Press, Washington, 1986.

37. K. R. Dittrich, editor. *Advances in Object-Oriented Database Systems*. Lecture Notes in Comp. Sc. 334. Springer Verlag, Berlin, 1988.

38. M. Atkinson, F. Bancilhon, D. DeWitt, K. R. Dittrich, D. Maier, and S. B. Zdonik. The Object-Oriented Database System Manifesto. In W. Kim, J.-M. Nicolas, and S. Nishio, editors, *Proc. Int. Conf. on Deductive and Object-Oriented Database Systems*, pages 40–57, Kyoto, Japan, December 1989.

39. W. Kim and F. H. Lochovsky, editors. *Object-Oriented Concepts, Databases, and Applications*. ACM Press/Addison-Wesley, New York, NY/Reading, MA, 1989.

40. A. Heuer. *Objektorientierte Datenbanken*. Addison-Wesley, Bonn (D), 1992. *In German*.

41. E. Verharen. Object-Oriented System Development—An Overview. In G. Saake and A. Sernadas, editors, *Information Systems—Correctness and Reusability*. Informatik-Bericht 91–03, TU Braunschweig, 1991.

42. D. C. Tsichritzis and O. M. Nierstrasz. Directions in Object-Oriented Research. In W. Kim and F. H. Lochovsky, editors, *Object-Oriented Concepts, Databases, and Applications*, pages 523–536. ACM Press/Addison-Wesley, New York, NY/Reading, MA, 1989.

43. U. W. Lipeck. *Zur dynamischen Integrität von Datenbanken: Grundlagen der Spezifikation und Überwachung*. Informatik-Fachbericht 209. Springer, Berlin, 1989.

44. H.-D. Ehrich, R. Jungclaus, G. Denker, and A. Sernadas. Object-oriented design of information systems: Theoretical foundations, 1993. *This volume*.

45. J. Fiadeiro and A. Sernadas. Logics of Modal Terms for System Specification. *Journal of Logic and Computation*, 1(2):187–227, 1990.

46. S. Schwiderski, T. Hartmann, and G. Saake. Monitoring Temporal Preconditions in a Behaviour Oriented Object Model. Informatik-Bericht 93-07, TU Braunschweig, 1993.

47. ISO. Information Processing Systems, Definition of the Temporal Ordering Specification Language LOTOS. Report N1987, ISO/TC97/16, 1984.

48. T. Hartmann, R. Jungclaus, and G. Saake. Aggregation in a Behavior Oriented Object Model. In O. Lehrmann Madsen, editor, *Proc. European Conference on Object-Oriented Programming (ECOOP'92)*, pages 57–77. Springer, LNCS 615, Berlin, 1992.

49. T. Hartmann and G. Saake. Abstract Specification of Object Interaction. Informatik-Bericht 93–08, Technische Universität Braunschweig, 1993.

50. G. Saake. *Objektorientierte Spezifikation von Informationssystemen.* Teubner, Leipzig, 1993.

51. R. Jungclaus. *Modeling of Dynamic Object Systems—A Logic-Based Approach.* Advanced Studies in Computer Science. Vieweg Verlag, Braunschweig/Wiesbaden, 1993.

52. R. J. Wieringa. *Algebraic Foundations for Dynamic Conceptual Models.* PhD thesis, Vrije Universiteit, Amsterdam, 1990.

53. B. Batory and A. Buchmann. Molecular Objects, Abstract Data Types and Data Models: A Framework. In U. Dayal, G. Schlageter, and L. H. Seng, editors, *Proc. 10th Int. Conf. on Very Large Databases VLDB'84*, pages 172–184, Singapore, 1984.

54. H.-D. Ehrich and A. Sernadas. Algebraic Implementation of Objects over Objects. In J. W. deBakker, W.-P. deRoever, and G. Rozenberg, editors, *Proc. REX Workshop "Stepwise Refinement of Distributed Systems: Models, Formalisms, Correctness"*, pages 239–266. LNCS 430, Springer, Berlin, 1990.

55. S. Conrad, M. Gogolla, and R. Herzig. TROLL *light*: A Core Language for Specifying Objects. Informatik-Bericht 92–02, TU Braunschweig, 1992.

GOAL,
A GRAPH-BASED OBJECT AND ASSOCIATION LANGUAGE

J. Hidders

Eindhoven University of Technology, Eindhoven, The Netherlands

J. Paredaens

University of Antwerp, Antwerp, Belgium

Abstract

A graph-based model for describing schemes and instances of object databases together with a graphical data manipulation language based on pattern matching are introduced. The data model allows the explicit modeling of classes and relations which contain objects and associations, respectively. GOAL consists mainly of two operations, the addition and the deletion. These perform on every part of the instance where a certain pattern is found. We will present the syntax and the semantics of the language, and show its computational completeness.

1   Introduction

In traditional database models like the Entity Relationship Model [1], NIAM [2] and the Functional Data Model [3], labeled graphs are used to represent schemes and sometimes also instances. It is well known that graphically represented schemes are often easier to grasp than textual ones. Moreover, with the introduction of more complex data models like the semantic and, more recently, object-oriented data models [4,5,6,7], this has become even more important. If we want to offer the user a consistent graphical interface to a database then it is desirable that there is also a graphical manipulation language. Unfortunately, the manipulation languages of these models are usually either textual or graph-based but with limited expressive power.

One of the first graph based data models that offered a graph based manipulation language that was computationally complete was GOOD [8] (Graph Oriented Object Database Model). The data representation of GOOD is simply a graph with labeled nodes and labeled edges between them. In PaMaL [9] the data model of GOOD was extended by labeling nodes explicitly as either objects, tuples, sets or basic values. Furthermore, the manipulation language was adapted to fit the meaning of these nodes. This made it possible to conveniently model complex objects in PaMaL.

In the data model of GOAL that we will present here, the data model of GOOD is extended in a slightly different way. In GOAL we distinguish three kinds of nodes being the value nodes, the object nodes and the association nodes. The value nodes are used to represent the so-called printable values such as strings, integers or booleans. The object nodes are used to represent objects and the association nodes are used to represent associations. Both, objects and associations may have properties that are represented by edges. The participants in an association are also considered to belong to the properties of the association. The main difference between associations and objects is that the identity of objects is independent of their properties, whereas associations are considered identical if they have the same properties. Properties may be either functional i.e. have only one value, or multi-valued i.e. consist of a set of values. The type of a property is not constrained in advance such that the property of an object or an association may be either a basic value, an object or an association. This is in contrast with the Entity Relationship Model where, usually, associations are only allowed to hold between entities.

The language of GOAL consists mainly of two operations, the addition and the deletion. Both are based on pattern matching i.e. the finding of all occurrences of a prototypical piece of an instance graph. Wherever such an occurrence is found the addition specifies which nodes and edges to add, and the deletion specifies which nodes and edges to delete. Furthermore, a fixpoint operation is introduced to enable some form of iteration.

The organization of this paper is as follows. In section 2 we introduce the data model of GOAL and how its schemes and instances can be represented as graphs. In section

3 we present the operations of GOAL. In section 4 we will give some extra examples of GOAL programs and discuss the expressiveness of GOAL. Finally, in section 5, we will compare GOAL to other data models and graph manipulation languages such as PaMaL.

2 The Data Model

The basic concept of GOAL is the finite directed labeled graph. It is used to represent schemes and instances as well as the operations on them. Therefore, we will begin with the formal definition of this concept.

Definition 2.1 A *finite directed labeled graph* with node labels L_n and edge labels L_e is $G = \langle N, E, \lambda \rangle$ with N a finite set of nodes, $E \subseteq N \times L_e \times N$ a finite set of labeled edges, and a labeling function $\lambda : (N \to L_n) \cup (E \to L_e)$ that maps nodes to node labels and edges to edge labels, where for all edges $\langle n_1, l, n_2 \rangle$ in E it holds that $\lambda(\langle n_1, l, n_2 \rangle) = l$.
□

Notice that it is not possible in a finite directed labeled graph that there are two edges between two nodes with the same label.

2.1 Object Base Schemes

To introduce the notion of scheme, let us consider the employee administration of a company. Figure 1 shows a possible database scheme of such an administration.

Here, the rectangular nodes represent classes, the rectangular nodes with a diamond shape in it represent relations and the round nodes represent basic value types. The single and double headed arrows that are labeled represent the properties of the objects and associations. If a labeled arrow has a single head it means that the property is functional e.g. the single headed edge *name* indicates that every person has only one name. If an arrow has a double head it means that the property is multi-valued e.g. the double headed edge *sections* indicates that a department may consist of more than one section. The double arrows that are unlabeled indicate the **isa** relation e.g. the arrow between manager and employee indicates that every manager is an employee.

Let us now look at the scheme of Figure 1 in more detail. Here we see the class Person which contains persons that have the properties name, date of birth and address. A subclass of Person is Employee which contains persons that are currently employed by the company. A subclass of Employee is Manager which contains employees that are considered fit to run a section or even an entire department. The second subclass of Employee is Engineer which contains employees that have technical skills in a certain domain. The class Department contains the several departments of the company that

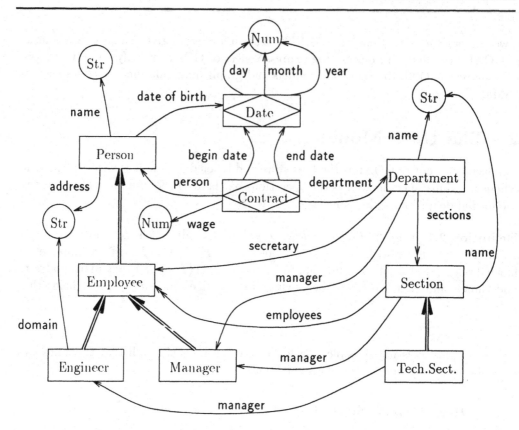

Figure 1: The employee administration database scheme

have a name, a secretary and a manager assigned to them. A department consists, furthermore, of several sections. The class Section contains these sections that have a name and a manager and a set of employees who work with it. A subclass of Section is the class Technical Section which contains sections where specialized technical work is done, and which have to be run by an engineer. The relation Contract records the contracts between a person and a department. Properties of a contract are the wage, begin date and end date. Finally, there is the relation Date which contains dates represented by a day, a month and a year.

The fundamental difference between objects and associations is that the identity of an object is not dependent upon its properties i.e. two objects with exactly the same properties are not necessarily the same object whereas two associations with the same properties are identical. Thus, the relationships of the Entity Relationship Model and the tuples of object oriented data models can be modelled in GOAL with the same concept i.e. association. Examples of this are the Contract relation and the Date relation in Figure 1.

Before we turn to the formal definition of a scheme we have to define a database context that contains the preliminary concepts which are system-given.

Definition 2.2 A *database context* is defined as $U = \langle B, V, \delta, C, R, F, M \rangle$ with B a finite set of basic types e.g. `int`, `str`, `bool` etc., V an enumerable set of basic values, $\delta : B \to 2^V$ maps every basic type to its domain i.e. an enumerable subset of the basic values, C an enumerable set of class names, R a countable set of relation names, F an enumerable set of functional edge labels and M an enumerable set of multi-valued edge labels. Furthermore, it must hold that B, C and R are pairwise disjoint and F, M and $\{\textbf{isa}\}$ are pairwise disjoint.
□

The database context is considered to be fixed for all the following definitions. We are now ready to define what exactly constitutes a scheme.

Definition 2.3 A *scheme* is a finite directed labeled graph $S = \langle N_S, E_S, \lambda_S \rangle$ with node labels $B \cup C \cup R$ and edge labels $F \cup M \cup \{\textbf{isa}\}$. Furthermore, it should hold that:

- all different nodes have different labels.

- edges may not leave from nodes labeled with a basic type.

- from a node there may not leave two edges with the same label except **isa** edges.

- the **isa** edges are only allowed between two nodes labeled with class names or two nodes labeled with relation names.

□

The nodes labeled with a basic type are called *basic type nodes.* and are represented by round nodes. The nodes labeled with a class name are called *class nodes* and are represented by rectangles. The nodes labeled with a relation name are called *relation nodes* and are represented by rectangles filled with a diamond. Edges labeled with a functional edge label or multi-valued edge label are called *functional edges* or *multi-valued edges* and are represented by single headed arrows or double headed arrows, respectively. Edges labeled with **isa** are called **isa** edges and are represented by double unlabeled bold arrows. Notice that **isa** edges are not only allowed between classes but also between relations.

If we look again at Figure 1 it can be verified that it presents a valid scheme except that it has several basic type nodes labeled with the same basic type. To be formally a scheme, these nodes would have to be merged but, informally, we allow the duplication of basic type nodes to increase readability.

The **isa** edges in Figure 1 indicate that every employee is a person, and that every manager is an employee. Evidently, it follows that every manager is also a person. Thus, the subtype relation can be easily derived from the **isa** edges.

Definition 2.4 The *subtype relation* $\preceq_S$ for a scheme S is a subset of $(B \times B) \cup (C \times C) \cup (R \times R)$ such that $l_1 \preceq_S l_2$ iff there are two nodes n_1 and n_2 in S with the labels l_1 and l_2, respectively, and a, possibly empty, directed path of **isa** edges from n_1 to n_2.

$\square$

Notice that the subtype relation holds between class names, relation names and basic types, and not between the nodes of the scheme. Also notice that since **isa** edges are not allowed between basic type nodes, the only subtype of a basic type is the basic type itself.

2.2   Database Instances

To introduce the notion of instance we present a small example of a weak instance of the employee database in Figure 2.

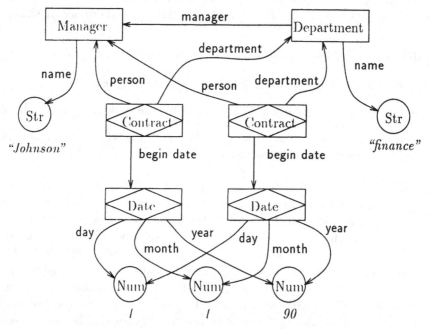

Figure 2: A weak instance of the employee database

The interpretation of the graph is reminiscent of the interpretation of a scheme graph. The rectangle nodes represent objects, the rectangle nodes with a diamond inside represent associations and the round nodes represent basic values.

Here we see a manager with the name "Johnson" who is the manager of the finance department. Apparently, Johnson has two contracts with his department, both with begin dates that have the same day, month and year.

Definition 2.5 A *weak instance* is a pair $I = \langle\langle N_I, E_I, \lambda_I\rangle, \nu_I\rangle$ where $\langle N_I, E_I, \lambda_I\rangle$ is a finite directed labeled graph with node labels $B \cup C \cup R$ and edge labels $F \cup M$. The partial function $\nu_I : N_I \to V$ maps nodes labeled with a basic type to their basic value. Furthermore, it should hold that:

- for every functional edge label there may at most leave one edge with that label from every node.

- exactly all the nodes labeled with a basic type are labeled with a basic value.

- the basic value of a node labeled with a basic type must belong to the domain of this basic type.

□

The nodes labeled with a basic type are called *value nodes*. The nodes labeled with a class name are called *object nodes*. The nodes labeled with a relation name are called *association nodes*. The λ-label and the ν-label of a node are said to be the *type label* and the *value label* of a node, respectively. Edges labeled with a functional edge label or a multi-valued edge label are called *functional edges* or *multi-valued edges*, respectively.

The graphical notation of weak instances is identical to those of schemes. It can be easily verified that the graph presented in Figure 2 is a valid weak instance.

We now turn to the question when a weak instance belongs to a certain scheme. Firstly, it may be clear that the weak instance may not contain objects and associations from classes and relations that were not mentioned in the scheme. Secondly, in GOAL we consider all properties to be optional e.g. the property date of birth of the class Person does not have to be defined for all persons. This enables us to conveniently model incomplete information. On the other hand, an object or an association may only have those properties defined that are prescribed for its type or for a supertype. Finally, the type of a property must be a subtype of all the types that are prescribed in the scheme by the type and the supertypes. For instance, in Figure 1 we see that the manager of a section must be a manager. It can also be seen that the manager of a technical section must be an engineer. Therefore the manager of a technical section must both be a manager and an engineer.

These intuitions about the typing of a weak instance can be formalized in the following way.

Definition 2.6 A *weak instance* I *is of scheme* S whenever:

- the type labels in the weak instance occur in the scheme.

- for every weak instance edge $\langle n_1, l, n_2\rangle$ there is a scheme edge $\langle n_1', l, n_2'\rangle$ such that $\lambda_I(n_1) \preceq_S \lambda_S(n_1')$.

- for every weak instance edge $\langle n_1, l, n_2 \rangle$ and scheme edge $\langle n_1', l, n_2' \rangle$ it must hold that if $\lambda_I(n_1) \preceq_S \lambda_S(n_1')$ then $\lambda_I(n_2) \preceq_S \lambda_S(n_2')$.

□

From the intuition of the typing of weak instances it may already be clear that the weak instance presented in Figure 2 is a weak instance of the scheme in Figure 1.

If we look at the weak instance of Figure 2 we see two Date associations with the same properties. Because the identity of an association depends fully upon the properties it has, these two associations should be merged. But then the properties of the two contracts would also become identical. Therefore, they would have to be merged also. Informally speaking, two nodes should be merged if they represent the same value.

Definition 2.7 Two nodes n_1 and n_2 are said to be *value equivalent* or $n_1 \cong_I n_2$ iff for all $i \in \mathbb{N}$ it holds that $n_1 \cong_I^i n_2$ where $\cong_I^i \subseteq N_I \times N_I$ is defined as:

- $n_1 \cong_I^0 n_2$ iff n_1 and n_2 are association nodes with the same type label or if they are the same class node or if they are value nodes with the same type label and the same value label.

- $n_1 \cong_I^{i+1} n_2$ iff $n_1 \cong_I^i n_2$ and for every edge $\langle n_1, l, n_1' \rangle$ there is an edge $\langle n_2, l, n_2' \rangle$ such that $n_1' \cong^i n_2'$ and vice versa.

□

Notice that if two nodes n_1 and n_2 are labeled with the same relation name, it holds that $n_1 \cong_I^0 n_2$. Furthermore, it can be observed that two value nodes are value equivalent iff they have the same type and value label, and two object nodes are value equivalent iff they are the same node.

Since we did not forbid associations to directly or indirectly refer to themselves, it is possible to represent certain infinite values in a weak instance. Consider, for example, the weak instance in Figure 3.

Here, the nodes n_1, n_2 and n_3 are association nodes that represent the same infinite list of 1's. They are therefore value equivalent. The nodes n_4 and n_5 both represent infinite lists with alternating 1's and 2's. They are not value equivalent because n_4 represents the list starting with a 2 and n_5 the one starting with 1.

We are now ready to define instances i.e. weak instances that respect the notion of associations without identity.

Definition 2.8 An *instance* is a weak instance I for which it holds that all different nodes are not value equivalent.

□

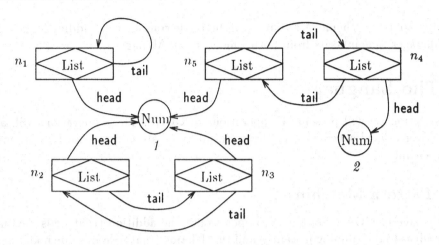

Figure 3: An instance with infinite values

Definition 2.9 For every weak instance there is an instance that can be obtained by merging nodes that are value equivalent. This instance is called the *reduction* of a weak instance.
□

For example, if in Figure 2 the two contracts, the two dates and the two value nodes with value label 1 would be merged, then we would obtain an instance.

2.3   Inheritance Conflicts

The scheme in Figure 1 has got a small problem. The manager of a section has to be a manager, but the manager of a technical section also has to be an engineer. In the GOAL data model, objects only belong to the class they are labeled with and its superclasses. This implies that an object can only belong to two classes at once if these classes have a common subclass. Since the classes Manager and Engineer do not have a common subclass there can not exist a manager that is an engineer as well. Formally, this does not present a problem since the manager of a technical section may always be left undefined, thus avoiding the contradiction. Of course, this is not what was intended with the scheme. Therefore, we introduce the notion of consistent scheme that prevents these problems.

Definition 2.10 A *consistent scheme* is a scheme S where for every two edges $\langle n_1, l, n_2 \rangle$ and $\langle n_1', l, n_2' \rangle$ in S for which $\lambda_S(n_1') \preceq_S \lambda_S(n_1)$ it holds that there is a node n_3 in S such that $\lambda_S(n_3) \preceq_S \lambda_S(n_2)$ and $\lambda_S(n_3) \preceq_S \lambda_S(n_2')$.
□

Notice that the scheme of Figure 1 can be made consistent by adding a class Technical Manager that inherits from both Engineer and Manager.

3   The Language

In this section we will present the operations of GOAL. These operations will all be defined over a fixed scheme S i.e. all begin, intermediate and final instances must be of this scheme.

3.1   Pattern Matching

The language of GOAL contains two operations: the addition (that adds new nodes and/or edges to the running instance) and the deletion (that deletes some nodes and/or edges from the running instance). Both operations follow the same principle: everywhere some "pattern" is found in the running instance, the operation is applied. A pattern has the form of a weak instance where not necessarily all value nodes have a value label.

Definition 3.1 A *pattern* is a weak instance but with the value function ν allowed to be undefined for some value nodes.
□

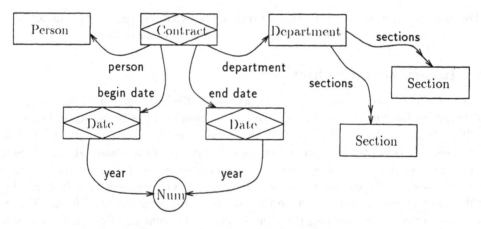

Figure 4: An example of a pattern

Figure 4 shows a pattern over the scheme of Figure 1, that represents all the persons that have a contract that is signed with a department with at least two sections and that has different begin and end dates with identical year.

Clearly a pattern can match with several parts of an instance. Each such a matching is called an embedding of the pattern into the instance.

Definition 3.2 An *embedding of a pattern J into a weak instance I* is a total injective function $\phi : N_J \to N_I$ such that:

- pattern nodes are mapped to weak instance nodes the type labels of which are subtypes.

- pattern nodes with value labels are mapped to weak instance nodes with the same value label.

- if the edge $\langle n_1, l, n_2 \rangle$ is in J then $\langle \phi(n_1), l, \phi(n_2) \rangle$ must be in I.

The set of all embeddings of J into I is denoted as $Emb(J, I)$.
□

Note that distinct nodes in the pattern are mapped to distinct nodes in the instance. Furthermore a node in the pattern is mapped to a node in the instance with the same type or with a subtype. Recalling Figure 1, an Employee node in the pattern can be mapped, for example, to a Manager node in the instance, indicating that the Manager node is considered here as of type Employee.

3.2 Additions

An addition is used to add new nodes and/or edges, for every embedding of a given pattern that is found in the running instance. The addition is represented by that pattern, J_m augmented with the bold nodes and/or edges that have to be added. These bold nodes and edges together with J_m have also to form a pattern, that is called J_a.

Definition 3.3 An *addition* is a pair $\mathcal{A}\langle J_m, J_a \rangle$ with patterns J_m and J_a where J_m is a subpattern of J_a and both patterns are of the scheme that the language is defined over.
□

Figure 5 represents an addition where a new employee Bergman and a contract that starts on 1-1-94 between Bergman and the finance department is added. Bergman also becomes an employee of the treasury section.

Actually, for every bold node (edge) a new node (edge) is created. But after the creation of the new nodes and/or edges, we obtain an instance that can be weak. Therefore the semantics of the addition ends with a reduction.

Definition 3.4 The *semantics* of an addition $\mathcal{A}\langle J_m, J_a \rangle$ applied to an instance I is defined as the reduction of I' the minimal weak superinstance of I such that every embedding $\phi \in Emb(J_m, I)$ has an extension $\phi' \in Emb(J_a, I')$ with:

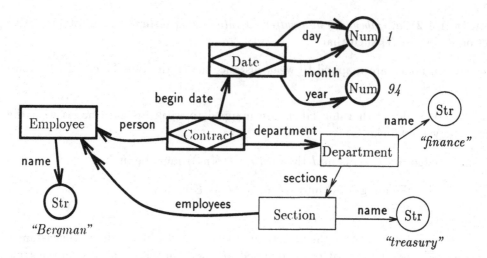

Figure 5: An example of an addition

- ϕ' is equal to ϕ on the nodes of J_m.

- each pattern node of $J_a - J_m$ is mapped by each extension to a different node, which does not belong to I.

□

Remark, that the addition of Figure 5 creates a new association node for the new contract. A new association node for the date 1-1-94 is also created, but it merges with the existing date 1-1-94, if the latter exists in the running instance. A new object node for Bergman is created of type Employee. If such a node would already exist this node will not merge with it. The basic values such as "Bergman", 1 and 94 are also drawn in bold because otherwise the pattern would not match if these values did not already exist in the object base and therefore nothing would be added.

Clearly the semantics is uniquely defined up to an isomorphism on the new object and association nodes. Notice that the semantics may sometimes be undefined e.g. when a person receives a new name without removing the old one. The result would then be a person with two names but since the property name is functional this is not possible in any instance.

3.3   Deletions

A deletion is used to delete existing nodes and/or edges, for every embedding of a given pattern that is found in the running instance. The deletion is represented by that pattern, J_m, where the nodes and/or edges that have to be deleted are drawn in dashed lines. The nodes and edges that are not dashed have to form a pattern, called J_d.

Definition 3.5 A *deletion* is a pair $\mathcal{D}\langle J_m, J_d \rangle$ with patterns J_m and J_d where J_d is a subpattern of J_m and both patterns are of the scheme that the language is defined over.

□

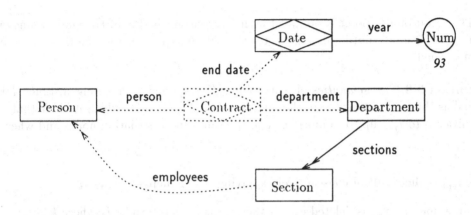

Figure 6: An example of a deletion

Figure 6 represents the deletion of the contracts that end in 1993 and removes the contracted employees from the sections that belong to the department the contract was with.

Actually, the deletion starts with the removal of the indicated nodes and/or edges. But after this removal we obtain an instance that can be weak. Therefore the semantics of the deletion ends with a reduction.

Definition 3.6 The *semantics* of a deletion $\mathcal{D}\langle J_m, J_d \rangle$ applied to an instance I is defined as the reduction of I' the maximal weak subinstance of I for which it holds that for all embeddings $\phi \in Emb(J_m, I)$:

- if a node n in J_m is not in J_d then $\phi(n)$ is not in I'.

- if an edge $\langle n_1, l, n_2 \rangle$ in J_m is not in J_d then $\langle \phi(n_1), l, \phi(n_2) \rangle$ is not in I'.

□

Clearly the semantics is uniquely defined up to an isomorphism on the association nodes that result from a merging during the reduction.

3.4   Recursion

A transformation is a finite list of additions, deletions (and fixpoints). In order to handle the recursion we define a fixpoint of a transformation.

Definition 3.7 A *fixpoint* is defined as $\mathcal{F}\langle T \rangle$, where T is a transformation, i.e. a finite list of additions, deletions and fixpoints.
□

The result of a fixpoint is obtained by first iterating the list of transformations on the running instance until a fixpoint is reached. If no fixpoint is reached the semantics is not defined.

Definition 3.8 The *semantics* of a fixpoint $\mathcal{F}\langle T \rangle$ applied to a strong instance I is defined as the first instance I_j in the infinite list $I_0, I_1, I_2, \ldots$ for which it holds that I_j is equivalent to I_{j+1} up to isomorphism on the value and association nodes and where:

- $I_0 = I$

- I_{i+1} is the result of consecutively applying the elements of T to I_i

- if a node n in I_i is deleted in I_{i+1} then it may not return in I_k where $k > i$.

□

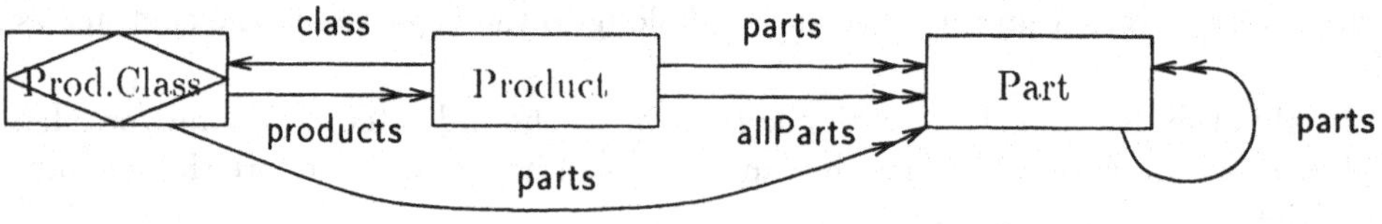

Figure 7: A scheme for products and parts

Figure 7 shows the scheme of a database that represents products that are built from parts, that in their turn are built from parts, and so on. In this scheme the edge labeled allParts represents all the parts needed to build a product recursively.

In Figure 8 a transformation is given that adds all the necessary allParts edges in a given instance. Remark that we separate the operations by semicolons and that we use { }* as a notation for the fixpoint.

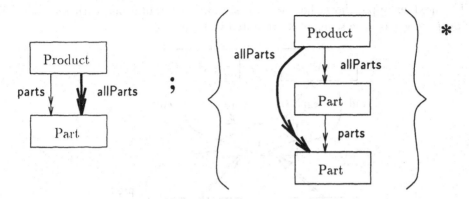

Figure 8: An example of the fixpoint operator

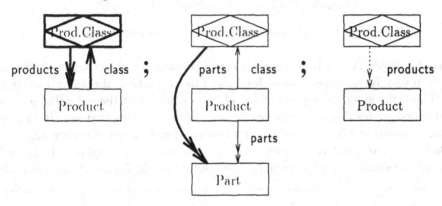

Figure 9: The computation of the Product Classes

4   More Examples

In this section we will give some more examples of GOAL transformations. The first example in Figure 9 presents the calculation of what is known in GOOD as an abstraction. The transformation is defined in the context of the scheme of Figure 7. Its intention is to create one Product Class node for every class of products where a class is defined as a set of products that contain the same parts. In the first operation, a product class is created for every product. Notice that these product classes all have a different products property. This prevents them from being merged into one node. In the second operation, the product classes obtain the same parts as the product they belong to. In the third statement, the product class is stripped of its products property. The only property now left is the parts property. Therefore, the product classes with the same parts will be merged. All products consisting of the same parts will now point to one and the same product class.

The next example shows how we can simulate computations with numbers. For this purpose we use the scheme as presented in Figure 10.

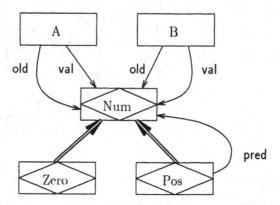

Figure 10: A scheme for numerical computations

Here the classes A and B are meant to each contain one object being the variables a and b, respectively. These variables have two properties, the value and the old value. The value gives the current value of the variable and the old value is used to hold intermediate results. The relation Number holds numbers that are either Zero or Positive. A positive number points to its predecessor, thus numbers are represented as a chained list of positive numbers ending with a zero. In Figures 11, 12 and 13 we present the simulation of some simple computations. In Figure 11 the value of a is

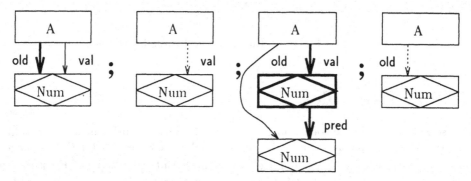

Figure 11: a becomes a plus 1

incremented by one. In Figure 12 the value of a is decremented by one. Notice that the old number is not removed because it may be shared with other variables. This is very likely because nodes that represent the same number are always merged. In Figure 13 the value of b is set to zero if the a is zero. Notice that the first operation of Figure 13 does not match if the value of b is already zero. This is because different nodes in

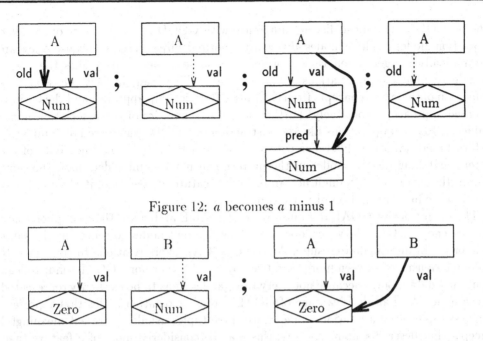

Figure 12: *a* becomes *a* minus 1

Figure 13: *b* becomes zero if *a* is zero

the pattern have to be embedded upon different nodes in the instance. The following addition would not cause any changes either because the edge it tries to add would already exist. The total result would therefore be identical to what was intended.

Finally, some remarks about the completeness of GOAL. From the previous examples we can observe that together with some form of iteration that can be simulated using the fixpoint operation, GOAL can simulate all computable functions on numbers. However, since GOAL is meant as an object database manipulation language, it is more interesting to know whether all "reasonable" manipulations can be computed. Since GOOD is known to be complete in this sense, [10] we can make the following observation.

Theorem 4.1 GOAL is computationally complete.

Proof: All operations of GOOD can be simulated in GOAL. The technical details of this will be omitted here.

□

5   Conclusions

In this paper we presented a graphical object-oriented database model and a graph-based manipulation language. This model is the result of the continuing research done on GOOD. The most distinct difference with GOOD is the presence of so-called association nodes. These nodes differ from normal object nodes because they are automatically merged when they represent the same value. This makes them very suitable to model both relationships and tuples. They can, in fact, be seen as a unification of these two concepts from the Entity Relationship approach and the Object-Oriented approach, respectively. Furthermore, the semantics of the association nodes enables us to avoid operations like the abstraction in GOOD, which are not completely pattern based. Another difference with GOOD (and PaMaL) is the injectivity of the pattern matching i.e. two nodes in the pattern can not be embedded upon the same node in the instance. Although not an essential feature we feel that it gives in many cases a more intuitive notion of pattern matching.

The operations of GOAL resemble those of PaMaL and share their simplicity and expressiveness. GOAL, however, does not allow different nodes to represent the same tuple or set in intermediate results. Moreover, GOAL offers relations to conveniently model relationships between more than two objects. Furthermore, GOAL tends to lead to succinct data models because not every tuple and set has to be explicitly represented with a node. A small disadvantage of GOAL is that association nodes that represent nameless tuples need a relation name. Since these tuples usually represent meaningful concepts that deserve a name anyway, this may be considered more of a feature than a bug. Finally, GOAL provides multiple inheritance, even between relations, and a mechanism to detect inheritance conflicts.

References

[1] Chen, P.P.: "The Entity-Relationship Model: Toward a Unified View of Data", *ACM Transactions on Database Systems*, 1 (1976), 9–36.

[2] Nijssen, G.M. and T.A. Halpin: *Conceptual Schema and Relational Database Design: a fact oriented approach*, Prentice Hall, Sydney, Australia, 1989.

[3] Shipman, D.W.: "The Functional Data Model and the Data Language DAPLEX", *ACM Transactions on Database Systems*, 1 (1981), 140–173.

[4] Abiteboul, S. and R. Hull: "IFO: A formal semantic database model", *ACM Transactions on Database Systems*, 4 (1987), 525–565.

[5] Abiteboul, S. and P.C. Kanellakis: "Object Identity as a Query Language Primitive", *Proceedings of the 1989 ACM SIGMOD International Conference on Management of Data*, Portland, pages 193–204, 1985.

[6] Lécluse, C., P. Richard and F. Velez: "O_2, an object-oriented data model", *Proceedings of the Fifteenth International Conference on Very Large Data Bases*, Amsterdam, pages 411–422, 1989.

[7] Beeri, C.: "A Formal Approach to Object-Oriented Databases", *Data & Knowledge Engineering*, 4 (1990), 353–382.

[8] Gyssens, M., J. Paredaens and D. Van Gucht: "A Graph-Oriented Object Database Model", *Proceedings of the 1990 ACM Symposium on Principles of Database Systems*, Nashville, pages 417–424, 1990.

[9] Gemis, M. and J. Paredaens: "An Object-Oriented Pattern Matching Language", *JSSST, International Symposium on Object Technologies for Advanced Software*, Kanazawa, Japan, pages 339–355, 1993.

[10] Van den Bussche, J., D. Van Gucht, M. Andries and M. Gyssens: "On the Completeness of Object-Creating Query Languages", *Proceedings 33rd Symposium on Foundation of Computer Science*, pages 372–379, 1992.

DATABASE DESIGN STRATEGIES

B. Thalheim
Cottbus Technical University, Cottbus, Germany

thalheim @ informatik.tu-cottbus.de

Abstract

Database design methodologies and tools should facilitate database modeling, effectively support database processing, database redesign and transform a conceptual schema of the database to a high-performance database schema in the model of the corresponding DBMS. Since the late 1970's, various tools for database design have been introduced. Most of them, however, are dependent on the knowledge, comprehension and experience of the database analyst and their knowledge in normalization theory. The systems $(DB)^2$ and RAD developed in our groups do not require the user to understand the theory, the implementational restrictions and the programming problems in order to design a database scheme. A novice designer can create a database design successfully using the system. These tools are based on an extended entity-relationship model. The entity-relationship model is extended to the *Higher-order Entity-Relationship Model* (HERM) by adding structural constructs and using integrity constraints and operations. The system RAD has a component which enables the user to choose his design strategy according to his experience and abilities. Different database design methodologies are developed based on the HERM approach. This paper demonstrates how different database design strategies can be developed and supported. This paper surveys further the strategy support of the design system RAD and proposes the design methodology *Design-By-Units*.

This paper has been partially supported by DFG Th 465/2.

1   Database Design

The problem of database design can be stated as follows: Design the logical and physical structure of a database in a given database management system to contain all the information required by the user and required for an efficient behavior of the information system.

The implicit goals of database design are:

- to meet all the information (content) requirements of the entire spectrum of users in the given application area;
- to provide a "natural" and easy-to-understand structuring of the information content;
- to conserve the whole semantic information of the designers for a later redesign;
- to achieve all the processing requirements and achieve a high degree of efficiency of processing;
- to achieve the logical independence for query and transaction formulation on this level.

The most important issue of database design is a **high-quality schema** within the restriction of the model and the class of DBMS or more general within the restrictions of the modeling paradigms. Low-quality schemes are hard to use, to maintain, and to adjust and tend to corruption.

A schema is called **high quality** or **conceptually adequate** if:

1. It describes the concepts of its application **naturally**.
2. The schema contains **no** or very little or necessary **redundancy**.
3. The schema does **not impose implementational restrictions**.
4. The schema covers as **many integrity constraints** as necessary for an efficient implementation on different platfroms.
5. The scheme is **flexible** according to later changes.
6. The concept is **conceptually-minimal**.

While on the one hand the inputs to the process are so informal, the final output of the database design is a database definition with formal syntax and with qualitative and quantitative decisions regarding such problems of physical design like physical placement, indexing and organization of data. This adds additional complexity to the database design process. A formal design must be turned out from, at times, extremely informal available information. The main complexity of the design process is already given by the complexity and number of items included in the database scheme, and further by the semantics defined for the database and the operations.

In database modeling three different perspectives can be identified. Different models stress only some of those. The *structure-oriented, semantic perspective* focusses on what kind of data are stored in the database, what constraints apply to these data, and what kinds of data are derivable. The *process-oriented perspective* is concerned with the processes or activities performed in the application area. The *behavior-oriented perspective* is concerned with how events in the real world trigger actions in the database systems. Database modeling should consider all three perspectives. The following strategy supports this approach and is an extension of [1],[4],[14],[17].

There are several additional requirements to support for database design, e.g.,

- Database design tools need to be **adaptable** to a wide range of designers.
- Database design could be viewed as a special *knowledge representation process*.
- The **reusability** of design decisions is another important feature of modern design tools.
- A database changes also its structure over its lifecycle.
- Database design is based on one or more data models.

Therefore, database design methodologies have to meet the following criteria [6]:

1. The methodology is a *step-by-step procedure*.
2. *Roles* and *responsibilities* have to evaluated carefully.
3. The methodology distinguishes clearly between *generic* and product-specific design techniques.
4. The methodology supports the generation of *data dictionaries*.
5. The methodology should be based on *database theory*.
6. *Checkpoints* should be established throughout the design process.
7. The *semantical and behavioral information* should be integrated.
8. The methodology uses simple *graphical representation* techniques.

Beside these criterias, special design challenges could be addressed:

- If possible, access to data through views is supported.
- Data security is considered throughout the design process.
- Very large databases and rather small databases are distinguished by the design strategy.
- Database evolution is considered during the design process and during implementation.
- Database technology is developing too. The methodology anticipates the technology evolution.

Based on an analysis of systems supporting database design we have developed a database design system $(DB)^2$ [32] which is supporting a high-level efficient database design. The system is using an extension of the entity-relationship model for the structural design and the graphical interface. Further, a high-level language for specification of integrity constraints and operations has been developed. Constraint declarations include: attribute data types, non-null attributes, attribute combinations forming primary and candidate entity keys, functional dependencies, multivalued dependencies, and inclusion dependencies. They also include relationship cardinalities and other dependencies. The chosen constraint set is powerful enough to capture the constraints in each schema, and to support the generation of equivalent schemes. Without constraints, there are only trivial equivalences between schemes. Without equivalence, it is impossible to justify transformations as provably preserving the information content of a schema. Furthermore, using the design information procedures for the maintenance of the database can be generated. The design can be translated to different DBMS according to characteristics of the DBMS and can be used for the generation of an interface builder if the design is to be translated to a multi-paradigm and multi-system environement. At present, we are developing another tool RAD in a joint project in different groups [2]. The system is based on the experience of four year of extensive utilization of $(DB)^2$ in more than 100 different user groups. It has a better user support system especially for the more difficult design steps like design of integrity constraints, refinement and rebuilding the schema.

Last but not least, the database design strategies had to be adapted to the model and the purposes of database design processes. This paper will report these results. For an automatic adaption of the design system to the chosen user strategy, the known database design strategies have been generalized. Further, we have developed our own database design strategy using approaches known in computer science.

The paper is divided into five parts. In section 2, the database design process is to be briefly discussed. Properties of database design are presented in section 3. Different classical design strategies are to be reviewed in section 4. Further, we introduce the design by units design process which is a unifies modular and object-oriented database design in section 5. Due to the space limitations, the paper presents a partial example on database design in the appendix. The paper summarizes the experience of intensive utilization of the design tool $(DB)^2$ for more than four years by almost 100 different user groups. One outcome of the project is presented in the paper: The theoretically based design strategy. An extended version of this paper is presented in [33].

2 Components of the Database Design Process

The database design process can be described according to the information units which are necessary:

- The *requirement description* is an informal description of the application and the goals (mission) to be achieved.
- The *interface* is the description of the organizational structure and the distribution of the database.
- The *structure* of the database objects is described by different classes of objects and their typing systems.
- The *semantics* describes the static properties of objects and object classes. Thus, the semantics is used for restricting the set of possible databases.
- The *views* describes the different subschemata for different parts of the application.
- The *operations* describe how the database should operate.
- Based on the semantical, structural and view information *cooperating views* can be defined for the different sub-databases.
- Using abstraction *query forms* describe in general the database information retrieval processes for the user.
- The *behavior* specifies the dynamic constraints of a database.
- The *transactions* are used for the specification of database programs.
- Finally, the *database modul* collects and re-organizes the information.

These units are not independent. The description of views depends from the structural, semantical and interface information. The complete dependency graph is displayed in Figure 1. Based on these information units different design decisions can be generated.

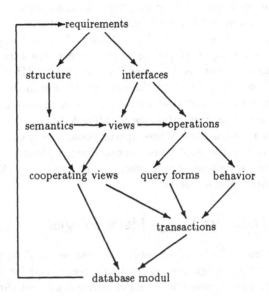

Figure 1: The Information Acquisition in Database Design

The database design activities can be differently organized by different methodologies in accordance to the *information systems life cycle*. For instance, we can use the commonsense knowledge on platforms first for *feasibility studies*. Then *requirements* can be collected, analysed, structured and grouped. Based on this information the *design* is performed. Further, a *prototype* is developed. The prototype allows the user to verify that the information system satisfies their needs. This can lead to an additional requirement collection and analysis. If the prototype satisfies the requirements the *implementation* of the design is performed. Implementation is concerned with the programming of the final, operating version. During the *validation and testing* process the developer assures that phase of the process is of acceptable quality and is an accurate transformation from the previous phase. *Operation* starts with the initial loading of data and terminates when the system eventually becomes obsolete and has to be replaced. During operation, maintenance is required for adopting the system to other requirements (conditions, functions, structures) and for correcting errors that were not detectted during validation.

The *design process* is mainly concerned with the requirement acquisition, requirement analysis and conceptual design. We can distinguish different *phases* in database design. Based on the waterfall and/or fountain models of software development the classical scenario for *structure-driven database design* distinguishes between conceptual, logical and physical design. During *conceptual design* a high-level description of the database (structure, semantics, operations, distibution) is developed using the data and operations requirements. This description is *independent* from the platforms or the database management systems which are later used. Conceptual design results in a conceptual schema which is kept, for instance, for later database maintenance. During *logical design* a conceptual schema is translated to a logical schema which describes the structure, operations, semantics and distribution of the database according to a class of database management systems (or according to a single system or, in general, according to a set of paradigms). The logical schema is transformed into the physical schema during *physical design*. The storage structures, access methods, the organization in secondary memory is developed for a specific DBMS.

Alternatively, the *processing-driven database design* starts with the *processing analysis* of requirements which generates a functional schema. This is used during *high-level application design* for the generation of the application specification which describes the behavior of the database in a high-level abstraction. These specifications are transformed into a detailed program specification during the *application program design* phase.

Modern, more recent approaches try to unify and to combine both the structure-driven and the processing-driven database design.

3   Properties of Database Design Methodologies

A design methodology could be based on monotone reasoning. Each design step is adding certain information. During design the information already modeled is not changed. This does not mean that structures, operations and constraints are not changed. However, the new design step does not abandon already obtained information. Each design step needs to satisfy certain restrictions:

- Each design step is *content-preserving*, i.e. there exists a query q such that for each database $db' \in SAT(S')$: $q(db') \in SAT(S)$ for S, S' and $Step(S) = S'$.

- Each design step is *constraint-preserving*, i.e. $\Sigma' \models \Sigma$ for $S = (Struc, Ops, \Sigma)$, $S' = (Struc', Ops', \Sigma')$ and $Step(S) = S'$.

- Each step is *minimally content-preserving*, i.e. the design step does not add derived types; there does not exist a query q such that for each database $db' \in SAT(S')$ there exists a database $db \in SAT(S)$ such that $q(db) = db'$ for S, S' and $Step(S) = S'$.

Furthermore, there are some desirable restrictions:

- Each step is *minimally constraint-preserving*, i.e. $\Sigma \models \Sigma' |_{Struc}$ for $S = (Struc, Ops, \Sigma)$, $S' = (Struc', Ops', \Sigma')$ and $Step(S) = S'$.

- Each step is *nearly free of path tuple-generating constraints*. When a path tuple-generating constraint is present it often requires that the path has to be computed to check whether the constraint holds in the database.

Notice, that inclusion constraints can be maintained in a database using only projections. Path inclusion constraints are still based on joins. The last restriction is often too strong. It can be replaced by the following restriction. This restriction requires an effective management of basic database operations.

- Each step is *update simplicity-preserving*, i.e. if for S the complete set of basic update operations is defined without join operations then $Step(S)$ has this property too.

A schema is *lexical-minimal* is it uses as few lexical units as possible. For instance, the attribute DepartmentName of the type *Department* is can be replaced by Name (the corresponding identifier is Department.Name).

It should be mentioned that several known normalization algorithms do not fulfill the above requirements. However, there are 4NF algorithms which preserve all properties.

A methodology needs also **rules** in which case which concept is going to be applied. One rule which could be considered as the basic rule is that independent objects are to be represented by entity sets.

A database design is similar to database lifetime. Each design step can be modeled by some transaction. The database is designed step by step using one of the given transactions. Each transaction commits or aborts the actions taken since the last last transaction committed. Therefore, the design strategy can be considered to be simple if the design is performed by a sequence of transaction. Often, design strategies are proposed which consists of one complex transaction. Such strategies are prone to errors. Errors and wrong assumptions made at the beginning are corrected only at the end. However, several implications have been derived during design from those assumptions. Therefore, error deletion or revision of assumptions lead in such cases to revision of the entire design process. We need to distingiush between wrong assumptions and errors. Wrong assumptions have several reasons. Errors are detectable at a certain stage of the design procedure. The princip should be that the detection should happen during the most early step.

- A database design step is *closed* if errors which could have been made during this step must be corrected before this step is going to be completed.

Checkpoints are an instrument to develop design strategies with closed steps.

In order to achieve closed design strategies a set of general **design bussiness rules** can be developed. Design consistency is maintained by enforcing these rules during database design. Design business rules can fall into the following categories:

Model-specific. Each database model has a certain set of implicit structural constraints and integrity constraints which are satisfied by each schema. Examples of such constraints are the existence of a primary key based on the key uniqueness and the entity integrity.

Schema-specific. Certain models allow or permit the existence of cyclic constructs. If, for instance, derived attributes are designed then a certain set of operations must be designed too. In this case, any change to the schema should not violate the schema-specific constraints.

Application-specific. Organizational policy, laws and general structure of the application affect the design strategy. If, for example, the application under design is highly heterogeneous then the strategy could use that and begin with design of different views. If main requests to the database require computation over different views then the conceptual schema needs to be designed with special care.

The database design methodology developed in [21] is an example of such a strategy driven design business rules. Another example which considers mainly application-specific design rules is discussed in [9]. The rules discussed in [6] are model-specific design rules.

4   On Design Methodologies

4.1   Design Perspectives

In software design and in database design we distinguish different design perspectives.

1. The *structure-oriented perspective* focusses on the structural description of the data. Almost all known database design approaches are based on the structure-oriented perspective. Sometimes, the structure-oriented perspective is unified with the semantical perspective. In this cases, the design of the structure is to be combined with the design of static integrity constraints. The different strategies based on the structure-oriented perspective are shown in Figure 2.

2. The *behavior-oriented perspective* (called in [10] *integrity-centered*; see also [12]) is concerned with the behavior of the database during its lifetime. It can be based on event approaches [12] or on Petri-net approaches [15,16] and predicate transition systems.

3. The *process-oriented perspective* is concentrated on the database operating. This perspective has been considered mainly for software design. Several strategies have been developed. Only recently it got attention by the database designers.

The structure-oriented perspective is discussed in a large variety of papers. The process-oriented perspective can reuse approaches known in software engineering. The behavior-oriented perspective is a high-level descriptive approach to an integrated specification of structures and operations. Database design is considered to be a transformation process carried out on integrity constraints. Database behavior is specified by stepwise reification.

The structure-oriented approach is currently well developed for relational models and was directly generalized to semantical models like entity-relationship models. It is, however, possible to develop for semantical models more specific methodologies which are using the specific properties of these models. One specific methodology is discussed in the next subsection. Generally, a methodology consists of a strategy, a set of primitives to be used and guidelines on the application of each strategy step and each primitive. A methodology should be, from one hand side, *rigorous*, i.e. suggesting a strategy which is to be used, and, from the other hand side, *flexible*, i.e. applicable to a variety of applications. These requirements are contradictory in general. A design tool should be flexible enough to be adaptable to different design styles and should be rigorous enough to be well-based.

The building block of a methodology is the design strategy. Known strategies are, for example, the bottom-up and top-down appraoch. Most of the known strategies are considering only the structural part of a schema. The strategies are based on different primitives. Most of these primitives can be considered to be generalizations of the known algebraic operations of the relational model.

4.2 Design Primitives

In [3] design primitives were introduced. We distinguish between structural abstraction and graphical abstraction. The last one is understood as a kind of representational abstraction. In this case, we define a mapping from the set of possible schemata to the set of graphs. This mapping is called *injective* if each graph image corresponds only to one preimage. The mapping is called *basic* if it is defined as the extension of the mapping from primitive types (entity, relationship and attribute types) to primitive graphical units (rectangles, diamonds with arrows, points with lines; may be with names). The structure is context-sensitive because the corresponding entity types must exist for component types of relationship types. However, the context sensitivity follows the order of the types. Therefore, the mechanism for defining a structure are not equal-order-context-sensitive. The mapping mechanism for the presented extended ER-model is injective and basic. The mapping mechanism used in most ER books is injective but not basic. The reason for this is that subtypes and their supertype need to be mapped together. If the mapping mechanism is not basic then during database design the design of the database structure needs to be combined with the graphical representation. Since in such design languages the graphical structure is on the equal-order-context-sensitive the graphical structure can change strongly for even very simple changes. Tools based on such approaches are more complex.

Further, since database design can be considered to be database management on a schema database we can compare the design primitives with operations in the design database system. In the nested relational model different operations are used:
projection, selection, partition, join, θ-join or the join via a coercion function, union, nest, and unnest.
Additionally, concepts can be added to the schema.
The operations can be seen also as decomposition/composition pairs:

selection / union,

partition / union,

nest / unnest,

projection / product (or join).

We have mentioned already that each database model needs its own primitives according to the constructors used in the definition of types. In HERM we are using the type constructors **product** (generating tuple-sets) and **union** (generating clusters or generalizations of subtypes). Therefore, for a complete set of design primitives we need only primitives defining the generation of products (i.e. product and concatenation to components (The last can be expressed via the first operation. However it might be sometimes more convenient to have this operation too.)) and the generation of union types. Further, we need operations for initializing the design (in our case, generating basic attribute types and generating basic entity types but not for the generation of relationship types). We define now these general design operations. For that we assume a set C of type constructors. Using this set we can define a set of terms and subterms for each term. For instance, if the C consists of union $\cup$ and product $\times$ then the set T of terms is defined by the consecutive application of these operators and the subterms are defined by selection and projection operators. Further, we assume $\perp \in T$ for the empty term.

Composition. Given the constructor C, a new name t and types $t_1, ..., t_n$. The composition $compose(t_1, ..., t_n, C, t)$ defines a new type t using the constructor C.

Decomposition. Given a type t and terms $e_0, e_1, ..., e_n$ and (possibly empty) names $N_0, ..., N_n$. The decomposition $decompose(t, e_0, e_1, ..., e_n, N_0, N_1, ..., N_n)$ defines new types which are generated by e_i and are labeled by N_i.

Extension. Given a type $t = (t_1, ..., t_m, \{A_1, ..., A_n\})$ of order i ($m \geq 0$ ($m = 0$ for entity types), $n \geq 0$), an attribute A' and a type t' of order j, $j < i$ then
$extend(t, A)$ is the type obtained from t
adding A' to the attribute set and
$extent(t, t')$ is the type obtained from t
adding t' to the component sequence.

For our purposes entity types are types of order 0.

Initialization. *generate(E)*, *generate(A)* generate an entity type labeled by E without attributes and an attribute type labeled by A.

4.3 Dimensions in Database Design

Database design has been based in the past on relational design techniques. Two main approaches have been developed: top-down approaches (decomposition) and bottom-up approaches (synthesis). The first strategy begins with a set of basic types and builds new types using decomposition. The second approach begins with a set of descriptions or attributes and then group those in types.

The relational decomposition approach starts with a given schema of relation types and decomposes it to smaller relation types until certain properties such as normal form and losslessness are satisfied. The starting schema can be a universal relation type or a near-normal-form set of types. In the synthesis approach to designing relational databases, we assume the application is described by a set of attributes and functional dependencies among them. The functional dependency (FD) is the main vehicle in synthesizing relation types out of lists of attributes. In this case, we start with a minimal cover of FDs. Normally, the two strategies are not applied in their pure form. Database design could be performed by mixing the two strategies which is sometimes called mixed strategy.

These two approaches could be considered as approaches with different design **directions**.

Design strategies can be distinguished also by their **control mechanism**. One control mechanism rules the step-by-step development of types. Control strategies decides which rules to use in a given situation. The inside-out strategy selects first one central type and then develops the associated type by a discrete neighborhood function. The next type to be developed is a new type with the smallest neighborhood value according to the central type. Another control mechanism exploits another more abstract schema of the database. This mixed strategy is controlled by a sketch of the database schema (the so-called skeleton). Alike in second-order grammars this control mechanism can be generated by another grammar. The skeleton schema is representing the control information of the database design.

Relational database design has been considered mainly for the design of conceptual schemata according to the three-level architecture of a database. The conceptual schema unifies the different views of external users. The database design could also begin with the view design [6]. The views are later composed into the conceptual schema. This approach can be useful for the design of homogeneous view sets. Since view integration is undecidable the applicability of this approach is limited. The modular design strategy *Design-by-units* extends this approach. For each subschema which could be considered to be a module alike in software technology the interface is defined for each unit. Units can be associated only by their units. We can define also other kinds of scoping rules in database design. This dimension of database design uses the **modularity** concept. Modularization is based on implementation abstraction and on localization abstraction. *Implementation abstraction* is to selectively hide information about structures, semantics and the behavior of concepts defined by the previous two abstraction mechanisms. Implementation abstraction is a generalization of *encapsula-*

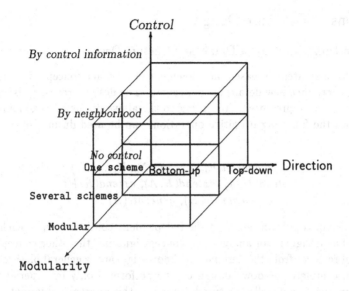

Figure 2: Main Dimensions in Structure-Oriented Design

tion and *scoping*. It provides *data independence* through the implementation, allowing the private portion of a concept to be changed without affecting other concepts which use that concept. *Localization abstraction* to "factor out" repeating or shared patterns of concepts and functionality from individual concepts into a shared database / knowledge base application environment. Naming is the basic mechanisms to achieve localization. Parametrization can be used for abstraction over partial object descriptions.

Another dimension not represented in the figure is the **representation form** for design results. For instance, the ER model uses rectangles, diamonds as nodes of a graph. The IFO model uses more sophisticated node types and different types of edges. The representation is more compact but also more complex. The NIAM model uses object nodes for abstract objects and relationship nodes for the representation of associations among objects and relationships nodes. The graphical representation differs from model to model. The most important issue is, however, that the graphical representation has to be based on a well-founded semantics. Often, especially in the ER literature and for ER-based tools, design is considered as drawing graphs leaving semantic issues aside.

The power of abstraction principles comes from their orthogonality and their generality. All these mechanisms can be combined with more specialized mechanisms, like exception and default rules.

If we compare different strategies then we can relate them to known **search strategies in AI**. Search strategies are characterized by direction, topology, node representation, selecting rules and heuristic functions. Other design strategies can be developed based on this analogy.

We could search forward or backward.

5   Directions of Database Design

5.1   The Top-Down Strategy in Database Structure Design

The pure top-down strategy is based on refinement of abstract concepts into more concrete ones. Each step introduce new details in the schema. The design process ends when all structural requirements are represented. According to the above discussed taxonomy of database design operations the following primitive operations can be used during top-down design:

$$decompose(t, e_0, e_1, ..., e_n, N_0, N_1, ..., N_n)$$
$$extend(E, A), \ extend(R, A), \ extend(R, E)$$
$$generate(E), \ generate(A)$$

The advantage of top-down design is the independent consideration of each type during a design step. The designer can analyse one concept ignoring the other concepts. However, top-down design requires from the designer the knowledge on the general picture of the design first. Therefore, complete top-down design can be performed only by experienced designers if the application area is not well-structured. Based on this approach, different primitives are developed [33].

5.2   The Bottom-Up Strategy Database Structure Design

Bottom-up design was first developed for the relational model. During bottom-up design each step introduces new concepts not considered before or modify existing ones. During each step the designer checks whether all features of requirements are covered. The designer start from elementary concepts and builds more complex out of them. The advantage of the bottom-up approach is its simplicity. The main disadvantage of the bottom-up approach is that this approach requires restructuring. Therefore, the strategy is not monotone.
Primitive operations are discussed in [33]. The following primitive operations can be used during top-down design:

$$compose(t_1, ..., t_n, C, t)$$
$$extend(E, A), \ extend(R, A), \ extend(R, E)$$
$$generate(E), \ generate(A)$$

6   Control Strategies

6.1   The Inside-Out Strategy in Database Structure Design

The classical inside-out strategy restricts the bottom-up approach by controlling the order of primitives application. This strategy is still complete. We choose the most important concept first, design it and then proceed by moving as an oil stain does, designing first concepts that are conceptually closed to the already design. The order of refinements is disciplined. The designer navigates from the central type to the more distant ones. It is easy to discover new concepts which are to be designed next. However we loose abstraction capabilities. The global schema is built at the end only.

This strategy can be generalized now as follows:

Given a set of concepts C to be designed and a neighborhood function F on C, i.e.

$$F : C \times C \rightarrow NatNumber .$$

This function is used for the design agenda. In this case we use the following algorithm for a given central concept c:

Algorithm   *Bottom-up version*

1. Agenda $:= \{c\}$; Designed $:= \emptyset$.

2. *Repeat until Agenda* $= \emptyset$

   (a) *Repeat until Agenda* $= \emptyset$

      i. *Choose* $c \in$ Agenda

      ii. *Design* c *using the bottom-up strategy*

      iii. Agenda $:=$ Agenda $\setminus c$
         Designed $:=$ Designed $\cup \{c\}$

   (b) $m := min\{F(c,c') \mid c \in C \setminus$ Designed$, c' \in$ Designed$\}$
      Agenda $:= \{c \in C \setminus$ Designed $\mid F(c,c') = m$ *for some* $c' \in$ Designed$\}$

For the top-down variant of the algorithm, step 2.(a).ii is used for the design in top-down fashion. This algorithm can be refined. For instance, if the set of concepts is unknown at the beginning then a substep is added to step 2 which looks for extensions of C and of F in each iteration.

6.2   The Mixed Strategy in Database Structure Design

Another controlled approach is the mixed approach. This approach mixes the top-down and the bottom-up approach. First, a skeleton schema is to be designed (using one of the previous approaches). This schema represents the main classes (or units) and their main associations. Then each of the units is refined and later integrated with other designed units. Using the skeleton schema the bottom-up integration of concepts is simpler. Since the complete requirements set is now partioned the design of each unit is less complex. The success of the strategy depends from the design of the skeleton schema. Therefore, this method is applicable if the application is already well-recognized.

7   Modular Design by Units

7.1   Design by Units - Structural Design

In [34,27,24] another new design methodology was developed: **Design-by-units**. Most of the well-known design methodologies think as in the relational approach. But each of the database models should have its own methodology. It is surprising that most of the proposed models do not have its own design methodology. If the model is getting richer in construct the methodology should be deepen. The proposed methodology support also extensibility since using this methodology an existing design and implementation can be extended without introducing changes to it. It promotes reuse and inheritance as well as behavioral extension. To some extend, this approach is similar to modular design known in software engineering. The orientation is different only. We are first interested in the data representation part and then in the processing part since a part of the processing part is based on generic operations which are defined according to the structure. However, if we consider modularization, parametrization and inheritance to be the kernel concepts of object-oriented design then this design approach can be considered to be complety object-oriented.

This approach has further other advantages: it is easier to detect similarities among design units and to reuse parts of design units in other units; changes to the scheme and to parts of units are directly reflected in all other units which are using the changed. The new methodology supports directly the above discussed distinction between kernel and dependent object. This is especially useful, if abbreviation techniques [20] are used in query forms [34]. It is a recursive method. Each step is based on the above discussed eight design steps. This methodology is not following the classical waterfall model with iterations but rather supporting a high level inside-out-strategy [3]. Experience in utilization of (DB^2) has shown that this methodology was the most often choosen for practical design.

Design-by-units

1. *basic step.*
   Design the types for the independent kernel object classes.

2. *Recursion step.*
   Repeat until the schema is not changed.
   Either reification :

   - *Refine the units introducing subtypes (in HERM represented by unary relationship types).*

   - *Refine the relationship types according to the subtypes.*

   or generalization of units:

   - *If there are associations among units then introduce a new unit containing the associated units and the relationship type according to the association.*

   - *Add other relationship types if there exist new associations.*

7.2   Design by Units - Process Design

As already discussed in the previous section, the data design and the process design can not be separated from each another. We need the process information as well as the structural information. For this reason the process design and the structural design need to be integrated. We use a dataflow approach [3]. A process is an activity of the information system. The dataflow is an exchange of information between processes. The processes use information from the database and create temporary databases necessary for the process. Since processes use different databases and these databases are usually not fully integrated, interfaces are to be used for view cooperation. Generally, the interface is the description of the cooperation between different users (originator/receiver of the dataflow).

One of the difficult tasks in processing modeling is to evaluate whether the designed data structures are appropriate for an effective processing of data. It is known already that relational normalization can contradict effective processing. Sometimes unnormalized relations can be used simpler. For handling this we need a cost model for processes. The cost model can be based on models of complexity for operations and on priority functions for queries and transactions. Therefore, we need a representational and a graphical language for the representation of processes. We decided to use three different languages, one high-level abstract language which is directly supported by the modular design-by-units-strategy, another one for a more detailed procedural description and and another more dataflow oriented which shows the level of the database directly. A *transaction* is a (nested) sequence of database operations which transforms consistent databases into consistent ones. They can be described like queries. However, modeling of transactions provides additional information about the relationship and the order of database operations. In the same manner, an application program can be viewed as a structure of queries and/or transactions that manipulate a database or several databases.

8   Derived Design Strategies

The experience of $(DB)^2$ utilization shows that different database designers use also very different design strategies. The system RAD supports this variety of design strategies. For each user, a specific database design strategy can be developed which is derived from abilities and experience of the specific user. This chapter demonstrates two derived strategies. The variety of possible design strategy is much larger.

8.1   Relational Database Design Combining Mixed and Bottom-Up Design

We show now that a closed relational database design strategy can be derived which is based on entity-relationship modeling (For detailed description, see [33].).

Mixed strategy on user views. The user view represents the data requirements of a single user. The skeleton under developement contains only the most important aspects of data requirements.

Bottom-up design: A - Identification. Now we add detail information to the developed user views.

Bottom-up design: B - Characterization. Each object of a certain type has normally beside its identification also characterized properties.

Integrity control: A - Validation. The normalization of relational schemes has been generalized to ER schemes. Normalization is a theory that addresses analysis and decomposition of data structures into a new scheme that has more desirable properties.

Bottom-up design: C - Domains. Now constraints on valid values that attributes may assume are added.

Integrity control: B - Behavior. The specification of the database is used for the generation of the behavior of the database.

Bottom-up design: D - Combination and Integration. Each view developed so far models the information requirements for one special application. They are now comprehensive, correct, and unambiguous. Now these views should be integrated.

Integrity control: C - Stability and Extension. The database is changing also its structure during its lifetime. This needs to be supported. Scheme evolution is similar to view integration.

The next steps will be only mentioned. For those, we can develop complete descriptions in the same manner.

Translation and Validation

Optimization: A - Access.

Optimization: B - Indexes.

Optimization: C - Controlled redundancy.

Reconsideration and redefinition

Coping with challenges: A - View updates.

Coping with challenges: B - Security.

Coping with challenges: C - Very large databases.

Coping with challenges: D - Access change.

Coping with challenges: E - Future technology.

8.2   Modular Object-Oriented Design Based on Top-Down-Directions

Modular object-oriented design is based on a database model which encorporates structural, semantical, and behavioral model. The model developed and used in [21] could be used as one of such. The designer specifies the types, classes and methods of the given application. Similar to the previous strategy, we assume that kernel types and classes are specified. Then the specified scheme is refined by adding information on the database and changing the structure of the database or refining types in the schema. This change can be considered [21] as reification of the scheme and its types. This approach allows the development of generic class libraries for application areas. The types in the library are general enough to be used again after reification according to the specific applications of the given application area. This approach quickens the development of schemes. For modular developement of schemes, we specify the type, its interface, its semantics and meaning and its behavior within the database. The reification follows that specification. Therefore we can distinguish the following categories of reification:

Reification by Specialization. Refinement by specialization introduces new subclasses and reorganizes associated relationships. Moreover, it may involve to replace a structure expression such that the new type will be a subtype of the old type and the new implicit and explicit constraints will imply the old ones.

Reification by Splitting. Refinement by splitting also leads to new types. But their type corresponds to parts of an existing type which in turn is replaced by references.

Reification by Completion. Refinement by completion means the definition of new types, constraints, methods, and behavioral constraints.

Reification by Instantiation. The schema may contain undefined parameters, attributes, and types. Refinement by instantiation provides definition for those concepts. The same applies to class parameters. Reification by instantiation may introduce new parameters as well.

In all these cases, additional changes to methods are required.

9   Conclusion

The goal of database modeling is to design an efficient and appropriate database. Some important criteria are performance, integrity, understandability, and extensibility. We have developed a theoreical basis for different database design methodologies together with an extension of the entity-relationship model. Based on this extension a new approach to database design has been developed which is effective in meeting these goals. Based on the theory and the methodology the design system $(DB)^2$ was developed. This approach shows that a strong theory can be developed and applied for important practical problems. The history of database management systems demonstrates that a lacking theoretical basis leads to poor and difficult to apply technologies. The presented model and systems have the foolowing advantages:

1. The model has a strong theoretical basis [29].

2. The modeling is more natural and can be applied in a simple manner. Only necessary facts are to be expressed [25,34].

3. The theory is applicable to practical needs [23,24,27,34].

4. The results of the design are much simpler than in other approaches [34,30].

5. The model is easy understandable, simple and perceivable [27] and can be used as a basis for design tools [2,24,29].

This paper aims to demonstrate how a well founded theory can be used for the development of a concise, understandable and useful approach to the database design. Based on this theory, design strategies can be developed and suppported by design systems.

References

[1] S. Abiteboul and R. Hull. IFO: a formal semantic database model. Proc. PODS 84, 3, 119–132.

[2] P. Bachmann, W. Oberschelp, B. Thalheim, and G. Vossen. The design of RAD: Towards an interactive toolbox for database design. RWTH Aachen, Fachgruppe Informatik, Aachener Informatik-Berichte, 90-28, 1990.

[3] C. Batini, S. Ceri, and S. Navathe, Conceptual database design, An entity-relationship approach. Benjamin Cummings, Redwood, 1992.

[4] P. P. Chen. ER – A historical perspectives and future directions. Entity Relationship Approach For Software Eng., B.V.(North Holland), pp. 71–78, 1983.

[5] R. Elmasri and S. H. Navathe, Fundamentals of database systems. Benjamin/Cummings Publ., Redwood City, 1989.

[6] C.C. Fleming and B. von Halle, Handbook of relational database design. Addison-Wesley, Reading, 1989.

[7] A. Heuer. Equivalent schemes in semantic, nested relational, and relational database models. LNCS 364, Springer, 1989, 237–253.

[8] R. Hull. Four Views of Complex Objects: A Sophisticate's Introduction. In Proc. Conf. on Nested Relations and Complex Objects in Databases (Eds. : S. Abiteboul, P.C. Fischer, and H.J. Schek), Lecture Notes in Computer Science, 1989, 361, 87–116.

[9] ISOTEC, Methoden des Fachkonzepts. PlönzkeInformatik GmbH, Wiesbaden 1991Ω

[10] U.W. Lipeck and S. Braß. Tools for integrity-centered design of database applications. Internal report of the Computer Science Department, University Dortmund, 1990 (in German).

[11] Y.E. Lien, Relational database design. In S.B. Yao: Principles of database design, Volume I: Logical organizations, Prentice-Hall, 1985, 211–254.

[12] U.W. Lipeck. Dynamic integrity of databases. Informatik-Fachberichte 209, Springer, 1989.

[13] S.B. Navathe and M.K. Pillallamarri, Toward making the E-R approach object-oriented. Proc. Seventh Int. Conf. on Entity-Relationship Approach, 1988

[14] G. M. Nijssen and T. A. Halpin. Conceptual schema and relational database design - a fact oriented approach. Prentice Hall, Sydney 1989.

[15] A. Oberweis. Checking database integrity constraints while simulating information system behavior. Proc. of 9th European Workshop on Applications and Theory of Petri Nets, Venice, 1988, 299–308.

[16] A. Oberweis. Time structures for information systems. PhD Thesis, University Mannheim, 1990 (in German).

[17] N. Rishe. Database Design Fundamentals. Prentice-Hall, Englewood-Cliffs, 1988.

[18] J.F. Roddick, Schema evolution in database systems - An annotated bibliography. SIGMOD RECORD, 21, 4, 1992, 35 – 40.

[19] J.W. Schmidt and F. Matthes. Language technology for post-relational data systems. LNCS 466, 1990, 81–114.

[20] E. Sciore, Abbrevation techniques for entity-relationship query languages. Proc. 10 ER-Conference (ed. T. Teorey), 1991, 129-145.

[21] B. Schewe, K.-D. Schewe, and B. Thalheim, Object-oriented design of data intensive business information systems. Proc. 23 German Computer Science Conference, Dresden 1993. (In German)

[22] R. Spencer, T. Teorey, and E. Hevia. ER standards proposal. Proc. 9th ER Conference, ed. H. Kangassalo, 1990, 405–412.

[23] K.-D. Schewe, J. W. Schmidt, B. Thalheim, I. Wetzel. Extensible safe object-oriented design of database applications. Submitted for publication, 1991.

[24] B. Thalheim. The higher-order entity-relationship model and (DB)^2. LNCS 364, Springer 1989, 382–397.

[25] B. Thalheim, Generalizing the entity-relationship model for database modeling. JNGCS, 1990, 3, 3, 197 – 212.

[26] B. Thalheim. Dependencies in Relational Databases. Leipzig, Teubner Verlag 1991.

[27] B. Thalheim, Concepts of the database design. In: Trends in database management systems, (eds. G. Vossen, K.-U. Witt), Oldenbourg, München, 1–48 (in German).

[28] B. Thalheim, Extending the entity-relationship model for a high-level, theory-based database design. LNCS 504, Springer 1991, 161 - 184.

[29] B. Thalheim, Foundations of entity-relationship modeling. Annals of Mathematics and Artificial Intelligence, 6, 1992.

[30] B. Thalheim, Semantics in entity-relationship models. Proc. Workshop "Semantics of Programming Languages and Model Theory" (eds. E. Börger, M. Droste, J. Gurevich), Morgan Kaufman, 1992.

[31] B. Thalheim, Fundamentals of Entity-Relationship Modeling. Springer, Heidelberg, 1992.

[32] B. Thalheim, Design with the database design system $(DB)^2$. In Fourth Int. Conference "Putting into practice methods and tools for information system design" (ed. H. Habrias), Nantes, France, 1992, 155 – 174

[33] B. Thalheim, A survey on database design strategies. Report CB-CS-1-93, Computer Science Department, Cottbus Technical University, 1993, 92pp.

[34] M. Yaseen and B. Thalheim. Practical Database Design Methodologies. Kuwait University, Faculty of Science, 1989, 256p.

SEMANTICAL CONSTRAINTS FOR DATABASE MODELS

B. Thalheim
Cottbus Technical University, Cottbus, Germany

Abstract

Modeling of semantics is one of the most difficult tasks in database design. Constraints are used to express database semantics. They are used differently in database models. They express domain restrictions, specify relationships between components and state database behavior. The utilization depends on the richness of the type system used in the model. The relational model is using a simple type system and has a very large set of integrity constraints. Semantical models are using richer type systems which express also different types of integrity constraints. At the same time, the theory of integrity constraints is more complex. Object-oriented models use either a simple type system or type systems like the semantical models. The theory of integrity constraints is still under development. This overview tries to give a unifying framework on integrity constraints.

1 Introduction

The goal of this overview is to provide a systematic and unifying introduction to the theory of constraints in database systems. The first step of the foundation of database theory is the precise definition of data models. Without a precise definition, the database concepts cannot be understood for purposes of the design, analysis, and implementation of schemata, transactions, and databases. A *database model* is a collection of mathematically sound concepts defining the intended structural and behavioral properties of objects involved in a database application. In the axiomatic approach, a database model is defined by the properties of its structures and operators. The semantics is given by *axioms* or *constraints* which characterize the databases and the sequences of databases to be accepted.

One of the most important database models is the relational model. One of the major advantages of the relational model is its uniformity. All data are seen as being stored in tables, with each row in the table having the same format. Each row in the table summarizes some object of relationship in the real world. The benefits and aims of the relational model are: to provide data structures which are very simple and easily to be used; to improve logical and physical independence without references to the means of access to data; to provide users with high level languages which could be used by non-specialists in computing; to optimize access to the database; to improve integrity and confidentiality; to take into account a wide variety of applications; to provide a methodological approach for schema design and database design.

These benefits are based on a powerful theory the core of which is the theory of integrity constraints and dependencies in the relational model. Database constraints can be regarded as a language for specifying the semantics of databases. They express the different ways by that data are associated with one another. Since many different associations of data exist, a lot of different classes of dependencies (more than 100) are considered in the literature. By studying their respective properties it can be shown how different types of dependencies interact with one another. These properties may be considered as inference rules which allow to deduce new dependencies from given constraints as well as to generate the closure of all dependencies. Solving this problem, we can test whether two given sets of dependencies are equivalent or whether a given set of dependencies is redundant. A solution for these problems seems to be a significant step towards automated database schema design, towards automated solution of the above-mentioned seven aims and towards recognizing computational feasible problems and the unfeasible ones.

At present we know at least five fields of application of dependency theory:

1. normalization for a more efficient storage, search and modification;

2. reduction of databases to equivalent sub-databases;

3. utilization of dependencies for deriving new relations from basic relations in the view concept or in so-called deductive databases;

4. verification of dependencies for a more powerful and user-friendly, nearly natural language design of databases;

5. transformation of queries into more efficient search strategies.

Integrity constraints are developed in most cases only for relational models. More advanced models use richer typing systems which can define directly integrity constraints based on the structure. Generally, a database model can be seen as a framework like those used for the definition of abstract data types, i.e. the model is specified by the definition of the structure, the operations and the semantics. In database models, operations are specified generically or explicit. Generic operations are defined by the structure. Examples of such operations are the *Insert, Delete* and *Update* operations.

The theory of the relational model can be inherited by most of the other models. The current stage of the development of the theory is very different for different database models. Further, for early models like network and hierarchical models a theory was not developed.

1. **Relational models** use a simple structure, a simple algebra and a rich set of integrity constraints. The algebraic and structural theory is simple and is used for efficient implementations. However, the more complex associations in the database can be modeled only by semantical constraints. Since the enforcement of integrity constraints is complex and should be avoided if possible in practical databases the relational database design uses different approaches for the generation of equivalent structures of the application with simpler sets of integrity constraints.

2. **Semantical models** use a rich type system for the definition of the structure of a database. This type system specifies also parts of the semantical description of the database. In some applications, this set of integrity constraints is powerful enough. Most of the semantical models are used as mediators in databases design, i.e. for the description of the structure. For this reason, a general theory on operations was developed only for some models. An extended theory of integrity constraints was not developed for most of the semantical models.

3. A general theory of **object-oriented models** is currently under development. The structure of these models is either based on simple labeled graphs or on type systems like for semantical models. The operations are either specified completely by the user or are partially specified by the user under use of generic operations. The theory of integrity constraints is mostly inherited from relational and semantical models.

The paper is organized as follows. The second chapter gives a short introduction to database structures, database algebra and integrity constraints in general. The third chapter is devoted to structural and algebraic constraints. We consider the identification of objects in databases and the key concepts, study algebraic constraints and examine class constraints. The fourth chapter discusses different classes of constraints in different models. Using a general framework, constraints in relational, semantical, object-oriented and deductive models are introduced and formally treated. The fifth chapter is devoted to applications of constraint theory in databases. We discuss how constraints can be used in database systems, how complex constraint sets can be and consider the integrity enforcement.

There are several books and overview papers which could be used for extending this overview on semantics in databases [50,56,66,67], on theoretical fundamentals of (deductive) databases [26,31,32,53,71], on logical foundations [5,28,29], on type and specification theory

[54,75] and on database and knowledge base systems [18,21,24,25,44,45], [47,7]. The bibliographies in these books and [60] contain references to more recent research. The bibliography [42] is a source on research until 1980. For length restrictions a representative bibliography (it would cover more than 3000 papers) can not be attached to this review. The used theorems are collected from [66,67]. Further, each chapter close with additional bibliographical remarks.

2 Modeling Databases

2.1 Algebraic Fundamentals

There are three layers in any database and database system. The first layer is the data environment called data scheme which is supplied by the system or is the assumed set of available atomic data. The second layer is the schema of a given database. The third layer is the database itself representing a state of the application's data and knowledge.

The second layer is treated differently in most database models. Nevertheless, there are common features, especially type constructors. For their discussion we introduce a general type definition framework. A common approach in most models is the generic definition of operations according to the structure of the type. Several object-oriented models omit generic operations and use user-defined operations.

2.1.1 Type Systems

A **type constructor** is a function from types to a new type. The constructor can be supplemented

- with a *selector* for retrieval (like *Select*) and *update functions* (like *Insert*, *Delete*, and *Update*) for value mapping from the new type to the component types or to the new type,

- with *correctness criteria* and rules for validation,

- with *default* rules,

- with one or several *user representations*, and

- with a *physical representatation* or properties of the physical representation.

Further, functions can be defined on each type and used in other type constructors. The set of constructed types and functions can be taken as the signature of a logical language. The logical language can be used for the representation of semantical information and for the definition of derived data and knowledge.

The type constructors define type systems on data schemes, i.e. a collection of constructed data sets. In some database models, the type constructors are based on a pointer semantics.

For instance, the set type is based on another type and uses an algebra of operations like union, intersection and complement. The retrieval function can be viewed in a straightforward manner as having a predicate parameter. The update functions like *Insert, Delete* are defined as expressions of the set algebra. The user representation is using the braces $\{,\}$.

The tuple constructor $(,)$ is a variadic function on a list of types with a simple retrieval function using the number of the component in the list (or if the used types are different then the component type name can be used). The projection of a tuple is a function which maps tuples to tuples on another tuple type. This operation needs to be generalized.

There can be introduced also other types. A type is called *bulk type* if it can have instances of arbitrary large size. Another conception closely related to bulk types is *comprehension* [74].

For a type system, a parametric iterator *map* that restructures each element on a given type can be used. For instance, it takes one function parameter, say f, and when applied to a set S, it returns $\{f(s) \mid s \in S\}$. Operations like *nest* can be defined in the same manner. The *nest* operation is based on two functions, say f, g. It partitions the elements of a set according to common values for f and combines each such value with the set of g values for these elements. The *filter* operator is another typical function. Given a set L of formulas and the type T. Then we define *filter* $: T \times L \to T$ by $filter(R^t, \alpha) = \{t \in R^t \mid \alpha(t) = 1\}$.

Further, a general aggregator, called in [10] *pump*, can be applied successively to a set starting and a binary function with a given element u. For instance, given types T_1, T_2, T_3 and functions $g : T_1 \to T_2$ and $h : T_2 \times T_3 \to T_3$. Then the aggregator can be defined for relations consisting of tuples from T_1 by the iteration rules

$$pump(\{t\}) = h(g(t), \lambda) \qquad pump(\{t\} \cup R^t) = \begin{cases} h(g(t), pump(R^t)) & \text{if } t \notin R^t \\ pump(t, R^t \setminus \{t\}) & \text{if } t \in R^t \end{cases} .$$

Examples of such operations are *sum* which starts with 0 and applies + for the function.

Another very useful modeling construct is *naming*. Each concept and each concept class has a name. These names can be used for the definition of further types.

Some types can be used in other types under certain restrictions. Such restrictions can be formulated as precondition for the use of instances of this type and as postconditions for rejection of the result of application of this type.

The set of types can be organized into a hierarchy of types so that the corresponding concepts are in a is-a-relationship. Types may have multiple supertypes.

2.1.2 The Relational Model

Let us first consider the relational database model. This model has a strong theory which can be reused in most of the other database models.

A *data scheme* $DD = (U, \underline{D}, dom)$ is given
by a finite set U of *simple attributes*,
by a set $\underline{D} = \{D_1, D_2, ...\}$ of (not necessarily disjunct) *domains*,
and by a *domain function* $\qquad dom : U \longrightarrow \underline{D}$
which associates with every simple or atomic attribute its domain.

Now, the *relational schema* $R = ((B_1, ..., B_n), \Sigma)$ can be defined as a tuple of simple attributes and a set of (local) integrity constraints (which are discussed in the next section; for the purpose of this section we can use $\Sigma = \emptyset$, i.e. $R = ((B_1, ..., B_n), \emptyset)$). The set of attributes of R is denoted by $attr(R) = \{B_1, ..., B_n\}$.

For a given set $X \subseteq U$, a tuple t on X is defined as a function assigning a value from $dom(A)$ to each $A \in X$. A *finite* set R^t of tuples on $(B_1, ..., B_n)$ is a valid instance (relation) of the relational schema R if Σ is valid in R^t.

The set of all valid instances of the relational schema R is denoted by $SAT(R)$.

These definitions can be extended to collections of different relational schemata which are called *database schema DS*, i.e. $DS = ((R_1, ..., R_n), \Psi)$ where Ψ is a set of (global) integrity constraints on DS.

Similarly, database instances on DS etc. can be introduced.

Based on DS generic operations *Insert, Delete* and conditional *Update* are defined for adding tuples to instances, deleting tuples from instances and modifying tuples in instances if a certain condition is valid. These operations are extended to the relational algebra which is based on the set algebra.

For two relations R^t, R'^t on a relational schema $R = ((B_1, ..., B_n), \emptyset)$ the operations $R^t \cup R'^t$ (union), $R^t \cap R'^t$ (intersection) and $R^t \setminus R'^t$ (set difference) are defined as usual.

For a relation $R^t \in SAT(R)$, $A, C \in \{B_1, ..., B_n\}$, a value $a \in dom(A)$, a comparison operator $\theta \in \{\leq, \geq, \neq, =, <, >\}$, the *selections* $\sigma_{A\theta a}$, $\sigma_{A\theta C}$ are the subsets $\{t \in R^t \mid t(A)\theta a\}$ and $\{t \in R^t \mid t(A)\theta t(C)\}$ of R^t respectively. For a given tuple t on X the restriction of R^t to t is defined by $\sigma_t(R^t) = \{t' \in R^t \mid t'[X] = t\}$. These operations are defined on R with the range R.

There are several operations defined between schemata. For a tuple t on $\{B_1, ..., B_n\}$ and a subset $X \subseteq \{B_1, ..., B_n\}$ the projection of t to X, denoted $t[X]$, is the restriction of the function t to X.

The *projection* $R^t[X]$ of a relation R^t on $R = ((B_1, ..., B_n), \Sigma)$ to a subset X of $\{B_1, ..., B_n\}$ is the set $\{t[X] \mid t \in R^t\}$.

Given two schemata $R = ((B_1, ..., B_n), \emptyset)$, $R' = ((B'_1, ..., B'_{n'}), \emptyset)$ and relations R^t, R'^t on R, R'. The *(natural) join* $R^t \bowtie R'^t$ of R^t, R'^t is the relation $\{t \mid t[\{B_1, ..., B_n\}] \in R^t, t[\{B'_1, ..., B'_{n'}\}] \in R'^t\}$ defined on $\{B_1, ..., B_n\} \cup \{B'_1, ..., B'_{n'}\}$. For a schema $R = ((B_1, ..., B_n), \emptyset)$, two attributes $A \in \{B_1, ..., B_n\}$, $B \in U \setminus \{B_1, ..., B_n\}$ and a relation R^t on R the renaming $\varrho_{A|B}(R^t)$ is the relation $\{t \mid for\ some\ t' \in R^t : t(B) = t'(A), t[\{B_1, ..., B_n\} \setminus \{A\}] = t'[\{B_1, ..., B_n\} \setminus \{A\}]\}$ on $(\{B_1, ..., B_n\} \setminus \{A\}) \cup \{B\}$.

There can be defined more operations.

The operations can be applied several times. The expressions of the relational algebra over a database schema DS are the expressions generated by the above presented operations.

The relational algebra can be used for the support of procedural languages. It has a declarative counterpart, the *relational calculus*. A relational schema with n attributes and a relation symbol in logics with arity n are similar concepts. Using this translation the database schema $DS = ((R_1, ..., R_n), \Psi)$ can be represented by a set of relation symbols $\{R_1, ..., R_n\}$. The formulas of the relational calculus with equality over the alphabet $\{R_1, ..., R_n\}$ and an infinite set of variables are built out of atomic formula of the form $x = y$ and $R_i(x_1, ..., x_{m_i})$, $1 \leq i \leq n$ (where R_i is m_i-ary) using the connectives $\vee, \wedge, \neg$ and the quantifiers $\forall, \exists$. Every relational algebra expression can be translated, in polynomial time of its size, into an equivalent relational calculus formula. Every relational calculus formula can be translated, in time polynomial in its size, into an equivalent relational algebra expression (using also the set complement operation which is based on the data scheme). A formula is called domain-independent if the evaluation of an DS database db is not changed whenever the underlying data scheme is expanded. The class of domain-independent formulas is not recursive. There are known several recursive subclasses of the class of domain-independent formulas. The relational calculus can be also defined using tuple variables (tuple relational calculus) instead of domain variables (domain relational calculus).

The relational model has been implemented based on the set semantics. However, often the model is implemented on a *bag semantics*. SQL is in this case also based on a bag semantics. This mixing leads to problems in the interpretation and the meaning of database operations.

2.1.3 Other Models

The models can be distinguished also by the kind of type definition. Type definitions can be recursive or strongly hierarchical. Recursive type definitions like for instance the type definitions in functional or object-oriented models need additional correctness criterias. In the other case, the instances of types are infinite. Type definitions can reuse parts of other types or can tight concepts to different types. Such conceptions like shared attributes or shared concepts need a special treatment of inheritance or sharing. Inheritance is one of the main inference mechanisms in advanced database systems. It has to be distinguished from hierarchical organization.

More complex database models are based on advanced attribute sets. For a given set $Names$ of names we can construct now the set $NestAttr$ of nested attributes with the basic property $\{\emptyset\} \cup U \subseteq NestAttr$ and applying recursively the following step:
If $X_1, ..., X_n, Y$ are distinct elements from $NestAttr$ and $X \in Names$ then $X(X_1, ..., X_n)$ is a (tuple-valued) nested attribute in $NestAttr$ and $X\{Y\}$ is a (set-valued) nested attribute in $NestAttr$.
On the basis of this definition the corresponding value sets are defined.

In the style of the relational approach, other database models can be defined. Their definition depends on whether recursive definitions are allowed or not and whether structures can be reused or not.

The **nested relational schema** can be defined by a tuple of nested attributes and a set of integrity constraints.

The **entity schema** is defined as a set of (nested) attributes together with a set of integrity constraints. The **relationship schema** is defined by a sequence of entity schemata and a set of (nested) attributes together with a set of integrity constraints. The extended entity-relationship model (e.g. in [67]) allows hierarchical definition of relationship types, i.e. a relationship schema of order i is defined by a sequence of relationship schemata of order less than i and a set of (nested) attributes together with a set of integrity constraints whereas entity schemata are considered to be relationship schemata of order 0. The entity-relationship model could be also defined by entity schemata as above and relationship schemata based on references. In this case, the meaning of integrity constraints changes. However, the last treatment of schemata can be mapped to the first. For this reason, we use here the set semantics for the entity-relationship model.

The **network model** uses lists of tuples and references. Its type system is nonrecursive. Often, the network model is considered to use sets of tuples and relationship sets. However, this interpretation is not used in systems. The first definition of the network model does not allows to consider the entity-relationship model to be a generalization of the network model.

The basis of the **functional model** are objects and functions. An object is an individual concept. Functions map objects onto other objects and data values. Relationships between objects, attributes of objects, and procedures associated with objects are represented by functions.

The identifier is one of the main conceptions of **object-oriented models**. The algebra of operations changes completely for such models. For instance, the *map* function which is not injective should be supported on the identifier level. The projection is an example of such operation. If two tuples t, t' are mapped to the same projection tuple $t"$ then the value $t"$ is associated with two identifiers. Other conceptions to be developed for object-oriented databases are according to [1]: overriding, overloading and late binding; computational completeness; extensibility; persistence; secondary storage management; multiple inheritance; type checking and type inferencing; design transactions; versions. More research is necessary for the clarification of these concepts.

Scripts are an extension of frames using also functions with pre- and postconditions in the intensional part of event concepts.

Deductive databases are considered to be an important case of *knowledge bases*. The database theory was presented up to now using the model theoretic approach. The proof theoretic approach is used in deductive databases. A database can be seen as a set of facts or ground formulas and queries can be evaluated by proving theorems on the fact set. In this case, three closure assumptions should be stated explicitly.

The *domain closure assumption* postulates that the individuals occuring in
   the database are all and only existing individuals.

The *unique name assumption* requires that individuals with different names
   are different.

The *closed world assumption* presumes that the only possible individuals
   are those which are implied by the database.

The proof theoretic approach provides a correct treatment of query evaluation even in the case of null values, a correct enforcement of integrity constraints, and can cover more real world semantics in conceptual modeling. Since all relational operations are expressable by formulas and the transitive closure can be expressed by formulas but not in the relational algebra this calculus is more powerful than the relational algebra for query evaluation. Since queries, integrity constraints, facts and operations are represented in the same language this approach is uniform. Further, since logic can be used as a knowledge representation language (or knowledge model) this approach allows the direct extension of databases to knowledge bases.

A deductive database can be defined by a set of formulas of the first-order predicate logic. A formula can be represented by a Skolemized clause of the form
$$\gamma = ((\alpha_1 \wedge \alpha_2 \wedge .... \wedge \alpha_n) \rightarrow (\beta_1 \vee \beta_2 \vee ... \vee \beta_m))$$

where α_i, β_j are atomic formulas (may be closed (using only constants)). This treatment can be extended to formulas with negation in the premise, i.e.

$$\gamma = ((\alpha_1 \wedge \alpha_2 \wedge \dots \wedge \alpha_n \wedge \neg\alpha_{n+1} \wedge \dots \wedge \neg\alpha_k) \rightarrow (\beta_1 \vee \beta_2 \vee \dots \vee \beta_m)).$$

The introduction of negation in premises increases the expressive power of deductive databases. However, negation in programs raises problems in the definition of declarative semantics of such programs. These can be solved for classes which declarative semantics is well-defined (e.g. stratified rule sets) or by reducing the meaning of semantics by many-valued logic models.

A *deductive database* is the triple $DDB = (Facts, Rules, Integrity\_Constraints)$. The set of facts is the extensional database and the set of rules can be used for the generation of the intensional database. This model can be extended to models which use formulas as facts and higher-order logics for the specification of constraints.

The logical data language (LDL) extends the above discussed Datalog approach by adding functional symbols to the language, using built-in-functions, sets and composition of objects to complex objects. Then the safety conditions, the stratification etc. should be modified.

Higher-order logics [55] can be used for the specification of meta-information on the predicates (Is-A-associations etc.).

2.2 Integrity Constraints

Logic is used for the specification of constraints in databases and for the specification of intensional or derivable relationships. The best understood set of constraints is the set called dependencies. These are discussed in the first subsection. The logical language used for the specification of derivable relationships is richer than the algebraic and needs a special evaluation strategy. These problems are addressed in the second subsection.

If a database is viewed as a set of tuples over some domain values then missing semantics should be specified additionally. These semantic specifications are called integrity constraints. They specify which databases are meaningful for the application and which are meaningless. In the relational model of particular interest are constraints called (data) dependencies. During the last two decades a lot of different classes of integrity constraints have been discussed (for an overview of most classes known in the relational model see [66]).

Before introducing some special classes let us discuss the general structure. Generally, we distinguish between

- *static integrity constraints* (for the representation of semantics of all possible instances of the database)
  and

- *dynamic integrity constraints* (for the representation of the behavior of the database during its lifetime, e.g. correctness of sequences of states of the database).

Static integrity constraint classes can be classified according to their function in the scheme:

1. structural constraints, i.e. constraints which are used in reality for the database design and express conditions on the structure, e.g. inclusion, exclusion, functional dependencies;

2. semantic constraints. i.e. constraints which are used in reality for the database design and are semantic restrictions, e.g. functional, multivalued dependencies;

3. representation constraints, i.e. constraints which are used for the representation of the database, e.g. inclusion, join, tuple-generating dependencies;

4. design constraints, i.e. constraints which can be used for a user-friendly schema design [66], e.g. general functional and generalized functional dependencies.

It can be shown that these constraints can be used in dynamic integrity constraints. Dynamic integrity constraints are useful for the maintenance of the database system. At present, there is no general framework for the utilization of dynamic integrity constraints. Dynamic integrity constraints can be classified according to thier functionality:

1. transition constraints, i.e. constraints which restrict the application of database operations and database state transformations, e.g. pre- and postconditions for update operations;

2. temporal formulas, i.e. constraints on state sequences [58].

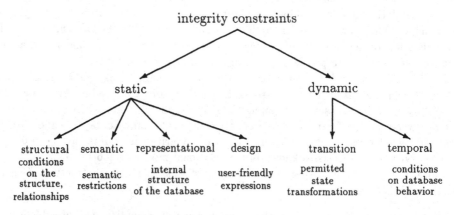

Figure 1. The classification of integrity constraints

This classification includes both inherent and explicit constraints. The distinction between inherent and explicit constraints depends on the model used. In the relational model, all integrity constraints are represented together. This comixing leads to difficulties in classification. In [11] a classification of dependencies by their role is proposed. The consideration of the set of all constraints has the advantage that we need only one unique derivation procedure. However, there is no axiomatization for different sets of integrity constraints, e.g.

for functional and inclusion dependencies. Therefore in this case, only the axiomatization known in first-order predicate logic could be applied. But this is fairly complex. The mixing leads also to a mismatch of constraint types. Especially, in relational database design dependencies are intending to express both basic relationships and semantic relationships. In the entity-relationship approach, structural constraints are modeled by inherited constraints like inclusion dependencies which are defined on the structure of the scheme. In most extensions of the entity-relationship model different types of functional constraints like one-to-one or one-to-many relationships or cardinality constraints are considered. The advantage of those constraints is that they are easy to specify and that they are design dependencies.

We can restrict the utilization of integrity constraints to the following mappings:

1. $f_1 : \{DesignDep\} \hookrightarrow \{StructInt\} \bigcup \{SemanticInt\}$,
2. $f_2 : \{StructInt\} \hookrightarrow \{RepresentInt\}$,
3. $f_3 : \{SemanticInt\} \hookrightarrow \{RepresentInt\}$,
4. $f_4 : \{StructInt\} \bigcup \{SemanticInt\} \bigcup \{RepresentInt\} \hookrightarrow \{DynamicInt\}$.

Therefore, the design process could be considered as a process of schema transformations [38]. In the first step a schema consisting of a structure and a set of design constraints is defined (*design schema*). Using the function f_1 a new schema consisting of the same structure and a set of design, structural and semantic constraints is generated (*conceptual schema*). Using f_2 and f_3 this schema is translated to a schema which is more efficient (*database schema*). Then using f_4 we generate the corresponding insert, delete and update operations. These operations maintain consistent states under consideration of dynamic integrity constraints (*management schema*).

Integrity constraints are to be specified according to their environment. They can be valid in a subschema (unit) only. They can be partial or exceptional [8]. They should be maintained during the lifecycle of the database and are enforcing several operations in the case of validation. Furthermore, they can be considered as active rules. Therefore, a complete specification of integrity constraints includes also the environment:

> *Integrity Constraint* φ
> [Localization: < unit_name>]
> [Partiality: < validity condition >]
> [Exception: < exception condition >]
> [In-Context: (< enforcement rule > , < enforcement event >)]
> [Out-Context: < conditional operation>] .

There are several other ways to classify integrity constraints.

- Integrity constraints can be classified according to their application area. They can be applied to one tuple, two tuples, several relations etc.

- Integrity constraints can be distinguished according to their logical form, e.g. tuple-generating and equality-generating dependencies.

- Integrity constraints can be separated by their invariants, e.g. stability under renaming.

Further, we can distinguish special classes of integrity constraints by their validity area. For instance, semantic integrity constraints can be enterprise-dependent. They can represent laws of nature or belong to commonsense knowledge.

For the purpose of this overview we use the model-theoreticc interpretation of formulas. For deductive databases, it may be useful to consider the proof-theoretic interpretation of integrity constraints. In this case, we distinguish satisfiability and entailment for integrity constraints. This can be accomplished by completion requirements like the closed world assumption. Formulas of epistemic modal logic cover all these different proof-theoretic approaches.

Bibliographical remarks

The algebraic background is reviewed in standard textbooks like [21,50,56], [72] and in the overview [43]. The extensions of the relational model are discussed also in [7,24,27,40,59]. Distributed schemes [19] can be defined by database schemata with a set of allocation constraints defined on a network.

The general approach to integrity constraints is developed in [66,67] and uses extensions from [8].

3 Algebraic and Structural Constraints

3.1 Identification and Keys

The notion of the "key" is a predecessor idea of the concept of the identifier. According to the usage of the term "key" we can identify several utilizations of the term:

Identification of objects The key is defined as a non-empty set of attributes which uniquely identifies a particular object. To eliminate redundant keys, the key definition may be restricted to the minimum number of attributes that characterize the object uniquely.

Existence of objects The "key" is an indication of the existence of the object. The object-oriented database system maintains an identity for each object by an object identifier, which is generated by the system and is independent of any key attributes. Hence, any attribute of an object that can be updated without destroying its identity. The value-oriented representation of the key concept leds to the concept of the surrogate. The surrogates have, then, the following additional properties:

- Surrogates are system-controlled. They can be created, duplicated or invalidated only by the system at the command of a manager.

- The equality operation is the only basic function that is available for surrogates.

Integrity constraint The "key" is also used to preserve the uniqueness of a set of objects. For example, in relational database theory the key dependency $X \longrightarrow U$ for $X \subseteq U$ implies that the relation $r(U)$ is a set of tuples which can be uniquely identified through the value of $(r(U))[X]$.
We notice here that the uniqueness property is an intrinsic characteristic of the relation, whereas the identification property is an extrinsic characterization used by the system.

Accessibility We can physically order the records of a file based on the values of a set
of attributes. This leads to the concept of an ordered file. This ordering has several
advantages over unordered files.

The notion of the key as it is used in the area of database systems is associated with the
concept of **distinguishability**, i.e. having different identities.

This notion can be extended to object-oriented databases. An object is represented in
the database by its identifier, its values and references to other objects and by methods. The
representation of values is structured by the type system. We distinguish like [10] between the
structural representation and the behavior of objects. The object level is used to represent the
structure of objects. The method level is used for the representation of dynamic properties
of objects.

identifier is used for the representation of object identity. This concept can be considered
as a generalization of the classical key concept. However, object identifiers are system-
maintained. They are invisible to the user. There are no operations available for the user
which can be used to manipulate or display them. The user can only ask whether two objects
are equal or not. Identifiers are internally used to determine which of the objects are equal
and which not. The identity is visible through the object's interface [12]. The identifier may
be considered as being immutable. However, from a systems oriented view permutations or
collapses of identifiers without changing anything else should not affect the behaviour of the
database.

For the user the abstract identifier of an object has no meaning. Therefore, a different
access to the identification problem is required. The unique identification of an object in a
class leads to the notion of *(weak) value-identifiability* [62], where weak value-identifiability
can be used to capture also objects that do not exists for there own, but depend on other
objects. The stronger notion of *value-representability* is required for the unique definition of
generic update operations. The identification of identifiable objects can be based on their
value type. In this case, object identifiers can be dropped and replaced by values of referred
objects. This value representation type is unique up to isomorphism. An object is called
weakly value-identifiable if it can be identified by values of referred objects and by references from weakly value-identifiable objects. The weak value-representation type of objects
is unique provided it exists. Value-representability implies weak value-representability. Moreover, each weakly value-representable class is also weakly value-identifiable and vice versa.
The (weak) value-representation is computable. An object is uniquely identifiable [12] if its
orbit in $G(\mathcal{D})$ is trivial. A class has the unique identification property if for all instances all
objects are uniquely identifiable. A class C has the unique identification property iff C is
weakly value-identifiable [12,62].

3.2 Algebraic Constraints

A formal system for reasoning about different kinds of constraints can be based on expressions
defined in the relational algebra. A relational expression is any well formed expression built
up from relation schema names and relational operators. These expressions can be considered
to be queries which are evaluated for a given database. For instance, for relations $R_1^t, ..., R_m^t$
on $R_1, ..., R_m$ the join $\bowtie_{i=1}^m R_i^t$ is the set generated by the expression $(((R_1^t \bowtie R_2^t) \bowtie R_3^t)... \bowtie$

R_n^t). For a cover $\{X_1, ..., X_m\}$ of $\{B_1, ..., B_n\}$ a relation R^t on $\{B_1, ..., B_n\}$ has the *lossless join property* (can be decomposed without loss of information into $R^t[X_1], ..., R^t[X_m]$) if $\bowtie_{i=1}^m R^t[X_i] = R^t$.

Expressions of the relational algebra can be compared for containment and equivalence. Containment and equivalence of relational expressions are undecidable. Containment equalities can be used for the specification of integrity constraints (e.g. for the lossless join property). The relational algebra can be understood as a cylindric algebra [78].

Based on this language algebraic integrity constraints can be defined. Algebraic dependencies are considered to be a unifying approach to the theory of dependencies in relational databases. Algebraic dependencies are introduced for extended schemata with an infinite collection of copies of relation schema names. This class is equivalent to the later defined class of BV-dependencies.

For a given relation schema R and algebraic expressions e_1, e_2 on R defined on attribute subsets X, Y on R, the following algebraic dependencies are valid:

$$(e_1[W])[V] = e_1[V] \quad \text{for} \quad V \subseteq W \subseteq X \qquad\qquad e_1[X] = e_1$$

$$e_1 \bowtie e_1[W] = e_1 \quad \text{for} \quad W \subseteq X \qquad\qquad (e_1 \bowtie e_2)[X] \subseteq e_1$$

$$(e_1 \bowtie e_2)[V \cup W] \subseteq (e_1 \bowtie e_2[W])[V \cup W] \quad \text{for} \quad V \subseteq X, W \subseteq Y$$

$$(e_1 \bowtie e_2)[V \cup W] = (e_1 \bowtie e_2[W])[V \cup W] \quad \text{for} \quad V \subseteq X, W \subseteq Y, X \cap Y \subseteq W$$

$$(e_1 \bowtie e_2)[W] = (e_1[X \cap (Y \cup W)] \bowtie e_2[Y \cap (X \cup W)])[W]$$

$$e_1[W \cup V] \subseteq (e_1[V] \bowtie e_1[W]) \quad \text{for} \quad V, W \subseteq X$$

Further, the join operation is commutative and associative.

Inclusion dependencies are special algebraic dependencies. The inclusion dependencies can be generalized to *nondeterministic inclusion dependencies*. This generalization is important if the model permits clustering. A *generalized inclusion dependency* is an expression of the form

$$R_1[X_1] \cap ... \cap R_n[X_n] \subseteq S_1[Y_1] \cup ... \cup S_m[Y_m]$$

for compatible sequences X_i, Y_j and is valid in a database $(..., R_i^t, ..., S_j^t, ...)$ if $R_1^t[X_1] \cap ... \cap R_n^t[X_n] \subseteq S_1^t[Y_1] \cup ... \cup S_m^t[Y_m]$.

For $n = m = 1$, the generalized inclusion depdendency is called inclusion dependency.

A special class of algebraic constraints are key based inclusion dependencies, i.e. inclusion dependencies $R[X] \subseteq S[Y]$ where Y forms a key of S. These are called *referential integrity constraints*.

The class of exclusion dependencies [66] is another important class of algebraic integrity constraints. Given two schemata R, S and names of attributes $R.A_1, ..., R.A_n, S.B_1, ..., S.B_n$ defined on these schemata. An **exclusion dependency** is an expression of the form

$$R[R.A_1, ..., R.A_n] \parallel S[S.B_1, ..., S.B_n]$$

and is valid in a database $(..., R^t, ..., S^t, ...)$ if for all $r \in R^t$ and all $s \in S^t$

$$r \mid_{A_1, ..., A_n} \neq s \mid_{B_1, ..., B_n}.$$

The class of exlusion and inclusion dependencies is axiomatizable like in [66].

Axioms

$$XY \subseteq X \qquad X \subseteq X \cup Y$$

Rules

$$\frac{X_1...X_n \subseteq Y \cup W_1 \cup ... \cup W_m \qquad Y Z_1...Z_n \subseteq V_1 \cup ... \cup V_l}{X_1...X_n Z_1...Z_n \subseteq V_1 \cup ... \cup V_l \cup W_1 \cup ... \cup W_m} \qquad l \neq 0$$

$$\frac{X_1...X_n \subseteq Y \cup W_1 \cup ... \cup W_m \qquad Y Z_1...Z_n \parallel V}{X_1...X_n Z_1...Z_n V \subseteq W_1 \cup ... \cup W_m} \qquad m \neq 0$$

$$\frac{X_1...X_n \subseteq Y, \qquad Y Z_1...Z_n \parallel V}{X_1...X_n Z_1...Z_n \parallel V}$$

$$\frac{X \parallel X}{X \parallel Y} \qquad \frac{X \parallel X}{X \subseteq Y} \qquad \frac{X_1...X_n \parallel X_0}{X_0 X_1...X_{n-1} \parallel X_n}$$

$$\frac{X_1...X_n \subseteq \zeta}{X_{\pi(1)}...X_{\pi(n)} \subseteq \zeta} \qquad \text{for each permutation } \pi$$

$$\frac{X_1...X_n \parallel Z}{X_{\pi(1)}...X_{\pi(n)} \parallel Z} \qquad \text{for each permutation } \pi$$

The implication problem for exclusion and (generalized) inclusion constraints is NP-complete.

The algebraic constraint $(R[X_1] \bowtie ... \bowtie R[X_n])[X] \subseteq R[X]$ for $X \subseteq X_1 \cup ... \cup X_n \subseteq attr(R)$ is called *projected join dependency* and denoted by $(X_1, ..., X_n)[X]$. Since $(R[X_1] \bowtie ... \bowtie R[X_n])[X] \supseteq R[X]$ the projected join dependency is equivalent to $(R[X_1] \bowtie ... \bowtie R[X_n])[X] = R[X]$. If $X = X_1 \cup ... \cup X_n$ then the projected join dependency is called *X-join dependency*. If $attr(R) \neq X_1 \cup ... \cup X_n$ the projected join dependency is called embedded otherwise total. *Join dependencies* are total X-join dependencies. Binary ($n = 2$) join dependencies are equivalent to multivalued dependencies. The binary X-join dependency is also called embedded multivalued dependency. The set of binary join dependencies is axiomatizable. The set of join dependencies is not axiomatizable. Join dependencies are template dependencies. Template dependencies are axiomatizable.

For $X, Y, Z \subseteq attr(R)$ and $Y \cap Z = \emptyset$ the projected join dependency $(R[X \cup Y] \bowtie R[X \cup Z])[Y \cup Z] \subseteq R[Y \cup Z]$ is called *transitive dependency* and denoted by $X(Y, Z)$. Transitive dependencies are axiomatizable by the following system:

Axioms

$$XY(Y, Z)$$

Rules

$$\frac{X(Y, Z), Y(Z, T)}{X(Z, T)} \qquad \frac{X(Y, Z), X(T, Z), Z(T, Y \cup Z)}{X(Y \cup T, Z)}$$

$$\frac{X(Y, Z)}{X(Z, Y)} \qquad \frac{X(Y \cup T, Z)}{X(Y, Z)} \qquad \frac{X(Y, Z)}{X \cup T(Y, Z)}$$

The extended transitive dependency is defined by

$$(\overset{p}{\underset{i=1}{\bowtie}} \quad \overset{q}{\underset{j=1}{\bowtie}} \quad R[X_i \cup Y_j])[\overset{q}{\underset{j=1}{\bigcup}} Y_j] \subseteq R[\overset{q}{\underset{j=1}{\bigcup}} Y_j]$$

for pairwise disjoint sets X_i and Y_j.

Bibliographical remarks

The books [66,78] give an impression on the algebraic treatment of dependencies.

4 Logical Constraints

4.1 Dependencies in Relational Models

Dependencies form a large class of constraints in the relational model. We need some formal notions.

Let $R = ((B_1, ..., B_n), \emptyset)$ a relational schema on a data scheme DD and X, Y subsets of $attr(R) = \{B_1, ..., B_n\}$. A relation $R^t \in SAT(R)$ satisfies the *functional dependency* $X \to Y$ when for all tuples t, t' in R^t if $t[X] = t'[X]$ then $t[Y] = t'[Y]$. A relation satisfies a set of functional dependencies if it satisifies all the dependencies in this set. A subset X is called key of R^t if $X \to attr(R)$ is valid in R^t. Minimal such subsets are called *minimal key*.

Given now a cover $X, Y_1, ..., Y_m$ of $attr(R)$ where the sets $Y_1, ..., Y_m$ are pairwise disjunct. The *hierarchical dependency* $X \to\to Y_1 \mid Y_2 \mid ... \mid Y_m$ is valid in R^t if for tuples $t_1, t_2, ..., t_m$ from R^t which are equal on X a tuple t exists in R^t for which $t[X \cup Y_i] = t_i[X \cup Y_i]$ for all $i (1 \le i \le m)$.

If $m = 2$ the hierarchical dependency is called *multivalued dependency*.

Functional dependencies are an example of equality generating dependencies:
$$\forall(x_{1,1}, ..., x_{m,n})$$
$$(P_R(x_{1,1}, ..., x_{1,n}) \wedge ... \wedge P_R(x_{m,1}, ..., x_{m,n}) \wedge F(x_{1,1}, ..., x_{m,n}) \quad \to$$
$$G(x_{1,1}, ..., x_{m,n}))$$
where $F(x_{1,1}, ..., x_{m,n}), G(x_{1,1}, ..., x_{m,n})$ are conjunctions of equalities of the form $x_{i,j} = x_{i',j'}$ and P is the predicate symbol associated with R. Equality generating dependencies have some useful properties. For instance, if a equality generating dependency is valid in a relation then it is valid also in any subset of this relation. If we allow in F and G arbitrary formulas on equalities and $m = 2$, the dependency is called *generalized functional dependency*.

Multivalued and hierarchical dependencies are examples of tuple generating dependencies:
$$\forall(x_{1,1}, ..., x_{m,n})\exists(y_{i_1}, ..., y_{i_k})(P_R(x_{1,1}, ..., x_{1,n}) \wedge ... \wedge P_R(x_{m,1}, ..., x_{m,n}) \wedge F(x_{1,1}, ..., x_{m,n})$$
$$\to P_R(y_1, ..., y_n) \wedge H(y_1, ..., y_n, x_{1,1}, ..., x_{m,n}))$$
where $F(x_{1,1}, ..., x_{m,n})$ is a conjunction of equalities of the form $x_{i,j} = x_{i',j'}$ and $H(y_1, ..., y_n, x_{1,1}, ..., x_{m,n})$ is a conjunction of equalities of the form $y_j = x_{i',j'}$ and $y_{i_1}, ..., y_{i_k}$ are the variables of the premise which do not appear in H.

A tuple generating dependency is called *full* if all y_i are bounded by equalities in H.

Typed equality or tuple generating *dependencies* use only equalities with $j = j'$.

Join dependencies can be represented by full, typed tuple generating dependencies with equalities in F only for those variables which are used in H. Join dependencies represent a decomposition of a relation. Hierarchical dependencies are join dependencies.

Any set of relation schemata $\mathcal{R} = \{R_1, .. R_n\}$ has an associated set of predicate symbols $\mathcal{P}_\mathcal{R} = \{P_{R_1}, .. P_{R_n}\}$ which forms together with the constants $C_{DD} = \{c_{d,D} \mid d \in D, D \in \underline{D}\}$ of the data scheme DD the signature of the first-order predicate logic $L = L(\mathcal{P}_\mathcal{R}, C_{DD})$. This logical language can be used to express *database constraints* on $\mathcal{R}$ and C_{DD}. Database constraints can be restricted to formulas without scheme constants. For two data schemes DD and DD' a formula α from $L(\mathcal{P}_\mathcal{R}, C_{DD}) \cup L(\mathcal{P}_\mathcal{R}, C_{DD'})$ is said to be domain-independent if for all databases $DB^t = (R_1^t, ..., R_n^t)$ on DD and $DB'^t = (S_1^t, ..., S_n^t)$ on DD' with $R_i^t = S_i^t$ for all i DB^t satisfies α if and only if DB'^t satisfies α. A database $DB^t = (R_1^t, ..., R_n^t)$ which relations have at most one element is said to be trivial. Domain independent formulas which hold in any trivial database are called *dependency*. The set of dependencies is recursively enumerable only in the case $n = 1$. The problem to decide whether a given formula is a dependency is recursively unsolvable. Therefore, special classes of dependencies are of interest.

A formula is uni-relational if it is built from one predicate. A formula is typed if variables are not used in two different argument positions of the same predicate symbol and only variables which occur in the same argument position of a predicate symbol can be used in an equality.

A *general embedded implicational dependency* is a formula of the form

$$\alpha = \forall y_1 ... \forall y_k \exists z_1 ... \exists z_l ((\beta_1 \wedge ... \beta_p) \longrightarrow (\gamma_1 \wedge ... \wedge \gamma_q)$$

where all β_i, γ_j are atomic formulas, at least one β_i is a predicate formula $P_R(\bar{x})$, the set of variables occuring in the β_i is the same as the set of variables occuring in predicated β_i and is exactly $\{y_1, ..., y_k\}$, and the set of variables occuring in the γ_j contains $\{z_1, ..., z_l\}$ and is a subset of $\{z_1, ..., z_l, y_1, ..., y_k\}$. General embedded implicational dependencies can be classified as follows:

dependency	k	l	p	q	restrictions for β_i	γ_j	α
inclusion			=1	=1	predicates	predicates	
BV-dependency		=0					uni-relational
tuple-generating		=0			predicates	predicates	uni-relational
embedded template				=1	predicates	predicates	uni-relational many-sorted
template		=0		=1	predicates	predicates	uni-relational typed
equality-generating		=0			predicates	equalities	uni-relational typed
functional		=0	=2		predicates	equalities	uni-relational typed
total BV-dependency		=0					uni-relational
embedded tuple-generating					predicates	predicates	uni-relational

The following proof procedure can be used to check whether a set of total general implication dependencies (with $q = 1$ and $l = 0$) imply another one. This proof procedure can be written in a tableau. Then the procedure corresponds to a step by step generation of new rows. For template dependencies in this representation the proof procedure is called chase of a tableau.

Given a set of total general implication dependencies Σ and a total general implication dependency $\alpha = \forall((P_{i1}(\bar{x}_{i1}) \wedge ... \wedge P_{im}(\bar{x}_{im})) \to \beta)$. Then the following closure can be defined inductively:

$$Cl_0(\Sigma, \alpha) = \{P_{ik}(\bar{x}_{ik}) \mid 1 \leq k \leq k\}$$

$\tilde{Cl}_{k+1}(\Sigma, \alpha)$ is obtained from $CL_k(\Sigma, \alpha)$ by applying the following unification:
　　　for $\forall(P_{l1}(\bar{u}_1) \wedge ... \wedge P_{lp}(\bar{u}_p) \to y_i = y_j$ in Σ and
　　　a substitution ς such that $P_{ls}(\varsigma(\bar{u}_s)) \in Cl_k(\Sigma, \alpha)$ for $1 \leq s \leq p$
　　　then identify $\varsigma(y_i)$ and $\varsigma(y_i)$ in $Cl_k(\Sigma, \alpha)$;

$$Cl_{k+1}(\Sigma, \alpha) = \{P_{l0}(\varsigma(\bar{u}_0)) \mid \forall(P_{l1}(\bar{u}_1) \wedge ... \wedge P_{lp}(\bar{u}_p) \to P_{l0}(\bar{u}_0) \in \Sigma$$
$$\text{a substitution } \varsigma \text{ such that } P_{ls}(\varsigma(\bar{u}_s)) \in Cl_k(\Sigma, \alpha)$$
$$\text{for } 1 \leq s \leq p \}$$
$$\cup \tilde{Cl}_{k+1}(\Sigma, \alpha) \quad ;$$

$$Cl(\Sigma, \alpha) = \bigcup_{k = 0}^{\infty} Cl_k(\Sigma, \alpha)$$

Since there is a finite number of atomic formulas composed of α $Cl(\Sigma, \alpha)$ can be finitely computed and there is a k such that $Cl_k(\Sigma, \alpha) = Cl(\Sigma, \alpha)$. It can be proven that $\Sigma \models \alpha$ if and only if $\beta \in Cl(\Sigma, \alpha)$ or y_i and y_j are unified in $Cl(\Sigma, \alpha)$ for $\beta = y_i = y_j$.

The *closure dependency* $X@Y$ is a uni-relational formula on R of the following form

$$\forall x_1...\forall x_n \forall y_1...\forall y_n \exists z_1...\exists z_n ((P_R(x_1, ..., x_n) \wedge P_R(u_1, ..., u_n) \longrightarrow P_R(v_1, ..., v_n))$$

where for $1 \leq i \leq n$

$$u_i = \begin{cases} x_j & \text{if } A_j = C_k \text{ and } B_k = A_i \text{ for some } k \\ y_i & \text{otherwise} \end{cases}$$

$$v_i = \begin{cases} x_i & \text{if } A_i = B_k \text{ for some } k \\ y_i & \text{if } A_i = C_k \text{ for some } k \text{ and for no } l\ B_l = A_i \\ z_i & \text{otherwise} \end{cases}$$

for sequences $X = B_1, ..., B_m$, $Y = C_1, ..., C_m$ of attributes from $attr(R) = \{A_1, ..., A_n\}$ where attributes in the sequences are disctinct from each other.

This constraint states that the relation R^t is obtained by its transitive closure on X and Y. Closure dependencies are commutative. This property forms the axiomatization of this class. Closure dependencies and functional dependencies together are not axiomatizable. The generalized closure dependency drops the restriction that the attributes in sequences are different.

For multivalued dependencies four equivalent definitions can be used:
1. The multivalued dependency $X \longrightarrow\!\!\!\rightarrow Y \mid Z$ is valid in R^t.
2. The algebraic equality $R^t = R^t[X \cup Y] \bowtie R^t[X \cup Z]$ is valid.
3. For all tuples t from R^t it holds that $(\sigma_{t[X]}(R^t))[Y] = (\sigma_{t[X \cup Z]}(R^t))[Y]$.
4. The relation R^t can be represented by the nested relation $\nu(\nu(R^t, Y, A), Z, B)$ where $\nu(S^t, V, C)$ maps the relation S^t on U to a nested relation on $U \setminus (V), C\{V\}$.

The equivalence of the first two definitions is well known. The third condition states that the Y-values of X-restricted tuples are completely independent from their Z-values. This condition describes the meaning of multivalued depdencies. The last condition associates multivalued dependencies to horizontal decomposition of relations and to representations by nested nested relations.

These constraints can be generalized to database schemata.

One important interrelational constraint is the inclusion dependency. Given two relational schemata R, R' and two sequences X, X' from $attr(R), attr(R')$, respectively of the same length. The *inclusion dependency* $R[X] \subseteq R'[X']$ is valid for relations R^t, R'^t on R, R', respectively if $R^t[X] \subseteq R'^t[X']$.

If the length is 1 then the inclusion dependencies are called unary.

Most of the papers in dependency theory deal with various aspects of the finite implication problem, i.e. the problem of deciding for a given set of dependencies Σ and a dependency α whether Σ logically implies α (denoted $\Sigma \models_{fin} \alpha$, i.e. all r in which Σ is valid satisfies α). The general implication property (denoted $\models$) is defined on all (finite and infinite) tuple sets on database schemata. Relational databases are a collection of finite relations. The finite implication property and the general implication property can or can not coincide on dependency sets. For instance, they coincide on inclusion dependencies, full tuple generating dependencies and equality generating dependencies. The two implication properties do not coincide for tuple generating dependencies, even for typed. They do not coincide for functional and inclusion dependencies. The implication problem can be (not) solvable and not decidable or (P- or NP-) decidable. The two implication problems for typed full tuple generating dependencies are unsolvable. The two implication problems for inclusion dependencies are equivalent and PSpace-complete. However, the implication problems for functional and inclusion dependencies are unsolvable. For functional dependencies and unary inclusion dependencies they are solvable in polynomial time. For functional and join dependencies the implication problem is solvable in exponential time. Testing whether a set of multivalued dependencies implies a join dependency is NP-hard. Testing whether a join dependency and a set of functional dependencies imply a join dependency is NP-complete. If the implication problems are solvable we can search for an axiomatization. For the set of join dependencies there does not exist a Hilbert type axiomatization [57] but there is a Gentzen type axiomatization. For the class of functional and multivalued dependencies the following Hilbert type axiomatization is sound and complete.

Axioms

$$ X \cup Y \rightarrow Y \; ; \quad X \cup Y \rightarrow\!\!\!\rightarrow Y \mid Z $$

Rules

$$ \frac{X \rightarrow Y}{X \cup V \cup W \rightarrow Y \cup V} \qquad \frac{X \rightarrow Y, Y \rightarrow Z}{X \rightarrow Z} $$

$$ \frac{X \rightarrow\!\!\!\rightarrow Y \mid Z}{X \rightarrow\!\!\!\rightarrow Z \mid Y} \qquad \frac{X \cup Y \cup Z \rightarrow\!\!\!\rightarrow V \mid W \cup U, \; X \rightarrow\!\!\!\rightarrow Y \cup V \cup W \mid Z \cup U}{X \cup Y \rightarrow\!\!\!\rightarrow V \mid Z \cup W \cup U} $$

$$ \frac{X \rightarrow Y}{X \rightarrow\!\!\!\rightarrow Y \mid Z} \, Z = attr(R) - (X \cup Y) \qquad \frac{X \rightarrow\!\!\!\rightarrow Y \mid V, \; Z \rightarrow W}{X \rightarrow W} \, W \subseteq Y, Y \cap Z = \emptyset \; . $$

The implication problem can be solved by transformation of dependencies to other languages for which the implication problem is solved. One example is the class of all functional and hierarchical dependencies. This class can be represented by formulas of propositional logic and has therefore a simple solution of the implication problem.

Let us represent attributes A from $attr(R)$ by p_A and subsets $X = \{C_1, ..., C_k\}$ by $\tau(X) = p_{C_1} \wedge ... \wedge p_{C_k}$. Further, $\tau(X \rightarrow Y) = \tau(X) \rightarrow \tau(Y)$ and $\tau(X \rightarrow\!\!\!\rightarrow Y_1 \mid Y_2 \mid ... \mid Y_m) = \tau(X) \rightarrow\!\!\!\rightarrow (\tau(Y_1) \vee \tau(Y_2) \vee ... \vee \tau(Y_m))$. Then for a set $\{\alpha_1, ..., \alpha_k, \beta\}$ of functional and hierarchical dependencies

$$ \{\alpha_1, ..., \alpha_k\} \models \beta \text{ iff} $$
$$ \{\tau(\alpha_1), ..., \tau(\alpha_k)\} \models \tau(\beta) \text{ iff} $$
$$ (\tau(\alpha_1) \wedge ... \wedge \tau(\alpha_k)) \rightarrow \tau(\beta) = 1 \, . $$

Another class which axiomatization can be expressed by propositional logic is the class of generalized functional dependencies.

The dependency theory is very rich for the relational model. [66] introduces 95 static dependency classes. Most of constraint classes are used by vertical decomposition. However, especially for distributed databases, horizontal decomposition has the same importance. Horizontal decomposition is useful for the treatment of exceptions as well.

Conditional functional dependencies can be used for horizontal decomposition. A *conditional functional dependency* $X \rightarrow Y \supset\!\!\!\rightarrow X \rightarrow Z$ holds in R^t if for any $t \in R^t$ whenever $X \rightarrow Y$ is valid in $\sigma_{t[X]}(R^t)$ then $X \rightarrow Z$ is valid in $\sigma_{t[X]}(R^t)$. If conditional functional dependencies are valid in a relation then this relation can be partioned into a subrelation which fulfills all functional dependencies and a subrelation for the exceptions.

Union constraints express that a relation can be horizontally decomposed into two sub-relations such that the original relation can be generated by the sum of a projection of the first subrelation and of the second subrelation.

An *afunctional constraint* $X \not\!\!/\!\!\rightarrow Y$ is valid in R^t if for any tuple t from R^t another tuple t' exists in R which coincides with t on X and is different from t on Y. If an afunctional constraint holds in R^t then R^t can be partioned into R_1^t and R_2^t such that the union of R_1^t and R_2^t is R^t and the functional constraint $X \rightarrow Y$ is valid in R_1^t and the afunctional dependency holds in R_2^t. Afunctional constraints can be generalized to *(p,q)-constraints*. A (p,q)-constraint is satisfied by R^t if for any tuple t from R^t $p \leq | \{t' \in R^t \mid t[X] = t'[X]\} | \leq q$. If the (1,3)-constraint $X \rightarrow_{(p,q)} Y$ is valid in R^t then R^t can be partioned into R_1^t, R_2^t, R_3^t such that the functional dependency is valid in R_i^t for $1 \leq i \leq 3$.

Excluded functional constraints $X \not\!\!\rightarrow Y$ state that the functional dependency $X \rightarrow Y$ is not valid. They are useful for acquisition of constraints during database design by example.

Functional dependencies can be generalized to *interrelational functional dependencies*. They specify when does one of the database relations satisfy a certain functional dependency. Given a database schema consisting of relation schemata $R_1, ..., R_n$ on $attr(R_1), ..., attr(R_n)$ and a set F of functional dependencies on $attr(R_1) \cup ... \cup attr(R_n)$. A relation R^t on $attr(R_1) \cup ... \cup attr(R_n)$ is a weak universal relation for the database $(R_1^t, ..., R_n^t)$ on $R_1, ..., R_n$ if $R_i^t \subseteq R^t[attr(R_i)]$ for all i. A database $(R_1^t, ..., R_n^t)$ globally satisfies F if there is a weak universal relation for it.

These properties can be considered also for relations with null values, i.e. with tuples which contain the value 'unknown' for certain attributes. In this case, for instance, the key notion is extended to key families. For a given relation schema R and its attribute set $attr(R)$ a set K of subsets of $attr(R)$ is called *key set* and is satisfied in a relation R^t if for each pair of tuples t, t' from R^t there is an element K in K such that both tuples are completely defined on K and $t[K] \neq t'[K]$. Known algorithms and approaches can be extended to key sets.

Disjunctive existence constraints $X \Rightarrow Y_1, Y_2, ..., Y_n$ specify that if a tuple is completely defined on X then it is completely defined on Y_i for some i. There is an axiomatization for disjunctive existence constraints. They can be represented by monotone Boolean functions.

Dependencies can be generalized to relations containing null values. Two tuples t, t' are strongly equivalent with respect to X (denoted by $t \approx_X t'$) if both are defined on X and are equal on X. They are weakly equivalent on X (denoted by $t \sim_X t'$) if they are both equal on A whenever both are defined on A for any $A \in X$. They are equivalent on X (denoted by $t \simeq_X t'$) if they are both equal on A whenever both are defined on A and both are undefined in the other case for any $A \in X$. Now we can define different kinds of validity of the functional dependency $X \rightarrow Y$ in a relation R^t with null values. We mention some of them.

- The relation R^t 1-satisfies the functional dependency $X \rightarrow Y$ if all pairs of strongly X-equivalent tuples are Y equivalent.

- The relation R^t 2-satisfies the functional dependency $X \rightarrow Y$ if all pairs of strongly X-

equivalent tuples are strongly Y equivalent.

- The relation R^t 3-satisfies the functional dependency $X \to Y$ if all pairs of weakly X-equivalent tuples are weakly Y equivalent.

- The relation R^t 4-satisfies the functional dependency $X \to Y$ if all pairs of strongly X-equivalent tuples are weakly Y equivalent.

- The relation R^t 5-satisfies the functional dependency $X \to Y$ if all pairs of weakly X-equivalent tuples are strongly Y equivalent.

3-satisfiability implies 4-satisfiability. 1-satisfiability implies 4-satisfiability. 2-satisfiability implies 1-satisfiablity. 5-satisfiability implies 2-satisfiability. The above mentioned axiomatization for functional dependencies can be directly applied to the axiomatization of 2- and 3-satisfiability. The augmentation axiom $X \cup Y \to Y$ is not valid for 4-satisfiability and for 5-satisfiability. The transitivity rule is not correct for 1-satisfiablity, i.e. the 1-satisfiability of $X \to Y$ and $Y \to Z$ in a relation R^t does not imply the 1-satisifablity of $X \to Z$. A key K is called *sure key* of R^t if R^t 5-satisfies $K \to attr(R)$. The key is called *possible key* of R^t if R^t 2-satisfies $K \to attr(R)$.

In the same manner multivalued, join and other dependencies can be generalized for relations with null values.

There are several kinds of null values which should be distinguished in this case depending on whether a property is applicable to an object or not, whether a property is under change (incomplete, not committed) or not, whether a value is available or not, whether a value is stored or not, whether a value is derivable from inconsistent or incomplete data or not and whether a value is secured or not. Context-dependent null values [66] are semantically defined null values.

There have been various approaches proposed in literature for modeling dynamics of databases. Examples of these approaches include:

1. active databases and production systems;

2. various mechanisms for specifying database evolution over time, e.g. action triggering mechanisms and specifying transactions by pre- and post-conditions or by transaction specification languages;

3. temporal logic programming, deductive databases, and other applications of temporal logic for specifying database dynamics;

4. deontic and modal logics; and

5. Petri net based approaches.

Let us consider two of those approaches.

A production system is defined by its database schema, a set of rules for that schema, and an controller that specifies how the rules are applied and how they change the database state. Production rules are defined on the basis of a (finite) set Ops of database operations (e.g. $Insert(R_5, (a_1, ..., a_n))$ is an insert operator for the relation schema R_5 and a tuple $(a_1, ..., a_n)$). Let ";" be the sequence operator, i.e. $o_1; o_2$ means that these operators are executed according to some conflict resolution strategy. Then the format of a production rule is

$$\alpha \longrightarrow o_1; o_2; ...; o_n$$

where α is a formula which expresses a certain condition on the database. The controller specifies how rules are applied in a recognize-act-cycle and how new database states are generated as a result of it. The controller can apply rules either in parallel and resolve conflicts or sequentially using a selection strategy.

Temporal formulas can be used to specify database behavior. Temporal logics extends predicate logic by special operators ($next$, $after$, $\forall_{future}$, $\forall_{past}$, $\exists_{future}$, $\exists_{past}$) relating database states within sequences of admissible states, e.g.

$$(\delta_{start}, \delta_1, ..., \delta_{current}, \delta_{c+1}, ...)$$

for a linear discrete time model. *Transition constraints* describe the allowed database state transitions by restricting (δ_i, δ_{i+1}) of successive states. In temporal logic they can be expressed in the following way: $\alpha \to next(\beta)$ where α, β are static integrity constraints. Temporal integrity constraints can be represented by transition graphs which are a kind of finite state machine.

Static dependencies $\alpha = (\gamma \to \theta)$ can be expressed by transition constraints in the following way: It is assumed that the first database state is correct. Then the transition constraint $\alpha \to next(\alpha)$ expresses that the dependency is not violated after the starting state.

Algebraic properties of dependencies are of importance especially for generalizing dependencies to other database models. For a relational operation o and a formula α a relation r which satisfies a formula α is called (o, α)-invariant if α is valid in $o(r)$.

If a functional dependency $X \to Y$ is valid in r then r is (o, α)-invariant for the following operations: projection, selection, difference, intersection with relations of the same type, join with any relation, product with any relation, union with any relation r' for which it holds that $r(X) \cap r'(X) = \emptyset$, and sum in restricted cases.

Relations are not $(o, X \to\!\!\to Y \mid Z)$-invariant for multivalued dependencies if projections including X, selection, joins, intersection, sum, and difference are considered. They are product-invariant and restricted union-invariant. The same results can be extended to join dependencies.

According to the left side of an inclusion dependency, relations are $(o, R[X] \subseteq S[Y])$-invariant for selection, joins with other relations, intersection, difference, product, and projection outside of X. According to the right side, relations are invariant for union, product, sum.

For the inverse of a relation none of the invariance properties is valid.

4.2 Constraints in Semantical Models

The meaning of constraints changes also from model to model. For instance, the inclusion constraint $R[X] \subseteq S[Y]$ has for ER-schemata at least two meanings. In IsA-relationships it requires key inheritance. Together with a key property the constraints specifies a referential integrity constraint. Together with cardinality constraints it specifies an identification property.

Models which are based on richer type systems have also larger sets of implicit integrity constraints. For instance, if the ER-model is based on set semantics then relationship schemata are based on component schemata, i.e. for a relationship schema $R = (..., R', ..., attr(R), ...)$ the inclusion dependency $R[R'] \subseteq R'$ is inherited from the schema definition.

According to the above presented invariance properties, dependencies can be generalized to semantical models. For instance, functional dependencies are generalized to path functional dependencies in entity-relationship models. Given a schema $ERDec = \{E_1, ..., E_n, R_1, ..., R_m\}$. A sequence $p = P_1 - ... - P_k$ of types from $ERDec$ is called $ERDec$-path (or briefly path) if for each i, $1 \leq i < k$ either P_i is a component of P_{i+1} or P_i has the component P_{i+1}.

For pathes the of attribute identifiers [67] can be extended. For pathes only such identifiers are of importance which are used in the path. For this we distinguish leaves and roots of the path. Given a path p and the set $attr(p)$, $X, Y \subseteq attr(p)$ of attribute identifiers of the path. A *path functional dependency* is $p : X \to Y$. The validity of path functional dependencies is defined like for functional dependencies for the relation p^t which is defined as the relation generated over the path p from the relations in $ERDec^t$. We can also invert pathes. Since the attribut notation of pathes depends on the order of the path we can also introduce the inversion of a path. The set of path functional dependencies is axiomatizable by the following calculus.

Axioms

$$X \supseteq Y : \quad p : X \to Y \qquad\qquad X = p' \star Y : \quad p : p' \to X$$

Rules

$$\frac{p : X \to Y}{p : X \bigcup Z \to Y \bigcup Z} \qquad\qquad \frac{p : X \to Y , \quad p : Y \to Z}{p : X \to Z}$$

$$\frac{p : X \to Y}{p' \star p : p' \star X \to p' \star Y} \qquad\qquad \frac{p : X \to Y}{(p : X \to Y)^{-1}}$$

It can be proven that this system is sound and complete for implications of path functional dependencies. The proof is based on invariance properties of functional dependencies.

Cardinality constraints are already discussed over a longer period. They are very powerful constraints. Using this powerful class of constraints in a proper manner requires a deep knowledge of the theory behind. The differences in treatment, definition, representation and terminology (calling cardinality constraints, for instance, complexity, relative cardinality, connectivity, degree, uniqueness constraint or specifying the information on cardinality constraints by other constraints, e.g. key constraints) shows that there is a need in a unification of the definition and in a formal treatment. For $R = (R_1, ..., R_k, attr(R))$ where R_i is an

entity or a relationship schema and for each $i, 1 \leq i \leq k$, the *cardinality constraint*
$$comp(R, R_i) = (m, n)$$
specifies that in each database state an item e from R_i^t appears in R^t at least m and at most n times.

For binary relationship schemata $R = (R_1, R_2, attr(R))$ between two entity or relationship schemata R_1, R_2, traditionally there are introduced special cardinality schemata: One-to-One, One-to-Many, Many-to-One and Many-to-Many. For instance, the many-to-one relationship schema is characterized by:
Each item in R_2^t is associated with any number of items in R_1^t, each item in R_1^t is associated with at most one item in R_2^t, , i. e. $comp(R, R_1) = (0, 1)$ or $comp(R, R_1) \leq (1, 1)$ and $comp(R, R_2) \in \{(0, m), (1, m)\}$. This notation can be extended also to arbitrary relationships.

The most general form of general cardinality constraints is the following:
Given a relationship type $R = (seq, attr(R))$ for a sequence of component types and an interval I of natural number with 0. Let seq_1 be a subsequence of seq, seq_2 a non-empty subsequence of seq_1 and $SEQ_2 = seq_{2,0}, seq_{2,1}, ..., seq_{2,n}$ a partition of seq_2 into subsequences or an empty sequence. seq_1 is called root expression. seq_2 is called component expression.
The *general cardinality constraint* $comp^{seq_{2,1},....,seq_{2,n}}(R[seq_1], seq_2) = I$
specifies that items from $R_{j_h}^t$ for $seq_{2,0} = R_{j_1}...R_{j_k}$, $1 \leq h \leq k$ and items from $R^t |_{seq_{2,i}}$ for $1 \leq i \leq n$ appear in the projection of $R^t |_{seq_1}$ i times for $i \in I$.

Using this notation, the other generalizations are unified.
For instance, for $R = (E, F, G, H, \emptyset)$

$comp^{\lambda}(R[EFGH], EF) = \{0, 1, 2\}$	is equivalent to	$comp(R, EF) = (0, 2)$,
$comp^{E,F}(R[EFG], EF) = \{1, 2, 3\}$	is equivalent to	$comp^*(R[EFG], EF) = (1, 3)$,
$comp^{EF}(R[EFG], EF) = \{1, 2, 3, 4\}$	is equivalent to	$comp^+(R[EFG], EF) = (1, 4)$,
$comp^E(R[EFGH], E) = \{1\}$	is equivalent to	$comp^*(R, E) = (1, 1)$

and to $comp^+(R, E) = (1, 1)$.
$comp^{EG,F}(R[EFGH], EFG) = \{0, 1, 2, 3\}$ can not be expressed by other forms.
The empty sequence is denoted by λ and can be omitted.

Cardinality constraints are not axiomatizable. The same is valid for general cardinality constraints. However, there are several useful properties.
The cardinality functions are monotone decreasing for both component sequences and root expressions. The minimum and maximum of I in Int-cardinality constraints is monotone decreasing for both component sequences and root expressions. The lower bound is preserved for root expressions.
Given the relationship type $R = (R_1, ..., R_k, attr(R))$.
The cardinality constraint $comp(R, R_1'...R_m') \leq (1, 1)$ is valid if and only if the functional dependency $R_1'...R_m' \longrightarrow R_1, ..., R_k$ is valid in. R .
The constraint $comp(R, R') \geq (1, 1)$ is valid if and only if the inclusion dependency $R' \subseteq R[R']$ is valid in the scheme.
$comp^*(R, R_1'...R_m') = (1, 1)$ if and only if $R_1'...R_m' \longrightarrow R_1, ..., R_k$ is valid in R.
The cardinality constraint $comp(R, R') = (0, .)$ can be used as a default value. It is not a restriction.

Cardinality constraints are constraints and not dependencies. A database dependency is a formula which is satisfiable in all databases containing only relations with single elements. Generally, each ER scheme with a set of cardinality constraints is satisfiable by the empty database. However, if the set of cardinality constraints is not well-specified then the empty database may be the only finite instance of the scheme. If the ER-scheme is using only cardinality constraints but not generalized cardinality constraints and is hierarchical then the scheme has also finite non-empty instances.

An ER-scheme $\underline{S}$ with a set of cardinality constraints $\underline{C}$ is called **consistent** (strongly satisfiable) if there exists at least one finite database $DB = (r_1, ..., r_k)$ in $SAT(\underline{S}, \underline{C})$ in which all r_i are not empty.

In general, it can be proven that an ER-schema is consistent if and only if each cycle has a weight greater or equal 1. The weight is computed by the maximum cardinality within the direction of the directed cycle and by the inverse of the minimum cardinality (or ∞ if $comp(R, R_i) = (0, m)$ for some m) against the direction of the directed cycle. In the above discussed example the weight of one cycle is $2 \cdot \frac{1}{3} < 1$.

The weight can be furthermore used for the simplification of schemata. If the cycle has only adjacent cardinalities from $\{(0, 1), (0, .), (1, 1), (1, .)\}$ then cycles with weight 1 indicate that all adjacent cardinalities are $(1, 1)$.

4.3 Constraints in Object-Oriented Models

There are several approaches to object-oriented models.

1. Object-oriented models are based on a model which is simple enough to discover the phenomenons. One of such is the graphical model used in [12].

2. Object-oriented models are generalizing semantical models. Additionally one class is added, the class of object identifiers (e.g. [63]). In most publications, object models are based on semaantical models.

Both approaches are semantically equivalent. Generally, an object is a unit of structure and behavior. An object can be composed to form complex objects. It has an identity which persists through change. This identity is encoded in implementations by an identifier which can differ in different implementations and systems. Objects communicate with each other. They are classified by object schemata and collected into object classes.

The basis of object graphs $B = (AV, Labels)$ is defined by the (finite) set of atomic values AV and the (finite) set of labels $Labels$ with $AV \cap Labels = \emptyset$.

The *object graph* G on $(AV, Labels)$ is the pair $(Nodes, Edges)$ where $Nodes$ is the union of finite disjoint sets of atomic elements: a set AV of atomic values, a set CV of complex values, and a set O of objects. $Edges$ is a relation $Edges \subseteq (O \cup CV) \times Labels \times (AV \cup CV \cup O)$.

If the relation $Edges$ represents a function, i.e. $\forall u \forall s \forall u' \forall u''((u, s, u'), (u, s, u'') \in Edge \Rightarrow u' = u'')$ then we use the derived function
$Edges^f : (O \cup CV) \times Labels \nrightarrow AV \cup CV \cup O$ and the object graph $G = (Nodes, Edge^f)$ is called *simple object graph*.

Notice that nonfunctional relations represent set-valued graphs, i.e. for some nodes u and some labels s there exists a set of adjacent via s nodes for u. If the adjacent nodes cannot be distinguished they can be replaced by one node and the *Edge* relation of the new graph is functional for u.

The set *Edge* can be also a bag or multiset. In this case, there are elements in *Edge* which are repeated. However, treating *Edge* as a bag is a representation which is difficult to handle. For this reason, we choose the representation of bags via sets with additional information on the number of repeated elements.

The *extended object graph* G on $(AV, Labels)$ is the triple $(Nodes, Edges, \mu)$ where $(Nodes, Edges)$ is an object graph and μ is a function from *Edge* to $\mathcal{N}$ assigning to each edge its multiplicity where by $\mathcal{N}$ is denoted the set of natural numbers.

Using a simple extension, classes can be represented in object graphs. If $\underline{C} = \{C_1, ..., C_k\}$ is the set of classes then we add to the basis $\underline{C}$ and to the labels the special label $\in$. Since an object can belong to different classes at the same time the object graph on the extended basis is not simple. Furthermore, we can add constraints to the definition of object graphs like 'for each object o there is a class C such that $(o, \in, C) \in Edge$' or 'no complex value belongs to a class'. In the same manner, hierarchies between classes can be modeled.

Based on this simple model we can develop an approach to modeling of classes.

One of the main concepts of OODB is the concept of object identity. Only if we can distinguish clearly between individual objects is it possible to treat object concepts like inheritance and interaction in a sound way: inheritance relates aspects of the *same* object, interaction relates *different* objects. Each object can be uniquely identified. This concept is implemented by means of object identifiers. Identifiers are implementation-dependent atomic items whose principle purpose is to characterize objects uniquely. Each object has an encapsulated internal state that can be observed and manipulated exclusively through an object 'interface'. Identifiers are internally used to determine which of the objects are equal and which are not. Since OODB approaches put emphasis on the observable structure of objects (through attributes, for instance) and identifiers are an internal concept, the identity of objects should be visible through the object 'interface'. Therefore, the identity should be definable on the object 'interface'. The identity concept in databases is based on the indiscernability concept. Two objects that cannot be distinguished should be considered to be identical. Therefore, the identity concept depends also from the language that is used for the definition of object properties. This language is based on structural constructs and can have also a richer functionality like counting etc.

The schema derived from the structure expression S of a class by replacing each reference and each subreference by the schema ID is called the *representation type* V_C of the class C, the schema $U_C = (ident : ID, value :: T_C)$ is called the *class schema* of C.

An object-database on a structural schema S assigns to each class schema C a set of objects such that the following conditions are satisfied:

Uniqueness of identifiers: For every class C^t the identifiers are unique.

Inclusion integrity: Identifiers used in a subclass C^t of C'^t we are used in C'^t. Moreover, if V_C is a subschema of V'_C with subschema function $f : V_C \rightarrow V'_C$, then $(i, v) \in C^t$ implies $(i, f(v)) \in C'^t$.

Referential integrity: If an object refers to a corresponding object in another class then this object exists in the other class.

Local referential integrity: If two objects refers to the same object in a part class then these objects are equal.

Based on this assumption, we can now formulate several kinds of integrity constraints. An *integrity constraint* on a schema $\mathcal{S} = \{C_1, \ldots, C_n\}$ is a formula from the logic defined by this schema.

For class schema C, the *uniqueness constraint* on C states that if objects are equal on their representation type then they are equal.

A *functional constraint* on C is a constraint of the form $X \to Y$ for substructures X, Y of C.

An *inclusion constraint* on C_1 and C_2 is a constraint of the form $C_1[X] \subseteq C_2[Y]$ for compatible for substructures X, Y of C_1 and C_2, respectively.

An *exclusion constraint* on C_1, C_2 is a constraint of the form $C_1[X] \| C_2[Y]$ for compatible for substructures X, Y of C_1 and C_2, respectively.

In the same manner, we can generalize the constraint theory of other models as well.

Inequality constraints are defined on the class level. Given the value representation schema V_C of a class schema C and a substructures X, Y of V_C ($X \sqsubseteq V_C$; $\sqsubseteq, \sqcup, \sqcap$ are operations and predicates on substructures). The *inequality constraint* $C(X \nparallel Y)$ holds in the class C^t if it it not possible to have two objects in C^t that aggree on the X-value and also agree on the Y-value. Obviously, X, Y can be used for identification of objects in C^t. Therefore, this object-oriented concept is similar to the concept of key sets. There can be easily defined a system of formal implication rules, e.g.

$$\frac{C(X \nparallel Y)}{C(Y \nparallel X)} \qquad \frac{C(Y \nparallel X)}{C(Y \sqcup Z \nparallel X)} Z \sqsubseteq V_C \qquad \frac{C(X \nparallel Y, Z \to X)}{C(Z \nparallel Y)}$$

Additonally, rules which specify the semantical inheritance for subclasses and for mapping functions, for instance, prefix extension or path extension, can be added to the above mentioned rules.

Constraints in object-oriented databases is an active research area. Several special problems are still not solved. One of such is the mismatch between classes and subclasses since logical languages based on the pure first-order predicate logic lack in the ability to deal with inheritance [48].

4.4 Constraints in Other Models

Most constraints introduced for other models are some kind of generalization of constraints known already for the relational database model. One exception is the set constraint which has to be used in all models which use lists or references whenever a set property has to be modeled. Such set constraints could be specified in the following form:

$y_1 = (\bar{x}), y_2 = (\bar{x}) \in R^t \Rightarrow y_1 = y_2$.

Element-generating dependencies are a generalization of tuple-generating dependencies. Such types of constraints are necessary whenever the typing system of a models is richer than the one of the flat relational model. For instance, we can define that whenver for a map operation a certain set exists then another element exists in the structure which satisfies another property, i.e., more formally, given types T, T_1 and a function $f : T \to T_1$. A *generalized element-generating constraint* (Ω, ω) is given by a set $\Omega \cup \{\omega\}$ defined on T_1. The constraint (Ω, ω) is valid in a relation R^t on T if whenever there is a subset S^t of R^t with $f(S^t) = \Omega$ then there is an element r in R^t with $f(r) = \omega$.

Analoguously, the generalized equality-generating constraint can be defined in the following way: Given types $T_{i,j} = T_{j,i}, 1 \le i,j \le m$, $T'_{i,j} = T'_{j,i}, 1 \le i,j \le m$ and functions $f_{i,j} : T \to T_{i,j}$, functions $f'_{i,j} : T \to T'_{i,j}$. Let $F = \{f_{i,j} \mid 1 \le i,j \le m\}$, $F' = \{f'_{i,j} \mid 1 \le i,j \le m\}$. Then a class C^t on T satisfies the *generalized equality-generating constraint*

(F, F') if whenever for m elements $r_1, ..., r_m$ of C^t
$$\bigwedge_{i=1}^{m-1} \bigwedge_{j=i+1}^{m} f_{i,j}(r_i) = f_{j,i}(r_j)$$

then
$$\bigwedge_{i=1}^{m-1} \bigwedge_{j=i+1}^{m} f'_{i,j}(r_i) = f'_{j,i}(r_j) \ .$$

If the functions $f, f_{i,j}, f'_{i,j}$ are based on substructures of T and $T_1, T_{i,j}, T'_{i,j}$ are substructures of T then the chase procedure can be extended to generalized element-generating and generalized equality-generating constraints. For other cases, the axiomatization depends on the properties of $f, f_{i,j}, f'_{i,j}$, especially some kind of general injectivity.

Usually an object o which is existence dependent from another object o' cannot be be added before o' is added, and o can not be removed before o is removed. o blocks the removal of o' and o' blocks the addition of o. Furthermore, the meaning of existence constraints can be refined also by distinguishing the cases above from the rule that whenever a removal from S^t violates the constraint null values are used for such elements in R^t. This leads to the following separation [51]:

1. The *block existence constraint* is an inclusion dependency $R[X] \subseteq S[Y]$ which disallows an insert on R^t unless the corresponding element in S^t exists and which disallows a delete on S^t if the constraint would be violatet. Updates on R^t and on S^t are cascaded.

2. The *trigger existence constraint* is an inclusion dependency $R[X] \subseteq S[Y]$ which requires that whenever an element is to be inserted into R^t a corresponding element has to exist in S^t or it should be inserted as well and that whenever an element is deleted from S^t the elements in R^t which existence depends only from that element are deleted too.

Integrity constraints are separated from the generation rules in the intensional part of a deductive database. They can be used for the translation to Prolog programs and for improving the performance of a logic program. For instance, functional dependencies can be used for the automatic insertion of cuts in logic programs. It has been shown that integrity checking in logical data models is not more difficult than in the relational model. The data complexity (the size of SAT(DS)) is still LogSpace and the expression complexity (the number of all constraints implied by a database) is still PSpace.

The maintenance of deductive databases includes the validation check on integrity constraints. This can be infeasible. Therefore, we use reduced or simplified sets of integrity constraints. For each generic operation the infected integrity constraints are selected, modified and then added to the preconditions of the generic operations. The unnecessary and phantom preconditions can be omitted. Integrity constraints can be also used to optimize user queries.

Bibliographical remarks

The theory of dependencies is discussed in [3,6,50,56,66,73]. The extension of this theory to other database model is developed in [4,36], [37,39,67] for semantic models and in [2,13,30,35,46], [62] for object-oriented models. The book [78] gives an impression on the algebraic treatment of dependencies. A survey on deductive databases is presented in [20],[72]. Further, the papers [14,16,17], those cited in [33] and in [53] cover several special topics. Dynamic integrity constraints are surveyed in [49].

5 Applying Constraints

5.1 Using Constraints

The *maintenance simplicity* is one of the main quality criterias in design. The maintenance is simpler if there is less redundancy in the data, if data and knowledge are so organized that the basic generic operations like Insert can be applied effectively. One solution to the maintenance problem is *normalization* which is mainly used for the reduction of redundancy. The theory of dependencies is applied to the normalization of relations. To represent a relation by a number of subrelations is known as a normalization. There are three approaches to normalization: vertical decomposition, horizontal decomposition [34,61] and deductive normalization [64]. These three approaches can be uniquely represented using category theory and morphisms on partially ordered sets. Vertical decomposition is based on the operations projection and join; horizontal decomposition requires the use of the operations selection and union; deductive normalization is based on the reduction of a relation to a minimal generating subset (called deductive normal form) and on generation of the relation from the deductive normal form by a formula. In normalized relations redundancy is minimized and the update problem is solved. Horizontal normalization is used in databases for optimization of deduction and evaluation.

Different normal forms are defined for vertical decomposition. They are using functional, multivalued and join dependencies. There are two methods for vertical normalization: normalization through vertical decomposition from first normal form up to project-join normal form using multivalued and join dependencies, and normalization through synthesis from first normal form up to elementary key normal form or to Boyce-Codd normal form. The relational schema used here is in first normal form. A relational schema is in elementary key normal form if for every functional dependency $X \rightarrow \{A\}$ which is implied by the schema the set X is a key or A is an element of a minimal key K so that for none $B \in attr(R) - K$ and none $C \in K$ the constraint $K - \{C\} \rightarrow \{B\}$ is implied by the schema. A schema is in Boyce-Codd normal form if for every functional dependency $X \rightarrow \{A\}$ which is implied by the schema X is a key. There are polynomial time bounded synthesis algorithms so that each schema can be decomposed into a database schema where each schema is in elementary key normal form. The problem of determining that there is no Boyce-Codd normal form decomposition representing all given functional dependencies (i.e. preserving the original set of functional dependencies) is NP-hard. There are schemata such that no decomposition exists which is in Boyce-Codd normal form and preserves the dependencies.

The vertical normalization is based on the (weak) universal relation assumption which states that there is a universal relation (with null values) of which all of the relations in a database are projections. In this case, access path independence is achievable, a simple user interface can be defined, the uniqueness of dependencies is guaranteed and axiomatizations can be developed. A set of dependencies is called consistent in a database if this set is valid in the weak universal relation. There is no effective test for consistency of dependencies. The consistency test for full dependencies is ExpTime-complete. The consistency test for functional dependencies is solvable in polynomial time. Similar results can be shown for other such assumptions.

Hypergraphs are used for the representation of vertical decompositions of a database. They are useful for a simple representation if a hypergraph exists for the database schema (This is not the case if multiple relationships are defined on the same set of attributes.). It has been shown that the hypergraph is acyclic iff it is obtained by decompositions which are using only multivalued dependencies. Acyclic hypergraphs allow a simpler query evaluation (for instance, polynomial time instead of NP-completeness).

An alternative approach is the top-down approach developed in different database models starting from atomic, clearly meaningful relational schemes, and working towards all other relational schemes that are desirable in a better schema. They end up with a database schema which is a view of the conceptual schema and relate constraints to these. This approach removes the need for assumptions like the problematic universal relation assumption.

Normalization is not universally recommended. In some cases, non-normalized relations are desirable. For instance, if typical queries are evaluated on the basis of several joins then the database schema should be tuned with systems performance.

Normalization requires desirable structures. Acyclic, dependency preserving, 4Nf schema exists if and only if the set of functional and multivalued depdencies has an extended conflict-free cover [77].

Interesting studies have also been conducted concerning the correctness of updates on views. View updates are possible in some database schemata if some derived dependencies are valid in the view.

These theories can be extended to other database models. The differences and specialities of these models should be considered in such extensions. For instance, keys in nested models are to be defined using different equality concepts [4]. In models using relationships or references path constraints can be defined. There properties are similar to the properties of dependencies [67]. The dependency theory can be extended to constraints on classes.

The first-order predicate logic should be extended for such advanced models. Object-oriented models can be based on F-logic [46].

An example of such theory application is the ER theory. Let us consider one specific application. Binary relationship schemata are classified according to the complexity of components in the relationship. Containment relationships among relationship schemata are of a special interest. An *IS-A relationship schema* is a special binary relationship schema $R = (R_1, R_2, attr(R))$ which is syntactically characterized by the integrity constraints $comp(R, R_1) = (1, 1)$ and $comp(R, R_2) = (0, 1)$. But the integrity constraints above can be used to represent semantically different relationship schemata. Let us consider this for the case of relationship schemata.

1. The original Is-A relationship defines a subtype hierarchy or a subset hierarchy.

2. The Role-Of-relationship defines a subtype hierarchy without attribute inheritance, i. e. the attribute and identifier sets can be different and the relationship of the entities is defined by some relationship between the identifiers.

3. The Is-Synonym-Of-relationship states models objects which have the same lifetime but in different environment different functions, operators and attributes with a different structure can be connected by an I-S-O-relationship.

4. The Is-Kind-Of-relationship between schemata allows schemata to be defined to be of the same behaviour.

If we do not want surrogate attributes for clusters then normally clusters are restricted to key-equal schemata. This restriction is too strong for applications. In most cases, we need only the functions of the clustered schemata for further database programming. In this case, the Kind-Of-type is the weakest type which could be used.

Since user-specified operations are a part of the schema definition there are several other total-partial one-to-one relationships which could be considered in the design. For instance, the Is-Property-Of, Has-Effect-Of, Has-Function-Of, Is-Subobject-Of and Is-Homonym-Of relationships [67] can be used for the efficient representation of schemata. If schemata are sharing methods then this should be implementable. In this case generic operations are definable. The Is-Homonym-Of-association between attributes can be understood as the opposite of the Is-Synonym-of-association. In the same manner, this relationship kind can be treated for schemata.

Furthermore, for the Is-A-relationship there are four different approaches for the representation. Let us consider an example.

Event-nonseparation approach Students and professors are a role of persons.

Event-separation approach Students and professors are different persons. They can be treated independently.

Union approach If only professors and student are represented then *Person* is the cluster of *Professor* and *Student*.

The universal relation approach Professors and students are represented by one schema using additional boolean attributes for their distinction. This requires the use of null values and additional integrity constraints like "if a person is a student then the students number is defined, in the other case it is null".

It should be noticed that there are one-to-many and one-to-one relationships which can be treated like Is-A-relationships. Normally, Is-A-relationship schemata can be omitted by introducing the corresponding subtype instead of the subordinate schema.

The equivalence problem is undecidable and not axiomatizable. However, this problem can be solved 'partially'. It is possible to identify special schemata for which equivalent schemata exist. The ER theory can be applied for generating equivalent schemata. These equivalence can be also used for view integration and view cooperation in schemata.

The schema $ERS = (\{E_1, ...E_n, R_1, ..., R_m\}, C)$ is included in the schema $ERS' = (\{E_1', ...E_{n'}', R_1', ..., R_{m'}'\}, C')$ (denoted by $ERS \subseteq ERS'$)
if each ERS-database DB can be mapped to an ERS'-database DB' and the database DB' can be mapped to its preimage DB, i.e. more formally there exist formulas $\varphi_{E_1'}, ..., \varphi_{E_{n'}'}$, $\varphi_{R_1'}, ..., \varphi_{R_{m'}'}$ defined on ERS and formulas $\varphi_{E_1}, ..., \varphi_{E_n}, \varphi_{R_1}, ..., \varphi_{R_m}$ defined on ERS' such that for each ERS-database DB the database
$DB' = \{\varphi_{E_1'}(DB), ..., \varphi_{E_{n'}'}(DB), \varphi_{R_1'}(DB), ..., \varphi_{R_{m'}'}(DB)\}$ is an ERS'-database and
$\{\varphi_{E_1}(DB'), ..., \varphi_{E_n}(DB'), \varphi_{R_1}(DB'), ..., \varphi_{R_m}(DB')\} = DB$.

The schemata ERS and ERS' are equivalent if $ERS \subseteq ERS'$ and $ERS' \subseteq ERS$.

The equivalence of schemata can be considered for simple schemata with integrity constraints from a restricted set. Expecially, cardinality constraints, inclusion, functional and equality dependencies can be used for the transformation of the schemes.

5.2 Complexity of Modeling

The complexity theory is mainly developed for the relational database model. However, the main results can be easily extended to other models. We discuss in this chapter complexity results concerning the size of different constraint sets and the size of relations. The complexity of derivations in deductive databases is out of scope in this paper and is reviewed in several articles and books on logic programming [5].

There are certain reasons why complexity bounds are of interest. First, most of the known algorithms, e.g. for normalization, use the set of all minimal keys or nonredundant sets of dependencies. Therefore, they depend from the cardinality of these sets. Second, the maintenance complexity of a database depends on the number of integrity constraints which are under consideration. Therefore, if the cardinality of constraint sets is large the maintenance becomes infeasible (Two-tuple constraints like functional dependencies require $O(m^2)$ two-tuple comparisons for relations with m elements.). Furthermore, they give an indication whether algorithms are of interest for practical purposes since the complexity of most known algorithms is measured by the input length. For instance, algorithms for the construction of a minimal key are bounded by the maximal number of minimal keys. The problem of deciding whether there is a minimal key with at most k attributes is NP-complete. The problem of deciding whether two sets of functional dependencies are equivalent is polynomial in the size of the two sets and therefore exponential.

The complexity theory of relational databases is using the tight relationship of relational databases to algebras of Boolean functions, to Sperner sets (sets of incomparable subsets of a certain set) and to lattice theory.

Keys

The number of keys of a relation is determined by the maximal number of elements in a Sperner set. More precisely, given a relational schema $R = ((B_1, ..., B_n), \emptyset)$ and a relation r from $SAT(R)$. Then r has at most

$$\binom{n}{\lfloor \frac{n}{2} \rfloor}$$

different minimal keys. This estimate is sharp. However, if the domains in the data scheme are bounded this estimate is lower. Suppose that $| dom(B_i) | \le k$ $(1 \le i \le n)$ where $k^4 < 2n + 1$. Then the number of minimal keys cannot exceed

$$\binom{n}{\lfloor \frac{n}{2} \rfloor} - \lfloor \frac{n}{2} \rfloor .$$

This estimate is not sharp.

For practical purpose, keys are of different meaning and complexity. Domains for attributes have very different complexity. The maximal number of minimal keys in relations with nonuniform domains is also precisely exponential in the number of attributes. It is different in order from the maximal number of minimal keys on domains with the same complexity.

These results can be extended to relations with null values [66].

Since the set of minimal keys can be very large it is of interest in which cases this set is small. Let for a relation schema R and a set F of functional dependencies, $ExtrAttr(R, F) = \{A \in attr(R) \mid F \not\models attr(R) \setminus \{A\} \to \{A\}\}$. Then the schema has one minimal key iff $ExtrAttr(R, F)$ is a minimal key.

Dependencies

These considerations can be extended to sets of functional dependencies. A set of functional dependencies is called nonredundant if none of the dependencies of this set is implied by the remaining dependencies in this set. The maximal size of nonredundant sets of functional dependencies is bounded by 2^n for schemata on n attributes. A nonredundant set is called basic if for all dependencies in the set the replacement of this functional dependency $X \to Y$ by a dependency with either a smaller left set $X' \subset X$ or a larger right set $Y \subset Y'$ in the original set leads to a non-equivalent set. The maximum number $N(n)$ of basic sets of functional dependencies for schemata on n attributes is determined by the estimation

$$2^n \left(1 - \frac{4 \log_2 \log_2 n}{\log_2 e \log_2 n}\right)(1 + o(1)) \le N(n) \le 2^n \left(1 - \frac{\log_2^{\frac{3}{2}} n}{150\sqrt{n}}\right) .$$

Minimal generating sets of functional dependencies are also so complex. Given a family of functional dependencies $\mathcal{F}$ which is closed under implication. The size of the smallest subset of $\mathcal{F}$ which implies $\mathcal{F}$ is denoted by $M(\mathcal{F})$. Let $M(n)$ denote the maximum number of $M(\mathcal{F})$ for all $\mathcal{F}$ on n attributes. Then

$$\binom{n}{\lfloor \frac{n}{2} \rfloor} \le M(n) \le 2^n \left(1 - \frac{\log_2^{\frac{3}{2}} n}{150\sqrt{n}}\right) .$$

The minimum number of functional dependencies generating the worst case of $M(n)$ remains exponential even in the case of relations with $O(n)$ elements. It can further be shown that two different generating sets of functional dependencies do not differ in size by a factor not greater than $n - 1$.

The same kind of results can be obtained for sets of multivalued dependencies.

A subset Σ of a dependency class $\mathcal{C}$ is called closed if all dependencies from $\mathcal{C}$ which follows from Σ belong to Σ. We can ask how many different closed subsets has a class. Let us denote by $Cl(\mathcal{F}, n)$ the number of closed subsets of functional dependencies on relational schemata with n attributes. Then

$$2^{\binom{n}{\lfloor \frac{n}{2} \rfloor}} \le Cl(\mathcal{F}, n) \le 2^{\binom{n}{\lfloor \frac{n}{2} \rfloor}(1+o(1))} .$$

An asymptotic estimate is not known.

Armstrong Relations

Armstrong relations are of practical use as they can effectively code the entire information on a class of dependencies, i.e. for a class $\mathcal{C}$ of dependencies and a subset Σ of $\mathcal{C}$ a relation r is called Armstrong relation if such and only such dependencies from $\mathcal{C}$ are valid in r which follow from Σ. Armstrong relations can be used as a design tool and a source of sample data for program testing. By inspecting the Armstrong relation it can be decided whether a dependency is a consequence of a set of dependencies or not. Several classes of dependencies have Armstrong relations for each subset, for instance the class of functional dependencies and the class of keys. Therefore the size (the number of tuples) of Armstrong relations can be considered as a complexity measure of the class. For each subset Σ there exists an Armstrong relation of minimal size. Let us denote by $L(\Sigma)$ the size of one minimal Armstrong relation of Σ and by $L_{\mathcal{C}}(n)$ the maximum number for all subsets of $\mathcal{C}$ where $\mathcal{C}$ is defined for relational schemata with n attributes. Now we get the following estimates for the classes $\{key\}$, $\{key(k)\}$, $\mathcal{F}$ of all key sets, of all key sets of length k ($4 \le k \le n - 3$), and of all functional dependencies.

$$\frac{1}{n^2}\binom{n}{\lfloor \frac{n}{2} \rfloor} \le L_{\{key\}}(n) \le \binom{n}{\lfloor \frac{n}{2} \rfloor} + 1$$

$$c_1 n^{\frac{k-1}{2}} \le L_{\{key(k)\}}(n) \le c_2 n^{\frac{k-1}{2}}$$

$$\frac{1}{n^2}\binom{n}{\lfloor \frac{n}{2} \rfloor} \le L_{\mathcal{F}}(n) \le \binom{n}{\lfloor \frac{n}{2} \rfloor}\left(1 + \frac{c_3}{\sqrt{n}}\right)$$

where c_1, c_2, c_3 do not depend on n.

The estimates for $L(\Sigma)$ can be refined for functional dependencies using minimal generating sets of closed subsets [9]. For a given set of functional dependencies F a subset X of $\{B_1, ..., B_n\}$ is F-closed if from $F \models X \rightarrow Y$ follows $Y \subseteq X$. Since the intersection of F-closed subsets is an F-closed subset the set M of all F-closed subsets can be generated from a minimal subset $Gen(F)$ of M by intersection. Every minimal Armstrong relation for a set F of functional dependencies contains at least $\lceil (1 + \frac{1}{2}\sqrt{1 + 8r}) \rceil$ and at most $r + 1$ tuples, where r is the number of elements in $Gen(F)$.

The complexity of finding an Armstrong relation, given a set of functional dependencies, is precisely exponential in the number of attributes.

Average Complexity

There are only several results on the average complexity. For instance, in allmost all relations with l tuples on domains with $|dom(B_i)| = 2$ $(1 \leq i \leq n)$ the average length $av_n(l, 2)$ of minimal keys is bounded by

$$\lfloor \log_2 l \rfloor \leq av_n(l, 2) \leq 2\lfloor \log_2 l \rfloor .$$

5.3 Integrity Enforcement

Traditionally, integrity constraints in database systems are maintained either by rolling back any transaction that produces an inconsistent state or by disallowing or modifying operations that may produce an inconsistent state or repairing inconsistent states.

In general, for a given database schema polymorphic update operations are defined. Then, canonical update operations are generated by functions $Insert_{gen}$, $Delete_{gen}$, $Update_{gen}$ with signatures:

$$Insert_{gen} : DatabaseSchema_{rep} \times ClassSchema_{rep} \rightarrow Meth_{rep}$$
$$Delete_{gen} : DatabaseSchema_{rep} \times ClassSchema_{rep} \rightarrow Meth_{rep}$$
$$Update_{gen} : DatabaseSchema_{rep} \times ClassSchema_{rep} \rightarrow Meth_{rep}$$

Integrity constraints can be maintained in restricted cases by term rewriting systems. For instance, for each inclusion dependency $R \subseteq S$ or class constraint $R \ IsA \ S$ two additional term rewriting rules are generated:

$insert_R(x) \Rightarrow insert_R(x); insert_S(x)$; $delete_R(x) \Rightarrow delete_S(x); delete_R(x)$.

In general, tuple generating dependency of the form

$\forall \exists ((P_1(\bar{x}_1) \wedge ... \wedge P_n(\bar{x}_n) \rightarrow Q(\bar{y}))$

generates conditional methods for *Insert*:

if $(P_1(\bar{x}_1) \wedge ... \wedge P_{i-1}(\bar{x}_{i-1}) \wedge P_{i+1}(\bar{x}_{i+1}) \wedge ... \wedge P_n(\bar{x}_n)$
   then $insert_{P_i}(\bar{x}_i) \Rightarrow insert_{P_i}(\bar{x}_i); insert_Q(\bar{y})$.

For *delete* we obtain non-determinstic methods or methods which can be selected by a controller. For instance, the constraint above generates n methods one of which is selected by the controller:

if $(P_1(\bar{x}_1) \wedge ... \wedge P_{i-1}(\bar{x}_{i-1}) \wedge P_{i+1}(\bar{x}_{i+1}) \wedge ... \wedge P_n(\bar{x}_n)$
   then $delete_Q(\bar{y}) \Rightarrow delete_Q(\bar{y}); delete_{P_i}(\bar{x}_i)$.

General dependencies of the form

$\forall \exists ((P_1(\bar{x}_1) \wedge ... \wedge P_n(\bar{x}_n) \rightarrow (Q_1(\bar{y}_1) \vee ... \vee Q_n(\bar{y}_m))$

generate non-determinstic methods. Using this approach, the exclusion constraint $R\|S$ affects the *insert* operation as follows:

$insert_R(x) \Rightarrow insert_R(x); delete_S(x)$.

Additionally, contraction rules are added to this system:

$insert_R(x); delete_R(x) \Rightarrow delete_R(x)$; $insert_R(x); insert_R(x) \Rightarrow insert_R(x)$;

$delete_R(x); delete_R(x) \Rightarrow delete_R(x)$; $delete_R(x); insert_R(x) \Rightarrow insert_R(x)$.

This approach can be refined to specific triggering rules:

> *Trigger Rule* < rule name>
>> [Localization: < unit_name>]
>> [Operations: < list of operations to be triggered >]
>> [If: < condition >]
>> [Then: < list of actions >]
>> [Precedes: (< list of rules > , < enforcement event >)]
>> [Follows: < list of rules>] .

Term rewriting of operations can be applied as long as the obtained system is confluent and terminating. However, this is not the case for schemata with cycles in structure and constraints. The restrictions of the term rewriting approach are based on three problems:

1. Though the rules behave nice with respect to one constraint, they do not with respect to the conjunction. In the example above the required solution *fail* can not be written in the form $T_1; R$, where R is a database transformation corresponding to the term rewriting system.

2. The approach can be only applied to strictly hierarchical schemata.

3. Even if the first problem does not occur, we are hardly interested in integrity enforcement with respect to primitive update operations rather than consistent transactions. For term rewriting systems it has to be shown how events (and actions) can be extended to the really interesting case of transactions.

In [63], in order to exceed these limits an operational approach has been introduced, which aims at the computation of consistent specializations. Thus, the problem is to find the *greatest consistent specialization* (GCS) $T_{\mathcal{I}}$ for each given database transformation T and each integrity constraint $\mathcal{I}$. The greatest solution with respect to specialization is required, since otherwise *fail*, which is always undefined, would certainly define a solution. Note that *fail* corresponds in a natural way to the classical rollback.

The theoretical basis of this approach is formed by an extension of Dijkstra's calculus that is used to give an axiomatic semantics for database transformations. On this basis specialization and consistency have been formalized, a precise definition of a GCS was given and results on the existence and uniqueness (up to semantic equivalence) have already been proven.

Furthermore, the compatibility of the GCS construction with respect to the conjunction of constraints can be proven, i.e. on consistent initial states with respect to $\mathcal{I}_1 \wedge \mathcal{I}_2$ the transformations $(T_{\mathcal{I}_1})_{\mathcal{I}_2}$ and $T_{\mathcal{I}_1 \wedge \mathcal{I}_2}$ are semantically equivalent. This enables us to compute GCSs successively. Moreover, the GCSs for basic update operations with respect to distinguished classes of constraints are known. Their structure is closely related to the elementary rules used in term rewriting sytems.

Idle updates are implicit insertions or deletions which does not effect the database state.

In this case, there is no need in propagation. Using the GCS approach, local idle updates can be removed from transactions. Phantom updates are updates which are rolled back. The examples above show that the GCS approach can handle this case.

Bibliographical remarks

A survey on normalization is given in [56,72,76], for horizontal normalization in [34,56]. Most of the books on the entity-relationship model can be used as a source on approaches to vertical normalization. The papers in [26,31], [33,68] discuss the impact of logic to database theory.

Most of the results on complexity reported in this section are discussed in [41], [66] and proven there or in [9,22,23,52]. We have reported only some of the main results. An overview on the complexity of algorithms can be found in [43,50]. For instance, it is known that the complexity of expressions is typically one exponent higher than the data complexity. The average complexity of Armstrong relations, families of functional dependencies and of key sets is still open. However, there is some indication [41,66] that the average complexity is polynomial for Armstrong relations.

The results on integrity enforcement are taken from [62]. This approach extends integrity enforcement approaches developed for deductive databases.

References

[1] M. Atkinson, F. Bancilhon, D. DeWitt, K. Dittrich, D. Maier, S. Zdonik, The object-oriented database system manifesto. Proc. Conf. DOOD 89, Kyoto 1989, 40 - 57.

[2] S. Abiteboul, P.C. Kanellakis, The two facets of object-oriented data models. IEEE Data Engineering Bulletin 14, 2, 1991, 3-7

[3] S. Abiteboul and V. Vianu, Transactions and integrity constraints. Proc. of Database Systems, 1985, 193-204.

[4] S. Al-Fedaghi and B. Thalheim, The key concept in database models. Information systems, 1992.

[5] K.R. Apt, Logic programming. In Handbook of Theoretical Computer Science (ed. J. van Leeuwen), Vol. B, Formal Models and Semantics, Elsevier, Amsterdam, 1990, 493 – 574.

[6] P. Atzeni and V. De Antonellis, Relational database theory. Benjamin Cummings, Reading, 1993.

[7] C. Batini, S. Ceri, and S. Navathe, Conceptual database design, An entity-relationship approach. Benjamin Cummings, Redwood, 1992.

[8] A.P. Buchmann, R.S. Carrera, and M.A. Vazquez-Galindo, A generalized constraint and exception handler for an object-oriented CAD-DBMS. IEEE Conf. 1986, 38–49.

[9] C. Beeri, M. Dowd, R. Fagin, R. Statman, On the structure of Armstrong relations for functional dependencies. Journal of ACM, Vol.31, No.1, January 1984, 30-46.

[10] C. Beeri, New data models and languages - the challenge. Proc. ACM PODS, 1992.

[11] C. Beeri, M. Kifer, An integrated approach to logical design of relational database schemes. ACM TODS, 11, 1986, 159–185.

[12] C. Beeri, B. Thalheim: Can I see your identification, please?, manuscript in preparation, 1993

[13] J. Biskup and P. Dublish, Objects in relational database schemes with functional, inclusion and exclusion dependencies. Proc. MFDBS - 91, LNCS 495, 1991, 276 – 290.

[14] N. Bidoit, Negation in rule-based database languages: A survey. Theoretical computer science 78, 1991, 3 - 83.

[15] M.L. Brodie, J. Mylopoulos, and J.W. Schmidt, On conceptual modeling. Springer, Heidelberg, 1984.

[16] F. Bry, Query evaluation in recursive databases: Bottom-up and top-down reconciled. ECRC Report IR-KB-64, 1989.

[17] F. Bry, Intensional updates: Abduction via deduction. Proc. 7th Int. Conf. on Logic Programming, 1990.

[18] R.G.G. Cattell, Object data management: Object-oriented and extended relational database systems. Addison-Wesley, Reading, 1991.

[19] S. Ceri and G. Pelagatti, Distributed databases: Principles and systems. McGraw-Hill, New York, 1984.

[20] S. Ceri, G. Gottlob, A. Tanca, Logic Programming and databases. Springer 1991.

[21] C. Delobel and M. Adiba, Relational Database Systems. North-Holland, Amsterdam 1985.

[22] J. Demetrovics, G.O.H. Katona, Combinatorial problems of database models. Colloquia Mathematica Societatis Janos Bolyai 42, Algebra, Cominatorics and Logic in Computer Science, Gÿor (Hungary), 1983, 331-352.

[23] J. Demetrovics, L.O. Libkin, and I.B. Muchnik. Functional dependencies and the semilattice of closed classes. Proc. MFDBS-89, LNCS 364, 1989, 136–147.

[24] R. Elmasri and S. II. Navathe, Fundamentals of database systems. Benjamin/Cummings Publ., Redwood City, 1989.

[25] R.A. Frost, Introduction to knowledge base systems. MacMillan, New York 1986.

[26] II. Gallaire and J. Minker, Logic and databases. Plenum Press, New York, 1978.

[27] S.K. Gadia, C.-S. Yeung, A generalized model for a relational temporal database. Proc. ACM SIGMOD 1988, June 1988, Chicago, p. 251-259.

[28] M.R. Genesereth and N.J. Nilsson, Logical foundations of artificial intelligence. Morgan-Kaufman, los altos, 1988.

[29] M. Ginsberg, Nonmonotonic reasoning. Morgan-Kaufman, Los Altos, 1988.

[30] G. Gottlob, G. Kappel, and M. Schrefl, Semantics of object-oriented data models - The evolving algebra approach. LNCS 504, Springer 1991, 144–160.

[31] H. Gallaire, J. Minker, and J.-M. Nicolas, Advances in database theory, Vol. I, Plenum-Press, New York, 1981.

[32] H. Gallaire, J. Minker, and J.-M. Nicolas, Advances in database theory, Vol. II, Plenum-Press, New York, 1983.

[33] H. Gallaire, J. Minker, J.M. Nicolas, Logic and databases: a deductive approach. Computing Surveys 16, June 1984, 153-185.

[34] S.J. Hegner, Decomposition of relational schemata into components defined by both projection and restriction. ACM SIGACT-SIGMOS-SIGART Sym. 1988, 174-183.

[35] A. Heuer. Equivalent schemes in semantic, nested relational, and relational database models. LNCS 364, Springer, 1989, 237–253.

[36] R. Hull and R. King, Semantic database modeling: Survey, applications, and research isues. ACM Computing Surveys 19, 3, 1987, 201 -260.

[37] R. Hull. Four Views of Complex Objects: A Sophisticate's Introduction. In Proc. Conf. on Nested Relations and Complex Objects in Databases (Eds. : S. Abiteboul, P.C. Fischer, and H.J. Schek), Lecture Notes in Computer Science, 1989, 361, 87–116.

[38] T. Imielinski, W. Lipski Jr., A systematic approach to relational database theory. ICS PAS Reports 457, Warszawa, 1982.

[39] B.E. Jacobs, On database logic. Journal of ACM, 29, 2, 1982, 310 - 332.

[40] G. Jaeschke, H.J. Schek, Remarks on the algebra of nonfirst-normal-form relations. Proc. First ACM SIGACT-Sigmod Symposium on Principles of Database Systems, 1982, 124-138.

[41] G.O.H. Katona and J. Demetrovics, A survey of some combinatorial results concerning functional dependencies in relational databases. Annals of Mathematics and Artificial Intelligence, 6, 1992.

[42] Y. Kambayashi, Database, a bibiliography. Computer Science Press, Rockville, 1981.

[43] P.C. Kanellakis, Elements of relational database theory. In Handbook of Theoretical Computer Science (ed. J. van Leeuwen), Vol. B, Formal Models and Semantics, Elsevier, Amsterdam, 1990,

[44] L. Kerschberg (ed.), Expert database systems. Benjamin Cummings, Menlo-Park, 1987.

[45] W. Kim and F.H. Lochovsky (eds.), Object-oriented concepts, databases, and applications. Addison-Wesley, Reading, 1989.

[46] M. Kifer and G. Lausen, F-logic: A higher-order language for reasoning about objects, inheritance and schema. Proc. ACM SIGMOD Conf. 1989, 134 – 146.

[47] I. Kobayashi, An overview of database mangement technology. In Advances in Information System Science, ed. J.T. Tou, Vol. 9, Plenum Press, New York, 1985.

[48] M. Lenzerini, D. Nardi, and M. Simi (eds.), Inheritance hierarchies in knowledge representation and programming languages. John Wiley, Chichester, 1991. 5J. ACM 29, 2, April 1982, 333-363.

[49] U.W. Lipeck and B. Thalheim (eds.), Modelling Database Semantics, Springer Series Workshops in Computing, 1992.

[50] D. Maier, The theory of relational databases. Computer Science Press, Rockville, MD, 1983.

[51] V.M. Markowitz, Referential integrity revisited: An object-oriented perspective. Proc. VLDB 1990, 578 – 589.

[52] H. Mannila and K.-J. Räihä, On the complexity of inferring functional dependencies. Discrete Applied Mathematics, 1992.

[53] J. Minker (ed.), Foundations of deductive databases and logic programming. Morgan Kaufman, Los Altos, 1988.

[54] J.C. Mitchell, Type systems for programming languages. In Handbook of Theoretical Computer Science (ed. J. van Leeuwen), Vol. B, Formal Models and Semantics, Elsevier, Amsterdam, 1990, 365 – 458.

[55] J.F. Nilsson, Knowledge base property combinator logic. Information Processing 89 (ed. G.X. Ritter), Elsevier, Amsterdam, 1989, 661 – 666.

[56] J. Paredaens, P. De Bra, M. Gyssens, and D. Van Gucht. The structure of the relational database model. Springer, Berlin, 1989.

[57] S.V. Petrov, Finite axiomatization of languages for representation of system properties: Axiomatization of dependencies. Information Sciences 47, 1989, 339-372.

[58] G. Saake, Descriptive specification of database object behaviour, Data and Knowledge Engineering 6 (1991), 47 – 73

[59] H.J. Schek, M.H. Scholl, Evolution of data models. Proc. Database Systems of the 90s, LNCS 466, 1990, 135-153.

[60] J.W. Schmidt and C. Thanos (eds.), Foundations of knowledge base management. Springer, Heidelberg, 1989.

[61] D.-G. Shin and K.B. Irani, Fragmenting relations horizontally using a knowledge-based approach. IEEE Transaction on Software Engineering, 17, 9, 1991, 872–883.

[62] K.-D. Schewe, B. Thalheim, I. Wetzel and J.W. Schmidt, Extensible safe object-oriented design of database applications. University Rostock, Computer Science Department, Preprint CS-09-91, 1991.

[63] K.-D. Schewe, B. Thalheim, and I. Wetzel, Foundations of object-oriented concepts. Technical Report, Computer Science Department, Hamburg University, FBI - HH - B - 157/92, Aug. 1992.

[64] B. Thalheim, Deductive basis of relations. Proc. MFSSSS 84, LNCS 215, 226-230.

[65] B. Thalheim, On the number of keys in relational and nested relational databases. Discrete Applied Mathematics, 38, 1992.

[66] B. Thalheim. Dependencies in Relational Databases. Leipzig, Teubner Verlag 1991.

[67] B. Thalheim, Foundations of entity-relationship modeling. Annals of Mathematics and Artificial Intelligence, 6, 1992.

[68] B. Thalheim, Fundamentals of cardinality constraints. Proc. Conf. on Entity-Relationship-Approaches, LNCS 645, 7–23, 1992.

[69] B. Thalheim, Database design strategies. This volume, 1993.

[70] B. Thalheim, Fundamentals of Entity-Relationship models. Springer, Heidelberg 1993.

[71] A. Thayse (ed.), From modal logic to deductive databases. John Wiley, vol. 1: 1989, vol. 2: 1990.

[72] J. D. Ullman. Principles of database and knowledge-base systems. Computer Science Press, 1989.

[73] M.Y. Vardi, Fundamentals of dependency theory. In Trends in Theoretical Computer Science (ed. E. Börger), Computer Science Press, Rockville, 171 – 224.

[74] P. Wadler, List comprehensions. Chapter 7 in P. Jones, The implementation of functional programming languages. Prentice Hall, New York, 1987.

[75] M. Wirsing, Algebraic specification. In Handbook of Theoretical Computer Science (ed. J. van Leeuwen), Vol. B, Formal Models and Semantics, Elsevier, Amsterdam, 1990, 675 – 788.

[76] C.-C. Yang, Relational databases. Prentice Hall, Englewood Cliffs, 1986.

[77] L.-Y. Yuan and Z.M. Ozsoyoglu, Design of desirable relational database schemes. JCSS 1992, 45, 3, 1992, 435 – 470.

[78] M.S. Zalenko, Modeling semantics in data bases. Science, Moscov, 1989 (in Russian).

A BRIEF TUTORIAL INTRODUCTION TO DATA STRUCTURES FOR GEOMETRIC DATABASES

T. Ohler and P. Widmayer
ETH Zentrum, Zürich, Switzerland

1 The setting

It is a well established fact that traditional — such as relational — database systems are inappropriate for a large class of nonstandard applications. On the one hand, modeling and querying nonstandard data may be unnatural in a traditional system, and on the other hand, the resulting inefficiency — such as a long response time to a geometric query — may render the system altogether useless. The management of geometric objects, for instance in CAD or cartography, is a prime example of an application where efficiency is the bottleneck; this bottleneck cannot be eliminated without the help of suitable access structures (see also [1]).

In this brief tutorial, we present the basic concepts of current geometric access structures and the efficiency arguments involved. Until today, there is no precise understanding of what the building blocks of access structures really are or how they interact with the common goal of achieving maximum efficiency. Hence, here we aim at an intuitive understanding, with as little formalism as possible involved. Our presentation is in the spirit of [2], with a preliminary version of the first part of this tutorial having appeared in the first part of [3].

1.1 Geometric objects

A geometric object is characterized by a geometric component that determines shape and position of the object in space. In CAD for VLSI, for instance, aligned rectangles of the different layers of a chip describe the physical chip layout; in cartography, a partition of space into polygons describes land uses or political entities. Geometric objects may be complex in two ways [4]: On the one hand, the complex geometry makes geometric algorithms complicated and slow; on the other hand, the representation of an object may be complicated and long. Since the problems resulting from geometric object complexity are not the topic of this tutorial, we will restrict our discussion to simple geometric objects with a short description and easy and fast geometric algorithms; these objects may serve as containers for more complex objects.

1.2   Operations

Geometric operations refer to the spatial position of objects, most often to spatial proximity. A range query asks for all objects that intersect a given query range. A nearest neighbor query asks for an object in the database that is closest to a given query point. This query may be posed, for instance, to let a user pick an item with the cursor on the screen. As examples for proximity queries, these two types of operations will suffice for our purposes. Since the set of objects changes dynamically, insertions and deletions, and hence exact match queries, must also be supported.

1.3   Data structures

Data structures support geometric queries by realizing a fast but inaccurate filter for the response: The data structure allows to identify a superset of the set of desired objects. In a refinement step, each object returned by the data structure needs to be inspected. One reason for this approach is the complex geometry of objects that suggests the conservative approximation of each object by a simpler object of a fixed type, a container. The smallest aligned rectangle enclosing an object, the bounding box, is the most famous container: A data structure for aligned rectangles can be used to support geometric operations on arbitrary objects. For simplicity, we assume that a data item representing a geometric object is given by its geometric key; for a bounding box, the geometric key is the coordinates of the left, right, lower and upper rectangle boundary. We refrain from discussing the problems of maintaining object descriptions of variable length; for simplicity, we even assume that the description of the data item is fairly short.

Since the number of objects in an integrated geometric database easily goes into the millions [5], we assume that the data are stored on a secondary storage medium with fixed size blocks that can be addressed directly, such as a magnetic disk. Here lies the other reason for the filtering and the refinement step: Since blocks on external storage can be accessed only as a whole, it is in general unavoidable to access objects that do not belong to the response of a query. The data structure for secondary storage supports the filtering step only, that is, the selection of all blocks to be accessed.

As a consequence, we focus on secondary storage access structures for multidimensional aligned rectangles (or, equivalently, multidimensional intervals), or even multidimensional points in special cases. In order to support range queries efficiently, these data structures should respect the spatial proximity of objects by distributing objects physically on disk according to their location in space. Therefore, it is not enough to organize a suitable extra index on the data; the geometric data structures need to be the primary data organization, with its effect on the physical clustering of objects in blocks.

1.4 The problem

Let us now define the data maintenance problem more precisely as follows. Let d be the dimension of the space we consider, and let U_i be the universe in dimension i, $1 \leq i \leq d$. Let $U = U_1 \times U_2 \times \ldots \times U_d$ denote the d-dimensional universe of all geometric objects. Each geometric object g in an arbitrary set G of geometric objects is given by a d-dimensional bounding box b and other attributes that are not relevant for geometric operations. For each dimension i, $1 \leq i \leq d$, a bounding box b is the interval with left boundary l_i and right boundary r_i, $l_i, r_i \in U_i$, $l_i \leq r_i$. In total, $b = (l_1, r_1, l_2, r_2, \ldots, l_d, r_d)$ represents the d-dimensional interval $[l_1, r_1] \times \ldots \times [l_d, r_d]$. We use dot notation (as known from records in programming languages) to denote components; that is, component l_i of bounding box b is denoted by $b.l_i$, and similarly for $b.r_i$ and $g.b$. For brevity, we write $g.l_i$ or $g.r_i$ for $g.b.l_i$ or $g.b.r_i$. We are interested in a secondary storage access structure S that supports the following operations for a set G of geometric objects efficiently:

- *range query* $(w, S(G))$:
  For the query range (window) w and the set of objects G stored in S, return each object $g \in G$ whose bounding box $g.b$ intersects w. Here w is a d-dimensional interval, and the intersection of two topologically closed objects is defined as the closure of the intersection of the interior of the objects (as proposed by Tilove [6] to avoid certain anomalies);

- *exact match query* $(b, S(G))$:
  For bounding box b and set G of geometric objects stored in S, return an object $g \in G$ with $g.b = b$;

- *insert* $(g, S(G))$:
  For the geometric object g and the set G of geometric objects stored in S, add g to G; the result is $S(G \cup \{g\})$;

- *delete* $(b, S(G))$:
  For bounding box b and set G of geometric objects stored in S, delete an object g with $g.b = b$ from G; the result is $S(G \setminus \{g\})$.

We are not interested in treating special cases explicitly, such as ambiguities in exact match queries, insertions or deletions; we will therefore assume uniqueness whenever this facilitates our discussion. Our examples to illustrate the data structures are chosen for $d = 2$ and $U_1 = U_2 = [0, 1]$, unless stated otherwise.

2   Basic concepts

The operations exact match, insert, and delete do not refer to the location of objects in space, in spite of the geometric key. They can be supported efficiently with traditional secondary storage access schemes, such as B-trees [7, 8] or dynamic hashing [9], by simply concatenating the $2d$ key components of a d-dimensional bounding box lexicographically into a single key. Only in range queries, spatial proximity comes into the picture; we refrain from discussing other spatial queries explicitly, since range queries suffice to illustrate the basic concepts.

Since external storage access operations are far slower than main memory accesses or computation steps, usually the number of block accesses needed to answer a range query measures the complexity of that operation. Rarely, a closer look is taken towards the constituents of block access time, namely disk seek time, latency time and block transfer time [10, 11]. Here, seek plus latency time exceeds transfer time by far on standard magnetic disks. If we consider the blocks on a disk to be arranged in a total linear order with relative addresses $0, 1, \ldots$, and if we assume that block $i + 1$ can be transferred immediately after the transfer of block i without any extra seek or latency time, then it is obvious that there may be an advantage to reading more than one block in a sequence. This can be achieved by defining a logical block to consist of a number of physical blocks (Dröge et al. [12] investigate the situation where storage clusters are allowed to consist of a variable number of blocks), or even by systematically distributing data items on blocks in such a way that few sequences of blocks must be accessed in response to a range query [13, 14]. In any case, a block that needs to be read should contain as many desired data as possible. For range queries, this implies that all objects stored in a block should be neighbors in space; we call this *local order preservation*. The requirement that objects in nearby blocks should be close in space, called *global order preservation*, can be achieved even less strictly in general, but may nevertheless increase efficiency for appropriate circumstances.

2.1   Associating objects with blocks

To preserve local order, geometric objects are associated with blocks according to their geometric key, the bounding box. This is achieved by means of geometric regions: With each block B_j in a set B of blocks, we uniquely associate a region $R_j \subseteq U$ in a set R of regions, $1 \le j \le m$, where m is the current number of blocks. Typically, a block's region is the bounding box of the objects stored in the block [15] or a part in a partition of the universe [16]. We also denote R_j by $R(B_j)$, and B_j by $B(R_j)$. A block in this context may consist of a number of logical blocks, such as overflow blocks, without further structure.

With each geometric object g, a set $R(g.b) \subseteq R$ of regions is associated uniquely via its key $g.b$. To illustrate this principle, let us look at point objects in some detail. Here we have $g.b.l_i = g.b.r_i$ for all objects $g \in G$ and all dimensions i, $1 \leq i \leq d$; we write $g.p$ (point) instead of $g.b$ and $p = (p_1, p_2, \ldots, p_d)$. In this case, usually R is chosen such that the regions partition U. With each geometric object g, we associate the region containing point $g.p$. Region boundaries are uniquely associated with one of the regions bounded.

The freedom of choosing regions is limited: on the one hand, regions should in some way match the objects (not a problem for point objects), and on the other hand, regions themselves need to be maintained, just like geometric objects. Qualitatively, the situation is similar to what we know from one-dimensional access structures: If regions adapt to objects in a more flexible way (such as B-trees do, as against linear hashing), the management of regions becomes a heavier burden (such as the internal nodes in a leaf-oriented B-tree, as against a counter in linear hashing), but the number of blocks needed to store the objects decreases. We distinguish between region definitions that are based only on the number of objects and not on their geometry, and those that take the geometry into account. The former allow for data structures without much overhead for region management, i.e., structures without directory, whereas the latter make a directory (of more than constant size) necessary.

2.2   Data structures without directory

For multidimensional linear hashing, the management of regions is as simple as possible: the number n of objects fully determines the partition of the universe into regions. Since the storage space capacity of a block is assumed to be a constant, say $c \in \mathbb{N}$ objects, the number m of regions is determined by a fixed, desired storage space utilization of $\alpha = n/(c \cdot m)$. This number of regions is reached by repeatedly cutting a region into two new regions, according to a fixed scheme; the initial region is the universe. For maintaining the partition of the universe into regions, it is therefore sufficient to keep track of the number of cuts that have taken place since the beginning. Hence, we do not need an extra data structure — a directory — for maintaining the partition. On the other hand, the partition cannot adapt to the *set* of objects; therefore, in general, a fixed size block will not be large enough to store all objects in its region, and hence overflow blocks will be necessary. As a result, query efficiency will be acceptable only if geometric objects are distributed rather evenly in space.

2.3   Data structures with directory

Structures that adapt the regions to the set of objects do need a directory to maintain the set of regions. At least for point objects, the region maintenance problem may be the hardest part of the data structuring problem. As in the one-dimensional case, a directory can be built on a mixture of the address computation (as in hashing) and the key comparison (as in trees) techniques. For illustration purposes, assume $U_i = [0, 1)$ for each i with $1 \leq i \leq d$. In address computation techniques, we represent a coordinate value $x \in [0, 1)$ (for p_i, l_i or r_i) by the bit sequence $b_1 b_2 b_3 \ldots$ (of conceptually infinite length) of the fractional part of the binary representation of x, i.e., $x = \sum_{j=1}^{\infty} b_j 2^{-j}, b_j \in \{0, 1\}$. Depending on our needs, we pick a finite prefix with value $x_k = \sum_{j=1}^{k} b_j 2^{-j}$; its length k is called *resolution*, the sequence itself is called a *binary radix sequence*. In dimension i with resolution k_i, a *binary radix interval* I_i is an interval that can be created from U_i by repeated cutting in halves; such an interval has a left end point x_h and a length 2^{-j}, for $0 \leq h \leq j \leq k_i$. For d binary radix intervals $I_1, \ldots, I_d$, call $I_1 \times \ldots \times I_d$ a *binary radix region*. Almost all geometric data structures based on address computation arrive at regions through set operations on binary radix regions, where a region is viewed as a point set. Mostly, the union operation is enough; sometimes, e.g. for the BANG file, set difference is used in addition. The resolution of binary radix regions is chosen only as large as necessary to avoid overflow blocks (or other undesired phenomena, such as lack of balance in the BANG file).

In contrast to address computation, key comparison based data structures allow for a free choice of region boundary positions. Hence, regions fit objects more closely, but the expected effort to maintain regions increases. Mixtures of address computation and key comparison techniques try to make use of both, good worst case behavior in trees and fast expected access by hashing. Typically, each node in the tree is an external storage block whose interior is organized by hashing; data structures of this type are sometimes called *hash trees* [17, 18].

Since a directory must be designed to support range queries, we request for simplicity that for each object g associated with a region, $g.b$ intersects the region. Clearly, each object is associated with at least one and at most all of the regions intersected by its bounding box; for point objects, there is no reason to choose more than one region. Hence, to answer a range query, it suffices to access all blocks whose regions intersect the query range.

2.4   Associating rectangles with regions

Whereas it is fairly obvious how to associate point objects with regions, this is not true for rectangular objects: in a partition of the universe into regions, a rectangle need not be enclosed in any one region (Fig. 1 (a)). In that case, the only way of handling range queries efficiently requests that the rectangle is associated with each of the regions it intersects, and hence that the object is stored in each of the corresponding blocks; this technique is known as *clipping*. This can lead to reasonable performance in cases where the geometric object behind the bounding box can be cut at the region boundaries, such as those cartographic applications in which objects are polygons with lots of corners [19, 20]. In these cases, clipping has the advantage over most other techniques to be conceptually simple, easy to implement, and to preserve the geometry of the situation for any proximity query. In general, however, clipping may degrade performance substantially, since the number of objects (copies) to be stored increases, which in turn increases the number of regions, thereby again increasing the number of copies, a vicious circle [21, 22]. In the worst case, clipping can even become bad enough to cut through a linear proportion of all rectangles, even with the best possible cut line [23, 24, 25].

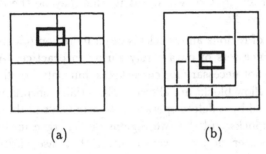

(a)   (b)

Figure 1: Associating rectangles with regions

If we allow instead that regions may *overlap* without any restriction, we can define for each rectangle at least one region that encloses the rectangle (Fig. 1 (b)). To answer range queries efficiently, it is then sufficient to associate a rectangle with one of the regions that enclose it. However, if the directory does not tell with which of these regions a rectangle is associated, an exact match query may become quite inefficient, since all candidate regions may have to be inspected; this is the case with the R-tree [15]. In addition, if regions tend to overlap too much, the geometric selectivity of the access structure suffers, with a negative effect also on range query performance [26].

As a third possibility, a rectangle may be viewed as a *point* in some parameter space. For simplicity, most often a d-dimensional rectangle $b = (l_1, r_1, \ldots, l_d, r_d)$ is viewed as a $2d$-dimensional point $p = (p_1, \ldots, p_{2d})$, with $p_{2i-1} = l_i$ and $p_{2i} = r_i$ for $1 \leq i \leq d$. A range query in the original space maps into a half-open range query in parameter space, i.e., a range query whose query region extends to half the boundaries of the parameter space. Many arguments and experiments have been made to reveal the performance that can be expected from parameter space transformations [27, 28, 29, 30, 31], with promising steps being taken in the recent past [32].

All known data structures for rectangles are limited to these three basic ingredients: clipping, overlapping regions, and point transformations [21, 22, 31]. Therefore, data structures for points do not only cover a special case of objects, but can also be used to maintain sets of parameter points.

2.5 Growing and shrinking

The association of regions with objects changes dynamically: Upon insertion or deletion of an object we check by means of a growth or shrinkage criterion whether the number of blocks and, hence, of regions, should increase or decrease. Growth is typically induced by reaching a prespecified storage space utilization (for structures without directory) or by a block overflow (for structures with directory). To realize growth, we select an appropriate block and split its region into two; then, we associate two blocks with the new regions (one of the two blocks may be the old one that was split, but at least one new block is added). The function that associates an object with a set of blocks tells where to store the objects in the block that was split. In case this growth step preserves the criterion for growth, we repeat it; this may be the case if a block split does not eliminate an overflow.

Shrinking the number of regions and blocks is often more complicated, but fortunately also less important, since sets of data rarely shrink in practice. Also, in many data structures shrinking is not necessary for correctness, but only for efficiency; the same is true for growing, if overflow blocks are allowed. Essentially, shrinking reverses growing: a shrinking step, induced by a delete operation, selects two suitable blocks and merges them. Both, the two blocks and the two regions, are merged into one. Two suitable regions and blocks, however, do not always exist; in that case, shrinking is impossible. To remain efficient, data structures have to make sure that for a decreasing number of objects, eventually a sufficient number of shrinking steps is possible. In this tutorial, we will not be concerned with further details of shrinking steps from now on.

2.6 Design decisions

The efficiency of operations is considered to be determined by the number of external block accesses, or, far less frequently, by the number of disk seek operations. Spatial access structures aim at a good average case efficiency for range queries, without even clearly defining what *average* means. Stochastic geometry [33, 34, 35, 36, 37] has shown that it is by no means easy to talk about a random geometric situation in a reasonable way; we do not expect a mathematical model of typical situations in CAD or cartography to be found in the near future. Except for some very rare cases in which analytical results are available [38, 39, 40], statements about the efficiency of operations in data structures must be based on plausibility arguments and experiments.

To define a particular data structure, we obviously need to make at least the following decisions:

1. How should regions look like? What is a split strategy and what is a merge strategy to achieve this dynamically? In case block addresses must be associated with regions so as to preserve global order, which rule should be applied?

2. How should objects be associated with regions?

3. What should be the criterion for growth, what should it be for shrinking? How should blocks be selected for split and for merge operations?

4. How can we maintain regions in a way that supports all necessary operations on regions efficiently?

These questions serve as our template for the definition of data structures; in the following, we will describe data structures for rectangles according to this template. As to the shape of regions and the split and merge strategies, including growing and shrinking, most data structures for rectangles are strongly based on multidimensional data structures for points. These, in turn, are most often generalizations of one-dimensional data structures to higher dimension. For instance, multidimensional order preserving linear hashing with partial expansions [41] is based on linear hashing [42]; the grid file [16] is based on extendible hashing [43], and the hB-tree [44] is based on the B-tree [7]. The outstanding textbooks by Samet [45, 46] discuss all of these structures in detail.

3 Rectangles as points in parameter space

A rectangle can be transformed into a point in some parameter space in a number of ways. The transformation should aim at describing the image point with few parameters to keep the dimension of the image space low, and at transforming range queries in such a way that data structures for points in space support the transformed queries in image space efficiently. The two most visible transformations proposed in the literature are the *corner transformation* and the *center transformation*. We illustrate both transformations at the example of one-dimensional rectangles, i.e., intervals on the real line.

The corner transformation maps the d-dimensional rectangle $b = [l_1, r_1] \times \ldots \times [l_d, r_d]$ into the $2d$-dimensional point $p(b) = (l_1, r_1, \ldots, l_d, r_d)$. In our example of $d = 1$, for $b = [l, r]$ we get $p(b) = (l, r)$. Since $r \geq l$, all image points lie above the diagonal (in Fig. 2 (a) we have $p_j = p(b_j)$).

The coordinates of points, hence, are not independent in the dimensions; therefore, they cause more or less severe efficiency problems in many data structures for points. In addition — and this seems to be far more severe —, the intuitive concept of proximity in original space is not preserved. The Euclidean (or Manhattan) distance may serve to illustrate this point: it is different from 0 (and thereby largest) in the example in Fig. 2 (a) only between b_1 and b_3; in image space, however, the distance is smallest between p_1 and p_3.

The center transformation that associates with $b = [l_1, r_1] \times \ldots \times [l_d, r_d]$ the image point $p(b) = ((r_1 + l_1)/2, (r_1 - l_1)/2, \ldots, (r_d + l_d)/2, (r_d - l_d)/2)$ does not solve this problem (Fig. 2 (b)). Nevertheless, it has the advantage over the corner transformation to separate parameters for the location of the object in space from parameters for the size

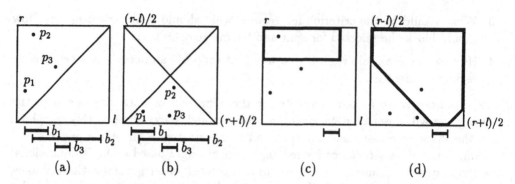

Figure 2: Corner transformation (a) and center transformation (b) for intervals and for query ranges (c), (d)

(and shape) of the object. In spite of this property, any of the typical grid partitions of the point data structures seems to fit neither the distribution of image points (lying close to an axis in parameter space for small rectangles in original space, a common situation) nor the shape of query ranges. Fig. 2 (d) shows the image of a query range. For a small upper bound on the size of query ranges that is known beforehand, the data space partition can be adjusted accordingly, leading to acceptable efficiency even for range queries (Seeger et al. [31] make use of *asymmetric* partitions and PLOP-Hashing). The corner transformation appears to be preferable to the center transformation, as far as the adaptivity of data regions to query ranges is concerned (Fig. 2 (c) shows a query range and its image).

For multidimensional image points of rectangles, a highly adaptive data structure has been developed that supports range queries efficiently, the local split decision tree (*LSD-tree* [28, 29]. The LSD-tree generalizes the k-d-tree by not prescribing strictly the change of the split dimension from level to level, but instead leaving the decision about which dimension to choose completely open. A special paging strategy that can be applied to arbitrary binary search trees makes the LSD-tree suited for external storage [27]. According to Henrich [29], the LSD-tree beats the R-tree [15] for a large spectrum of data distributions and split strategies, especially when query ranges tend to be small. The LSD-tree has been used quite successfully as the geometric access structure in the extensible database system Gral [47] and in the relational database system Oracle [48].

For the special case in which range queries are the only type of proximity queries, other good transformations have recently been found [32]. These transformations use the parameters volume and aspect ratio to cluster rectangles that is quite appropriate for flexible point data structures such as the LSD-tree. Nevertheless, we feel that a transformation cannot be general enough to preserve the geometry of the original situation entirely, and, as a consequence, will not be able to support all types of proximity queries well.

4   Data structures for rectangles

In another straightforward way of using point data structures for storing rectangles, a reference point is chosen for each rectangle — typically its center —, and the rectangle is associated with the block in whose region its reference point lies. This works only if we keep track of the extensions of the rectangles beyond the region boundaries. In a range query, the region to be considered for a block is not the region defined by the partition of the data space, but instead the bounding box of all rectangles actually associated with the block. The latter may in general be larger than the former, and not all data structures will easily accomodate that extended region information. Hierarchical structures such as k-d-trees [49, 50], the BANG file [51], or PLOP-hashing [18, 31] can be used for that purpose. Even though this approach works well whenever only small rectangles are to be stored, it is inefficient in general, because no attempt is made to avoid the overlap of search regions, and therefore geometric selectivity is lost easily.

4.1   The R-tree family

With the explicit goal of high geometric selectivity, the R-tree [15] has been designed to maintain block regions that overlap just as much as necessary, so as to make each rectangle fall entirely into a region. Its structure resembles the B^+-tree, including restructuring operations that propagate from the leaf level towards the root. Each data region is the bounding box of the rectangles associated with the corresponding block. Each directory block maintains a rectangular subspace of the data space; its block region is the bounding box of the subspaces of its children. As a consequence, on each level of the tree, each rectangle lies entirely in at least one block region; since block regions will overlap in general, it may actually lie in more than one region (see Fig. 3, in which rectangles E and F lie in regions A and B, referenced by the root block). This fact may distort geometric selectivity: In an exact match query, we cannot restrict the search for E to either A or B, but instead we need to follow both paths (in the worst case, with no hint as to which one is more likely).

R-tree regions are created as a result of the sequence of insertions and the association of rectangles to regions during insertion. For a rectangle b, the insertion operation determines a path from the root to a leaf of the R-tree, representing a data region, the *insertion path*. The insertion path proceeds from a directory region to *the* region referenced in the directory block whose area needs to be enlarged as little as possible to accomodate b. In the best case, the necessary enlargement is 0; if this is true for more than one of the referenced regions, an arbitrary one of them is chosen. Otherwise, the new boundaries of the enlarged region are stored in the directory block, to correctly guide future queries. In case the data block identified by the insertion path does not overflow, due to the insertion of b, the insert operation terminates. Otherwise, the block is split into two regions, with the aims of distributing entries among the two new blocks evenly, and of keeping the new block regions small, with little overlap. As in

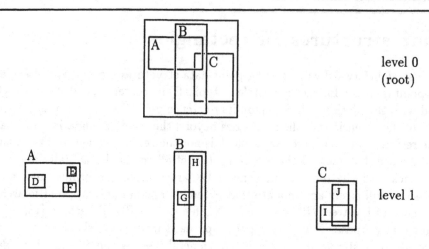

Figure 3: An R-tree partition with two levels and a directory block capacity of three regions

B^+-trees, the structural change propagates up the tree.

Since it is essential for the R-tree to avoid excessive overlap of regions, a surprisingly large number of reports on strategies of splitting an overflowing block into two exist. The initial suggestion [15] has been to aim at the minimum of the sum of the areas of both resulting regions, under the condition that each of the two blocks receives at least a fixed number of entries. Since n regions can be partitioned into two subsets in 2^n ways, realistic values for n of roughly 50 do not permit to consider all these possibilities. Instead, Guttman [15] proposes two heuristics, one with linear and one with quadratic runtime (expressed in n).

In the meantime, other measures to be optimized and other heuristics have been proposed. Beckmann et al. [52] suggest to heuristically aim at optimizing a combination of the sum of the areas, the sum of the perimeters, and the area of the intersection of both regions. They report that, together with repeated restructuring operations (reinsertion in [15]) from time to time, this R-tree variant, the so-called R^*-tree, is superior to the heuristics proposed in [15] and in [26]; even as point data structure, the R^*-tree outperforms the grid file, according to [52]. Surprisingly enough, Becker et al. [53] have shown that for all of these criteria, it is not necessary to resort to heuristics, but instead all of them can be optimized efficiently. Six et al. [3] and Pagel et al. [54] have come up with explanations as to why mixed criteria such as those the R^*-tree may lead to high performance.

For specific purposes, a number of variants of the R-tree have been proposed. The R^+-tree avoids overlapping directory regions by clipping rectangles as necessary [55, 56]. Sellis et al. [56] come to the conclusion that the R^+-tree is superior to the R-tree; Greene [26] does not find a significant difference between both in an experimental performance comparison. Since the R^+-tree suffers somewhat from the conceptual and implementation complexity and the slight inefficiency caused by forced splits propagating downwards, similar to k-d-B-trees, Greene [26] prefers the R-tree. Smith et al. [57] arrive at a similar conclusion; their experiments do not give a total order, as far as efficiency is concerned, among the R-tree, the R^+-tree, the grid file (for transformed rectangles), and the locational key [58] stored in a B^+-tree. For a static situation, in which almost no insertions or deletions take place, and therefore queries dominate the picture, the R-tree can be packed densely so as to increase effciency in time and space (the *packed R-tree* [59]). Ohsawa et al. [60] combine the R-tree with the quad tree partition mechanism.

4.2   Multilayer structures

Geometric selectivity is higher whenever the overlap of regions is lower. This observation has been the starting point for a number of techniques that operate with overlapping regions. Multilayer structures [21, 22] cover the data space with more than one partition. In this method, any suitable point data structure that partitions the universe can be used for each of the partitions. Multiple instantiations of this point data structure, each with a modified split strategy so as to yield *different* partitions, form *layers* of the multilayer structure. The layers are ordered, from *lowest* to *highest*. The partitions of the various layers are chosen in such a way that each rectangle that needs to be stored is contained entirely in a region of at least one partition. If split positions are chosen appropriately, this is possible for small d-dimensional rectangles with at most $d + 1$ layers (the technical term *small* has a precise meaning [21, 22]). If large rectangles are to be stored as well, and the number of layers should be limited, one might decide to clip all rectangles that do not fit entirely into any region. Fig. 4 shows a three-layer grid file with data block capacity $c = 3$, where the split positions can be chosen freely for each layer; they are maintained in the grid file scales.

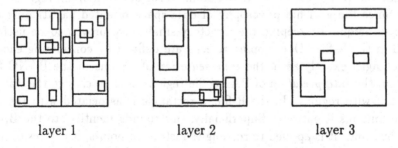

layer 1   layer 2   layer 3

Figure 4: The partitions of a three-layer grid file

A rectangle is associated with the region of the lowest layer that contains it entirely. This association of rectangles with regions is unique, in contrast to the R-tree. For exact search, this implies that first, the layer of a rectangle is determined by looking at the partitions, and second, the search for the rectangle in the corresponding layer is carried out, as defined by the point data structure. A range query, on the contrary, must be carried out on each layer. Six et al. [21, 22] show experimentally that the loss of efficiency is small, as compared with a point data structure, whenever the query range has at least a certain size.

The efficiency of multilayer structures crucially depends on the adaptivity of the partitions of the various layers, with respect to the set of rectangles to be stored, as well as with respect to each other. Six et al. [21, 22] propose to choose a new split position in such a way that its distance to all existing parallel split lines, no matter on which layer, is maximum. For several different definitions of the term distance, we get several different concrete split strategies. Fig. 4 illustrates that for a suitable split strategy, regions of higher layers tend to be larger; as a consequence, large rectangles also have a chance to be stored without clipping, even if the number of layers is limited to a constant.

Hutflesz et al. [14] show how the multilayer technique can be used to arrive at data structures for rectangles that inherit other desirable properties from point data structures, at the example of dynamic z-hashing. In addition, multiple layers realize the advantages of recursive linear hashing [61] without its overhead, because the layers can be used to avoid overflow blocks. This makes bookkeeping somewhat complicated, but pays off in terms of efficiency: Experiments show that range queries in multilayer dynamic z-hashing are extremely fast, even though the number of block accesses is roughly the same as in other data structures for rectangles [14].

4.3   The R-file

Since the search parameters are the same for each layer (e.g. in a range query), it might be desirable to somehow integrate all the directories into just one directory. This is exactly what the R-file [62] does. It maintains a set of overlapping regions with one directory. Since the grid file philosophy of data-space oriented partitioning and the BANG file technique for keeping the directory small have proven to be useful, both are applied in the R-file. Overlapping regions are defined by considering each region to be a rectangle, exactly as in the *representation* of regions in the BANG file, but different from the *interpretation* of BANG file regions, and to change the way objects are associated with regions. In the R-file, a rectangle is associated with the smallest region that contains it entirely. Superficially, this sounds identical to the BANG file technique, but since it is applied to rectangles instead of points, it creates overlapping rectangular regions instead of a partition into orthogonal polygonals. Fig. 5 shows an R-file pattern of four regions (a), compared with a grid file partition with clipping (c) into seven regions, for the same set of rectangles and a data block capacity of $c = 3$.

Because all rectangles associated with the region of the universe intersect the central vertical split line, it pays to distinguish insertion regions from search regions. If too many rectangles intersect this split line, it may happen that too large a number of

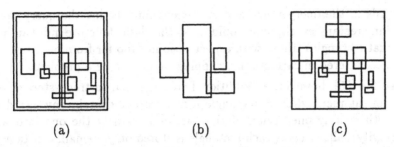

Figure 5: An R-file pattern of insertion regions (a), the corresponding search regions (b), and a grid file partition with clipping (c)

rectangles should be associated with the corresponding region. In that case, a lower dimensional R-file stores these rectangles; the one dimension in which all of these rectangles intersect the split line can be disregarded. Fortunately, no extra data structure is needed for the $(d-1)$-dimensional R-file; instead, a simple skip of dimension d in the cyclic turn through all dimensions will do. Experiments [62] have shown the R-file to be an extremely efficient data structure for cartographic data. It suffers, however, from the disadvantage of being somewhat complicated to implement, with extra algorithmic difficulties (but not inefficiencies) such as a forced split downwards. Nevertheless, it is a good basis for a data structure that supports a varying degree of detail, in addition to spatial proximity queries (the PR-file, see [63, 64]).

4.4 Guard files

Remember that the difficulties in maintaining rectangles as opposed to points comes from the fact that a rectangle may intersect more than one region of a space partition, that is, it may intersect a split line (or more than one) in a dynamic data structure. In the R-file, for instance, rectangles intersecting a split line may be handled separately. But there is no a priori reason why split lines should be chosen to differentiate between two types of rectangles, those that intersect and those that don't. Guard files make use of this inherent freedom by choosing other geometric objects that guard the rectangles to be stored, in the sense that rectangles that intersect a geometric guard are treated separately from those that don't. Nievergelt et al. [65] suggest to let the guards be the corner points of the regions of some regular space partition.

To make range queries efficient, we impose a hierarchy on the guards: For a quad tree partition, for instance, the level of a guard is the level of the largest quad tree region of which the guard is a corner point, with the root of the tree having the highest level. Now, a rectangle containing a guard is stored with the highest level guard that it contains; if it contains no guard, then it might be clipped and stored with all regions (of the partition, that is, at the leaf level of the quad tree) that it intersects. As a consequence, a range query would be carried out by inspecting the rectangles associated with all guards in the query range and all regions intersecting the query range. For long and skinny rectangles, clipping would make this data structure quite an inefficient one, but for fat rectangles (those with aspect ratio not too far from one) such as those most often encountered in cartography, clipping would not be a problem.

In the guard file [65], however, an additional step is taken to trade storage space for query time for fat rectangles: A rectangle that does not contain any guard point is associated with exactly one region of the partition, namely the one into which its center (of gravity) falls. Hence, each rectangle is stored only a small, constant number of times, the number depending only on the type of regular partition being used. In a range query, it is no longer sufficient to inspect the regions that intersect the query range: Adjacent regions also need to be inspected. The halo by which a query range must be extended depends entirely on how fat the stored rectangles are: the fatter the rectangles, the smaller the halo. For various types of regular partitions and various bounds on the fatness (in a precise, technical sense for arbitrary, convex geometric objects), it has been shown [65] that the guard file is conceptually simple, easy to implement, and efficient at the same time.

5   Concluding remarks

The set of spatial data structures and paradigms has grown to a respectable size. There is a multitude of concepts that may serve as building blocks in the design of new spatial data structures for specific purposes. A number of convincing suggestions indicate that, for instance, these building blocks can be used in the design of data structures for more complex settings. Becker [66], Brinkhoff et al. [67], Günther [68], Kriegel et al. [69], and Shaffer et al. [70], among others, show how various kinds of set operations, such as spatial join, can be performed efficiently by using a spatial index. For objects and operations going beyond geometry, Ohler [71] shows how to design access structures that involve non-geometric attributes in a query. In a closer look to the needs of cartography, a data structure of weighted geometric objects is proposed that efficiently supports queries with a varying degree of detail, as specified by the user [64]. For the special case in which the objects to be stored are the polygons of a planar partition, and access to entire polygons (in containment queries with points, for instance) as well as access to the polygon boundaries (for drawing a map) is needed, there are suggestions that consider both external accesses and main memory computations as important cost factors [72, 73]; other suggestions aim at making queries efficient without storing polygon boundaries twice [74]. In addition, hierarchical spatial access structures can be designed to support queries into the past [75, 76, 77]. It can be seen from this list that even though a fair number of concepts of data access are readily available, it is mosten often a considerable effort to bring any two of them together without losing key features, especially efficiency.

In all of the above suggestions, the arguments to the efficiency of data structures are only of an intuitive nature. An average case analysis is rarely given ([38, 39, 40, 78, 79] are exceptions), because a probability model for sets of geometric objects and queries is very hard to get [33, 34, 36, 37]. Even experiments [57, 80, 81] that clarify some of the efficiency aspects tend to reveal not too much about the contribution of the building blocks of data structures to their overall efficiency. Some small first steps towards a clarification of what is the best possible efficiency and how to achieve it, with consequences for the data structure design, have been taken [3, 54, 82], but many more are needed to shed enough light on the inner workings of spatial data structures. In the meantime, the designer and programmer of spatial data structures should be aware of the existing building blocks and use them with expertise and intuition, bringing them together wherever possible.

Acknowledgement

Thanks go to the Deutsche Forschungsgemeinschaft DFG, the Swiss National Science Foundation SNF, the European Community with the ESPRIT program, the Landesanstalt für Umweltschutz in Baden-Württemberg, and the Umweltministerium Baden-Württemberg for their support of the work of and their cooperation with the authors in the field of spatial data structures and geographic information systems over many years. In particular, the authors are grateful for having learned a lot about spatial data structures and GIS in discussions with B. Becker, P.G. Franciosa, F. d'Amore, S. Gschwind, O. Günther, R.H. Güting, A. Henrich, A. Hutflesz, M. Müller, V.H. Nguyen, J. Nievergelt, Th. Ottmann, T. Roos, H. Samet, B. Seeger, H.-W. Six, and G. Thiemt.

References

1. Günther, O. and A. Buchmann: Research issues in spatial databases, IEEE CS Bulletin on Data Engineering, Vol. 13, No. 4, 1990, 35–42.

2. Widmayer, P.: Datenstrukturen für Geodatenbanken, in: Entwicklungstendenzen bei Datenbank-Systemen (Eds. G. Vossen, K.-U. Witt), Oldenbourg Verlag, 1991, 317–361.

3. Six, H.-W. and P. Widmayer: Spatial access structures for geometric databases, in: Data Structures and Efficient Algorithms (Eds. B. Monien, T. Ottmann), Final Report on the DFG Special Joint Initiative, Lecture Notes in Computer Science, Vol. 594, Springer-Verlag, Berlin 1992, 214–232.

4. Kemper, A. and M. Wallrath: An analysis of geometric modelling in database systems, ACM Computing Surveys, Vol. 19, No. 1, 1987, 47–91.

5. Crain, I.K.: Extremely large spatial information systems: a quantitative perspective, Proc. 4th International Symposium on Spatial Data Handling, Zürich, 1990, 632–641.

6. Tilove, R.B.: Set membership classification: A unified approach to geometric intersection problems, IEEE Transactions on Computers, Vol. C-29, 1980, 874–883.

7. Bayer, R. and C. McCreight: Organization and maintenance of large ordered indexes, Acta Informatica, Vol. 1, No. 3, 1972, 173–189.

8. Comer, D.: The ubiquitous B-tree, ACM Computing Surveys, Vol. 11, No. 2, 1979, 121–138.

9. Enbody, R.J. and H.C. Du: Dynamic hashing schemes, ACM Computing Surveys, Vol. 20, No. 2, 1988, 85–113.

10. Wang, J.-H., T.-S. Yuen and D.H.-C. Du: On multiple random access and physical data placement in dynamic files, IEEE Transactions on Software Engineering, Vol. 13, No. 8, 1987, 977–987.

11. Weikum, G., B. Neumann and H.-B. Paul: Konzeption und Realisierung einer mengenorientierten Seitenschnittstelle zum effizienten Zugriff auf komplexe Objekte, GI-Fachtagung Datenbanksysteme für Büro, Technik und Wissenschaft, Informatik-Fachberichte, Vol. 136, Springer-Verlag, Berlin 1987, 212–230.

12. Dröge, G. and H.-J. Schek: Query-adaptive data space partitioning using variable-size storage clusters, 3rd International Symposium on Advances in Spatial Databases, Singapore, Lecture Notes in Computer Science, Vol. 692, Springer-Verlag, Berlin 1993, 337–356.

13. Hutflesz, A., H.-W. Six and P. Widmayer: Globally order preserving multidimensional linear hashing, Proc. 4th International Conference on Data Engineering, Los Angeles, 1988, 572–579.

14. Hutflesz, A., P. Widmayer and C. Zimmermann: Global order makes spatial access faster, Geographic Data Base Management Systems, ESPRIT Basic Research Series Proceedings, Springer-Verlag, Berlin 1992, 161–176.

15. Guttman, A.: R-trees: a dynamic index structure for spatial searching, Proc. ACM SIGMOD International Conference on the Management of Data, Boston, 1984, 47–57.

16. Nievergelt, J., H. Hinterberger and K.C. Sevcik: The grid file: an adaptable, symmetric multikey file structure, ACM Transactions on Database Systems, Vol. 9, No. 1, 1984, 38–71.

17. Otoo, E.J.: Balanced multidimensional extendible hash tree, Proc. 5th ACM SIGACT-SIGMOD International Symposium on Principles of Database Systems, Cambridge, Massachusetts, 1986, 100–113.

18. Seeger, B.: Entwurf und Implementierung mehrdimensionaler Zugriffsstrukturen, Dissertation, Universität Bremen, Germany, 1989.

19. Schek, H.-J. and W. Waterfeld: A database kernel system for geoscientific applications, Proc. 2nd International Symposium on Spatial Data Handling, Seattle, 1986, 273–288.

20. Waterfeld, W.: Eine erweiterbare Speicher- und Zugriffskomponente für geowissenschaftliche Datenbanksysteme, Dissertation, Fachbereich Informatik, Technische Hochschule Darmstadt, Germany, 1991.

21. Six, H.-W. and P. Widmayer: Hintergrundspeicherstrukturen für ausgedehnte Objekte, 16. Jahrestagung der Gesellschaft für Informatik, Berlin, Informatik-Fachberichte, Vol. 126, Springer-Verlag, Berlin 1986, 538–552.

22. Six, H.-W. and P. Widmayer: Spatial searching in geometric databases, Proc. 4th International Conference on Data Engineering, Los Angeles, 1988, 496–503.

23. d'Amore, F. and P.G. Franciosa: Separating sets of hyperrectangles, International Journal of Computational Geometry and Applications, Vol. 3, No. 2, 1993, 155–165.

24. d'Amore, F., T. Roos and P. Widmayer: An optimal algorithm for computing a best cut of a set of hyperrectangles, International Computer Graphics Conference, Bombay, 1993.

25. Nguyen, V.H., T. Roos and P. Widmayer: Balanced cuts of a set of hyperrectangles, Proc. 5th Canadian Conference on Computational Geometry, Waterloo, 1993, 121–126.

26. Greene, D.: An implementation and performance analysis of spatial data access methods, Proc. 5th International Conference on Data Engineering, Los Angeles, 1989, 606–615.

27. Henrich, A., H.-W. Six and P. Widmayer: Paging binary trees with external balancing, 15th International Workshop on Graph-Theoretic Concepts in Computer Science, Castle Rolduc, Lecture Notes in Computer Science, Vol. 411, Springer-Verlag, Berlin 1989, 260–276.

28. Henrich, A., H.-W. Six and P. Widmayer: The LSD-tree: Spatial access to multidimensional point- and non-point objects, 15th International Conference on Very Large Data Bases, Amsterdam, 1989, 45–53.

29. Henrich, A.: Der LSD-Baum: eine mehrdimensionale Zugriffsstruktur und ihre Einsatzmöglichkeiten in Datenbanksystemen, Dissertation, FernUniversität Hagen, Germany, 1990.

30. Hinrichs, K.H.: The grid file system: implementation and case studies of applications, Dissertation, ETH Zürich, 1985.

31. Seeger, B. and H.-P. Kriegel: Techniques for design and implementation of efficient spatial access methods, Proc. 14th International Conference on Very Large Data Bases, Los Angeles, 1988, 360–371.

32. Pagel, B.-U., H.-W. Six and H. Toben: The transformation technique for spatial objects revisited, 3rd International Symposium on Advances in Spatial Databases, Singapore, Lecture Notes in Computer Science, Vol. 692, Springer-Verlag, Berlin 1993, 73–88.

33. Harding, E.F. and D.G. Kendall: Stochastic Geometry, Wiley, New York 1974.

34. Matheron, G.: Random sets and integral geometry, Wiley, New York 1975.

35. Mecke, J., R.G. Schneider, D. Stoyan and W.R.R. Weil: Stochastische Geometrie, DMV-Seminar Band 16, Birkhäuser Verlag, Basel 1990.

36. Santalo, L.A.: Integral geometry and geometric probability, Addison-Wesley, Reading 1976.

37. Stoyan, D., W.S. Kendall and J. Mecke: Stochastic geometry and its applications, Wiley, New York 1987.

38. Devroye, L.: Lecture notes on bucket algorithms, Birkhäuser Verlag, Boston 1986.

39. Flajolet, P. and C. Puech: Partial match retrieval of multidimensional data, Journal of the ACM, Vol. 33, No. 2, 1986, 371–407.

40. Regnier, M.: Analysis of grid file algorithms, BIT Vol. 25, 1985, 335–357.

41. Kriegel, H.-P. and B. Seeger: Multidimensional order preserving linear hashing with partial expansions, Proc. International Conference on Database Theory, Lecture Notes in Computer Science, Vol. 243, Springer-Verlag, Berlin 1986, 203–220.

42. Litwin, W.: A new tool for file and table addressing, Proc. 6th International Conference on Very Large Data Bases, Montreal, 1980, 212–223.

43. Fagin, R., J. Nievergelt, N. Pippenger and H.R. Strong: Extendible hashing - a fast access method for dynamic files, ACM Transactions on Database Systems, Vol. 4, No. 3, 1979, 315–344.

44. Lomet, D.B. and B. Salzberg: The hB-tree: A multiattribute indexing method with good guaranteed performance, ACM Transactions on Database Systems, Vol. 15, No. 4, 1990, 625–658.

45. Samet, H.: The design and analysis of spatial data structures, Addison-Wesley, Reading 1990.

46. Samet, H.: Applications of spatial data structures, Addison-Wesley, Reading 1990.

47. Güting, R.H.: Gral: An extensible relational database system for geometric applications, Proc. 15th International Conference on Very Large Data Bases, Amsterdam, 1989, 33–44.

48. Henrich, A., A. Hilbert, H.-W. Six and P. Widmayer: Anbindung einer räumlich clusternden Zugriffsstruktur für geometrische Attribute an ein Standard-Datenbanksystem am Beispiel von Oracle, GI-Fachtagung Datenbanksysteme für Büro, Technik und Wissenschaft, Informatik-Fachberichte, Vol. 270, Springer-Verlag, Berlin 1991, 161–177.

49. Ooi, B.C.: A data structure for geographic database, GI-Fachtagung Datenbanksysteme für Büro, Technik und Wissenschaft, Informatik-Fachberichte, Vol. 136, Springer-Verlag, Berlin 1987, 247–258.

50. Ooi, B.C., R. Sacks-Davis and K.J. McDonell: Extending a DBMS for geographic applications, Proc. 5th International Conference on Data Engineering, Los Angeles, 1989, 590–597.

51. Freeston, M.W.: A well-behaved file structure for the storage of spatial objects, Symposium on the Design and Implementation of Large Spatial Databases, Santa Barbara, Lecture Notes in Computer Science, Vol. 409, Springer-Verlag, Berlin 1989, 287–300.

52. Beckmann, N., H.-P. Kriegel, R. Schneider and B. Seeger: The R*-tree: An efficient and robust access method for points and rectangles, Proc. ACM SIGMOD International Conference on the Management of Data, Atlantic City, New Jersey, 1990, 322–331.

53. Becker, B., P. Franciosa, S. Gschwind, T. Ohler, G. Thiemt and P. Widmayer: Enclosing many boxes by an optimal pair of boxes, Proc. 9th Annual Symposium on Theoretical Aspects of Computer Science STACS, Cachan, Lecture Notes in Computer Science, Vol. 577, Springer-Verlag, Berlin 1992, 475–486.

54. Pagel, B.-U., H.-W. Six, H. Toben and P. Widmayer: Towards an analysis of range query performance in spatial data structures, 12th SIGACT-SIGMOD-SIGART Symposium on Principles of Database Systems, Washington D.C., 1993, 214–221.

55. Faloutsos, C., T. Sellis and N. Roussopoulos: Analysis of object oriented spatial access methods, Proc. ACM SIGMOD International Conference on the Management of Data, San Francisco, 1987, 426–439.

56. Sellis, T., N. Roussopoulos and C. Faloutsos: The R+-tree: A dynamic index for multi-dimensional objects, Proc. 13th International Conference on Very Large Data Bases, Brighton, 1987, 507–518.

57. Smith, T.R. and P. Gao: Experimental performance evaluations on spatial access methods, Proc. 4th International Symposium on Spatial Data Handling, Zürich, 1990, 991–1002.

58. Abel, D.J. and J.L. Smith: A data structure and algorithm based on a linear key for a rectangle retrieval problem, Computer Vision, Graphics, and Image Processing, Vol. 24, 1983, 1–13.

59. Roussopoulos, N. and D. Leifker: Direct spatial search on pictorial databases using packed R-trees, Proc. ACM SIGMOD International Conference on the Management of Data, Austin, 1985, 17–31.

60. Ohsawa, Y. and M. Sakauchi: A new tree type data structure with homogeneous nodes suitable for a very large spatial database, Proc. 6th International Conference on Data Engineering, Los Angeles, 1990, 296–303.

61. Ramamohanarao, K. and R. Sacks-Davis: Recursive linear hashing, ACM Transactions on Database Systems, Vol. 9, No. 3, 1984, 369–391.

62. Hutflesz, A., H.-W. Six and P. Widmayer: The R-file: An efficient access structure for proximity queries, Proc. 6th International Conference on Data Engineering, Los Angeles, 1990, 372–379.

63. Becker, B., H. Six and P. Widmayer: Maßstabsunabhängige Verwaltung von Landschaftsdaten, Tagungsband II der 20. Jahrestagung der Gesellschaft für Informatik, Stuttgart, Informatik-Fachberichte, Vol. 258, Springer-Verlag, Berlin 1990, 487–496.

64. Becker, B., H.-W. Six and P. Widmayer: Spatial priority search: An access technique for scaleless maps, Proc. ACM SIGMOD International Conference on the Management of Data, Denver, 1991, 128–137.

65. Nievergelt, J. and P. Widmayer: Guard files: Stabbing and intersection queries on fat spatial objects, The Computer Journal, Vol. 36, No. 2, 1993, 107–116.

66. Becker, L.: A new algorithm and a cost model for join processing with grid files, Dissertation, Fachbereich Elektrotechnik und Informatik, Universität-Gesamthochschule Siegen, Germany, 1992.

67. Brinkhoff, T., H.-P. Kriegel and B. Seeger: Efficient processing of spatial joins using R-trees, Proc. ACM SIGMOD International Conference on the Management of Data, Washington D.C., 1993, 237–246.

68. Günther, O.: Efficient computation of spatial joins, Technical Report TR-92-029, International Computer Science Institute, Berkeley, 1992.

69. Kriegel, H.-P., T. Brinkhoff and R. Schneider: An efficient map overlay algorithm based on spatial access methods and computational geometry, Geographic Data Base Management Systems, ESPRIT Basic Research Series Proceedings, Springer-Verlag, Berlin 1992, 194–211.

70. Shaffer, C.A. and H. Samet: Set operations for unaligned linear quadtrees, Computer Vision, Graphics, and Image Processing, Vol. 50, No. 1, 1990, 29–49.

71. Ohler, T.: The multiclass grid file: An access structure for multiclass range queries, Proc. 4th International Symposium on Spatial Data Handling, Charleston, 1992, 260–271.

72. Kriegel, H.-P., P. Heep, S. Heep, M. Schiwietz and R. Schneider: An access method based query processor for spatial database systems, Geographic Data Base Management Systems, ESPRIT Basic Research Series Proceedings, Springer-Verlag, Berlin 1992, 273–292.

73. Schiwietz, M. and H.-P. Kriegel: Query processing of spatial objects: Complexity versus redundancy, 3rd International Symposium on Advances in Spatial Databases, Singapore, Lecture Notes in Computer Science, Vol. 692, Springer-Verlag, Berlin 1993, 377–396.

74. Becker, B.: Methoden und Strukturen zur effizienten Verwaltung geometrischer Objekte in Geo-Informationssystemen, Dissertation, Mathematische Fakultät, Albert-Ludwigs-Universität, Freiburg, Germany, 1993.

75. Becker, B., S. Gschwind, T. Ohler, B. Seeger and P. Widmayer: On optimal multiversion access structures, 3rd International Symposium on Advances in Spatial Databases, Singapore, Lecture Notes in Computer Science, Vol. 692, Springer-Verlag, Berlin 1993, 123–141.

76. Charlton, M.E., S. Openshaw and C. Wymer: Some experiments with an adaptive data structure in the analysis of space-time data, Proc. 4th International Symposium on Spatial Data Handling, Zürich, 1990, 1030–1039.

77. Xu, X., J. Han and W. Lu: RT-tree: an improved R-tree index structure for spatiotemporal databases, Proc. 4th International Symposium on Spatial Data Handling, Zürich, 1990, 1040–1049.

78. Nelson, R.C. and H. Samet: A population analysis for hierarchical data structures, Proc. ACM SIGMOD International Conference on the Management of Data, San Francisco, 1987, 270–277.

79. Rottke, T., H.-W. Six and P. Widmayer: On the analysis of grid structures for spatial objects of non-zero size, International Workshop on Graph-Theoretic Concepts in Computer Science, Staffelstein, Lecture Notes in Computer Science, Vol. 314, Springer-Verlag, Berlin 1987, 94–105.

80. Kriegel, H.-P., M. Schiwietz, R. Schneider and B. Seeger: Performance comparison of point and spatial access methods, Proc. Symposium on the Design and Implementation of Large Spatial Databases, Santa Barbara, Lecture Notes in Computer Science, Vol. 409, Springer-Verlag, Berlin 1989, 89–114.

81. Shaffer, C.A., H. Samet and R.C. Nelson: QUILT: A geographic information system based on quadtrees, International Journal of Geographical Information Systems, Vol. 4, No. 2, 1990, 103–131.

82. Henrich, A. and H.-W. Six: How to split buckets in spatial data structures, Geographic Data Base Management Systems, ESPRIT Basic Research Series Proceedings, Springer-Verlag, Berlin 1991, 212–244.

DATA STRUCTURES AND ALGORITHMS FOR GEOGRAPHIC INFORMATION SYSTEMS: SELECTED TOPICS

T. Ohler and P. Widmayer
ETH Zentrum, Zürich, Switzerland

1 Introduction

For the performance of geographic information systems, it has been widely recognized that efficient data structures and algorithms supporting proximity based access to spatial data are a crucial ingredient. Because of that, in the last years, a lot of data structures for storage of multidimensional non-point objects have been proposed in the literature (for an overview see our tutorial introduction in this volume). Almost all of these approaches are made to support queries based on spatial neighborhood of objects, so-called proximity queries. Common examples of such proximity queries are *range queries*, returning all objects intersecting a given (rectangular) region, or *nearest neighbor queries*, determining the object nearest to a given point. But a geographic or cartographic information system should also support queries that do not exclusively refer to the spatial neighborhood of objects. For example, different versions of spatial data must be organized such that proximity queries to any version of the data can be answered efficiently. Or, given a set of object classes, a spatial query that involves an arbitrary combination of these classes should also be supported. Because of the growing size of data sets to be handled in geographic information systems, an appropriate data organisation to support such and several other application-specific queries becomes more and more important. In this paper, we will present two approaches for access structures supporting the two types of queries mentioned above. Handling of versioned, spatial data is the topic of Section 2, while Section 3 discusses queries on some classes selected from the set of object classes stored in a geographic information system.

2   Handling multiversion data

2.1   Introduction: multiversion access structures

The importance of maintaining data not only in their latest version, but also to keep
track of their development over time has been widely recognized, not only for geo-
information systems but also for many other database applications. Version data in
engineering databases [1] and time oriented data [2] are two characteristic examples
for situations in which the concepts of versions and time are visible to the user. In
multiversion concurrency control [3, 4], these concepts are transparent to the user, but
they are used by the system (e.g. the scheduler) for concurrency control and recovery purposes. In this section, we are concerned with spatial and non-spatial access
structures that support version based operations *on external storage* efficiently.

We are interested in such access structures that support at least *insertions*, *deletions*,
exact match queries and *range queries*, in addition to application specific operations
like *purging* of old enough versions in concurrency control. We focus on the situation
in which a change can only be applied to the present version, whereas queries can be
performed on any version, present or past. Spatial or non-spatial access structures
fulfilling these requirements are called *partially persistent* [5] or *multiversion* access
structures [6, 7].

In the literature, several approaches for building multiversion access structures have
been presented, many of them proposing multiversion B-trees. In this section, we
will introduce an approach, proposed by Becker et al. [7], to build an asymptotically
optimal multiversion B-tree; a result which not has been achieved before, despite the
considerable interest this problem received in the literature. Moreover, the technique
presented to transform a (single version) B-tree into a multiversion B-tree can be
applied directly or modified to a class of hierarchical external access structures, to derive
multiversion capabilities at no extra cost, neither for storage space nor for runtime,
asymptotically in the worst case.

Let us assume each data item stored consists of a *key* and an *information* part; access
to data items is by key only, and the keys are supposed to be taken from some linearly
ordered set (such as locational codes for spatial cells). Then, more precisely, such a
multiversion access structure should support the following operations:

- *insert (key,info)*: insert a record with given *key* and *info* component into the
  present version; this operation creates a new version.

- *delete (key)*: delete the (unique) record with given *key* from the *present* version;
  this operation creates a new version.

- *exact match query (key,version)*: return the (unique) record with given *key* in the
  given *version*; this operation does not create a new version.

- *range query (lowkey,highkey,version)*: return all records whose key lies between the given *lowkey* and the given *highkey* in the given *version*; this operation does not create a new version.

Let us state the strongest efficiency requirements that a multiversion B-tree, designed to support these operations, can be expected to satisfy. To this end, consider a sequence of N update operations (insert or delete), applied to the initially empty structure, and let m_i be the number of data items present after the i-th update (we say, in version i), $0 \leq i \leq N$. Then a multiversion B-tree with the following properties holding for each i (all bounds are for the worst case) is the best we can expect:

- for the first i versions, altogether the tree requires $O(i/b)$ blocks of storage space (b denotes the *block capacity*);

- the $(i + 1)$-th update (insertion or deletion) accesses and modifies $O(\log_b m_i)$ blocks;

- an exact match query in version i accesses $O(\log_b m_i)$ blocks;

- a range query in version i that returns r records accesses $O(\log_b m_i + r/b)$ blocks.

The reason for the bounds being optimum is the fact that for each version i, the efficiency of all operations is the same as if the data present in version i would be maintained separately in its own B-tree, neglecting the cost of identifying the (root of the) appropriate B-tree.

These bounds assume that in a query, access to the root of the requested B-tree has only constant cost. Thus we separate the concerns of, first, identifying the requested version, and, second, querying the requested version. This separation of concerns makes sense because in an application of a multiversion structure, access to the requested version may actually be free of charge (like for instance in concurrency control), allowing the discussion to concentrate on querying within a version. To identify the requested version, basically any of a number of search techniques can be used. Note that if we do not separate these issues, but instead assume that the root of the requested B-tree needs to be identified through a search operation, $O(\log_b N)$ instead of $O(\log_b m_i)$ is a lower bound on the runtime of a query, since one item out of as many as N items needs to be found.

2.2   Approaches to build multiversion access structures

The problem in designing a multiversion access structure lies in the fact that data are on external storage. For *main memory*, there is a general recipe [5] for designing a multiversion structure, given a single version structure, asymptotically at no extra amortized time and space costs. Unfortunately, a direct application of this approach to external access structures does not model storage space appropriately: a block is viewed to store a constant number of items, i.e. block size is not taken into consideration. Even worse, the direct application of the recipe consumes one block of storage space for each data item; clearly an unacceptable space efficiency, which also entails an unacceptable time complexity.

In building multiversion structures, there is a general tradeoff between storage space, update time and query time. For instance, building an extra copy of the structure at each update is extremely slow for updates and extremely costly in space, but extremely fast for queries. Near the other extreme, [8] view versions (time) as an extra dimension and store 1-dimensional version intervals in 2-dimensional space in an R–tree, with 1-dimensional key intervals (instead of single keys) coming for free. This gives good storage space efficiency, but query and update efficiency may be as bad as $\Theta(\log_b N)$. That is, the time to answer a query on version i does not depend on the number of items in that version only, but instead on the total number of all updates.

In a slightly different setting, namely for storing multiversion data on both, magnetical and optical WORM disks, [6, 9] propose the time-split B-tree, based on the write-once B-tree of [10]. Focussing on the objective to support migration of data from magnetic to optical disk in a simple way, the authors accept fairly bad time efficiency for queries. One of the proposed split strategies may lead to a time-split B-tree with no selectivity according to versions, which is clearly unacceptable in our setting.

Several variants of multiversion B$^+$-trees that also allow updates in the past have been proposed in [11], based on the ideas on full persistence in [5]. This is a more general concept than ours; if simplified for our multiversion situation (in the past only queries, no updates), query efficiency depends only on the number of items that belong to the queried version, as desired. Storage space, however, may be as high as $\Theta(N)$ blocks, because each operation may copy an entire block; clearly an unacceptable space efficiency.

As a result, none of these and other B-trees for multiple versions presented in the literature so far achieve optimum performance in time and space like Becker et al.'s multiversion B-tree.

2.3   An Optimal Multiversion B-tree

To transform single version *external* access structures into multiversion structures at no extra cost asymptotically, Becker et al. [7] associate insertion and deletion versions with items, since items of different lifespans need to be stored in the same block. Let < *key, in_version, del_version, info* > denote a data item, stored in a leaf of the access structure, with a *key* that is unique for any given version, an associated *information*, and a lifespan from its insertion version *in_version* to its deletion version *del_version*. Similarly, an entry in an inner node of the tree is denoted by < *router, in_version, del_version, reference* >; the *router*, together with the *in_version* and *del_version* information on the *referenced* subtree, guides the search for a data item. For example, the B-tree uses a separator key as a router.

From a bird's eye view, Becker et al.'s multiversion B-tree is a directed acyclic graph of B-tree nodes that results from certain incremental changes to an initial B-tree. Especially, the multiversion B-tree embeds a number of B-trees; it has a number of B-tree root nodes that partition the versions from the first to the present one in such a way that each B-tree root stands for an interval of versions. A query for a given version can then be answered by entering the multiversion B-tree at the corresponding root.

Each update (insert or delete operation) creates a new version; the i-th update creates version i. An entry is said to be *of version i*, if its lifespan contains i. A block is said to be *live* if it has not been copied, and *dead* otherwise. In a live block, deletion version * for an entry denotes that the entry has not yet been deleted at present; in a dead block, it indicates that the entry has not been deleted before the block died. For each version i and each block A except the roots of versions, the number of entries of version i in block A must either be zero or at least d, where $b = k \cdot d$ for block capacity b and some constant k (assume for simplicity that b, k, d are all integers and b is the same for directory and data blocks); in [7] this is called the *weak version condition*. As given for B-trees, this condition makes sure that the number of entries for each block and each version stored in the block is proportional to the block capacity.

Update operations that do not entail structural changes and queries are performed in the straightforward way that can be inferred from the single version structure by taking the lifespan of entries into account. E.g., an entry inserted by update operation i into a block carries a lifespan of $[i, *)$ at the time of insertion; deletion of an entry by update operation i from a block changes its *del_version* from * to i.

Structural changes are triggered in two ways. First, a *block overflow* occurs as the result of an insertion of an entry into a block that already contains b entries. A block underflow, as e.g. in B–trees, cannot occur, since entries are never removed from blocks. However, the weak version condition may be violated as a result of a deletion; such a *weak version underflow* occurs, if an entry is deleted in a block with exactly d present version entries.

The structural modification after a block overflow copies the block and removes all but the present version entries from the copy. In [7] this operation is called a *version split*; it is comparable to a time split at the present time in [6] or the node copying operation of [5]. In general, a copy produced by this version split may be an almost full block. In that case, a few subsequent insertions would again trigger a version split, resulting in a space cost of $\Theta(1)$ block per insertion. To avoid this and the similar phenomenon of an almost empty block, we request that at least a number of insert operations or delete operations proportional to the block capacity, $\varepsilon d + 1$ to be precise, are necessary to arrive at the next block overflow or version underflow in that block, for some constant ε to be defined appropriately (assume for simplicity that εd is integer). As a consequence, the number of present version entries after a version split must be in the range from $(1 + \varepsilon)d$ to $(k - \varepsilon)d$; this condition is called the *strong version condition*. If a version split leads to more than $(k - \varepsilon)d$ entries in a block – i.e. a *strong version overflow* occurs –, a version independent split according to the key values of the items in the block – a *key split* – is performed. Similarly, if a version split leads to less than $(1 + \varepsilon)d$ entries – i.e. a *strong version underflow* occurs –, a merge is attempted with a copy of a sibling block containing only its present version entries. If necessary, this merge must be followed by a key split. A weak version underflow is handled by performing a version split and then processing the same steps as necessary to eliminate a strong version underflow.

In any case, a structural change for one block can be performed in time $O(1)$ and using space $O(b)$ entries. Since $O(b)$ updates must be performed after each structural change before the next structural change occurs, an amortized analysis can be used to show the desired bounds posed for an optimal multiversion B-tree.

3   The MCG-File: a first approach for an access structure to support multi class range queries

In geographic information systems, multi-dimensional geo-objects, structured into thematic classes, must be organized such that spatial queries to an arbitrary subset of these classes can be answered efficiently. A typical application of such queries is graphical browsing through the data by displaying on screen all objects, belonging to some of the thematic classes, which intersect a given rectangular region. The latter type of query has been called *multi class range query* [12]. In this section, we discuss some conventional approaches to support multi class range queries and present the *multi class grid file*, *MCG-file* for short, a first proposal for an access structure especially designed for the efficient support of such queries.

To describe the problem more formally, let d denote the dimension of the data space D. We assume that all classes have the same data space, a condition which easily can be fulfilled by defining D to be the union of the data spaces for all the classes. Each object belongs to exactly one class. Then, a point object (e.g. derived by transforming a $d/2$-dimensional rectangle into a d-dimensional point [13]) can be seen as a $(d + 1)$-tuple $(x_1, .., x_d; class)$ of its coordinates in D and an attribute *class*, the identifier of the class the object belongs to.

A *multi class range query* then can be defined as follows: Given a d-dimensional isothetic rectangle R and a set S of class identifiers, determine all those objects o, with $o.class \in S$, which are enclosed by R. Using one of the data structures, which have been proposed for efficient support of range queries to multi-dimensional points (e.g. [14, 15]), three straight forward approaches to support multi class range queries can be identified:

A first approach is to organize the objects of each class in its own d-dimensional data structure. So, range queries to a single class can be answered efficiently. For multi class range queries, no advantage is taken from the fact that the query range is the same for all classes. Since for each of the required classes at least one path in the directory tree of the corresponding data structure must be traversed, the query performance strongly decreases with increasing number of required classes.

To avoid the disadvantages of multiple directories, another approach is to store the objects of all classes in one d-dimensional data structure. Then, a multi class range query is answered by performing a range query to all classes and, afterwards, selecting those objects belonging to the required classes. This approach clearly suffers from the fact that no selectivity is given according to classes.

To store the objects of all classes in one data structure taking into account their class membership, a $(d+1)$-dimensional data structure can be used, organizing the objects in the $(d+1)$-th data structure dimension according to their class attribute values. For that it is necessary to define a total order on the class attribute values. This data organization is advantageous for supporting queries to a class set represented by an interval of class attribute values, but not really adequate for queries over an arbitrary set of class attribute values, as given for multi class range queries. The higher the distance between the class attribute values of two classes in the defined order, the higher is the probability that objects of the two classes, although they are lying in the same data space subrange, are indexed via different branches of the directory tree. Therefore, the performance of a multi class range query strongly depends on the combination of class identifier values specified in the query. To avoid this effect, it seems to be more adequate to organize the data such that objects of different classes, falling into the same subrange, can be accessed via a common directory path.

In [12], from the discussion of these three approaches the following desirable properties of a data organization for efficient support of multi class range queries are derived:

1. The objects of all classes should be organized in a single data structure to avoid the overhead in storage space and query time of multiple directories.

2. To organize each class according to its size and its object distribution as good as possible, the data space partitioning for each class should be done in the same way as in the approach with separate data structures.

3. The directory should be organized such that objects of different classes, which are neighboring in the data space, can be indexed via a directory path that is common, or at least common to a large extent.

The MCG-file is the only access structure which fulfills all these properties.

3.1 The MCG-file

The *MCG-file* uses the grid file [14] in its variant *multi level grid file* [16] as underlying data structure. In contrast to the grid file directory, the multi level grid file directory is a balanced tree, with directory blocks on secondary storage as nodes. Each node represents a partitioning of a rectangular region of the data space (the root partitions the data space itself) and stores entries, each consisting of a region description and a reference to another block. For inner nodes, this block is another directory block; leaf nodes contain references to data blocks which store objects falling into the corresponding region.

To illustrate the basic idea of the MCG-file, let us consider the example in Fig. 1. The figure shows the data space partitionings for two grid files, each of it storing a set of objects belonging to a class. We assume that a split strategy was used during insertion into the grid files, which guarantees that an arbitrary pair of regions from two different classes is either disjoint, equal or contained in each other. The basic, not data-driven grid file split strategies fulfill this condition.

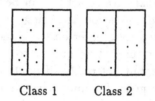

Class 1   Class 2

Figure 1: Objects of two classes stored in separate grid files.

The MCG-file exploits this fact to organize entries referring to data blocks of different classes, whose block regions are contained in the same subregion of the data space, in one directory block or along a directory path. More precisely, the MCG-file organizes objects of several thematic classes such that:

- Each class has its own data space partitioning and its own data blocks, but the entries referring to those data blocks are stored in a common directory tree. The data space partitioning is derived by the same split strategy for all classes; the split strategy must fulfill the conditions mentioned above.

- Entries referring to data blocks and entries referring to other directory blocks can be mixed in a directory block in a strictly controlled way.

- Let $cell(B)$ denote the region represented by a data block or a directory block. Then a MCG-file fulfills the following *invariant*: an entry referring to a data block B is, independent of its class, stored in the unique directory block B' for which $cell(B')$ is the smallest region enclosing $cell(B)$. That means that an entry referring to a data block B is stored in the same directory block or in a directory block on a directory level nearer to the root than entries referring to data blocks whose region is contained in the region of B.

- Since a directory may store entries referring directly or indirectly to data blocks of several classes, a directory reference contains the *region* of the block referred to and the *set of classes* stored in the referenced subtree. Such entries referring to directory blocks are organized as known from the multi level grid file.

Let us illustrate these concepts and the basic idea of the MCG-file algorithms in the following example (Fig. 2).

Fig. 2a shows the root directory of a MCG-file, containing entries which represent the data space partitioning for a class 1.

Insertion of an object *o* is done into the unique data block, representing the object's class *o.class*, whose region encloses *o*. The search to determine this data block, if it exists, is done as follows: Beginning at the root directory block, in each directory block *B* we follow the reference of the unique entry *d*, which is valid for class *o.class* and whose region encloses *o*. Search ends in a data block or, if no data block for class *o.class* exists, in the root directory. The latter case, insertion of an object of a new class, is shown in Fig. 2b. A new data block representing the whole data space for that class is created and an entry, referring to it, is added to the root directory.

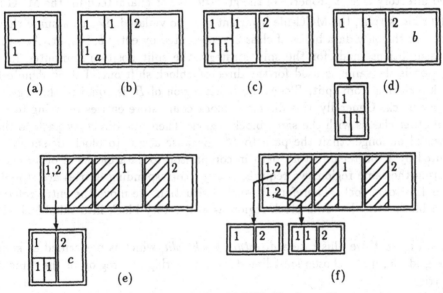

Figure 2: Example of MCG-file dynamics.

If the unique data block can be found, but insertion causes an overflow, a *data block split* is carried out as known from the grid file. Fig. 2c shows the situation resulting from a data block split of block *a* in our example.

Insertion of a new entry into a directory block, as e.g. resulting from a data block split, may lead to an overfull directory block (Fig. 2c). In the grid file, such a *directory block overflow* is managed by splitting the block, along a split line proposed by the split strategy, into two blocks. In the MCG-file this is not always possible as the example illustrates: For the situation considered in our example, let us assume that the split position is the middle of the interval resulting from the projection of the block region to the x-axis. As Fig. 2c shows, a directory block split as for the grid file is impossible, because the directory block contains one entry, the entry for class 2, whose region overlaps the given split line, and therefore cannot be assigned to one of the halves which would result from the split. To handle a directory block overflow in such a situation, in the MCG-file a new directory block is created, whose region is one half of the region of the overfull directory block, and all the entries contained in that half are shifted to it. The new block is inserted into the directory tree as a son of the previously overfull directory block (Fig. 2d). That operation is called *directory block shift out*. The background idea for this technique is to keep entries of different classes, contained in the same subrange of the data space, along the same directory path, by shifting the entries of the class(es) with finer data space partitioning to a lower directory level, if necessary. So, the objects of the different classes falling into the considered region can be reached via the same path in the directory tree, but now, the directory path to the classes with finer partitioning is longer. Because of the directory block shift out, the balanced directory tree, a property of the grid file, is not guaranteed for the MCG-file.

After data block split, the MCG-file invariant may be violated. Let us assume that in the next step the only data block of class 2, represented by entry b, is split. According to the assumptions made for the split strategy, the split position computed for its block region is the same as used for the directory block shift out. Let B^l denote the left block resulting from split. Then, the block region of B^l is equal to the region of a directory block. Generally, this directory block could store entries referring to data blocks of other classes with the same block region. Then, the directory path to these blocks would be longer than the path to B^l. Because access to block B^l should not be favoured by a shorter directory path in comparison to data blocks of other classes representing the same region, we require that the corresponding entries are stored in the same directory block. Therefore, in such a situation, we move the entry referring to a data block with the same block region as a directory block into this block (Fig. 2e).

Finally, in Figure 2f we illustrate a *directory block split*, which is performed as known from the grid file, if the chosen split line does not overlap any region of the directory block entries.

Applying the algorithms sketched above, the MCG-file fulfills the properties posed for an access structure to support multi class range queries efficiently. An experimental performance evaluation [12] showed that the MCG-file is a good choice for support of such queries to class data sets with not too extreme differences in their cardinality.

Acknowledgement

Thanks go to the Swiss National Science Foundation SNF and the European Community with the ESPRIT program for their support of the work of the authors in the field of spatial data structures and geographic information systems.

References

1. Katz, R.H.: Towards a unified framework for version modeling in engineering databases, ACM Computing Surveys, Vol. 22, No. 4, 1990, 375–408.

2. Clifford, J. and G. Ariav: Temporal data management: models and systems, in: New directions for database systems (Eds. G. Ariav and J. Clifford), Ablex Publishing Co., Norwood N.J. 1986, 168–186.

3. Bernstein, P.A., V. Hadzilacos and N. Goodman: Concurrency control and recovery in database systems, Addison Wesley Publ. Co., Reading 1987.

4. Barghouti, N.S. and G.E. Kaiser: Concurrency control in advanced database applications, ACM Computing Surveys, Vol. 23, No. 3, 1991, 269–317.

5. Driscoll, J.R., N. Sarnak, D.D. Sleator and R.E. Tarjan: Making data structures persistent, Journal of Comp. and System Sci., Vol. 38, 1989, 86–124.

6. Lomet, D. and B. Salzberg: Access methods for multiversion data, ACM SIGMOD International Conference on Management of Data, 1989, 315–324.

7. Becker, B., S. Gschwind, T. Ohler, B. Seeger and P. Widmayer: On optimal multiversion access structures, Proc. 3rd International Symposium on Large Spatial Databases, Springer Lecture Notes in Computer Science, Vol. 692, Springer-Verlag, Berlin 1993, 123–141.

8. Kolovson, C. and M. Stonebraker: Indexing techniques for historical databases, 5th IEEE International Conference on Data Engineering, 1989, 127–137.

9. Lomet, D. and B. Salzberg: The performance of a multiversion access method, ACM SIGMOD International Conference on Management of Data, 1990, 353–363.

10. Easton, M.: Key-sequence data sets on indelible storage, IBM J. Res. Development, Vol. 30, No. 3, 1986, 230–241.

11. Lanka, S. and E. Mays: Fully persistent B^+–trees, ACM SIGMOD International Conference on Management of Data, 1991, 426–435.

12. Ohler, T.: The Multi Class Grid File: An Access Structure for Multi Class Range Queries, Proc. 5th International Symposium on Spatial Data Handling, Charleston, 1992, 260–271.

13. Pagel, B.-U., H.-W. Six and H. Toben: The transformation technique for spatial objects revisited, Proc. 3rd International Symposium on Large Spatial Databases, Springer Lecture Notes in Computer Science, Vol. 692, Springer-Verlag, Berlin 1993, 73–88.

14. Nievergelt, J., H. Hinterberger and K.C. Sevcik: The grid file: an adaptable, symmetric multikey file structure, ACM Transactions on Database Systems Vol. 9, No. 1, 1984, 38–71.

15. Freeston, M.W.: The BANG-file: a new kind of grid file, ACM SIGMOD International Conference on Management of Data, 1987, 260–269.

16. Krishnamurthy, R. and K.-Y. Whang: Multilevel Grid Files, IBM Research Report, Yorktown Heights 1985.

GEOGRAPHIC INFORMATION SYSTEMS: AN EXAMPLE

T. Ohler and P. Widmayer
ETH Zentrum, Zürich, Switzerland

1   Introduction

Geographic information systems (*GIS* for short) are computer based information systems supporting input, storage, processing and output of spatial data. Spatial data means data objects characterized by its position and shape in a given application-specific data space, like e.g. a set of polygons describing the boundaries of political subdivisions of a country. Because of the large number of applications, in which spatial data must be stored and processed, the number of GIS installations has quickly grown in the last few years. Important application fields are e.g. land register, urban planning, cartography or environmental information systems based on GISs. In this paper, we will introduce a reader, not familiar with GISs, from the point of view of computer science into basic concepts of geographic information systems. We illustrate GISs at an example of an environmental information system.

2   Geographic information systems: Basic concepts

2.1   GIS data

Data objects handled in geographic information systems – *geo-objects* for short – basically are characterized by a *geometric* and *non-geometric* attributes. Non-geometric (also *conventional* or *thematic*) attributes are numbers (integers, reals), character strings, boolean values etc., like e.g. the name of a town and its number of inhabitants. A geometric attribute describes the geometric representation of an object, specifying its shape and its position in the data space, like e.g. the polygon of the boundary of a town.

Concerning object geometry, we basically distinguish between *raster* and *vector* data. Typical *raster* data objects are satellite raster images or raster data derived by scanning a printed map. Concepts of raster data handling are the topic of image processing and will not be discussed in this paper.

For *vector* data sets, the concept of vectors is used to describe position and shape of objects. Most of the approaches from literature and GIS implementations use the following three basic types of 2-dimensional shapes for the geometric attribute of vector data:

1. point (e.g. to represent the source of a river)

2. line, i.e. a sequence of line segments (e.g. to represent a river)

3. polygon (e.g. to represent the boundaries of a country)

In [1], Gueting presents the *geo-relational algebra*, a model and query language for 2-dimensional geometric databases, which covers the model of GIS vector data presented above.

In the next subsection, we describe the basic functionalities of a GIS and discuss operations on GIS data.

2.2   Basic functionalities of a GIS

As for each information system, the basic functionalities of a GIS can be classified into three types: *data input*, *data processing* and *data output*.

Data input is performed by loading data from file, using one of the file formats which have been defined for geometric and/or geographical data, by scanning a map or by digitizing. Digitizing means input of vector data geometry by specifying the coordinates of points either using a digitizing board or by onscreen digitizing. In the latter case, the map to be vectorized is scanned and the raster data loaded into the GIS can be digitized on screen manually or computer-assisted.

Data output in GIS basically supports the concepts of reports or business charts – as known from conventional database systems – but additionally the output of (thematic) maps on printer or plotter. Moreover, appropriate file formats allow the exchange of non-geometric resp. geometric data with spread sheet software resp. drawing programs.

Concerning **data processing** functionalities, a GIS basically supports the query processing functionalities of a conventional database system, like e.g. selection, projection and join for a relational database system. Additionally, for geometric attributes, geometric operators are available. For example, common geometric predicates are

- *equal*

- *inside* (e.g. point *inside* polygon)

- *intersects* (e.g. line *intersects* line)

Using these and other predicates, also a *spatial join* for two sets of geo-objects can be defined.

There are also a lot of spatial (geometric), more application-specific operators like e.g.

- *overlay* – computation of the overlay of two sets of polygons, creating a new set of polygons;

- *nearest neighbor* – returning those geo-objects which are the nearest to a given point;

- *length, area* – computing the length of a line resp. area of a polygonal geo-object;

- *buffer zone creation* – to compute a buffer zone with a given offset around a geo-object resp. a set of geo-objects;

- *network analysis* – e.g. computation of a shortest path or a minimum spanning tree in a street network.

A set of operators partially covering the operators mentioned above can be found in [1]; a formal specification of a large class of geometric operations is given in [2].

Further, important features for spatial data analysis are – possibly application specific – classification and aggregation operators.

Let us mention that interactive browsing of a spatial database, using the graphical user interface displaying a subspace of the dataspace, also results in a query performed on the underlying database. An example of such queries, typical for a GIS, are multiclass queries [3], which are used to display the geo-objects of a subset of all object classes stored in the GIS, intersecting a given region.

2.3 GIS as non-standard DBMS application

From the description of GIS functionalities in the previous subsection it is clear that no conventional (relational) DBMS directly and efficiently supports the desired data management features. E.g. neither conventional database languages are appropriate for spatial data and spatial queries nor efficient techniques for physical data organisation like spatial access structures are available in standard database systems. Therefore, geographic information systems can be seen as typical *non-standard database applications*. Because of the growing practical relevance of GIS, this type of information systems has been studied deeply in research on non-standard DBMS. In the following, we will summarize basic GIS architectures, presented in literature or used for implementation of commercial systems.

One approach is to build a GIS not using a DBMS but on top of a file system especially designed for geometric data handling (*non-DBMS GIS* [4]). This may lead to very good system performance; but since the data management capabilities of a GIS basically should fulfill all the requirements to a DBMS, this approach is not of high practical relevance.

To use a standard DBMS – mostly a relational database system – as a component to build a GIS, there are basically two approaches: The *dual* [5] or *partial DBMS architecture* [4] combines the DBMS for handling non-geometric data and a geometric storage manager. A system layer above integrates these modules into a GIS. The major disadvantage is that DBMS concepts like transactions, recovery and query optimization must be reimplemented in the integrating layer at very high cost. Performance of such a system suffers from the point, that geometric and non-geometric attributes of one object are stored in different storage managers, such that links between those representations become necessary, making access very expensive. Nevertheless, there are some commercial GIS products built on this approach. Oosterom [5] mentions *ArcInfo* [6] as an example.

To derive the DBMS features mentioned above directly from a given conventional DBMS, another system architecture approach builds a GIS upon a standard DBMS, using it to store non-geometric *and* geometric data. This approach has been called *layered architecture* [5] resp. *shell architecture* [4]. For storing geometric data in a standard relational DBMS, the following three techniques can be used. One approach is to define relations implementing the basic geometric types (point, line, polygon) and to link them by an appropriate key to the geo-objects itself. Clearly, this approach is expensive, because queries normally result in expensive join operations. Another approach is to assign to each geo-object a key value from a linearly ordered set, which approximates its spatial location [7]. Henrich et al. [8] present another interesting approach by building a geometrically clustering access method upon a relational DBMS, a technique which leads to good query performance for geometric queries. An example of a commercial system built using the shell architecture approach is *Primes System 9* [9].

Advanced database system technologies like extensible database systems or object-oriented databases allow an integrated approach to build a GIS by extending the database system with appropriate data types for geometric attributes. In an extensible DBMS, appropriate efficient access structures and application-specific extensions of the query language can also be introduced into the database system itself. This leads to very good performance although implementation of an abstract data type into the database system may be very difficult. Examples for such an *integrated* approach [5] are *GeoDASDBS* [10] and *Geo++* [5]. An integrated approach GIS built on an object-oriented DBMS is *GeO$_2$* [11].

A fairly new approach of building GIS applications is using the concept of *interoperability* [12]. Interoperability means the cooperation of heterogenous, autonomous components, forming service nodes in a network. To build a GIS, a database system, a geometric storage manager and other GIS specific services could be such service nodes. This approach is basically motivated by the idea that the functional power of GIS can be increased by cooperation of powerful components. A complete GIS application based on this approach up to now does not exist, but a prototype already has been implemented [12].

Finally, let us emphasize that the classification presented above of course is fairly schematic. Some GISs do not clearly fit into the schema but fulfill characteristics of several of the architecture approaches.

3 ALBIS: an environmental information system as an example application of a GIS

3.1 Introduction

Environmental protection to preserve our living conditions became one of the major topics in our society. Because of the huge amount of data which is relevant in the field of environmental protection, computer assisted information systems are absolutely necessary. Moreover, because most of this data is spatial data, geographic information systems are the appropriate tool for environmental data management.

As an example for a GIS, in this section we will introduce *ALBIS* [1] (in German: *Arten-, Landschafts-, Biotop-Informationssystem*) [13]. ALBIS is designed as an information system to support the second line management of the administration in the german state Baden-Württemberg with all ecological data in the field of species, nature reserves and biotopes. In the present prototype, ALBIS holds about 500 MBytes of data, including [14]

- biotopes (vector geometry),

- nature reserves (vector geometry),

- locations of occurrence for species of animals and plants,

- political divisions and its boundaries (vector geometry), like communities, districts, regions, and

---

[1] ALBIS was designed and implemented for the *Umweltministerium Baden-Württemberg (Department of the Environment Baden-Württemberg)*, Stuttgart, Germany, by members of the research group of P. Widmayer (ETH Zürich, Zürich, Switzerland) and the *isys software gmbh*, Freiburg, Germany.

- background data to support geographical orientation, including scanned topographical maps (scales 1:25000 and 1:50000) as raster data, and satellite images for land use classification.

The following examples stand for typical queries performed on the spatial data sets mentioned above [14]:

- Queries on non-geometric attributes:
  Which biotopes in Baden-Württemberg are strongly endangered? (object class: biotopes; attribute: endangered)

- Queries on spatial neighborhood (geometric attributes):
  Return all biotopes lying inside the boundaries of the community *Freiburg i. Br.*.

- Combined query (geometric and non-geometric attributes):
  Which biotopes inside the boundaries of region *Tübingen* are strongly endangered?

3.2   ALBIS as a part of a large information system in the field of environmental protection: the UIS Baden-Württemberg

ALBIS is a part of a large information system, the *UIS* (*Umweltinformationssystem* = environmental information system) *Baden-Württemberg*. This system gives the framework to provide all types of environmental data and to support handling of this data in the states administration. The following main goals and tasks are given for the UIS [15]:

- Presentation of relevant, possibly aggregated environmental data to political leaders, legislative, executive, administration and to the public;

- detection, analysis and prognosis of the ecological situation locally or in the state as a whole;

- support for management of emergency cases or to make provisions;

- support for effective management of administrative tasks concerning environment;

- coordination and integration of existing information systems with ecologically relevant data.

From the point of its system architecture, the UIS is built on basic components, like e.g. networks for control of ground, water or air pollution and radioactivity. Derived from the environmental data provided by these basic components, on a second level, information systems like ALBIS report about the environmental situation in the state. On top of the UIS stands an environmental information system providing highly aggregated data for political leaders and top management in administration [15].

3.3 Basic implementation concepts

The main implementation decision for ALBIS was to use a GIS as basic tool. Three major points were relevant for that decision: First, most of the data handled in ALBIS is spatial data. Second, many of the queries to be processed by the system include geometric predicates, and third, display of data as thematic maps on screen or as a plot is one of the major output functionalities of ALBIS. After an evaluation, the GIS *SMALLWORLD*[2] [16] and its integrated GIS development environment *SMALLWORLD Magik* had been chosen.

According to the classification presented in Section 2, *SMALLWORLD GIS* basically can be seen as an integrated system, although – comparable to the layered architecture – a relational data management component is used for storage of geometric and non-geometric data. The GIS supports object-oriented modelling features and includes the object-oriented programming environment *Magik*. *Magik* allows the system implementor to build an application upon the *SMALLWORLD GIS*, but also, since *SMALLWORLD GIS* itself is implemented in *Magik*, to modify the GIS itself. Basic features of *Magik* are:

- All elements of a *Magik* program are objects, belonging to a class which determines the structure and methods of the objects;

- (multiple) inheritance, i.e. a class can inherit features of (several) super classes;

- language constructs allow the definition of dependencies among objects;

- a large library of object classes, e.g. supporting window graphics or relational database access, is available.

The language *Magik* is interpreted by a *virtual processor*. By that, a GIS application built on *Magik* can directly be ported to all system configurations for which an implementation of this virtual processor exists.

The database of *SMALLWORLD GIS* is implemented by the *Virtual Database Manager* which allows transparent access to the internal relational database as well as to external relational DBMSs. The data model used to store geometric data is described in the next subsection. Geometric queries on this data are supported by assigning to each object geometry a spatial key [17, 18], which is chosen from a linearly ordered set and therefore can be handled in a conventional, one-dimensional access structure like the B-tree.

---

[2]SMALLWORLD Systems Ltd., Cambridge, England

3.4   ALBIS geometric-topological data model

In this subsection, we introduce the geometric-topological data model of *SMALL-WORLD GIS*, which is used to store object geometry in ALBIS. Since most of the concepts of this data model also can be found in other GIS implementations or data model proposals, it is a characteristic example how geometric data is modelled in a GIS.

The geometric-topological data model of ALBIS (Fig. 1) is based on strict distinction between topology and geometry. Basic geometric elements are *node* (i.e. point), *link* (i.e. line) and *polygon*; each stored by (the sequence of) its coordinates. Geometric elements can share other geometric elements, e.g. several *links* may share a *node*. Although not shown in the figure, the data model allows to model polygons with holes.

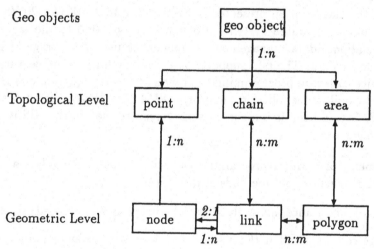

Figure 1: The geometric-topological data model of ALBIS

The topological elements, which are used directly to represent a geo-objects geometry, are *point, chain* and *area*. Each topological element corresponds to one or more geometric elements, and different topological elements can share the same geometric element. Now, geo-objects (or *Real world objects (RWOs)*, as *SMALLWORLD* calls them) have at least one, but possibly more topological representations; the relationships between geo-objects and its topological representation are 1:n-relationships with n fixed for each object and each topological representation. For example, this allows to model a polygonal object by its boundary and an in-point. Moreover, in *SMALLWORLD GIS* this is exploited to implement a simple form of scale-dependent representation of an object (*generalization*): e.g. a geo-object *town* may be represented by a polygon up to a scale of 1:100000 and as a point for smaller scales.

3.5   ALBIS user interface

The ALBIS graphical user interface was carefully designed to be simple and easy to use. It is based on the concept of a tree of windows, rooted at the *map window*. This window is used to display map graphics. It also contains the *main menu*, which supports functionalities on the map window, like e.g. zoom-in, zoom-out, and allows to open the following major windows, which themselves may have subwindows:

- *Legend window*
  The legend window shows a map legend for geo-objects and business charts drawn into the map window.

- *Overview map window*
  In an additional map window an overview map is displayed, e.g. showing the major political boundaries of the state Baden-Württemberg. To simplify geographic orientation, the subregion currently displayed in the main map window is represented by a highlighted rectangle.

- *Theme control window*
  The theme control window contains a list of all geo-object classes stored in ALBIS (*themes*) and their geometric attributes. The window allows to define which object geometry shall be displayed in the map window, whether an object class shall occur in the legend window and whether it is selectable using the mouse in the map window. By its settings, the theme control window supports graphical browsing through the object classes geometry.

- *Query window*
  The query window supports interactive definition and processing of queries. Details of query processing in ALBIS are described in the next subsection.

3.6   ALBIS query processing and data analysis

In ALBIS, a simple but sufficiently powerful concept to define and process queries is implemented. It can briefly be summarized as follows:

Processing of a query can be seen as a sequence of selection steps, performed on sets of geo-objects, and steps combining sets. Defining a query, first a base set, e.g. the set of all biotopes in Baden-Württemberg, is chosen. Afterwards, interactively geometric and non-geometric predicates are defined on the attributes of the base set objects. Two examples for important application-specific geometric predicates are

- all geo-objects intersecting a polygon, interactively specified in the map window by selecting an objects geometry or by input of the polygons base points, or

- all geo-objects inside the boundaries of a political division.

To define the final query condition, these geometric and non-geometric predicates can be combined using the boolean operators *and, or* and *not.* Let us mention, that the set resulting from such a selection step itself can be the base set for another selection step.

To create a new set, sets also can be combined in two different ways: First, two sets of the same class can be combined by the standard set operators union, intersection and difference. Second, two sets of different classes can be combined by polygon overlay.

Query evaluation is performed in background, such that definition of further query conditions or browsing of query results can be performed simultaneously.

For display of query results, ALBIS supports several comfortable methods. Non-geometric attributes of geo-objects in a result set can be browsed in separate windows, either the attributes of one object per window or a list of objects with their main attributes. For printer or file output, reports can be generated, using predefined or arbitrarily userdefined report formats. Object geometry can be displayed in the map window, e.g. highlighting selected geo-objects, or can be drawn into plots on paper. Moreover, possibly after applying aggregation or classification functions, numerical attributes can be visualized as thematic maps with business charts in the map window or in plots.

4   Discussion: GIS – Some open problems

Not only as an observation of the ALBIS project but for GISs in general, performance is a major topic for system designers and researchers in the next years. This is especially important because data sets to be handled in GISs are growing very fast [19]. For example, one major objective for the interdisciplinary *SEQUOIA 2000* project [20] is to develop an efficient way for storage of and access to spatial data sets of size in order of terabytes. More general, there is strong need for fast algorithms for data processing and efficient database support for large sets of geometric data, based on efficient algorithms and access structures. For simple geometric objects (rectangles) and elementary geometric queries (proximity queries) several efficient data structures supporting access to geometric data have been proposed in the literature. These approaches also can be used for geographic data, but over that, geographic applications are characterized by a lot of very application-specific features. In the following, we will mention some of those features and the problems they pose to methods of spatial data handling:

- *Generalization* – Geographic data shall be displayed in different scales showing different amount of details, like e.g. the number of edges of a polygon. Techniques must be found to store spatial data "scaleless" and to process queries defined for an arbitrarily specified scale. First proposals in that field have been made (see e.g. [21]).

- As mentioned in Section 2, special types of queries, like multiclass queries, must be processed in the field of geographic data processing. Access methods must be designed to support such queries efficiently.

- *Network analysis* – GISs often are used to handle network data, e.g. streets or pipelines. Techniques must be found how to store such networks on secondary storage such that the desired network analysis algorithms (e.g. shortest path) can be performed efficiently.

These are only some examples of problems the implementation of geographic information systems poses to computer science. Because these problems are both, interesting from a theoretical point of view and highly relevant for practice, geographic information systems are a very interesting field for research and development.

Acknowledgement

Thanks go to the Swiss National Science Foundation SNF and the European Community with the ESPRIT program for their support of the work of the authors in the field of spatial data structures and geographic information systems.

References

1. Güting, R.H.: Geo-Relational Algebra : A Model and Query Language for Geometric Databases, Proc. EDBT 1988, Springer Lecture Notes in Computer Science, Vol. 303, Springer-Verlag, Berlin 1988, 506–527.

2. Roman, G.-C.: Formal specification of geographic data processing requirements, IEEE Transactions on Knowledge and Data Engineering 2, 1990, 370–380.

3. Ohler, T.: The Multi Class Grid File : An Access Structure for Multi Class Range Queries, Proc. 5th International Symposium on Spatial Data Handling, Charleston, 1992, 260–271.

4. Bennis, K., B. David, I. Quilio and Y. Viemont: GéoTROPICS: Database support alternatives for geographic applications, Proc. 4th International Symposium on Spatial Data Handling, Zürich, 1990, 599–610.

5. van Oosterom, P. and T. Vijlbrief: The GEO++ system: an extensible GIS, Proc. 5th International Symposium on Spatial Data Handling, Charleston, 1992, 40–50.

6. Morehouse, S.: The Architecture of Arc/Info, Proc. Auto-Carto 9, 1989, 266–277.

7. Orenstein, J.A. and F.A. Manola: PROBE Spatial Data Modelling and Query Processing in an Image Database Application, IEEE Transactions on Software Engineering, Vol. 14, No. 5, 1988, 611–629.

8. Henrich, A., A. Hilbert, H.-W. Six and P. Widmayer: Anbindung einer räumlich clusternden Zugriffsstruktur für geometrische Attribute an ein Standard-Datenbanksystem am Beispiel von Oracle, BTW'91: GI-Fachtagung Datenbanksysteme für Büro, Technik und Wissenschaft, Informatik-Fachberichte, Vol. 270, Springer Verlag, Berlin 1991, 161–177.

9. Pedersen, L.-O. and R. Spooner: Data Organization in System 9, WILD Heerbrugg, 1988.

10. Schek, H.J. and W. Waterfeld: A Database Kernel System for Geoscientific Applications, Proc. of the 2nd International Symposium on Spatial Data Handling, 1986, 273–288.

11. David, B., L. Raynal, G. Schorter and V. Mansart: GeO$_2$: Why objects in a geographical DBMS?, Proc. 3rd International Symposium on Large Spatial Databases, Springer Lecture Notes in Computer Science, Vol. 692, Springer-Verlag, Berlin 1993, 264–276.

12. Schek, H.J. and A. Wolf: From extensible databases to interoperability between multiple databases, Proc. 3rd International Symposium on Large Spatial Databases, Springer Lecture Notes in Computer Science, Vol. 692, Springer-Verlag, Berlin 1993, 207–238.

13. Müller, M.: Entwicklung des Arten-, Landschafts-, Biotop-Informationssystems (ALBIS) als übergreifende Komponente des Umweltinformationssystems Baden-Württemberg, in: Umweltanwendungen Geographischer Informationssysteme (Eds. O. Günther, K.P. Schulz, J. Seggelke), Wichmann-Verlag, Karlsruhe 1992, 64–70.

14. Umweltministerium Baden-Württemberg (ed.): Benutzerhandbuch *ALBIS* Version 2.0, Edited by isys software gmbh and Chair Prof. P. Widmayer, Dept. of Computer Science, ETH Zürich, Switzerland, 1992.

15. Mayer-Föll, R.: Zur Rahmenkonzeption des Umweltinformationssystems Baden-Württemberg, in: Konzeption und Einsatz von Umweltinformationssystemen (Eds. O. Günther, H. Kuhn, R. Mayer-Föll, F.J. Radermacher), Informatik-Fachberichte, Vol. 301, Springer-Verlag, Berlin 1991.

16. Chance, A., R. Newel and D. Theriault: An object-oriented GIS - Issues and solutions, Proc. EGIS'90: First European Conference on Geographical Information Systems, 1990, 179–188.

17. Samet, H.: The design and analysis of spatial data structures, Addison-Wesley, Reading 1990.

18. Samet, H.: Applications of spatial data structures: computer graphics, image processing, and GIS, Addison-Wesley, Reading 1990.

19. Crain, I.K.: Extremely large spatial information systems – a quantitative perspective, Proc. 4th International Symposium on Spatial Data Handling, Zürich, 1990, 632–641.

20. Stonebraker, M., J. Frew and J. Dozier: The SEQUOIA 2000 project, Proc. 3rd International Symposium on Large Spatial Databases, Springer Lecture Notes in Computer Science, Vol. 692, Springer-Verlag, Berlin 1993, 397–412.

21. Becker, B., H.-W. Six and P. Widmayer: Spatial priority search: an access technique for scaleless maps, Proc. ACM SIGMOD International Conference on the Management of Data, 1991, 128–137.

Printed in the United States
By Bookmasters